ADULT LITERACY

SOURCE BOOKS
ON EDUCATION
(VOL. 14)

GARLAND REFERENCE LIBRARY
OF SOCIAL SCIENCE
(VOL. 346)

Source Books on Education

ADULT LITERACY
A Source Book and Guide

Joyce French

GARLAND PUBLISHING, INC. • NEW YORK & LONDON
1987

Library of Congress Cataloging-in-Publication Data

French, Joyce N., 1929-
   Adult literacy.
   (Garland reference library of social science ;
vol. 346. Source books on education ; vol. 14)
   Includes index.
   1. Literacy—United States—Bibliography.
   2. Elementary education of adults—United States—
Bibliography.   3. Functional literacy—United States—
Bibliography.   I. Title.   II. Series: Garland
reference library of social science ; v. 346.
III. Series: Garland reference library of social
science. Source books on education ; vol. 14.
Z5814.12F73   1987   [LC151]   016.374'012   87-21075
ISBN 0-8240-8574-4 (alk. paper)

Printed on acid-free, 250-year-life paper
Manufactured in the United States of America

To Susan and Richard
To Brent

CONTENTS

vii

PREFACE

Much has been written about adult illiteracy and functional literacy, about its impact on society and individuals, and about the steps we should be taking in this area. The purpose of this book is to broaden our thinking about illiteracy, putting it into the larger perspective of literacy and to organize our knowledge of the adult learner and the process of literacy acquisition. Finally, suggestions for future directions are made. The goal is positive: to develop literacy, not just to eliminate illiteracy. The emphasis is on action: to identify, understand, and use the elements necessary for positive and constructive decision-making in the establishment of alternatives for instruction, curriculum, and programs.

The examination of adult literacy and illiteracy is approached from both a theoretical perspective and a practical one. A review of the literature relating to definitions of literacy, models of reading instruction, and models of adult learning provides the framework for examining adult literacy in a variety of relevant contexts and is prerequisite to understanding and utilizing the information available in the field. The remainder of the text deals with specific adult populations in the United States as well as with adults in other countries. The discussion is directed toward that population of adults who cannot read or cannot read well, not toward those who can read but choose not to do so, those adults considered aliterate. For readers with a very specific interest or professional responsibility, the initial, theoretically oriented discussion can be combined with the relevant practical discussion of a particular target population. For readers

with a broad interest in the topic of adult
literacy and illiteracy, the text provides an
overview of the common threads that run through
all programs as well as a comparison of the
application of theory to particular populations.

The text is followed by an annotated
bibliography for each area. The problem of
separating entries in a bibliography into specific
categories can be a knotty one because authors
often include more than one issue or topic in an
article or monograph. However, use of the subject
index should provide access to pertinent
references in addition to those listed in the
bibliographic categories. The bibliographies were
developed from RESOURCES IN EDUCATION, CURRENT
INDEX TO JOURNALS IN EDUCATION, and BOOKS IN
PRINT. In addition, materials published by both
government and private agencies were examined.
The sources examined, for the most part, were
limited to those published in the United States.
The items are drawn primarily from the past five
years, although older items have been included
when they seemed relevant or were often cited by
others in the field. The aim in choosing items
was to provide both a cross-section of views and
ideas and a wide range of sources.

While this book provides a map for those
engaged in the process of decision making for
establishing, developing, executing, evaluating,
or refining programs, it is not intended as a how-
to manual for reading instruction. Although
specific teaching suggestions are included that
should be useful to the instructor, this text
should be combined with other sources for
specific, detailed information. My book, READING
AND STUDY SKILLS IN THE SECONDARY SCHOOL: A
SOURCEBOOK, for example, can provide those
specifics.

The position taken in this book is that
literacy difficulties exist here and now and that
we must deal with the situation as we find it. An
alternative way of meeting adult literacy
problems, of course, is to prevent them through
effective instruction in elementary and secondary
schools. While this would probably not alleviate

every difficulty, it would certainly help. This, however, is a topic beyond the scope of the present work though it is certainly being widely explored.

The book is intended for instructors and administrators in a variety of adult literacy programs. They constitute the front line, dealing directly with the problem and making the daily and long-range decisions that create programs. A second audience, no less important for the future of the field, consists of legislators in state and national governments, administrators and staff in agencies administering government funds, and those personnel concerned with awarding and reviewing the monies provided by public and private grants. These people, while not concerned with the specifics, certainly provide the lubrication that initiates programs and makes them work. They need an overview of the field as a reference in allocating funds. A third audience consists of those researchers, theoreticians and college professors who can have an impact on the field through thoughtful investigation and through the generation of new ideas, concepts, and programs developed, perhaps, by the germ of an idea included here. Finally, a fourth audience consists of students beginning their careers who may be inspired to work in this area and who may receive some guidance in doing so.

REFERENCE

French, Joyce N. READING AND STUDY SKILLS IN THE SECONDARY SCHOOL: A SOURCEBOOK. New York: Garland Publishing Inc., 1986.

Adult Literacy

ADULT LITERACY: AN EXAMINATION

An Overview: Literacy and Illiteracy

There is a widespread and growing concern in the United States and abroad in both the popular press (99) and in professional literature about illiteracy--the extent of it, the problems it presents, and the issues related to overcoming it. This concern is made more complex by the fact that we are attempting not only to raise the number of people considered literate but also to raise the quality of that literacy (6). The concern is matched by a widespread and growing resolve here and abroad to devote money and manpower to meeting and solving these problems.

First, let's put the problem of illiteracy and literacy into perspective. Is the problem in the United States more serious now than in the past? Aronowitz (8) responds firmly. "The assumption that the literacy problem is greater now than it was 20, 30, or 50 years ago is unfounded. There is no sound evidence to support that case" (p. 54). Hunter (79) asserts that "there has never been a time when so large a proportion of the population had such high levels of literacy as is true today" (p. 2). Micklos (90), after reviewing a variety of sources, also concludes that there is good news about basic and functional literacy levels and that "literacy is a healthy and growing part of American life" (p. 116). Mikulecky, Shanklin and Caverly (125) find, after comparing studies conducted over a 50 year period, that except for one study, "there seems to be an increase in adult's total reading time per day" (p. 32).

If the picture is so positive, why are we concerned? Why is there a national sense of

1

urgency regarding the problems of literacy and illiteracy? First, according to Rigg and Kazemek (226), "regardless of whether there is a 'crisis,' the problem of illiteracy does exist" (p. 24). By any count, as we will see, there is a substantial group of people who encounter difficulties in reading materials written for the average citizen (74, 91, 92, 170) and needed in everyday living. In addition, the newly literate (12) have skills that might have been sufficient 50 years ago but that are not now because of the new demands placed on them by society. Second, there is a substantial group of adults in the workplace who cannot read well enough to fulfill current on-the-job literacy demands (383, 393), let alone those of the future that can be expected to increase (8, 83, 93). Third, the fact that colleges and universities have put precious funds into remedial and supportive literacy programs is testimony to their concern for adults who, though they can read and are considered literate, cannot read sufficiently and/or easily enough to benefit from postsecondary education (471, 508). Finally, in all areas there is an increasing need for the adult who can read and reason critically, make inferences and judgments, and pose and solve problems, using literacy as a tool (12). If we link literacy, critical reading, and thinking, then Hovey (78) warns us "we would have to begin by recognizing that literacy is a serious problem" (p. 55). As we will see, the extent and implications of the literacy problems experienced by specific groups of adults demand a sense of urgency in the exploration of solutions. They also demand reflection and insight on the part of those charged with solving the problems. The urgency cannot dictate action without thought.

The Process of Decision Making for Literacy

The process of dealing with literacy issues and problems involves gathering information and making a series of decisions. First, planning in any area of adult literacy rests on three theoretical and research-based decisions:

1. What is your definition of literacy? Sounds simple. Everyone agrees on what literacy is. It is the ability to read. Why, then, do we

have reading programs for college students?
They can certainly read. What is functional
literacy and should that be our only or our
major concern? What definition of literacy is
appropriate for your population?

2. What is your view of reading and the reading
   process? Reading is knowing the letters and
   words and putting them together to read
   sentences and paragraphs. Programs for both
   adults and children have been based on this
   model. What other models of reading are there?
   How do they affect instruction?

3. What is your view of the adult learner and how
   does the adult learn? Is the adult a child
   grown up? What impact does the adult's
   knowledge and experience have on how he learns
   and how he is involved with his learning?

Second, you will need to make some specific,
program-related decisions. For any literacy
program, define the population and the extent of
the problem, then decide:

1. What are some effective instructional
   strategies? What kinds of materials can be
   used? Who will instruct? What training does
   the instructor need? Who will make the
   decisions regarding instruction and materials?

2. What curriculum alternatives are there that are
   appropriate for the particular population?

3. How can the program be developed to recruit and
   retain students and deliver services?

These two sets of decisions are closely
interrelated. Consider, for example, some of the
practical questions instructors and administrators
need to explore in setting up and running literacy
programs. If literacy is seen as a means of
surviving in a work setting, the materials used and
the skills taught will reflect that point of view.
If, on the other hand, literacy is defined as a
means of enjoying, contributing to, and benefiting
from life experiences, then the skills taught and
the materials used will probably be quite

different.

Since the teacher knows how to read and, presumably, the student doesn't have the same abilities, should the teacher be responsible for choosing the text, the skills, etc., and the student be the recipient of the teacher's knowledge?   On the other hand, should the student have a voice in determining what is to be learned based on the needs he identifies? Should he choose materials he wants or needs to read? Should these decisions be cooperatively made?   How such decisions are made will reflect the view of the adult learner that forms the basis for the program.

How will we teach adults to read and to improve and use their abilities? What, in fact, is reading?   Is it reading words or ideas or both? What is the impact of the experience, knowledge, and vocabulary that adults come to us with? How can this affect the materials we use?   Are adults interested in reading simple, easy materials? The instructional strategies used with adults will reflect the teacher's view of reading, of literacy, and of the adult as learner.

These are practical questions that must be answered in very practical ways on a day-to-day basis by those in the field.   It is easy to overlook the relevance of theory and research in our quest for how to get students and, once we have them, what to do with them on Monday evening. It is, however, the combination of theory, research, and practice that will give substance to programs and address the issues of literacy and illiteracy facing many of us individually and all of us as a society.

How appropriate our decisions are may well influence whether we get and keep students and raise the level and quality of literacy.   The efforts that have been made to date in the field of adult literacy education have produced somewhat mixed results and have certainly not been without their critics (30, 42, 83, 100). In an effort to meet the issues raised by illiteracy or by inadequate or inappropriate levels of literacy, we have been tempted to set up programs to meet

specific needs, not always taking into account the
larger picture or the impact of theory and
research. Eggert (248) warns us that "the
temptation is strong...to allow the decisions to
occur by default" (p. 27). We cannot allow this to
happen.

In this review of the literature, we will
first consider the literature related to the set of
decisions involved in defining literacy and
illiteracy as well as understanding and applying
models of the adult reading process and of the
adult as a learner. Second, we will look at the
literature related to specific populations,
considering for each group alternatives for
instruction, curriculum development and program
planning.

Literacy and Illiteracy: Definitions and Purposes

The problem that concerns society is the
problem of illiteracy. However, as Fingeret (103)
suggests, "illiteracy can be understood only in
relation to literacy; it is the absence or lack of
literacy, rather than a concept with its own set of
characteristics and standards" (p. 7). In
addition, the danger of focusing only on illiteracy
is, as Sticht (93) observes, that "the reification
of illiteracy has led too often to the initiation
of one-shot 'wars' in which large numbers of
students, workers, and teachers have set out to
'eradicate illiteracy', only to discover that each
new generation that fails to develop literacy leads
to a new 'crop' of illiterates" (p. 3). We will
look first at literacy.

Definitions of literacy have changed over time
(6, 113) and even today there is no common
definition of adult literacy (11, 30, 94) but
rather a number of definitions reflecting different
approaches and embodying different purposes. There
are two general approaches that are used in
defining literacy. One approach is to define
literacy in absolute terms, as an achievement or
grade level, and the other is to define it in
relative terms, often as the competency or ability
to perform literacy tasks in a particular
situation.

In defining literacy in absolute terms, we say
that the adult is reading on a particular level,
usually comparable to a level of schooling, or that
he has completed a certain number of years in
school (30). It is generally possible to document
whether an individual has completed a grade and,
presumably, mastered reading at that level. We can
establish a particular grade level as a benchmark
for literacy and determine whether an individual is
literate or not by whether he has completed that
level. We can change the level, as the U.S. Census
Bureau did in order to establish new expectations
for literacy, going from fourth grade in 1940 (11)
to sixth grade currently (24) as a cutoff for
determining functional literacy. Using an absolute
approach functional literacy is thus defined
quantitatively. Clifford (1), among others (22,
31, 36, 42), traces the use of this approach in the
United States, particularly by governmental
agencies, and determines that such use is probably
for "reasons of convenience" (p. 475). The need
for governmental agencies to "count illiterate
adults" (113, p. 7) is certainly linked to the use
of achievement or grade levels. Crane (13)
documents this use of "a national quantitative
definition" (p. 147) in Britain as well as in North
America.

There are, however, problems with using this
approach. We cannot assume that the adult has
mastered a set of skills just because he has
completed a certain number of years in school (42,
78). In addition, our expectations of achievement
at a particular grade level have changed over time.
Consider how this can affect our definition of
literate or illiterate and how it has in fact
affected the number of adults considered illiterate
(6) or functionally literate.

A further objection to the achievement level
approach is that standards "are set too low to
satisfy reading and writing requirements
encountered outside schools" (1, p. 476). Compare
for example the level of sixth grade used in the
1980 census with the reading level of essential
materials an adult must be able to read. A number
of studies (12, 74, 91, 92) have investigated the
reading levels of these materials and found them to

be difficult reading. Negin and Krugler (92), for
example, found that health and safety materials,
tax forms, and insurance policies are written on a
mean level of between grade 11 and 13 for the
documents analyzed. The message we give adults is
misleading. We tell them that if they learn how to
read at a sixth grade level they will be
functionally literate. Functional literacy implies
that the reader can function in society reading
everyday materials. The adult, often with a great
struggle, achieves this level and finds he still
can't read many of the documents he encounters.

What are some of the implications of using an
absolute approach to defining literacy? For one
thing, assessment becomes important. If we are to
evaluate programs and individuals on an achievement
basis, we must be able to determine accurately what
we mean by reading achievement at the completion of
a particular grade level and be able to determine
just as accurately if an individual has achieved
that level. However, as Chall (12) points out
"there are few tests specifically meant for adults"
(p. 3), and for those that are available "there
seems to be a hesitation in using them for
evaluating group or individual gains or for judging
the effectiveness of programs" (ibid.). The
literacy curriculum we choose if we are aiming at
raising the reading level based on school
achievement will probably have a broad, general
content with an emphasis on reading skills as
opposed to content. Harman (22) observes that "a
common program deficiency resulting from the
adoption of grade equivalencies is the transference
of actual grade school curricula to adult courses
.... the main effect is that adult illiterates are
often equated with children and treated as such"
(p. 237).

The second approach defines literacy within a
particular context, with an emphasis on the skills
needed to perform the literacy tasks in that
context. Fingeret (103) suggests that "literacy is
a shifting, abstract term, impossible to define in
isolation from a specific time, place, and culture;
literacy, therefore, is described as historically
and culturally relative" (p. 7). The key word here
is "relative." The context in which the literacy

demands occur is critical.

In what ways is literacy relative and context
critical? First, definitions of literacy can vary
according to setting or situation. Literacy can
vary "from country to country, and even from
regions within the same country" (32, p. 3), as
well as from urban to rural settings (36). It can
vary according to "the various milieus--the various
occupations, social, and intellectual settings--in
which our students will be expected or may wish to
function" (37, p. 11). Membership in particular
social or religious groups can affect the
definition and requirements of literacy (40).

This link between literacy and the setting or
situation can be seen in a few examples. The 1978
Adult Education Act combined absolute and relative
approaches to defining literacy by including in the
target population "not only those with less than a
high school diploma, but also those who lacked the
skills to function productively in American
society" (29, p. 51). One of the assumptions of
the Adult Performance Level project (34), a
competency-based program for basic literacy, was
that "literacy is a construct which is meaningful
only in a specific cultural context" (p. 43). The
demands of the context were identified and used in
literacy instruction. Programs have been developed
for work settings or for college settings on the
premise that there are particular demands within
these settings that the adult has difficulty
meeting.

Second, requirements for literacy can change
as a society changes (103) and as the individual
changes (21). As the society changes and becomes
more complex, the requirements for literacy also
change (2, 40, 106). Our standards of literacy
today are higher than in the past (6, 12) and "the
level of functional literacy required for effective
living and competence is ever increasing" (13, p.
148). "Literacy standards in the United States in
the 1990s will be both more demanding and more
widely applied than any previous standard" (6, p.
383). The requirements for literacy may also
change as the individual utilizes newly acquired
abilities and establishes new expectations for

himself. "The literacies that people need in order
to maintain and expand the groups in which they
live multiply as their aspirations are heightened"
(21, p. 352). Individuals who want or have
received a promotion encounter new literacy
requirements and may need help in meeting them
(408).

Third, literacy can be affected by the
materials being read and the purpose for the
reading (6, 19, 21, 31, 40). For example, you may
be highly literate reading this text on educational
matters but unable to read a legal document or an
article on advances in microbiology. The context,
in this case the text, has changed. You may find
yourself literate reading the article on
microbiology if your purpose is to identify the
general area of science related to microbiology.
If, however, your purpose is to identify and
compare four technical procedures used by
microbiologists, you may well find yourself
illiterate.

If we accept a relative approach to defining
literacy, then, as Cervero (11) suggests, "a common
operational definition is not attainable" (p. 52).
Even within a single context one definition may not
be possible because of the "values of the definers"
(ibid.). This last comment certainly helps explain
differences of opinions within programs.

In addition to approaching literacy from
either an absolute or a relative perspective,
definitions include a variety of purposes for
literacy and it is this variety, in fact, that has
given rise to an uncertainty in the use of
terminology. As Lehr (30) points out, the
"different terms--literacy, functional literacy,
competency-- ... are often used interchangeably"
(p. 176). Consider the following three major
purposes or functions of literacy:

1. Literacy for survival. Literacy enables the
   individual to "function" or to "survive" in a
   particular context. Scribner (38) refers to
   this as "literacy for adaptation" (p. 9).

   Kirsch and Guthrie (29): "Functional literacy

refers to how well a person can read materials
with 'survival' activities" (p. 505).

Clifford (1): Functional literacy might be
considered as the "possession of practical
competence adequate to the reading and writing
tasks faced in ordinary adult life" (p. 477).

Resnick and Resnick (6): "Functional literacy
has come to mean the ability to read common
texts such as newspapers and manuals and to
use the information gained, usually to secure
employment" (p. 383).

Fitzgerald (14): According to the U.S.
Department of Education, functional literacy
is "the ability of an individual to use
reading skills in everyday life situations--
reading street signs, reading and
comprehending written directions, labels,
applications and work-oriented information"
(p. 196).

Guthrie (393): A study of occupational
literacy found that "among professionals, many
of whom were in scientific areas such as
medicine, reading was usually regarded as
'critical for doing their own jobs well.' The
need to 'get information by reading' was rated
as critical" (p. 479).

2.   Literacy for empowerment. Literacy empowers
the individual to control his social context.
Scribner (38) uses the metaphor "literacy as
power" (p. 11).

Hunter and Harman (80): Functional literacy is
"the possession of skills perceived as
necessary by particular persons and groups to
fulfill their own self-determined objectives
as family and community members, citizens,
consumers, job-holders, and members of social,
religious, or other associations of their
choosing" (p. 7).

Hunter (26): "Literacy is closely related to
self-reliance and a sense of personal power
over conditions that affect one's life" (p.

138).

3. Literacy for human development. Literacy
    enables the individual to develop and grow
    within a particular context or into a new
    context. Scribner (38) calls this "literacy as
    social grace" (p. 13) and includes descriptive
    phrases such as "enlarges and enhances a
    person's essential self" (ibid.) and "literacy
    as a way of developing minds" (p. 14).

    Guthrie (18): Literacy is "a reaching out for
    understanding about the significance of the
    human experience" (pp. 451-452).

    Kazemek (141): "The functions of reading and
    writing cannot be separated from their social
    uses. Individuals use literacy in social
    situations not only to communicate and express
    themselves, but also to gain a deeper and more
    adequate understanding of themselves and the
    world. Truly, one uses literacy in social
    situations to help create oneself and one's
    world" (p. 334).

    Levine (31): The knowledge acquired through
    literacy is essential to the "opportunities--
    or 'life chances'--open to social classes" (p.
    263).

We certainly do not at the present time have a
single, common definition of literacy, functional
literacy, or functional competency even though a
single definition might be useful to federal and
state governments. A single definition would ease
the problem of determining membership in and size
of a target population for funding purposes and for
accountability. It would also be useful to the
publishers of books and tests. One set of
materials could be developed and distributed
economically and probably profitably to all
programs. However, according to Cervero (11), a
common definition and purpose would be useful to
neither the learner nor the teacher. Learners have
different needs and purposes in acquiring literacy
skills. Teachers need to be able to provide
different options. In fact, it is this relative
approach to literacy that has given rise to the

spectrum of programs available to a wide variety of
adults.   We   have   a   growing   sense--in   fact
conviction--that   there   should   be   different
definitions and purposes for literacy.

Although   most   programs   focus   on   one   or
possibly two purposes of   literacy,   Scribner   (38)
concludes   that   "ideal   literacy is simultaneously
adaptive, socially empowering, and   self-enhancing"
(p.   18).   The   adult   can do more than decode or
recognize   words   and   read   simple,   essential
materials.   He   reads,   comprehends,   thinks
critically,   and   acts.   He   functions   in   his
immediate   environment, participates in the life of
his community or the larger society, and   perceives
himself   as   becoming   enriched   as   a   person.
Literacy, thus, is more   than   a   specific   set   of
skills   useful for reading everyday or work-related
materials.

If these are the purposes   of   literacy,   what
are some of the benefits that accrue from literacy?
The   benefits   to   society may be economic, social,
religious, and political (2, 9, 24).   Crane   (13),
for   example, links literacy to "society's need for
skilled workers in order to function   smoothly   and
efficiently" (p. 149) and to its need for citizens
who act responsibly.

The benefits of   literacy   to   the   individual
cover   an   equally   broad   spectrum.   Literacy,
according to Bhola (9), enables the   individual   to
pursue job opportunities and to perform effectively
in   his   present job.   Northcutt (34) proposes that
"literacy is directly related to success" (p.   45).
However,   this   notion is not universally supported
(24,   505).   Levine   (31)   and   Weber   (42),   for
example,   find   little   evidence   to   support   the
relationship between literacy and economic benefits
to the individual.

A common belief is that literacy empowers   the
individual, enabling him to become an agent, not an
object (15,   17,   24,   26,   32).   Literacy, according
to Kazemek (28), liberates "people for intelligent,
meaningful, and humane actions about   their   world"
(p.   14).   Bhola (9) suggests that literacy enables
the individual to participate in political life and

that a "capacity for logical analysis and context-
independent abstract thinking" (p. 11) accrues from
literacy, along with "individualism, independence,
objectivity, holding individual opinion, ... a
sense of history and universalism" (ibid.). Hunter
(79) cautions us, however, that functional literacy
empowers the individual, but only when literacy is
taught within the "larger context of human
competence" (p. 4).

Kazemek (141) makes a distinction between
literacy training and literacy development that is
useful in connection with these purposes and
benefits. Literacy training enables the adult to
"manipulate certain types of surface language
conventions in a very restricted range of
situations; it results in 'survival' literacy
training or competency training of one kind or
another" (p. 333). Literacy development is a
"developmental, empowering process" (p. 334)
focusing on the individual, his needs, the social
context in which the literacy will take place, the
process of reading and writing, and "how the adult
relates all of these things to self and the world"
(p. 335). Instruction to enable the adult to
function at a survival level is literacy training.
Instruction to empower the individual and to enable
him to grow and develop is literacy development.
The distinction is worth keeping in mind in
planning instruction, curricula and programs.

These varying definitions and purposes of
literacy, of literacy as training and literacy as
development, require that we examine the stages of
literacy acquisition and the skills included in
instruction. Harman (22) suggests that literacy
occurs in three stages. "The first is the
conceptualization of literacy as a tool. The
second is literacy attainment, the learning of
reading and writing skills. The third is the
practical application of these skills in activities
meaningful to the learner. Each stage is
contingent upon the former; each is a necessary
component of literacy" (p. 228). The third stage,
in particular, is one that has not always been
included in basic literacy programs. We have not
consistently been concerned with what happens to
the newly acquired literacy after the adult leaves

the program. Yet Chall (12) identifies the newly
literate as the largest single group of adults
needing assistance. The college student who
appears at the skills center seeking help may also
be an example of someone in this third stage. He
may have the skills but not be able to apply them
under the pressure of a heavy reading load.

Chall (12) views adult literacy as occurring
in stages, analogous to the five stages of literacy
acquisition seen in children. These encompass word
recognition, decoding, language and thought,
multiple viewpoints, and the construction and
reconstruction of knowledge. "The course of
development of reading is essentially the same for
adults and children, although perhaps there is a
need for a somewhat different emphasis depending
upon maturity, and different text content" (p. 10).
Much of the emphasis in current programs has been
on Chall's first two stages of literacy
acquisition.

These views of literacy and of the extended
stages of literacy acquisition have given rise to a
range of needed skills and strategies that go
beyond decoding and recognizing words. Consider
these comments:

Miller and Shapiro (32), in viewing literacy
in relation to work, include "work habits,
motivation and teamwork" (p. 5) as skills to
be included in literacy instruction.

Northcutt (34), in discussing the APL project,
asserts that literacy skills go beyond basic
skills and include problem-solving and
interpersonal skills as well as the
application of skills to general knowledge
areas. Literacy is a two-dimensional process
including skill competencies and their
application.

Resnick and Resnick (6) state that "in order
to accommodate the changes in both the
literacy criterion and target population" (p.
385) we need to develop instructional
strategies focusing on comprehension, not on
"back to basics" (ibid.).

Levine (31) includes writing in the concept of functional literacy because it is the ability to write that allows the individual to initiate change by giving him "access to political mechanisms and the political process generally" (p. 262).

Aronowitz (8), Greene (17), Kazemek (28), and Oxenham (35) link literacy to critical and conceptual thinking. This connection cannot be made solely by emphasizing basic skills. Thinking must be included in literacy instruction at all levels, from basic literacy in the APL project to academic preparation for work (390) and college (493, 518, 519). Scribner and Cole (39) caution us that if we want to encourage analytic ability, we must include that component in reading and writing instruction; we cannot assume it will happen. Clifford (1) views literacy as a continuum with decoding skills at one end and reasoning, thinking skills at the other end.

Hirsch (25) includes another dimension in literacy instruction, that of insuring that the adult has the prior knowledge needed to comprehend the text. "Adult literacy is less a system of skills than a system of information" (p. 9).

Up to this point, the discussion has been concerned with literacy, its definitions and purposes, with almost no mention of illiteracy. If literacy is defined absolutely by levels of achievement, then the terms illiterate, functionally illiterate or semiliterate usually are related to an age or grade level. If the definition is relative such as that proposed by Levine (31), then the definition of illiteracy and the illiterate "is greatly widened--people without access to printed material relevant to their information needs, as well as those lacking rudimentary reading and writing skills, now count as illiterate" (p. 264). By such definition we might include the nursing home resident who wants to read the Bible but is unfamiliar with the words and the phrasing, the business executive who encounters difficulty reading and writing complex reports, or the college student who can't comprehend the philosophy text. Illiteracy, based on a relative definition of literacy, refers to those who cannot function within a particular context. Illiteracy and literacy as relative terms may be applicable to the same individual in different situations, reading different materials for different purposes.

In practical terms we are really talking about two broad groups of adults with literacy needs. The first group includes those adults who read on a low level of literacy by any standard. They cannot read the daily newspaper, necessary forms, or basic instructions and manuals needed on the job. The second groups includes those adults who, though not reading at a low level, cannot read sufficiently to meet the demands of the situation in which they find themselves or to which they aspire. This group can include business executives and college students, certainly not groups traditionally associated with literacy problems. A relative approach to defining literacy requires that we recognize the existence of this second group. In addition, we are beginning to recognize that within each group we cannot view an adult as either literate or illiterate but rather as being at some point on a continuum of literacy.

This relative view of literacy forces us to address a major issue. Are we aiming to wipe out illiteracy or to develop literacy? By focusing on literacy we "make possible the continuous development of literacy in both childhood and adulthood" (93, p. 3). The focus on literacy enables us to enlarge abilities and expand horizons, not just "eradicate" the problem of illiteracy with a single effort, no matter how substantial. A focus on literacy suggests looking at the social context and the particular demands of that context rather than focusing on a predetermined set of skills.

A focus on literacy allows for--in fact may require--much more than the development of basic survival skills. We begin to see literacy as comprehension, as a tool useful for many purposes, as the expansion, not merely the maintenance, of an

individual in his environment. Such a focus
permits teachers and students alike to think in
terms of providing instruction in a variety of
skills and strategies, using a variety of
materials, in a variety of settings. It suggests
work-related programs, programs for the elderly,
programs in colleges and universities which enable
students to benefit fully from available courses of
instruction. As Scribner (38) concludes,
"recognition of the multiple meanings and varieties
of literacy also argues for a diversity of
education approaches" (p. 18). Heath (24),
however, warns us that although "literacy has
different meanings for members of different groups,
with a variety of acquisition modes, functions, and
uses; these differences have yet to be taken into
account by policy-makers" (p. 132). The resolution
of the issue of whether to focus on literacy or
illiteracy is crucial to the development of our
national policy as well as to the future of many
adults.

Models of Reading

A second aspect of the decision making process
is a consideration of models of reading. In
general, these models fall into three main
categories: bottom-up, top-down, and interactive
(103, 148). In the bottom-up approach the emphasis
is on decoding the individual word, putting words
together and arriving at the meaning of one or more
sentences. This approach generally emphasizes the
importance of the teacher in imparting skills to
the student, in choosing materials, and in
developing curriculum. The top-down approach
starts with meaning, the meaning the reader brings
to the text and the meaning in the text itself.
Words are read as part of the whole meaningful text
or are predicted from the meaning. An interactive
model of reading "combines both top down and bottom
up, with an emphasis on the assumptions underlying
the top-down approach. That is reading is viewed
as a process of constructing meaning, and phonic
analysis is seen as one of a number of useful tools
for identifying specific words in the text" (103,
pp. 9-10). The reader's prior knowledge is seen
as critical for actively constructing the meaning
of the content and for understanding the structure

of the text. With this emphasis on meaning, it is
apparent that reading is viewed as a thinking
process, with the use of language and the self-
monitoring of the process included as critical
elements. In the last two models the student
becomes more active both in the learning process
and in the process of acquiring meaning from the
text. Because of this there is more room for
student involvement in the process of formulating
instructional goals, developing and choosing
materials, and structuring curriculum.

In many basic literacy programs, particularly
those oriented toward survival, a bottom-up
approach is used with an emphasis on decoding and
word reading. The adult is viewed as the recipient
not the agent in the process. When literacy is
seen as empowerment or human development, it
becomes more evident that meaning is critical and
that the adult must be a thinking, active
participant in the process, reflecting a top-down
or interactive model of reading. However, reading
instruction, even at the very basic level and
focusing on the attainment of survival skills, need
not, as we shall see, be limited to a bottom-up
model.

Adults as Learners

A third consideration that must go into the
decision making process is our view of adults as
learners. Kazemek (28) suggests that in order to
avoid "abstract and arbitrary definitions and
conceptions of adult literacy" (p. 10) and the
resulting "lists of 'required' skills which
individuals must supposedly master before they can
function adequately" (ibid.) we must learn about
and understand adults. This stress on the
importance of understanding the adult as a learner
is widely and well supported in the literature on
adult reading instruction (103, 106, 108, 111,
127).

The literature on adult development is broad
and complex; this is only an overview. The
references in the bibliography will provide breadth
and depth to the study of a critical area for those
who work with adults. It is an oversimplification

to say that theories of adult learning and
development fall into three categories dealing with
the differences between adults and children, the
phases in adult development that occur in response
to age-related changes in the adult's life, and the
stages in adult development that are sequential but
appear to be independent of the particular
conditions of the adult's life. All approaches
have implications for adult education, but it is
the differences between adults and children that
have been widely discussed, usually in terms of
andragogy and pedagogy.

Definitions, descriptions, and analyses of
andragogy and pedagogy, particularly the former,
abound in the literature on adult education (44,
48, 49, 50, 51, 56, 60, 62, 63, 64, 66, 67).
Darkenwald and Merrian (49) summarize the view of
adults that forms the basis for andragogy. Adult
learners are self-directed, have experience they
can use as a resource for learning, relate learning
and the readiness to learn to the tasks associated
with social roles, and are more problem-centered
than subject-centered. Andragogy, thus, refers to
a student-centered system in which the adult
learner group is designated as the agent in charge
of determining what levels and kinds of learning
are needed with the instructor acting as
facilitator. The teacher conducts a needs
assessment to determine what the learner wants and
needs to learn, becomes a facilitator of that
learning, involves the learner in educational
decisions, and provides for assessment of the
learning by the learner. Pedagogy refers to a
teacher-centered system of instruction in which the
responsibility for the learning resides in the
teacher and the institution. The teacher conveys
knowledge to the student, decides on the method and
organization of instruction, and conducts
assessment of the learning.

It has been suggested that perhaps adult
instruction should not be based on an either/or
approach but rather on a blend of the two. Beder
(44) proposes that the blend be done on the basis
of the knowledge to be learned. In
formal/segmented knowledge where information and
principles are cumulative, pedagogy is appropriate.

In problem oriented knowledge where the "information or skills an individual needs to learn in order to solve or cope with a problem posed by the environment or life situation" (p. 15) are critical, discrete and applied to experience, andragogy is appropriate.

Knowles, a major proponent of andragogy, has come to view the use of andragogy and pedagogy as a continuum determined by the material to be learned. In 1970 Knowles wrote a book subtitled ANDRAGOGY VERSUS PEDAGOGY; in 1980 he (64) stated that a pedagogical approach was appropriate when the material to be learned was "at the lowest level of complexity" (p. 3) and was material with which the learner was unfamiliar. Rachal (63) also suggests that andragogy and pedagogy present a continuum of possibilities for the teacher and learner based on the material to be learned as well as on the motivation of the student and the professional and ethical responsibilities of each party. Both approaches may be present in the same course or in the same class. Conti (47) suggests another alternative, a collaborative approach in which the learner and the teacher together determine the goals, methods, content, and evaluation of instruction.

Consider how these viewpoints might apply to literacy instruction. Much of the instruction that has taken place has been teacher-directed, particularly in programs designed to develop basic survival skills. It may be that survival material lends itself to teacher direction and decision-making. The danger is that all instruction will be based on pedagogy, while much of it could and should be based on andragogy. Adults can identify goals, make decisions about materials, and pose and solve problems. Hunter (79), in fact, states that "specific persons and groups are the only ones who can decide what functional literacy is for them" (p. 2). This seems especially relevant when the purpose of literacy is for empowerment and/or human development. The notion of a continuum or a collaborative approach is appealing.

Age-related phases, according to Lasker and Moore (58), relate to the developmental tasks that

are part of the various biological, social and
occupational situations and roles in which the
adult finds himself as he matures. Darkenwald and
Merriam (49) quote Havighurst as suggesting that
these roles are important because "educational
programs can be conceived to help people improve
their performance of [such] roles" (p. 91).
Programs for the elderly, for example, often
reflect age-related goals designed to enrich and
enhance the quality of life or attain wisdom at a
period in life when the senior citizen has the
time, inclination, and motivation to work on the
particular goal as opposed to an earlier goal of
earning a living.

Stage-related approaches, according to Lasker
and Moore (58), stress that adults develop
psychologically independently of the changing
conditions of their lives. It is these
"psychological systems through which adults make
sense of their realities and take action to meet
their needs" (58, p. 15). Lasker and Moore suggest
that these stages can be related to the instruction
of adult students in areas such as the social
climate of the classroom, the role of the teacher
and the learner, and the development of curriculum
that is appropriate to the stage of the adult.

If we are to apply learning theory about
adults to literacy instruction we need more
research in this area and we need to insure that
practitioners are familiar with these concepts.
Research is sorely needed in the field of adult
learning to establish and verify adult learning
strategies (65, 72). We cannot afford to assume
that adults and children have similar learning
needs and learn in the same way. It appears that
they may not. In addition, professional teachers
(72) and volunteers, both inservice (69) and
preservice (68), need to be trained in adult
learning theory (73) and have practice in applying
it to educational situations (71). In reading
about and planning literacy programs, we need to
consider how the instruction provided, materials
used, and program structure reflect current
thinking about adults.

Adult Literacy Practice

The traditional approach to adult literacy
programs is based on a school model, often on an
elementary school one. There may be two or three
groups in the room using the same text at different
rates, or possibly different texts. More likely,
the students are at desks, all using the same text,
with the teacher at the front of the room. In
adult basic literacy classes the materials are
those needed for survival in present-day society
such as employment forms, want ads, and
applications for bank accounts. The class may be
part of an Adult Basic Education program offered in
a school setting. It may be part of a program at
work and may deal strictly with materials that are
needed for the job. The class may be part of a
college skills program in which students are using
workbooks designed to prepare them to read text
required in courses. The teacher determines the
skills, strategies, and materials that will form
the core of the program and the methods of
assessing success or failure. Once the student
acquires the skills or the class is over, the
student leaves. Consider how this approach fits
with current notions of literacy, reading models
and views of adults as learners.

The assumption we make in traditional programs
is that the purpose of literacy is to function or
survive, probably in a specific environment with
success or failure determined by the institution.
Yet there is dissatisfaction with this goal. For
example, Eberle and Robinson (280), in describing
the clients of their program, conclude that
"perhaps what becoming more literate can do is give
a person the opportunity to make more choices,
rather than waiting in anxiety for someone else's
decisions" (p. 15). This suggests that for many
adults the goal of literacy is broader than to
survive.

In addition to a concern about the
incompatibility of the school model with the
literacy goals of adults, the school model of
instruction has been widely criticized because it
assumes that adults and children learn and learn to
read the same way (138). Malicky and Norman (124)

take strong exception to this notion. "Differences
between children and adults are sufficiently great
to indicate that the pedagogy of teaching reading
to children is not appropriate for the teaching of
adults" (p. 735). Weber (42) concurs, finding this
to be the "most persistent weakness" (p. 154) in
adult literacy programs and suggesting that this
instructional model may be a major reason why
adults are reluctant to enroll in programs, and
once in a program may not participate fully and may
fail to complete it.

        Finally, consider the implications of this
model for the adult student. "Learning for adults
does not happen most successfully in an environment
in which they feel they are being treated like
children" (280, p. 33). The physical environment,
the materials, the decision-making process, the
role of the teacher, and the role of the student,
all conspire to remind the student of previous
failures. Rigg and Kazemek (226) concur. "Is it
any wonder that programmes fail to retain many of
their students? Adults quickly realize when their
goals, plans, world views, and beliefs are given
little serious consideration by teachers" (p. 26).

        There is an increasing dissatisfaction with
the use of the school model in adult literacy
instruction while at the same time there is
uncertainty as to exactly what should be done. As
Beder points out "the issue of how adults should be
educated is central to the profession, eternal and
largely unresolved" (44, p. 14). Lindsay (72)
concurs, asserting that there is an "absence of
theoretical and tested empirical knowledge to guide
and verify the efforts of practitioners in this
field" (p. 50). However, Lindsay also points out
that the model just described "is antiquated and
increasingly incompatible with adults who must deal
daily with the realities of their work, their
family, and their community" (p. 51). We need to
examine a variety of alternatives in instruction,
curriculum, and program development.

Summary

        The matter would be simple indeed if we could
propose a model of adult literacy education that

would meet all the various literacy needs in our
society. We can't. As Fingeret (103) points out,
there is no one best approach. The needs of adults
are too diverse; the situations in which they find
themselves needing literacy skills are too diverse.

In order to approach the problems of literacy
and illiteracy from a manageable and practical
perspective we will consider adult basic literacy
in general, looking at instruction, curriculum, and
programming, then examine the needs of particular
groups who may have literacy needs at a variety of
levels, and finally review some general findings
from literacy programs abroad. As Scribner
suggests (38) "learning how literacy functions
among a people far removed from us culturally and
geographically may help us take a new look at its
functions here at home" (p. 15). In examining the
various contexts and purposes for literacy
instruction we need to consider the appropriateness
of the alternatives and suggestions in terms of the
three critical areas: definitions of literacy and
illiteracy, models of reading, and views of adults
as learners.

Adult Basic Literacy

The Extent and Implications of the Problem

Estimates of the number of adults in the
United States reading on low levels of literacy
vary, probably because of the differences in
definitions and measurement techniques (30, 36,
106). There is, however, an area of general
agreement. In 1983, the U.S. Department of
Education (98) estimated that "27 million people
are functionally illiterate today (A.P.L. 1) and an
additional 47 million do not function proficiently
(A.P.L. 2), for a total of 74 million Americans who
function at a marginal level or below" (p. 1).
(A.P.L 1 refers to adults with eight or fewer years
of education; A.P.L. 2 refers to adults with nine
to eleven years of schooling (225).)

Chall (12) in 1984 used somewhat different
categories but arrived at remarkably similar

totals, cautioning, however, that any figures must
be considered as estimates because of the lack of
national test data. The totally illiterate or
basic literacy group (up to 4th grade reading
level) numbered about one million people while the
functionally illiterate group (on the 4th to 8th
grade reading level) numbered approximately 23-26
million. These two groups were cited as having
made sizeable gains over the past few years. They
also correspond generally to the group of
functionally illiterate identified by the U.S.
Department of Education in both number of adults
and grade level achieved. The largest group Chall
identified was the newly illiterate, about 51
million. These adults have literacy skills but
they are not sufficient for the increasing demands
of our present-day society. Chall's third group
corresponds roughly to the second group identified
by the Department of Education in both number and
level.

Similar figures are available from other
sources (30, 76, 78, 83, 87, 89, 94), with some
differences occurring in numbers and levels
included in the groups. However, as Hunter and
Harman (80) point out, "the aggregate message of
all the statistics is more important than their
specific accuracy" (p. 56). We have a problem of
some magnitude.

Who is likely to be found in these categories
of adults with low literacy levels? The Department
of Education (98) states that "13 percent of White
and 56 percent of Hispanic seventeen year-olds are
functionally illiterate--and a recent study reports
that 47 percent of Black youth are illiterate" (p.
1). Members of other minorities, such as American
Indians and the handicapped, as well as the poor,
the unemployed, welfare recipients, prison inmates,
and the elderly are frequently identified as high
on the list of the illiterate (75, 78, 81, 85, 89,
94, 98, 100).

One of the difficulties, of course, when
examining groups with low levels of literacy is
teasing out what is cause and what is effect. Are
these groups part of the category of low literacy
levels as a result of being members of these

various groups or are they in the groups because of
their low literacy levels? Hunter and Harman (80)
present one perspective. "Research suggests that
the poverty and the power structure of society are
more responsible for low levels of literacy than
the reverse" (p. 9).

This list of groups having high rates of
illiteracy highlights some of the problems and
costs to society of illiteracy in terms of welfare,
unemployment, and incarceration to name a few (56,
76, 78, 83, 87, 226) as well as costs to business
and industry of jobs poorly done as a result of
literacy problems (78).

In assessing the costs to the individual and
the family the literature abounds with words and
phrases such as "powerless ... inadequate" (78, p.
3), "devastated concept of ... own self-worth" (94,
p. 6), "innate potential for anger and resentment"
(ibid.), "fearful" (ibid.), "resentful" (ibid.),
"stupid" (218, p. 8), "passivity" (ibid, p. 9),
"perplexities, frustrations" (280, p. 7). Kozol
(82) calls illiterates "Prisoners of Silence." The
impact of illiteracy falls not only on the
individual but also on the family (9, 106),
particularly the children in the family (83).
Mikulecky, Shanklin and Caverly (125) cite studies
showing the potentially adverse effect of adult
reading problems and habits on the children of the
family. Sticht (93) refers to this as the
"intergenerational relationship between the
literacy skills of adults and their children" (p.
9).

These costs, in fact, are so "staggering" (14,
p. 198) that Fitzgerald concludes we cannot afford
to allow volunteerism in adult basic literacy
education to continue. Adults do not have the
right to remain illiterate. Sticht (93) concurs
and goes even farther. Adults "have an obligation
to read and to develop the levels of literacy that
are needed to secure both personal and national
freedom" (p. 3).

Instruction

While there are many programs providing basic

literacy instruction for adults, there is no final, definitive theory of adult reading and relatively little basic research on how adults learn to read and to refine and apply the reading skills they have (103, 115, 119, 123, 124, 125, 132, 146). Much of the reading instruction that has been provided to beginning level adult students has been patterned after an elementary school model with a lagging recognition of the range of theoretical models of reading available and with minimal recognition of what we do know about adult readers (115). Although we do find some instructional programs for adults that emphasize reading as a thinking, meaning-gathering process, reflecting a top-down or interactive model, much emphasis in basic literacy instruction is placed on decoding and word recognition. The instructional model often adopted, whether recognized or not, reflects a bottom-up approach to reading.

Instructional Alternatives. In examining the critical issue of whether the emphasis should be placed on decoding or comprehending, consider some research findings. There is evidence that adult readers who have difficulty beginning the process of reading and/or make limited progress once they begin view reading as decoding or word calling, not as comprehending (116, 119, 149, 160). In addition, knowledge and use of the structure of the language appear to be important in obtaining meaning. Malicky and Norman (124), for example, found that readers in their study who did not make progress relied more heavily on decoding and word calling than on predicting words through their knowledge of the grammatical system of the language.

In terms of instruction, Sharpe and Ganschow (146) contend that in fact it is the emphasis on decoding that has failed with many adults. Thistlethwaite (148) also found that this approach is one that may have failed with adults when they were children. "Offering a comprehension-based model of reading to these adults gives them a new and different way of looking at reading" (p. 6). There is a widespread conviction that the focus of adult reading instruction should be firmly on comprehension (6, 119, 146, 148, 149, 159, 160,

182).   Rigg and Kazemek (226) conclude that
"comprehension--getting meaning--is not the result
of reading; it is reading.... Phonic drills and
word lists typify the materials that literacy
instructors should reject" (p. 28).

This focus on comprehension does not mean,
however, that everyone has discarded the notion of
teaching decoding and word recognition skills.
Chall (12), in discussing her five stages of
reading development, assures us that "both the 6
year old beginner and the 40 year old beginner need
to learn to recognize in print the words they know
when heard or spoken.... Most difficulties they
have in understanding what they read stem from
inadequate recognition of words.   It is their
limited knowledge of the alphabetic principle and
its automatic use that keeps them illiterates or
non-readers" (p. 10). She questions the emphasis
on "teaching concepts, ideas and knowledge from the
start" (ibid.) without providing instruction in
word recognition. She cites as an example the work
done by Paulo Freire which emphasizes political
consciousness but also teaches decoding and word
recognition using a carefully selected vocabulary.
Freire (136) would stress, however, that he "would
find it impossible to be engaged in a work of
mechanically memorizing vowel sounds.... Nor would
[he] reduce learning to read and write merely to
learning words, syllables, or letters" (p. 10).
His focus is clearly on meaning.

Boraks and Richardson (132) echo this concern,
stressing that "adults must be instructed in ways
which do not stress the abstract (letter/sound)
aspect of the reading process" (p. 12).   Instead,
we should "teach reading using functional or
language-experienced based symbols" (ibid., p. 13).
Again, the focus is on meaning!   However, Boraks
and Schumacker (116) did find that the ability to
"manipulate vowels and syllables" was useful in
making progress in literacy acquisition. Notice
the verb "manipulate." This implies an active role
in learning and using decoding cues.

For anyone, however, who has had experience
teaching adults, the question of automatic word
recognition is critical; the lack of it is the

source of enormous frustration to both instructor
and student. Chall (12) stresses that "clinical
experience in teaching adult beginners suggests the
need for teaching and learning word recognition"
(p. 11). Boraks and Richardson (132) stress,
however, that cues for word recognition should be
appropriate to the situation in which the adult
will meet the word. This implies that since words
will generally be found in context, not in
isolation, they should be taught in context, with
auditory and visual cues noted only after meaning
and syntax. Freire (136) contends that the words
used must be the student's words and the reading of
the words must be related to the student's world as
well as involve "critical perception,
interpretation, and re-writing what is read" (p.
11). Word recognition is put into the framework of
meaning.

A related and very practical question in adult
literacy instruction is whether we should teach
decoding and comprehension skills in a
predetermined sequence, probably using a
diagnostic-prescriptive approach, or whether we
should teach skills as needed, with the need
identified by the student and/or the instructor.
The sequential skill approach has been a
traditional one for some time in adult basic
literacy instruction (146). Lamorella, Tracy,
Hasse and Murphy (143), for example, describe a
diagnostic-prescriptive approach which emphasizes
sequential skill development with the decisions and
the instruction firmly in the hands of the teacher.

There is increasing criticism and rejection of
this approach for adults for a variety of reasons.
Sharpe and Ganschow (146) reject it for some adults
for practical reasons. It may have been tried
previously and not been successful. Jones (106)
bases his rejection on reading theory. Reading is
a meaning-oriented activity and a holist process.
Thus, the learner should learn only those skills
needed and not in any particular way or sequence
and should focus on meaning and content. Fingeret
(103) looks at the goals of literacy and suggests
that a diagnostic-prescriptive approach may
emphasize sequential skill development "at the
expense of reading enjoyment" (p. 31) as well as

comprehension. Rigg and Kazemek (226) also reject
this approach because of the implied view of adults
as learners. "In this situation teacher acts as
the Parent, and the student is treated as a Child"
(p. 26).

This perspective on teaching adult literacy
from a framework of meaning is consistent with
reading theory. This is not to say that adults
don't need some decoding skills and don't need to
recognize some essential words. They do. The
basic question is where to put the emphasis and how
to instruct. It may be that in the process of
focusing on meaning we make temporary compromises.
Rigg (145), for example, relates the experience of
tutoring a mature woman whose concept of reading
was getting the letters right. This contrasted
sharply with the tutor's emphasis on building
meaning. Because of the need to respect the adult
as a learner and as a person, a continuous
adjustment was made to accommodate both
perspectives. Some basic concepts of decoding and
some essential words were taught. In addition,
because of the nature of the material, following
the suggestion of Beder (44) and Knowles (64), it
might be useful to employ a pedagogical approach to
the teaching of decoding. The teaching of decoding
and meaning may provide a place to apply Rachal's
(63) concept of a continuum for using both pedagogy
and andragogy in adult literacy instruction.

If meaning is central to reading, what is the
role of the reader's background knowledge?
Literacy by its very nature, according to Hirsch
(25), requires relevant background knowledge
including knowledge of both language and concepts.
Prior knowledge appears to be critical in
comprehending text from a research perspective
(119, 120, 121, 129), a theoretical perspective
(103), and a practical orientation (280). Prior
knowledge also includes knowledge of text
structure. Boraks and Richardson (132), for
example, state that "students will comprehend
reading material better when they can focus on the
organization of the material" (p. 10).
Unfortunately, Gambrell and Heathington (119) found
that adult poor readers were often not aware of the
significance of text structure in comprehending

written materials.

In addition, adult students need to understand
the process of literacy acquisition (114) and the
function of the strategy they are learning (115,
149). Gambrell and Heathington (119) found that
adult poor readers "reported fewer strategies, more
misconceptions about strategies, and were not as
sensitive to how and when to use specific reading
strategies" (p. 220). These students lacked the
ability to monitor their own process. Boraks and
Richardson (132), in examining decoding skills,
concluded that "adults should be encouraged to
identify and organize their own approach to word
recognition" (p. 8). The key words here, of
course, are "identify and organize." Adults need
to develop an awareness of the decoding and word
recognition skills they are using as well as a
system for consciously using them. The emphasis is
on the student, not the instructor, ultimately
assuming responsibility for the process. Carmen
(167), in fact, believes that the most important
task for the instructor is to foster independence
and responsibility in the adult student. Consider
how this relates not only to reading theories but
also to theories of adult learning.

The picture that is emerging is one of adult
students assuming responsibility for their
learning, focusing on comprehension as the goal of
reading, and also using decoding and word
recognition strategies in an active, meaningful
manner. Boraks and Richardson (132) assert that in
view of what we know about adult learners we should
be moving from a "'present-recite-test' approach to
an 'active, thinking, using' approach" (p. 2).
Jones (106) concurs, proposing a language-thinking
approach to literacy instruction and basing his
proposal on a review of theories of reading. A
practical application of this approach can be seen
in a resource guide developed for the British
Columbia Department of Education (217) based on the
premise that reading is "both a language process
and a cognitive or thinking process" (p. 47). The
suggestions made in it focus on meaning. In making
instructional decisions, we need to consider
definitions of literacy, the role of the adult in
learning, models of reading, and the strategies of

the adult in acquiring literacy skills.

Let's consider some of the suggestions for
instruction that appear in the literature. Don't
settle on one suggestion and use it exclusively.
Students need a repertoire of skills and strategies
that they can use in a variety of situations.
Since poor readers tend not to have this repertoire
(119), one of the functions of teaching is to
increase the strategies available.

1. Don't assume that the adult understands that
    reading is comprehension. Provide experiences
    that will demonstrate this as well as provide
    an understanding of the process of reading
    (119, 149, 160). Use cloze activities with
    missing letters or words so the student can
    predict words and meaning based on both prior
    knowledge and the text. He does not need to be
    able to read every word in order to construct
    meaning.

2. Provide students with opportunities to monitor
    their process and progress (149). We need to
    focus on "both awareness and use of a
    repertoire of strategies" (119, p. 221).
    Bunner (152) provides an example of teaching a
    student to self-monitor during decoding by
    teaching the student to ask himself where he
    should look to decide why the word didn't sound
    right.

3. Develop or provide prior knowledge before
    reading through films, group discussions,
    questions, or advanced organizers (116, 121,
    123, 129). Background information might be
    developed through a language experience
    approach and then applied to commercial
    materials or functional materials. Enlarging
    the adult's social/cultural environment also
    serves to enhance prior knowledge in general
    (132).

4. Develop discussion and comprehension beyond a
    literal level (226) by using questions
    generated by the student and the instructor.
    Emphasize critical reading (159). If an adult
    is to benefit from all the advantages of

literacy he must read critically, evaluating the message of the text.

5. Encourage students to read for a variety of purposes, to fulfill more than one kind of literacy need, including enjoyment (103, 110, 133, 137).

6. Encourage students to make predictions about the text based on meaning (144, 146). This strategy is firmly related to the top-down and the interactive models of reading, yet many adult students are so afraid of being wrong (possibly because we have stressed the need to be absolutely right!) that they need reassurance that this is an acceptable strategy.

7. Teach the student to use text structure. Consider using Herber's leveled guide (132) in which the reader focuses on the text structure through the use of questions. Holland and Redish (158) confirm that forms, for example, have an identifiable text structure with particular characteristics, purposes and uses. We can plan instruction to teach these structures, using a variety of words and concepts (154).

8. Use text long enough for the meaning to be clear to the reader and for the reader to use the content and the text structure as sources of information (123).

9. Don't be afraid to teach some words to the level of automatic recognition. Because of the element of motivation and because of the need for students to be able to read certain high utility words, a number of lists have been developed particularly for adults. These include words drawn from government applications and forms (151), words categorized according to intent or meaning (153), words related to highway safety (155), and words identified as useful by adult students (157). The concern here is that word recognition will be the focus of instruction and that the words will be taught in isolation not in context. We

need to provide for recognition and practice of words in a meaningful context (132, 134, 137). In choosing the words to be emphasized, consider Freire's (136) caution that the words must come from the student's experience and reflect his needs.

10. Use a variety of strategies for word recognition, such as repeated readings, oral reading in order to allow "both teacher and student to become aware of errors and work together toward their solutions" (152, p. 147), or Prime-0-Tec, a technique combining listening to material read aloud, following the text, and reading along with the recording (156). The adult needs to develop individual approaches to word recognition, ones that work for him (132).

11. Provide direct instruction in decoding a word or group of words when this help is needed (12, 123, 148).

12. Include writing in literacy instruction. Adult Basic Literacy programs often stress writing as handwriting or as a way to practice vocabulary and sentence structure. However, these uses do not exploit the full potential of writing in a literacy program. Use writing to enable the reader to think like a writer, expand and explore his mind, analyze ideas, raise questions, become involved in the act of reading and writing, and develop language and self-confidence (106, 139, 140, 141, 146, 148, 167, 226). Kazemek (140) urges us to "incorporate writing instruction into each lesson, not as an adjunct to reading instruction but as an integral, equally supportive aspect of each lesson" (p. 618).

13. Use instructional strategies that foster learning. Model the process of learning and learning to read (116). Use simple, easily understood strategies (115). Avoid failure and try to insure success (115, 280). Insure that the student feels confident and at ease with himself (117, 280). Understand and respect the student (114).

How much time do we need to instruct the adult basic literacy student? The question, of course, is simplistic. We don't know what the student knows, needs to know, or wants to know. However, literacy programs often tend to be of short and defined time periods. The difficulty is that only limited progress is generally made in within relatively short periods of time. Sticht (128), for example, did not find substantial gains in the acquisition of literacy skills after brief, concentrated instruction in general literacy, although he did find more rapid learning when job-related materials were used than when general materials were used. Malicky and Norman (124) found that we cannot expect even, continuous progress by adults. This is certainly a disadvantage if the time period is defined and limited. Kazemek (141) firmly believes that literacy can't be acquired in a short time. She takes a very broad view of literacy, including in it the ability to "express and create as well as to analyze and communicate" (p. 335). This is certainly more than literacy for survival or literacy training.

These suggestions clearly go beyond having the instructor stand in the front of the room, drill the students on vowel sounds, and train them to memorize a list of essential sight words. Adult basic literacy students deserve more than that. In fact, they need more than that.

Materials. There is probably no issue of more immediate concern to both the student and instructor than the selection of reading materials to be used. In choosing materials, there are a number of questions you need to examine. Are you going to use readability levels and formulas as your basis for choice? You certainly don't want to give the student materials that are so difficult he can't possibly read them, but you also don't want to insult him with simplistic text. Are you going to use materials relevant to the student's world or are you going to try to expand his horizons? The materials chosen will reflect the purposes for acquiring and using literacy that form the basis of the program. Where will you obtain the materials? Will they come from commercial publishers, from the student's immediate environment, or from you or the

students themselves? Who will make the choice?
Remember the discussion of the variables in adult
learning. These questions are interrelated and need
to be considered in making the decision about
materials to be used.

The question of how much to rely on readability
formulas and levels underlies decisions regarding
materials. Readability formulas generally measure
the length of the words and sentences used in the
text (103). These formulas are often applied to
materials to determine reading level and are
frequently used in the writing of materials to
insure that they can be read by readers of a
particular reading level (161). The reading levels
of materials as determined by a formula are
frequently provided in listings of commercial
materials. The formulas are also relatively easy
for instructors to apply to materials in order to
obtain an indication of the level of difficulty and
to give support to their judgments.

The reliance on readability formulas has come
under serious question in recent years. Readability
includes more than word and sentence length. It
also includes language, style, organization of the
information, and visual format. Yet these are
generally not included in the computation of
readability levels (164). Another critical element
in readability is the appropriateness of the
material to the reader's background information
(103, 120, 164). Whyte (129), for example,
identifies the interaction between the text and the
reader's prior knowledge as an important source of
information for comprehension. Yet, this match or
interaction is often not considered when instructors
apply readability formulas and/or choose materials
(120). Finally, the use of formulas as a basis for
writing such materials has been criticized because
of the limitations imposed on vocabulary, concepts,
and meanings (103).

The use of a readability formula may provide a
broad measure of the appropriateness of a text, but
it needs to be combined with other considerations.
If instruction has stressed, for example, the
identification and use of text structure, the
student might be able to comprehend the text even

though the readability formula might indicate it was
a challenge. The content of the material also needs
to be considered in relation to readability.
Schnell (126), for example, found that instruction
using "materials chosen for their utility in daily
activities" (p. 102) without considering reading
level produced significantly higher gains in reading
than that using high-interest materials at an
appropriate level.

What should the content of materials be? This
issue is far from settled. In each case, consider
the relationship between the content and the purpose
of literacy. One suggestion is to use material
whose content is related to the student's
experiential background (120, 121, 123, 129).
Materials have been developed based on this premise-
-for example, using Biblical references (168) or
cultural and historical resources of the American
Indians (75, 181). Another alternative is to choose
materials needed by the student because of "their
utility in daily activities" (126, p. 102; 174, 178,
183) or their relevance to a job (128, 169, 171). A
different approach is to choose materials for
students that will "expand their goals and interests
by helping to redefine and redirect them" (132, p.
5).

No matter why the content is chosen, interest
in the material and motivation to learn are
important variables for adults (119, 120, 126, 132,
138). "'Readability' is nice, but it doesn't hold a
candle to interest in the material" (280, p. 31).
This recognition of interest as a variable also
requires recognition that it may require different
options for different adults and for the same adult
at different times (132) as interests and goals
change during the life cycle.

What are sources for obtaining materials? The
options here may be broader than you have
considered. Commercial materials specifically
developed for adult literacy students are available.
Cranney (102) has observed that in recent years the
materials available for adults have "increased in
quantity and somewhat in quality" (p. 421),
providing instructors with more options. How do you
know how to identify, evaluate, and choose

commercial materials? Before purchasing anything
check one or more of the many bibliographies
available which contain descriptions and/or reviews
of commercially prepared materials (162, 163, 167,
172).

Another source for materials is the student's
particular or general environment. Schnell (126)
believes that because of the interest and motivation
generated by these materials "no specially developed
instructional materials are necessary" (p. 104).
This approach is often taken in job-related programs
(401, 408, 409) and in community developed programs
(103). The purpose might be to develop job skills
or it might be to develop the adult's ability to
read needed forms (158). Consider using materials
such as the actual forms, magazines, newspapers
found in the adult's environment (176, 178, 183,
184).   These materials tend to promote a focused
view of literacy and literacy training with the goal
of enabling the student to survive in an
environment.

Other materials which may not have been
specifically developed for literacy students and
which don't have this focused, narrow view of
literacy can be used. Consider resources from the
local library such as a variety of nonfiction books
(166, 180), materials from the humanities (177), or
music or poetry (139, 141, 182, 185, 226). These
materials tend to foster literacy for empowerment or
for human development.   You might combine both
poetry and functional shopping lists as a way of
developing literacy skills for more than one goal
(140).   The materials used support the goal of
literacy chosen as the basis for instruction.

Before using any of these materials, evaluate
them using one or more of the guidelines or
checklists available (167, 172, 179, 180, 196). The
list developed by Newman and Eyster (179) for the
International Reading Association, for example,
includes: appeal, relevance, purpose, process, human
relations, evaluation, function, format, teacher
directions, and content. The guidelines compiled by
Rigg and Kazemek (182) have a somewhat different
focus. These authors stress that the material must
be meaningful and complete, have literary merit, be

readily available and inexpensive, and enable
students to integrate reading, writing, and
language.

    You might decide to have students create their
own materials or to create materials for them. An
advantage to the use of student-made and/or teacher-
made materials is that they can be based on the
student's vocabulary, language, and concepts (138).
The Language Experience Approach in which students
write their own material is widely suggested (106,
119, 123, 132, 134, 137, 148, 149, 182, 196, 216)
for adult basic literacy students. The adult is
actively engaged in the process of constructing and
reading the material. The vocabulary, content, and
concepts are appropriate and important to the
reader. The reader will be motivated to engage in
the process of reading. In addition, Longnion (123)
suggests that when using Language Experience adult
readers can "place more of their energy on the
graphophonic cueing system since they will be
processing print that contains their own syntax and
experiences" (p. 151). Singh, Singh, and Blampied
(147) advocate using repeated readings of Language
Experience material to develop automaticity in word
recognition skills. Escoe (135) suggests a
Communication Experience Approach in which material
is composed in a manner similar to the Language
Experience Approach but is written in response to an
identified need to communicate in a social
situation.

    The other option is for you to create materials
for students. Fingeret (103) warns us that
"unfortunately, many teacher-created materials
suffer from some of the same drawbacks as commercial
materials, due to the belief that the reading
difficulty of materials must be tightly controlled
through the use of 'readability' formulas" (p. 36).
Help is available to teachers in learning how to
write materials and in training writers to write
them (165, 175, 196). The materials written can
vary according to the needs of the program. Amoroso
(131), for example, proposes the use of an organic
primer, written by the instructor, in which the
emphasis is not on mastering a set of sequential
skills, but rather on reading stories with an
eclectic and appropriate content using natural and

predictable language. This approach is similar to
that developed by Freire and that used in the Cuban
Literacy Campaign. The materials you create will
reflect your view of literacy and your purpose for
instruction. You might create very practical
materials closely related to a job need (171) or you
might create humanities materials, designed to
expand horizons and experiences (175).

Finally, who will choose the materials, the
instructor, the student, or both? In most adult
basic literacy programs the instructor has
traditionally made the decisions on materials to be
used. There is a growing feeling that we should
bring the student into this decision. Jones (106),
for example, proposes that programs be developed
collaboratively with the instructor and the adult
student designing the course and choosing the
materials together. Others go farther, placing the
decision about materials in the hands of the student
(144). Hoffman (138) urges us to "find what the
learner wants to read and provide it" (p. 36). The
decision is the student's. Consider how the
decision as to who chooses the material reflects
views of the adult as learner.

There is no definitive, best set of materials
for us to use because of the differences in needs of
adults and the various definitions and purposes of
literacy. In practice, you may need to combine
materials. Harrison, Little and Mallett (137), for
example, suggest that instructors "balance
'instructional material' with the 'real reading' of
daily adult living" (p. 7). Rigg and Kazemek (182)
use country music, religious writings, poetry, and
language experience. The choice of materials is
inextricably linked to the other decisions to be
made in literacy instruction.

Assessment. Questions related to the
assessment of individuals have frequently loomed
large for literacy programs. We as a nation are
concerned about testing. We want to know levels,
skills, abilities, competencies. Probably, part of
this emphasis is a legacy from our definition of
literacy as a level of achievement. Unfortunately,
Chall (12) finds that "there are few tests
specifically meant for adults" (p. 3); Cranney (102)

labels the adult tests that are available as
"limited" (p. 418).

      One of the difficulties in developing tests and
in choosing the one or ones to use is that diverse
definitions of literacy and functional literacy
require different tests (186, 187). Do we want to
measure school literacy in adults? Do we want to
measure ability to function in a day-to-day world or
in a work world? Torres and Harnisch (194) suggest
that because of differences in definitions one test
may not suffice; we may need "highly specific tests"
(p. 13) to meet the various requirements.

      Another problem with formal testing is the
overemphasis on subskill testing (186, 191) without
a regard for the current view of reading as a holist
process. This emphasis on subskill evaluation may
present a practical problem for those programs that
do not focus on subskill instruction but rather on a
holistic view of comprehension (106).

      In the meantime, what are the alternatives? If
the decision has been or is made to use formal
tests, then examine the tests themselves as well as
current reviews of them (106, 172, 186, 187, 191,
193). Understand what the tests are testing, how
the information is obtained, and what kind of
responses the student is expected to make. Look at
information included in the tests on reliability and
validity. Consider patterns of responses and the
possibility that the error may be the result of an
information processing failure or carelessness and
may not be related to the level on which the student
is functioning (190, 194). In order to understand a
student's performance we need to know and understand
the tests that are used.

      Informal testing gives us a way of looking at
literacy from a more personal perspective, possibly
taking a holistic look at the individual, his needs,
and his progress toward reaching his goals (106,
137, 186). It also allows for the active
involvement and participation of the student in the
process of assessment (195). We might consider
assessing readiness skills and decoding skills
within the larger context of language, critical
thinking, and problem solving (192). We can use the

cloze procedure to assess literacy level and
potential for success in a particular text. It can
also be used to measure progress (161, 188, 189,
195). We can discuss a text with readers to find
out "what they have read and how they have read"
(137, p. 6). Examine and evaluate writing samples
in a holistic manner (187), not focusing on specific
skills, but rather on the writer's understanding of
writing as reading and as communication.

Another alternative is to encourage the student
to engage in his own assessment process. Eberle and
Robinson (280) state that:

> Our bias against tests derives not only from
> the fact that they scare people for whom they
> were a source of panic and focused failure in
> school, but more important, they reinforce the
> illusion created in school that learning is
> basically done for reasons external to the
> student--to please someone who will let the
> student know how well (s)he is doing. If a
> student's goals are her/his own, there is no
> need for testing to determine whether they are
> accomplished: the student knows whether the
> directions to assemble the kids' Christmas toy
> worked or not, or whether the curtains fit the
> windows. (p. 34)

In each case, consider how assessment relates
to views of literacy, reading, and the adult as
learner. Eberle and Robinson's notion of
assessment, for example, reflects a view of the
adult as taking an active, responsible part in his
own learning. Informal testing may allow us to
focus on reading as a process involving language and
thinking rather than as a set of subskills.

Instructors. As the field of adult basic
literacy instruction has become more professional
(94) we have begun to address issues related to
choosing and training instructors. First, who are
the instructors? Programs have been staffed
traditionally by part-timers, often volunteers, who
have a minimum of training and by a sprinkling of
professionals. Fingeret (103) found, for example,
that currently "the majority of ABE instructors are
employed part-time in literacy education, usually

with little or no formal training in adult literacy
instruction prior to their employment" (p. 28).
Jones and Lowe (204) express concern about the
prevalence of part-time tutors who work in relative
isolation with little professional contact with
each other or with full-time professionals.
However, Ulmer and Dorland (94), in reviewing the
field, found that since the 1960's there has been a
trend away from a reliance on part-time volunteers
toward the use of full-time adult instructors and
toward more training of such teachers. The
professionals have frequently come from elementary
schools, since those are the teachers most familiar
with initial reading instruction.

This trend reflects a concern that without the
use of professionals we will not be able to use
what we know about adult learning and about
literacy teaching in designing and providing
instruction (81). Burnett and Schnell (199) stress
that the trained reading teacher can bring a
variety of specific instructional skills to the
adult literacy setting including, for instance,
identifying reading behavior, preparing
instructional materials, and using reading
technology. In addition, Meyer (207) suggests that
professional reading teachers can disseminate
information about current literacy efforts, train
volunteers, and coordinate resources. Fingeret
(103) sees the professional as needed also for
management skills.

Not everyone concurs that a shift to using
professional instructors should take place. Waite
(96) advocates the use of volunteers, proposing a
program relying on a "massive utilization of
volunteers" (p. 4). Kozol (258) suggests using
volunteer youth who would receive a minimum of
training, would live within the community, and
would develop a sense of "common cause" (p. 18).
This sense of identification between the adult
learner and the volunteer is cited as an important
reason for using volunteer instructors (103),
particularly in community-based programs.

The decision about whether to use volunteers
or professionals is, of course, partly based on
program and community conditions, such as the pool

of financial resources and professional instructors available. It should also be a decision based on how we can provide the best instructional program for the students. In making this important decision, consider the following qualities and characteristics that adult literacy instructors should have.

1. A personality that will provide support to the student and respect for his needs as an adult (267). This is considered important by those who hire teachers (103), by teachers themselves (150), and by writers in the field (203, 205). However, as Ulmer (150) points out and Fingeret (103) concurs, "experience has taught continuing educators that placing an enthusiastic, caring teacher in the classroom will not, in itself, produce desired results" (p. 10). Instructors need more.

2. An understanding of the characteristics of adult learners and of teaching adult reading (94, 103, 127, 150, 205, 226) as well as of the learning process and the role of the instructor in it (43, 65, 66, 124, 125).

The first set of qualities is to some extent determined by the instructors themselves. The second, whether the staff is professional or volunteer, can be influenced by others. The value placed on teacher training is often related to whether the caring qualities of the instructor are of overriding importance or whether the knowledge and skill areas are of predominant or of equal importance. The qualities valued in instructors thus become part of the decision-making process involved in program development.

Even though Ulmer and Dorland (94) cite the training of professional instructors in adult basic literacy as one of the indications of the growing professionalism of the field, in fact not all adult literacy instructors have special training in teaching literacy. In a survey reported in 1980 (202) it was found that although 69% of the states require certification for adult education teachers, teachers of adult reading are generally not required to have any special reading training or

even any reading background beyond that required of
any adult basic education teacher. Programs
relying on the use of volunteers have sometimes
provided only minimal training, often as a result
of limited resources but sometimes as a result of
the philosophy of the program (258). There is,
however, a concern in many programs that training
in literacy instruction is needed for volunteers
(207). Cranney (102) cites this lack of consistent
professional standards as one of the problems in
the field.

What are the training options available for
volunteers and professionals? For volunteers,
training can be built into existing programs (196,
200, 206, 209). In fact, training volunteers can
have more than one purpose. It can, of course,
help insure that they will instruct and implement a
particular program (213); it can also help insure
that the volunteers once recruited will stay with a
program (209).

How can you go about providing onsite training
in the teaching of adult reading for both
volunteers and professionals?

1. Conduct a needs assessment among instructors to
   determine their needs (198).

2. Present workshops (200). These can take a
   variety of forms and approaches (201, 203,
   208), but they all should have as their goal
   the interaction of the instructors with theory
   and practice as it applies to their students.
   The workshops might be aimed at enabling the
   instructor to work with special populations
   such as the learning disabled (197, 210) or to
   use a particular instructional strategy or
   approach to teaching reading (212, 213).

3. Provide instructors with practical materials to
   be used as a basis for workshops or to
   supplement them (196, 201, 206).

4. Encourage and provide opportunities for
   interaction between and among the instructors
   (208).

5. Involve the instructors in the assessment of
    their own needs, in the establishment of their
    goals, and in the evaluation of their
    performances (204). This should be done in the
    spirit of staff development, not for teacher or
    program evaluation.

    The suggestions so far assume, as is generally
the case, that the training is done primarily by
the literacy program. Another source of training
is a college or university. While post-secondary
teacher education has traditionally had as its
major focus the training of elementary and
secondary teachers, it has recently been
increasingly involved in training adult literacy
instructors. As states contemplate reading
requirements for certification in adult literacy
education and as those in charge of hiring
emphasize graduate courses in reading (202), the
colleges and universities can expect to play an
increasingly significant role. In assuming this
role, however, they also must assume the
responsibility for conducting and collating
research on effective instruction and for preparing
teachers to incorporate this knowledge into their
own instruction (103). Finally, providing graduate
training alone is not sufficient. It must be
effective training based on current theory and
research and should include a practicum component.

    If we view reading as more than decoding and
word recognition and if we take into account what
we know about adults and about the reading process,
then we must seriously consider an increased role
for professionals in the process of designing and
delivering literacy instruction. We all have a
great deal at stake here. The demands on the
instructor are complex; much is required in terms
of personal and technical skills and knowledge.
While the professional has the skill and expertise,
particularly in the technical areas, the role of
the volunteer remains critical. The volunteer can
provide, given appropriate and creative training,
much good instruction, a model for the student, a
supportive environment, and a commitment to the
importance of literacy. Instead of thinking in
terms of either/or, we need to be thinking in terms
of the most appropriate mix of volunteers and

professionals for a particular program, with a particular population, in a particular community. There is room for and, in fact, a critical need for both.

Summary. The decisions to be made are coming into focus. Instruction must relate to and implement the definition of literacy, the model of reading, and the view of the adult that is adopted by a particular teacher or a program. Instruction cannot just occur or be provided in a certain way because it has always been done that way. We must firmly take the initiative and integrate these variables into an instructional program that can provide room for a variety of literacy definitions, not limiting the options to survival skills; that can instruct using all we know about reading models, not limiting instruction to decoding and word recognition; and that can incorporate all we know about adults as learners, not treating adults as children but giving them a significant role in the instructional process.

Curriculum and Program Alternatives

Literacy Curriculum: Choosing from Alternatives. Literacy instruction occurs as part of a literacy curriculum. Sometimes the curriculum is fully articulated, with a rationale provided for the purpose or purposes of literacy that is the goal of the curriculum and of the view of the reading process and of adult learning that forms the foundation for the instruction. More likely this rationale is not provided and, in fact, may not have been fully considered in the decision making process used in designing the curriculum. We will look at alternative models of curriculum and at a sampling of possibilities from the field. While examining each one, consider the definition of literacy it represents, the model of reading it advocates, and the assumptions about the adult learner it makes.

There are, according to Crandall (245), three basic aims that have been taken into account in the development of the content of literacy curriculum: to develop the ability of the individual to survive in a particular environment by stressing job-

related or general life skills; to empower the
individual to understand and control his learning,
his life, and his environment by examining relevant
issues; and to develop the human potential of the
individual by expanding horizons and enriching
experience. Note how each relates to the three
purposes of literacy. In addition, the curriculum
may include various instructional strategies, from
highly specific teacher-oriented ones to strategies
that put much more responsibility on the student in
the learning and decision making process. Remember
the andragogy-pedagogy continuum?

The first aim mentioned by Crandall has
traditionally been met by a combination of basic
skills and life competencies and/or job-related
skills. Such an approach may include a competency
based curriculum and/or diagnostic-prescriptive
instruction. A set of basic literacy skills, life
skills, and/or job skills is determined by the
instructor (or the curriculum developer).
Materials and tests relating to these skills are
developed for the program, purchased from a
publisher, or adapted from the environment by the
teacher. After an initial assessment the student
progresses through the program until he can
demonstrate mastery of or competency in the skills.
In programs that are not competency based, the
student is expected to complete the curriculum or
attend the program for its full duration.

The Adult Performance Level Project (34, 219,
220, 225) was one of the original and most
influential of the competency based, life skills
curricula. It is based on a two-dimensional
concept in which basic skills (reading, writing,
speaking, listening, viewing, computation, problem-
solving, and interpersonal relations) are applied
to knowledge areas (consumer economics,
occupational knowledge, health, community
resources, and government and law).

A testimony to the influence of the APL
Project is the amount of critical writing that has
been devoted to it (220, 222, 223, 224, 227).
Haney and David (223) provide a comprehensive
overview of the comments, including concerns about
the failure to incorporate relevant literature in

the formulation of the project, the inconsistencies
in the rationale for the project, and the incorrect
development and interpretation of test items and
results. It has been suggested that the APL
Project has been narrowly conceived, with success
defined "strictly in terms of income, education,
and occupational status" (ibid., p. 66) and with
right answers defined in terms of choosing one
answer from a multiple choice (ibid., pp. 74-75).
Rigg and Kazemek (226) criticize the project, as
well as all diagnostic-prescriptive approaches,
because of the heavy reliance on the teacher as the
"knower" (p. 26). Typically in these programs the
adult's "goals, plans, world views, and beliefs are
given little serious consideration by teachers"
(ibid.).

Why then has the APL approach been so
influential? Griffith and Cervero (222) suggest
that one of the major reasons is because "the APL
approach has been thoroughly and effectively
publicized and promoted by the U.S. Office of
Education" (p. 221). Haney and David (223) look
beyond this enthusiastic and "effective exercise in
marketing" (p. 72) and suggest that APL provides an
alternative to the traditional academic approach to
literacy, identifies a need, and provides a
framework for organizing literacy education.

Over the past ten years there have been many
spin-offs from the APL approach. Some of the
suggestions that have emerged from these programs
are that we ought to:

1. Keep the focus firmly on basic skills and
   functional competencies and at the same time to
   incorporate the adult's prior knowledge as part
   of the instructional process (221). Such a
   curriculum would develop materials from
   community resources rather than rely solely on
   commercial materials.

2. In addition to basic skills and life
   competencies, add specific pre-employment
   skills and incorporate elements of the
   student's culture in the content--native
   American culture in this particular case (216).

3. Recognize that the APL general knowledge
competencies may need to be changed or adapted
to a particular population and emphasize that
reading as one of the basic skills is "both a
language process and a cognitive or thinking
process" (217, p. 47).

Not everyone has adopted survival as the aim
in developing literacy curriculum. A second aim--
to empower the individual--is illustrated by
Ellowitch (218). He reports on a curriculum that
utilizes the experiences and background of the
student, enables him/her to understand and control
his/her environment, and activates and refines
critical thinking and decision making abilities.
The content is drawn from the work experiences of
the students. The materials are developed by the
students, based on vocabulary and content from
their environments. Word attack skills are taught
using multisyllable words from the text. There is
no one right answer to comprehension questions.
Group discussion is an integral part of the
curriculum. The student is expected to be an
active participant in the process of learning.

The third aim of developing the student's
human potential is illustrated by Belz (214). She
suggests a curriculum based on educational therapy
addressing both the affective and the cognitive
aspects of acquiring literacy. She advocates
recognizing and dealing with "the bonds of
insecurity, inadequacy and fear of failure and
success....by taking the client through the process
of educational therapy" (p. 103). This includes
four phases during which the responsibility shifts
from the therapist to the client. The phases
include: 1) exploration of academic strengths and
weaknesses and the adult's psychological view of
learning, 2) experimentation with success oriented
"distinct, measureable learning units" (p. 99)
including concrete decoding strategies, 3)
reflection on the reasons for past failures and the
"redefinition of self as learner" (p. 100) with
educational work secondary in this phase, 4)
working through or integrating the "adjusted self-
image into current action and thought" (p. 101).
This approach frees the adult to learn and, Belz
believes, can lead to increased assertiveness, risk

taking and decision making in all aspects of life.

The decisions are becoming more complex. When
we begin to identify, consider, and integrate all
the variables, there are many possibilities. Rigg
and Kazemek provide us with an example of this
process. In one article (226) they discuss the
variables in terms of theory and research; in
another article (411) they demonstrate a way of
integrating them in the field. When viewing adult
basic literacy from a theoretical perspective (226)
they advocate that the student and the teacher work
together to determine materials and instruction.
Their approach is based on a view of reading as the
deriving of meaning from the "complex interaction
between the author's thought, language and
experience and the thought, language and experience
of the reader" (p. 28). This suggests that the
focus of instruction will be on comprehension and
that there may be no one right answer to some
comprehension questions. They reject the
traditional drills on phonics and word lists.
Finally, they include writing as part of the
reading curriculum, but writing in a broad sense of
"structuring writing activities around a cognitive-
discovery model of the writing process" (p. 29).

Rigg and Kazemek (411) describe in vivid detail
the literacy curriculum that existed in a Job Corps
camp, the changes that were made in it, and the
process of making those changes. The original
curriculum relied heavily on word recognition and
on phonics drill and mastery using programmed
reading materials as well as other materials chosen
by the teachers for their relevance and interest.
Rigg and Kazemek view this as a continuation of the
limited kind of curriculum that had already failed
with these students. In addition, they believe
that this approach does "not develop effective
strategies which allow them [students] to function
as independent, proficient, self-monitoring readers
and thinkers" (p. 331).

The authors interviewed job corpsmen and
involved them in the process of identifying what
they currently read, what they wanted to read and
why they wanted to read. As a result, a wide
variety of materials were provided both in the

classrooms and in the barracks that were
interesting, motivating, and, most important,
wanted by the students. Stress was placed, not on
reading and answering questions, but on "reading,
sharing, debating, and listening" (p. 332).
Writing as a process of real communication, whether
letters home or poetry, was included in the
curriculum. A Writer's Club was started to "give
the corpsmen opportunities to tutor one another,
share their ideas and talents, and give them
confidence that they are language producers as well
as consumers" (p. 333). The goal was not solely to
increase literacy--it was also to give students
"the chance to become greater than they are"
(ibid.).

The curriculum designed for and by the
students in this particular program reflects the
theoretical bias of the authors. It encompasses a
broad view of literacy that permits "adult literacy
instructors to bridge the chasm between humanistic
conceptions of adult education and current research
findings on how people learn to read and write"
(226, p. 29). Finally, it reflects a view of
adults as agents and as active participants in the
process of learning. In addition, the students
developed the literacy skills needed to survive in
their environment.

Program Development. The Job Corps situation
is unique because the students are a captive
audience. This is certainly not true of the vast
majority of adult basic literacy programs. Because
adult programs are voluntary, it is mandatory that
we recruit and retain students, develop a delivery
system that will meet the needs of students and
instructors, as well as build a base of financial
and psychological support for the program.

One characteristic of the field of adult basic
literacy is the variety of program models that have
been developed, models which vary in a number of
aspects including the sponsoring agency, the method
of recruitment of students, the location of the
program, and the links to other agencies. These
aspects, of course, are in addition to the ones
already mentioned in the discussion of instruction
and curriculum.

Any discussion of basic literacy programs must recognize the influence and importance of Adult Basic Education (ABE) programs (80, 86, 103). The Adult Education Act (321, 322, 324, 327, 328, 330) provides funding for state administered Adult Basic Education programs as well as high school equivalency programs. The states are, according to Hunter and Harman (80), "largely disbursing agencies, responsible for allocating funds to individual communities" (p. 65). ABE programs are characterized by "local autonomy" (p. 64) and a "wide variety of cosponsorship arrangements" (p. 65). The overall content of ABE programs varies as can be seen from publications of the U.S. Department of Education (307, 308) although the literacy content often tends to focus on reading instruction designed to provide basic survival skills (86, 103). ABE programs will not be considered separately but will be included as examples of possible alternatives.

One of the first things to consider in terms of adult basic literacy programs is who sponsors them. The alternatives here are numerous:

1. National volunteer literacy groups (22, 80, 86, 103, 288) including Literacy Volunteers of America and Laubach Literacy Action International provide training, materials, and services to adult students and to other programs.

2. Libraries (80, 86, 103, 110, 243, 261, 271, 288, 293, 320), often under the broad sponsorship of the American Library Association, have developed a network of information and services available to other libraries, other agencies, and students.

3. Cultural and ethnic organizations (86, 288) as well as local neighborhood houses and social service agencies (86, 218, 288) support and provide a variety of community-based literacy programs aimed at specific populations and designed to meet specific needs.

4. State (272, 280, 283, 288, 291, 292), county (86, 255, 256, 287), and city governments (86,

278, 295) have identified problems and provided varying levels of literacy and literacy-related services. These might include providing a network of information, financial support, or direct services.

5. Local School districts (288, 302, 305) have identified needs and provided instruction, usually as part of an adult education program.

6. Community colleges, colleges and universities (273, 282, 284, 285, 287, 288, 289, 300, 304) have developed or cosponsored a variety of programs including basic research, teacher training, and direct delivery of services to adults. This involvement of higher education in the problems of basic literacy training has been an encouraging and promising development.

7. Employers and unions (80) have developed programs providing a variety of support services including funding to other programs and direct literacy instruction to adults on the job.

8. Almost all correctional institutions (80, 86, 103, 288) offer some literacy training.

9. The military provides literacy training for recruits (86).

The last three examples will be examined in more depth when we look at literacy in the world of work.

A relatively recent and potentially powerful development is the number of organizations cosponoring programs and working together to develop and implement them (81, 84, 85). Mark (87) strongly suggests that the solution to the literacy problem requires "locally built partnerships between all segments of the community" (p. 5). A few examples are offered to illustrate the variety of possibilities.

1. A state ABE program has agreements with the Literacy Volunteers of America for staff development and with colleges in the state to

enable teachers to obtain credit for "what they are doing and learning on the job" (280, p. 42).

2. A local community college provides tutoring and materials while a local racetrack provides the site and the students (298). The college and the racetrack share the costs of the project.

3. A school district provides "office space, telephones, reading lab space, salaries and mileage for the coordinator and the student-tutor coordinator" (305, p. 12). The local Literacy Council provides the volunteer tutors. Funding for materials is provided by a local charitable organization.

4. A borough-wide library system works with the Literacy Volunteers of America to provide direct services to adults (320). Mutual referrals are made with the local Adult Basic Education program. Funding and support come from a variety of sources.

All programs offering direct services must face certain problems. Students must be recruited and retained in the program and, while in the program, be motivated to attend and participate. First, let's look at some broad approaches to solving these problems and then at some specific solutions to particular problems.

One effective way to deal with such problems is to provide appropriate instruction. A recurrent theme in the literature is that the literacy instruction that failed with these students in their school experience is not appropriate for them as adults (42, 124, 138, 280, 411). We must develop more appropriate alternatives. Another broad suggestion is to respect the students as adults (103), to insure that they "own" the program by having them participate and collaborate in its development and execution and by allowing for a dialogue with the teacher during instruction (28, 82, 106).

Still another way of meeting these basic problems is to identify specific barriers to adult

learning and address them. These barriers,
according to Cross (30, 48), include situational
barriers (other responsibilities, cost, child care,
transportation), institutional barriers (amount of
time required, schedule of classes, red tape), and
dispositional barriers (the age of the adult, the
attitude toward school and studying). Many of the
specific suggestions in the various programs are,
in effect, strategies the program developers have
identified as useful in overcome the barriers.

In recruiting students we need to overcome
these barriers, particularly the dispositional
barriers. Use an advertising campaign based on the
motivational orientations of potential students
(260). Don't give negative reasons for beginning a
program (249). Use students to recruit students
(262). Use mass media in general (254, 255)
because potential students are influenced by the
media. Employ special techniques in the mass media
such as using folk heroes to recruit (270).

The location of the program can be chosen in
such a way as to overcome dispositional and
situational barriers. Traditionally, many classes
have been held in local schools, either as adjuncts
to school programs or because the location was
convenient for the teachers and administrators.
Brockett (46) suggests that we "use settings other
than formal educational institutions" (p. 18)
because of the negative experiences the student may
have had with school. The student may also be more
comfortable in a known social group or environment
(250, 251), thus helping to overcome a
dispositional barrier. Lack of access to programs
may be a serious barrier to many students (85) and
placing classes within the community is suggested
as a way of overcoming a situational barrier. The
program may be home-based (280), in a number of
various locations chosen because of student demand
(273, 278), or in one specific location because
that population is identified as needing and/or
wanting literacy education (298).

The student's attitude toward school and
schooling may certainly be a dispositional barrier
that is a hangover from earlier unsuccessful
schooling. The instructor's role in overcoming

this barrier is significant. Jones and Petry
(257), for example, found that along with other
variables the teacher's attitude, empathy, and
competence were identified as significant in
determining student attitudes toward the program.
Effective teacher recruitment and training is vital
in overcoming adverse student disposition.

The size of the instructional group might be a
barrier to learning. Much instruction in adult
literacy has been on a one-to-one basis, often in
programs stressing skill development, a diagnostic-
prescriptive approach, and/or individual growth.
For the beginning student who must take a great
risk in exposing the extent of literacy/illiteracy,
individual tutoring may be mandatory. For
practical, financial concerns some programs have
used small group instruction, but not
enthusiastically. However, small group instruction
allows for needed discussion particularly in
programs that stress empowerment and the expansion
of the individual's potential. Programs that view
reading as an interactive process have tended to
rely on small group instruction since this lends
itself to discussion and interaction. We must
consider using both individual and group
instruction in order to provide for current and
changing student and instructional needs (127).

The time commitment needed for a program and
the scheduling of that time can also be part of the
situational barrier. Solutions found in programs
include: allowing teacher and student(s) to
determine convenient meeting times (253),
establishing student control of the time and
duration of sessions (273), and providing an open-
entrance/open-exit plan in which students may enter
the program when it is convenient and leave when
they have reached a goal (265).

Can basic literacy programs have a positive
effect on literacy acquisition? There have been
many critics of these programs (30, 83, 100, 109).
McCullough (296), for example, in speaking of ABE
concludes that:

From its inception ABE has had some remarkable
successes, but also too many failures.

Untrained teachers, inappropriate materials, untrained and indifferent local supervisors, and no career-ladder incentives have combined to become the "tragic flaw" of the original ABE program--a laudable, necessary program, but a failure in eradicating adult illiteracy (p. 53).

However, there have been successes. Programs have demonstrated that adults can improve their skills, can maintain and use them, and can gain a sense of confidence and success (104, 105, 113, 117, 280). The National Adult Literacy Project (245), after reviewing successful programs, concluded that programs with a clear "commitment to integrate and systematically plan, implement and evaluate the educational process--those that create a coherent system of adult literacy instruction-- are the ones that are the most successful" (p. 5-1). Literacy programs must be the result of a conscious decision making process that is designed to "meet the learners' needs rather than those of the program designers and state administrators" (280, p. v). Two concepts emerge as key: commitment and decision making. Successful programs need both.

There is a growing feeling that while individual programs are meeting specific needs in specific areas, there is a need for a national commitment to adult basic literacy (81, 85, 252, 319). Kozol (82), for example, has certainly been a vocal advocate of the need for a total effort that would take the form of a massive campaign providing direct services, patterned after the Cuban and Nicaraguan campaigns. While, according to Fingeret (103) there is support for this concept in the U.S., "Kozol's plan may underestimate the complex nature of illiteracy in the United States; a multitude of small, locally operated programs may be more appropriate than a centralized, large-scale crusade" (p. 23).

Several current developments in the United States illustrate the directions in which national efforts are moving. These projects, while providing a national perspective and national contacts, do not negate the validity of local programs and local responsibility. In fact, they appear to strengthen local efforts by making information, program support, funding, and contacts available.

1. The National Adult Literacy Inititive (ALI) (99, 227, 319) was begun by the federal government and is a joint effort of public, private, voluntary, and military agencies to identify and address the problems of illiteracy. Under the auspices of the ALI the National Adult Literacy Project was organized as a collaborative effort of the Far West Laboratory for Educational Research and the Network of Innovative Schools, a collaboration that stretches from coast to coast. The project is designed to study successful projects and practices and disseminate information. The ALI sponsors pilot projects and cooperates with other organizations.

2. The Coalition for Literacy (86, 99, 227, 288) developed out of a proposal by the Advertising Council to initiate a campaign to inform the public about the extent of the literacy problem in the U.S. The Coalition is composed of a wide variety of organizations concerned with adult education, adult literacy, and adult reading. Broadly, its purpose is to provide training and support for programs, afford technical assistance to new groups, and act as a clearinghouse to encourage communication and disseminate information.

3. The Business Council for Effective Literacy, Inc. (310) is a foundation established under a private grant. The purpose of the foundation is to promote corporate awareness of literacy problems as well as to encourage participation in the solution of these problems.

Summary

We are currently reaching only a relatively small percentage of the group of adults who are potential candidates for basic literacy programs (42, 80, 226). Weber (42) asserts that "it is clear that illiterates in America have rejected the institutionalized patterns of education in large numbers by not joining, by withdrawing, or by participating only halfheartedly" (p. 155). We must reconsider the alternatives available to us in planning programs for this population. We must be prepared to offer a wide range of options (125, 142, 296) that can meet current literacy needs in a variety of situations as well as changing literacy needs evolving from new experiences and aspirations and new demands from society.

Literacy and The Older Adult

The Extent and Implications of the Problem

Older adults in this country currently constitute a sizeable and growing group (331, 353). In spite of its size it is a group that has traditionally not been involved in literacy activities (342). However, two areas of concern emerge here. First, we recognize that low levels of literacy exist in this group as in the rest of the population. The question we are now addressing is whether we should do anything about this and if so, how. Second, we are beginning to address the question of what role literacy activities can play in enhancing the quality of life for the older adult regardless of literacy level.

In considering these issues, we must remember that there is a scarcity of research on the patterns and levels of literacy particularly for those adults over 65 (331, 332, 342, 343, 348). This makes it difficult both to determine the size of the group needing and/or wanting literacy training or activities and also to develop instruction, curriculum and programs. There is an urgent need for more basic information regarding literacy and the older adult. In the meantime, we must examine what we do know.

First, we need to consider the size of the group of older adults with low levels of literacy. The problems already identified with differing definitions of literacy and ambiguous adult literacy test results apply to older adults as well as to the general population (332, 338). However,

there is a general consensus that a substantial
portion of these adults have low levels of
literacy. Lumsden (85) estimated in 1979 that 10
to 50 percent of the 22 million elderly were
illiterate. Kasworm and Courtenay (349) state that
those over 65 "represent the highest level of the
undereducated ... and have the highest levels of
functional illiteracy of any age cohort as defined
by the APL study" (p. 5). Courtenay, Stevenson,
and Suhart (332) found that "the current research
indicates the older adult has the greatest need for
literacy learning opportunities" (p. 350). Not
only is this the largest group of illiterates but
Kasworm (333) identifies this as the group with the
lowest level of participation in programs. We have
provided few literacy programs for older adults and
we have few people enrolled in them (333, 339, 348,
349, 354, 355).

    Why is literacy such a prevalent problem for
this group? The poor are highly represented in the
older adult population (331, 333) and the poor are
traditionally found in the ranks of the illiterate
and the functionally illiterate. In addition, the
older adults of today were in school "when times
were especially hard, and opportunities for getting
a good education were, to say the least, limited"
(85, p. 297). Also, as young adults during the
depression, their energies were spent on working,
not on going to school (333).

    Should we ignore the problem? We are
educating the young. Hopefully the problem will go
away. First, not everyone agrees that it will go
away. There is a concern about the level of
literacy and the decline in reading among the young
(85). Some of today's young people may well become
the illiterate older adults of tomorrow. In
addition, there is a philosophical dimension to the
issue (333) that Bhola (9) expresses strongly in
his statement that "literacy is a human right" (p.
21) and must be developed for all. This view was
recognized in the 1979 amendments to the Adult
Education Act where the older adult was
specifically targeted and included in the
provisions of the law as a result of findings of
the Commission on Civil Rights (333). Lumsden
(85), in discussing the older adult, expresses the

commitment felt by many that "illiteracy is a
personal and social ailment over which we must
maintain eternal vigilance" (p. 305). As
Courtenay, Stevenson and Suhart (332) conclude, "to
wait for improved measures and/or future
generations of older adults who are expected to be
'literate' is an injustice to the existing
generation of older persons" (p. 350).

Both the older adult without literacy skills
as well as those with skills can benefit from
programs. The implications of low levels of
literacy among the older adult can be serious.
These people may not able to take advantage of
community services and resources because they
cannot read the notices about the services or fill
out the application forms needed to avail
themselves of the resources (331). They may be
able to read but not well enough to alleviate a
sense of confusion about the plethora of written
material that seems to accompany many of our social
service programs. Those who read well may be
confused about new terms, new forms, new concepts
found in necessary written materials. This is
literacy for survival.

There is a growing recognition, however, that
the benefits of literacy programs are not limited
to those with low levels of literacy who need
survival skills in a sometimes hostile and
confusing environment. Literacy for human
development is a vital goal for the older adult.
For all older adults there are suggestions that
reading contributes to physical and mental health
(335), relieves loneliness and social deprivation
(339), and may be a means of "reversing a decline
resulting from a disuse of intellectual
capabilities...through reading activities in a
social setting" (353, p. 239). This is literacy
for human development and is a definition found
with increasing frequency in programs for the older
adult. With the growing political awareness and
activity of this group, with the emphasis on "gray
power" and "gray panthers," literacy will
undoubtedly become an avenue for empowerment.

These varying views of literacy apply to older
adults of all reading levels. The good reader who

is faced with an official document using technical language may need assistance in reading it in order to cope with the demands it makes on any reader. The poor reader benefits from enhancing the quality of life through literacy activities. We cannot limit one purpose to one category of reader but must think in terms of the needs and interests of the adult and the requirements of the context.

Instruction

In developing instruction for older adults we need to take into account the social context in which the individual or group exists (338) just as we do for the general population. In addition, the same concern for dealing with adults as adults applies to the older adult. Instruction must be appropriate (342) both in content and in the manner in which instruction is provided.

Instructional alternatives. Many of the issues already addressed concerning instruction for adult basic literacy students also apply to older adults, particularly those with low levels of literacy. Do we emphasize decoding or comprehension? DeSanti (346), in studying reading patterns of the elderly, concluded that automatic decoding was not required for comprehension since reading is the process of utilizing a variety of cues, including word, sentence, and text level cues as well as cues within the reader coming from background knowledge, language, and thought patterns. In fact, a "strong concern for accurate decoding was related to poor comprehension" (p. 276). The stress should be on meaning no matter what the older adult's purpose for reading is. Meaning, after all, is what reading is all about.

The importance of identifying and utilizing background information in reading comprehension is also stressed in the literature on older adults both for development and practice for those with low levels of literacy (347) and for the enhancement of the quality of life by sharing such background knowledge and experience in group literacy activities (343). If prior knowledge is scanty or not present it needs to be developed or provided. Walmsley, Scott, and Lehrer (344), for

example, found that simplification of social
service documents did not appreciably increase
their comprehensibility for the older adult.   The
authors suggest that "the source of their
comprehension difficulties must lie primarily
outside of the text itself" (p. 246) and go on to
cite factors associated with the use of the
documents.   It may be that the older adult is not
familiar with these social services and the uses
that can be made of them.   The implication is that
in instructing adults to read these documents we
may also need to build understanding of the
concepts and information on which they are based.
This concern is relevant whether we are working
with the older adult who has difficulty reading the
document at all or whether we are working with
the older adult who can read the document but cannot
make sense of it.

What are some of the difficulties encountered
by older adults in dealing with written materials?
Glynn and Muth (347) suggest that particular areas
of difficulty may be in discriminating relevant
from irrelevant information and processing "several
bits of information simultaneously" (p. 255).
Haase, Robinson, and Beach (348) found that older
adults may have problems organizing information in
order to understand and remember it. Spore (354)
identified a further difficulty. "Older students
are so accustomed to not understanding that they
may not ask questions or even stop when a sentence
or paragraph baffles them" (p. 17). They may not
monitor their own comprehension.   All of these
potential sources of difficulty represent
breakdowns in the process of reading.   These
difficulties may also help explain some of the
problems experienced in reading the social service
documents.

Suggestions for developing literacy and
literacy opportunities include some strategies that
can be used for older adults with various levels of
literacy whose aim may be to survive and/or to
enhance the quality of their lives.

1.   Insure that literacy instruction and activity
     are meaningful and presented in a meaningful
     context.   This might involve, for example,

providing basic skill instruction for some
older adults using materials such as health
related documents that they have identified as
needed (333) or it might mean using short
stories to enable the group to share
"remembrances of earlier days" (353, p. 241).
Meaningful instruction includes as well an
emphasis on "logical and critical thinking,
making inferences and application" (355, p.
69). A meaningful context may also be a
"problem-solving context" (ibid.).

2. Provide for group discussion and interaction,
   both to improve reading comprehension and also
   to increase social interaction and a feeling of
   worth and belonging (342, 343, 348, 350, 353).
   "A large part of meaningfulness for most aged
   persons is social interaction" (348, p. 233).

3. Teach strategies for organizing information,
   such as advanced organizers and prequestions
   that require the participants to organize
   information and ideas (347). The instructor
   may have to provide the organization, the
   categories, and the strategies (354).

4. Encourage the use of student-generated
   questions both as a means of insuring
   participation and involvement and as a means
   for self-monitoring comprehension (354). Group
   discussion lends itself to this.

5. Don't allow the process of acquiring literacy
   and/or using it to get bogged down by lack of
   progress or inconsistent attendance. For
   example, read to the group and then encourage
   discussion and rereading (353).

   Materials. The importance of choosing
appropriate materials is just as critical in
working with older adults as it is with any
population. The content must deal with the
concerns and interests of the reader (85). Rigg
and Kazemek (342) stress that we cannot assume we
know what older adults want; we must find out and
deal with their needs and interests. It may be
necessary to conduct a needs assessment to
determine the specific needs and interests of a

specific group in a specific context (336, 345).
We may find that we must deal with affective issues
as well as cognitive ones (85, 332). We may not
just be teaching students how to read and fill out
forms. We may also be developing self-esteem (333)
in a group of individuals who may perceive
themselves as useless and unwanted, on the
periphery of society.

What are some of the topics that have been
identified as interesting and important to older
adults? Interests may be related to whether the
individual is institutionalized or not. Murray
(340) found that institutionalized adults tended to
have narrower reading interests because they read
what was available to them and read to pass the
time. Non-institutionalized adults were interested
in a wide range of topics and read to gain
information. The range of topics that has been
identified is as wide and as diverse as the
individuals in the group (336, 342) and is
influenced by their background knowledge and
experiences (348). Topics related to coping and
surviving in old age include buying more food for
less money, obtaining and benefiting from home
health care, and using leisure time (333). Other
topics, chosen to enhance life and enlarge
horizons, relate to current events and spiritual
development (335).

Materials must reflect the diversity of
expressed interests (332). Because of this, a wide
range of materials should be available to those
working with older adults (348). Few materials
have been especially designed for this group (85,
339, 342, 349). In one sense this may present a
problem because it means that appropriate materials
are not readily available. On the other hand,
since one purpose of literacy activities for older
adults is to connect them to the larger society, it
might be an advantage to use the same materials
everyone else uses and to use materials readily
available from the adult's environment.

Current, easily available materials can form
the backbone of any instructional program whether
designed to enable older adults to survive and cope
or to enhance the quality of their lives.

Magazines and newspapers are often identified as the materials most read or most wanted to be read by them (336, 341, 351, 355). Short stories (353), speeches such as Martin Luther King's "I Had a Dream" (354) and modern fiction (352) provide opportunities to enhance life, both exploring current issues and connecting the present to the past.

Another source of literacy material is the student- or teacher-developed text designed specifically for a particular older adult group. Student-generated material using the Language Experience Approach (348, 354) is suggested for this group as well as for the adult basic literacy population. This approach has the social benefit of sharing experience and problems with others through group discussion (348). It also "encourages confidence" (354, p. 18) because the adult sees his own words and experiences as having value and worth. The adult is also able to focus on the task of reading since he already knows the content. A newsletter can be developed by either the class or the instructor and circulated to others as a form of Language Experience (355).

The specific needs of the older adult can be targeted in teacher-made materials such as those developed by a program in rural Vermont that emphasized "the problems of rural living" (355, p. 70). A program in South Carolina (355) found, after purchasing commercial materials, that "the most effective materials were developed by the teachers themselves in conjunction with the stated needs of the clients" (p. 63).

A recurrent suggestion is to use large size print (336, 340, 341, 351, 354). If the material is not available commercially in large size print, some part or all of it might be retyped on a primary typewriter (353).

Instructors. Again, we find the use of both volunteer and professional (355) instructors, often with the professional assuming responsibility for recruiting, training, and supervising the volunteers. One suggestion is to hire "retired teachers certified in ... Adult Basic Education"

(355, p. 63). The variable that seems critical
here is not so much whether the instructor is a
professional tutor or not, but whether the
instructor has the appropriate qualities. The
importance of caring instructors who have a
continuing contact with older adults (351) cannot
be overemphasized. It has even been suggested that
contact with the group should start with involving
instructors in the process of recruiting (333).

Instructors also need to know how to teach.
Kasworm and Courtenay (349) cite the importance of
"the teacher's role in building self-confidence,
giving encouragement, providing for flexible pacing
of instruction and giving opportunities for
frequent repetition and review" (p. 10). In
addition, the use of a wide variety of materials
requires that "instructors have a wide background
of literacy experience from which to draw" (348, p.
234). It is also important that instructors work
closely with other professionals associated with
older adults since they may have accurate
perceptions of their needs (336). Finally, the
same need for training exists with these
instructors as with any instructors. We must
provide inservice workshops to enable instructors
to understand particular needs and interests and to
create an atmosphere conducive to learning (337).

Curriculum and Programs Alternatives

Curriculum alternatives for older adults
generally emphasize two of the three purposes of
literacy: literacy for survival and literacy for
human development, with relatively few programs
developed for the purpose of literacy for
empowerment. Older adults need to be literate to
keep informed about services they can use to "cope
with aging" (335, p. 83) and to take advantage of
services and programs available to them (331).
Such curricula may use a competency-based format
with APL modules (355) or a more traditional
approach stressing "a priority subject like health"
(336, p. 15) and linking ABE to it. These programs
emphasizing literacy for survival are not
necessarily limited to those with low literacy
levels.

The emphasis on literacy for human development comes across strongly in the literature on literacy and older adults, perhaps more so here than in the literature dealing with other populations. Many older adults view literacy as a way of enhancing their lives. Wolf (345) studied members of a retirement home and found one purpose of literacy was related to the interests and needs of the inner person and the other purpose was related to the social needs of the individual. "Reading is a means to perpetuate an ongoing communication with life" (p. 15). This communication may mean reading for information, knowledge or recreation (335). Literacy is a way of involving one's self with a larger society and with others at a time when, for many older adults, the immediate world is shrinking (342, 345, 353). The act of sharing literacy experiences provides a means of enhancing social relations and contacts (352).

Lovelace (353) suggests that "the problems of [counteracting] withdrawal and enhancing the lives of nursing home patients and other elderly members of society become more serious as the number of aged increases" (pp. 242-243). One way of accomplishing this is through shared reading activities and discussions. Short stories are read either by the participants or by the instructor with the focal point of the activity on the discussion of the stories. The reading sessions are viewed as "social gatherings" (p. 240).

Gentile and McMillan (351) describe a program "designed to furnish continuous growth for the aged" (p. 215). The curriculum combines "invigorating reading, viewing, listening, and writing exercises" (p. 216). A wide variety of materials are used, including "extra-large printed books, cassette recorders and taped readings, various paperbacks, magazines, newspapers, and records" (ibid.). Group discussion is an important element in the execution of the curriculum.

Programs for older adults have been plagued with the same problems of recruitment, retention, and achievement found in other programs (85, 333). In order to overcome these difficulties, we can examine them again in relation to Cross's (30, 48) list of situational, institutional, and dispositional barriers. Many of the comments made regarding adult basic literacy students also apply here.

Adult students must be treated as adults and given a role and a stake in the development of the program. An easy trap to fall into with older adults is to "treat elders as 'old children'" (342, p 419). Murray (340) describes the attitude of "assumed passivity " (p. 17) found in the older adult, particularly in nursing homes. We cannot foster this attitude in literacy programs. The description of an ABE correspondence course for adults of all ages includes the statement that "the elderly are involved in exactly the same way as other students" (355, p. 70). This is important.

We also need to involve older adults in the decision-making process in planning programs. "They want and need some control over their destiny and having that control over their educational programs increases the likelihood of their continuing with the program" (348, p. 233). In addition, allowing "elders to participate in the actual program planning--which gives them control over the situations that affect their lives--has demonstrated that the 'diminished view' elders often have of themselves can dramatically change" (342, p. 421). This approach to program development may help overcome some of the dispositional barriers related to negative attitudes toward educational endeavors. In addition, involving the participants in the decision-making may aid in overcoming institutional barriers such as an inconvenient scheduling of classes or situational barriers such as an inconvenient location or transportation difficulties. Older adults themselves, by becoming involved in the planning of the program, can identify and overcome some of these potential barriers.

In recruiting participants, we must "explore more innovative methods of reaching these populations" (338, p.69) including many of the strategies for recruitment and retention already discussed. For example, mass media posters, formal and informal presentations by staff in places where older adults congregate (355) have been incorporated into programs in an effort to recruit them in a positive, non-threatening way. Recruitment might be part of a program in churches and community agencies designed to develop interest in reading activities (339).

Location of the program is a primary concern for older adults (332, 333, 349) and can represent a critical situational and/or dispositional barrier. Many older adults do not have the financial and physical resources to go to programs and may have negative attitudes once they get there. Yet, even for the older adult, "the basic unit of the American adult literacy experience has been and remains the classroom or some facsimile thereof" (85, p. 303). These classrooms have been patterned after a school model, with the students going to a location, chosen for its convenience for teachers and administrators. We must provide locations convenient and acceptable to the older adult.

Consider these alternatives. Provide programs in nursing homes, the individual's own home, churches, community centers, senior citizen centers, retirement adult communities and apartment complexes (333, 343, 353, 355). It is possible to develop innovative approaches to home-bound programs, for example, for those unable or unwilling to leave home. These might include using trained volunteers to go into the home to provide instruction, using the telephone to monitor progress and to enable participants to call in with questions, or developing a correspondence course using "relevant" readings from current newspapers and magazines (355).

If transportation is needed, try to provide funding to cover the cost. A program in South Dakota found that "the transportation component of the grant has also been an asset in the implementation of the program as many elderly no longer own or can drive a car, and many on a fixed or limited income cannot afford to travel within the community if a fee is involved" (355, p. 66). Location and convenience can also apply to

the availability of the reading material. Consider
using a mobile book cart to make books accessible
in a nursing home (340).

The amount of time involved and even the time
of day can be a significant institutional barrier
to participation and completion of a program.
Consider shorter time frames for individual
sessions (333) and courses offered in the mornings
(333, 349, 355).

One dispositional barrier that can be easily
overcome is the fear the individual may have of
school related procedures. Kasworm and Courtenay
(349) warn us that we should avoid lectures, timed
assignments, and grades.

Programs for older adults, as well as adult
basic literacy programs, have identified the need
to involve other community agencies and
organizations in providing tutors, materials, and
funds (351, 354, 355). We can use the existing
resources of Adult Basic Education programs which
often have links to social agencies serving older
adults (354, 355). This need to connect programs
is echoed in the need to include older adults in a
national endeavor and commitment to the development
of literacy (85).

Alternative proposals have been made for
providing literacy instruction such as reducing
readability levels of needed materials or providing
for alternative ways of disseminating and receiving
information, such as the use of recordings (331).
But these suggestions, while they might be
practical in the short run as a way of addressing a
particular problem, do not deal with a major
purpose of literacy for the older adult--the
enhancement of the quality of life. No matter what
the individual's level of literacy, we cannot lose
sight of the important role literacy can play in
enhancing the quality of life of the older adult.
This theme has been stated in a variety of ways,
from the role reading can play in creating "a zest
for living" (348, p. 235) to the fact that for the
older adult "emotional, psychic, spiritual and
corporal energy may be rekindled through the
avenues of literary enterprise, thereby opening an

aperture to a significant future" (351, p. 219).

All areas of adult literacy development call for more research and information, but probably none more so than the area of literacy for older adults. Some of the topics to be investigated include the specifics of acquiring and practicing basic reading skills and comprehension, choosing and developing materials, the effects of bibliotherapy, the changing purposes of reading during the life span, and the various effects of reading on the quality of life for the older adult (342, 343, 353).

Summary

Older adults with literacy difficulties and with literacy needs are part of our society. We cannot wait for future generations for these problems to, hopefully, go away. We must addresss them now by providing interesting, helpful, and innovative solutions to alleviate the older adult's literacy difficulties and enrich and enhance the quality of his/her life.

Literacy and The Speaker of English as a Second Language

The Extent and Implications of the Problem

Statistics on the size of the population of adults who speak English as a Second Language (ESL) vary somewhat but there is general agreement that the group is sizeable. Wallerstein (357) in 1984 estimated that we have 30 million U. S. residents who speak English as a second language and "two-thirds of these people who might come to ESL classes were born in the U.S., including Puerto Rico and U.S. territories" (p. 7). Sherman (370), two years earlier, put the size of the ESL population at 28 million. In looking at recent immigrants, Wallerstein (357) estimates that there have been "three to four million immigrants in the last decade, three-fourths from Latin America and Asia, and many illiterate or semi-literate in their own languages" (p. 6). Longfield (365) supports the conclusion that many immigrants from Latin

American and Asian countries "are functionally
illiterate in their own language" (p. 3).

ESL adults represent a variety of literacy
levels. There are those who are illiterate in
their native language, those who are semi-literate
or functionally literate in their native language,
and those who are literate in their native language
but who need to learn the Roman alphabet (367). To
this list can also be added those adults who are
considered preliterate (362) because they "speak a
language for which there is no written form or
whose written form is rare" (369, p. 1). Even
those ESL adults who are functionally literate in
their own language may not be able to meet the
basic literacy demands of their new country (354).
As we have seen, definitions and levels of literacy
occur within a particular context.

There is a sense of urgency related to the
literacy needs of ESL adults compared, for example,
to the needs of the elderly. ESL adults need work;
they need a place to live; they need social
services. These things are all easier to obtain if
you are literate in English. Thus survival is
generally seen as the prime goal of ESL literacy
programs. Literacy, however, can also be viewed as
a means of empowerment. Wallerstein (357) suggests
that functional literacy for survival is too narrow
a goal for this group, and perhaps for all adults.
ESL adults need to overcome problems of "a lack of
self-esteem, and crippling doubts of their
effectiveness to change and to bring about change"
(p. 4). In addition, literacy can be viewed in the
larger perspective of human development. Paul
(366), in working with Asian refugees, states that:

> While we certainly want to prepare our
> students to read and write survival messages
> and to do the exercises in ESL beginner texts,
> we don't want literacy training to stop there,
> abandoning the goal of lifelong literacy: that
> is the ability to receive and encode
> information and ideas in print. (p. 423)

It is a temptation to treat these adults as
less than adults because of their elementary or
non-existent literacy skills. We are cautioned

that "adult-adult relations between teachers and
students must be maintained, whatever the skill
levels of the learners" (362, p. 4). The ESL adult
learner must be active, in control of his learning
(376).

Instruction

Instructional issues and methods suggested
here, as with all adult literacy groups, reflect
the various purposes for literacy, models of
reading, and views of the adult as learner. There
are in addition two points that are particular to
ESL students. One is the order of oral and written
instruction and the other is the acquisition of a
new language structure and a new culture.

Should oral (listening and speaking) language
instruction in English precede written (reading and
writing) language instruction? Oral language
development certainly precedes written language
development in children and oral language
instruction has traditionally preceded written
language instruction for ESL adults (362). Savage
(369) asserts that there is consensus that it
should. However, the issue is not settled. For
example, both Bright (362) and Longfield (365)
point out that this order assumes the student is
literate in his native language. This is not
necessarily so. Longfield goes on to say that it
is not necessary for a student to be proficient in
spoken English in order to be able to understand
written English. Reading and writing may
"parallel" (p. 23) oral language development.

A related question is whether we should teach
ESL students who are illiterate in their own
language to read that language first and then
transfer the skill of reading to English (365).
The students could thus acquire literacy skills in
a familiar language environment. This procedure
is, as Longfield (ibid.) points out, not practical.
We do not have the financial or instructional
resources to do this and the students don't have
the time. Their need is to learn to read English
now.

We must recognize too that in addition to

acquiring literacy in English these adults may also
be coping with the problems of learning to speak a
second language as well as adjusting to the new
demands and expectations posed by a second culture
(367, 370). The difficulties encountered by
speakers of other languages in understanding
written (as well as spoken) English are compounded
by the many exceptions to the rules in decoding and
spelling words, the meanings of idioms and
hyperboles, and the problem of interference by the
native language (365). The text structure may well
be different from that used in text written in
their native language (366). The grammatical
structure of English is undoubtedly different from
that of the native language, contributing further
to the difficulties encountered. The problems
engendered by the lack of knowledge of the new
culture are perhaps more subtle but also more
complex. The role of background knowledge in
reading comprehension has already been documented.
The written materials of our culture assume
knowledge of many aspects of the culture which
these adults may not have. The problem is
compounded by a certain tension engendered by the
need and desire to acquire the new culture and the
reluctance to abandon the old (357).

With all these difficulties, can these
students succeed? Bright et al. (362) state that:

> Experienced ESL literacy teachers caution that
> not everyone who enters an ESL class will
> eventually become literate. The sincere
> belief in the power of instructional systems,
> that most teachers begin with, may be soon
> laid aside in favor of a more realistic,
> lowered set of expectations. (p. 4)

Remember, the adults who come to these classes to
gain literacy come with the same kinds of problems
that all illiterate or low level readers come with.
They have not mastered the intricacies of reading.
Possibly they haven't been taught. They may come
from a culture where literacy is not available or
valued (365). They may have a handicapping
condition such as learning disabilities (362, 365).
According to the Development Interdependence
Hypothesis, "the second language competence is

partially a function of first language competence
at the time of exposure to the second language.
This may account for the modest success of ESL
literacy programs" (365, p. 21).

In addition, consider the stresses and
tensions the adults may be meeting such as
prejudice, job insecurity, or emotional scars from
past educational experiences (357, 365, 366). The
picture is deliberately painted with a black brush
so as not to underestimate the difficulties.
However, as many students have demonstrated, these
difficulties can be overcome. We have had, as
Longfield (365) cites, "modest success" but that
does not mean that we have to settle for modest.

Instructional alternatives. Let's examine
some of the instructional issues related to
literacy as they apply to this group, keeping in
mind the need for more research in this area (365,
370). The question of whether to emphasize
decoding or comprehension is as important here as
it is in working with any group of adults that has
a low level of literacy. Traditionally, as with
other kinds of basic literacy instruction, we have
emphasized decoding. Recently Savage (369) has
identified a trend away from the earlier synthetic
approach where we worked on the parts and put them
together to form a whole toward an analytic
approach in which the emphasis is on meaning. This
emphasis on meaning is also cited by other
practitioners. Paul (366), for example, rejects
"isolated words and sentences out of context" (p.
423) in favor of paragraphs and stories that are
culturally relevant and that require the use of
thinking skills to comprehend, to resolve
uncertainties, and to identify and integrate
relationships.

The stress on meaning is reinforced by
research. After studying a group of ESL students,
Wilson (360) concluded that "when poor readers rely
too heavily on graphic and syntactic information,
their attention needs to be refocused" (p. 12).
The focus should be on passage-level cues, not
individual word cues. Chang and Lare (359)
compared a group of ESL Navy recruits with a group
of recruits who were functionally literate native

English speakers (NES) to determine reading
performance. They concluded that the significant
differences found in interpretative abilities did
not come from decoding difficulties or lack of word
knowledge on the part of the ESL recruit. Instead
they suggested that the differences might come from
an inability to organize information between
sentences and paragraphs, a failure to use context
to determine appropriate word meaning, a tendency
to translate individual words into the native
language, or a lack of appropriate background
information. The authors concluded that "providing
the ESL recruits with training in performing
higher-level comprehension and integration tasks is
where we are likely to obtain the greatest reading
improvements" (p. 8).

We are beginning to see in the area of ESL
literacy instruction a growing awareness of the
need to stress reading as meaning and to provide
literacy instruction that reflects an interactive
model of reading. The reading process for ESL
adults, as for other adults, is viewed as a process
of critical thinking, risk-taking, and problem
solving (357, 360, 366). The recognition of the
importance of background information in
understanding and of using both content and text
structure (361) is particularly critical because in
many cases the background knowledge of the ESL
adult does not match the demands of the text.

Now consider some of the suggestions that have
been made for instruction.

1. Listen to students in order to identify their
   interests and concerns. Use these in
   developing lessons and curriculum (357). Don't
   avoid the emotional and cultural issues that
   surface (366). These can be serious blocks to
   learning and need to be addressed.

2. Identify and develop specific needed background
   information through pictures, questions,
   discussions, and prereading activities (361).

3. Develop the general cultural knowledge that
   students are lacking (366). This might be done
   through field trips, movies, discussions, and

in-class observations of holidays and events.

4. Develop critical thinking and the ability to pose problems and suggest solutions (357, 366) through questioning, and group discussion and interaction.

5. Involve the student actively in the process of reading, using strategies such as the cloze procedure, strip stories, and scrambled words (365, 366, 369).

6. Stress the use of context to develop word meaning and comprehension of ideas using paragraphs and stories that are culturally relevant (360, 361, 366).

7. Phonics and sight word instruction should emphasize meaning and meaningful words, perhaps chosen by the student (369).

8. Teach basic skills such as left-to-right movement on the page and the correspondence of words to objects and ideas to preliterate adults who have no experience with the written word (369).

   Materials. The question of the kinds and availability of instructional materials is here again paramount to teacher and student. Be particularly aware of the background information assumed in the content of the materials. Either choose materials that match existing information in order to teach literacy skills (366) or choose material that will supply information that is missing (363). Be cognizant of tensions between new and old cultures that can cause misunderstandings. Wallerstein (357) asserts that "although many competency-based curricula are excellent for teaching living skills, some are superficial to the point of unwittingly reinforcing learning conflicts" (p. 8) because they fail to recognize these tensions. In addition, at times it is important to recognize the sense of urgency felt by many of these adults and relate the text to their concerns and the content of their lives (365, 369), whether the acquisition of literacy is for

the   purpose   of   survival,   empowerment,   or
enrichment.

        Commercially   prepared   literacy materials for
ESL students have   been   criticized   both   for   the
assumptions   they   make   about   the student and for
their content.   Longfield   (365)   identifies   two
assumptions   often made about the student which are
not true for many ESL adults.   The   first   is   that
the   student is literate in his native language and
is transferring skills.   The   second   is   that   the
adult   is   proficient   in   speaking   English.   She
concludes that "few   materials   are   available   for
teaching   literacy   skills   to   the limited English
Proficient Speaker"   (pp.   15-16).   Two   concerns
about   the   content   are   particularly   disturbing.
Wallerstein (357) suggests that teaching   materials
fail   to address the issues of vital concern to ESL
students   such   as   conflicts   between   cultures,
prejudices in the social and economic environments,
and   difficulties in employment.   Paul (366) points
out that many ESL materials do not involve thinking
skills,   but   rather   stress   memorization   and
vocabulary development.

        Suggestions   have   been made to overcome these
problems.   Consider the following.

1.   Use materials written   by   other   ESL   literacy
     groups that have been designed to meet specific
     needs.   For   example,   consider   a   magazine
     written for and by adults that focuses   on   the
     problems   of   acquiring   literacy   in   a second
     language, or materials written to   explore   the
     problems   of   living in a multi-cultural, multi-
     racial community (379).

2.   Involve   both   students   and   teachers   in   the
     process of developing materials based on common
     experiences   and   issues of concern (357, 367).
     Instructors   might   visit   sites   familiar   to
     students   and   take   pictures.   Through group
     discussion   stories   and   articles   can   be
     developed   and   critiqued.   This   is   closely
     related   to   the   Language   Experience   approach
     that   is   widely   suggested   for   use   in   ESL
     literacy classes (360, 361, 363, 365, 367, 369,
     371, 379).

3. Use teacher-adapted or created materials (365, 366).

   Instructors. Literacy instructors for ESL adults need the same personal and professional qualities required of other literacy instructors (365). They need patience, flexibility, enthusiasm, and respect for the adult learner. They also need to know how to teach. There is an important additional quality needed by these instructors. Wallerstein (357) quotes Alatis's observation that "the ESL teacher is not simply a technician. The most important quality for teachers to have is the cultural sensitivity and the ability to start from [the] learner's needs" (p. 9). In addition to understanding the student's culture, the teacher must be able to present the American culture to the student (365). Longfield (365) suggests that the ESL literacy instructor "must practically walk on water" (p. 17).

   The question of training is taken very seriously by writers in this field. Longfield (365) wants teachers with degrees in "Adult Education, ESL and/or Linguistics" (p. 17). She also identifies a need for teacher certification and for teacher training programs in this field. These professional teachers would form the core of the program with volunteers used as additional tutors. In any case, staff development for both the professional and the volunteer is considered important (365, 374) with a variety of models and programs available (379). Suggestions for training include, for example, conducting a needs assessment of those in the field to determine training needs (375), presenting regional conferences and workshops sponsored by successful literacy groups (357), and using video tape training programs (379).

Curriculum and Program Alternatives

   The same range of approaches to the development of curriculum and programs is found in literacy programs for ESL adults as is found in programs for other populations. In reviewing possibilities, consider how the curriculum developer juggled the three areas of decision

making: choosing a purpose for literacy to form the
focus   of   the   curriculum,   identifying   and
incorporating a model of reading, and utilizing
theories of adult learning theory.

Many   programs   develop   curricula   based   on
literacy for survival--often with the skills and
strategies   chosen   by   the   instructor   or   the
curriculum developer. A common approach is to use
a competency-based curriculum (364, 373, 379),
perhaps modeled on the APL project, in which life
skills   are   identified by the curriculum developer
and   taught   to   the   students,   using   either
commercially available materials or ones developed
for the program.

Longfield (365) suggests another alternative
for   a   curriculum   designed   to   develop   survival
skills.   She advocates combining ESL training with
vocational   training   and literacy training. These
are linked together because the "command of English
and   the   development   of   functional   literacy   are
essential" (p. 36) for both society and for the
survival of the   individual   in   the   new   society.
Instruction   is   based   on   a bottom-up approach to
reading   because,   according   to   Longfield,   these
adult   students   need   to develop prereading skills
followed by the recognition of letters, sounds, and
words.   Then they will "move from phonetic analysis
to comprehension at increasingly higher   levels   of
difficulty" (p. 19).   The skills, in this case,
have been predetermined by the instructor.

A   different   approach   to   curriculum
development,   still focusing on survival skills, is
seen in a program described   by   Craige   (372)   for
Haitian   farmworkers in which their culture and the
context in which they are living and   working   form
the   basis   for the content, the materials, and the
approach used in instruction. Here the focus is on
the student, his needs, his culture, and   his   role
in the process of acquiring literacy.

A   curriculum   designed   to   develop   literacy
empowerment   is   discussed   by   Wallerstein   (357).
Through   a   community approach to literacy in which
problems   are   identified   and   solutions   suggested,
students   "have   the social support in the group to

think critically about themselves in their community, and to discover new ways to address the problems" (p. 4). A dialogue develops, based on teacher questioning, that clarifies issues, develops critical thinking, and suggests action. Note the role the adult learner plays in this approach to developing literacy. The learner is active, in charge of learning, choosing issues and developing materials. The content of the program arises from the needs and concerns of the group and it enables the adult to identify, address, and change problem areas.

Paul (366), in viewing literacy as a life-long goal, includes emotional as well as intellectual responses, values clarification as well as problem solving, and examines cultural differences and tensions. The reading model on which Paul basis his approach is an interactive one, involving "sampling, predicting, testing, and confirming linguistic structures and content" (p. 423). The emphasis is on reading as thinking using a variety of strategies that can be applied to a variety of materials. The materials used are "culturally relevant paragraphs and stories, instead of isolated words and sentences out of context" (ibid.).

All of these approaches share a common element. They are all concerned with facts, ideas, issues, and concepts that are important and relevant to the students. This strategy is critical for overcoming the problems of student achievement in the long run and of student recruitment and retention in the short run. These three problems have plagued ESL literacy programs as they have other literacy programs. As has already been suggested, an appropriate, meaningful curriculum that incorporates student concerns and problems is one way to overcome these problems (357).

What are some of the other suggestions that have been made to address the problems of recruitment, retention and achievement? Remember Cross's (30, 48) barriers to adult learning? There is an urgent need to locate programs within the community (365) in order to overcome dispositional

and situational barriers. In addition, we need to
join with other community agencies (365, 379) in
offering these programs. Wallerstein (357) urges
us "to break out of the institutional mode and
conventional ways of thinking" (p. 15), to "de-
emphasize educational institutions by incorporating
literacy into existing community programs" (p. 17)
and by choosing community sites. An advantage of
community sites is that community agencies, already
working with these adults and their families, will
have connections to them, making the job of
recruitment easier. Literacy programs need to
become part of existing groups--part of church
groups, food cooperatives, housing projects,
migrant camps. Consider developing more programs
for teaching literacy skills on the job, and
enrolling business and industry for support, funds,
and space (365). We are already using many of
these sites (379), but it may behoove us to
consider more of them. "We need creative thinking
on student recruitment and on developing community
sites for classrooms" (357, p. 14).

The situational barriers for ESL adults are
often so great that we may need to consider
providing an open entry/open exit program (366) to
enable the student to fit the program into the
changing currents of his life. In addition, in
order to overcome situational barriers such as
child care and lack of transportation, we may need
to provide a variety of support services such as
day care, transportation, social workers, and
assistance with government agencies (357, 365) just
to make the acquisition of literacy possible.

Summary

The call for interagency cooperation and for
national planning (365) is heard here as elsewhere.
The need for careful decision-making is evident.
In dealing with these issues, we certainly must
consider the immediate need for literacy for
survival but in addition, we must look beyond that
goal and consider literacy for empowerment and for
human development. We need to think in terms of
literacy development, not just literacy training.
We are currently reaching a only small percentage
of those adults who could benefit from literacy

programs. In order to reach other adults we must
consider broader options in instruction,
curriculum, and program planning. The benefits of
literacy acquisition will accrue to society as well
as to the adult.

Literacy in the Workplace

The Extent and Implications of the Problem

Both the professional press and the popular
press identify work-related literacy as a problem
area. According to a report by the College Board
(390) "business people from coast to coast agreed
that inadequate reading levels among entering
employees is the largest single problem for
employers" (p. 2). McGowan (383) asserts that
"illiterates are actually in the work force in
spine-chilling numbers" (p. 38). Business and
industry is faced with people who cannot read or
read adequately while at the same time, reading
comprehension has been identified as the top
vocational skill by school administrators,
teachers, former students, and current employers in
a survey conducted by Baxter, Young, and Schubert
(380). Reading is the skill "on which future
learning is based" (p. 115) and is particularly
critical "in a period of rapid technological
change" (ibid.).

In looking at the results of low levels of
literacy in factory, blue, and white collar
workers, we find that corporate profits as well as
our defensive capabilities are effected (383, 385,
393, 396) because of errors committed and work not
done or completed. McGowan (383) looks at the
long-run consequences and states that "the literacy
crisis will undoubtedly threaten the future
strength of the economy" (p. 38). In addition to
the effects of low levels of literacy already cited
for adults in general, low levels of literacy on
the job can affect individual workers by causing
accidents, injury and death (383, 385, 392, 393).

While the concern centers on problems
associated with low levels of literacy, it is, in
fact, not limited to particular literacy levels,

jobs, or industries. Burkett and Hooke (389)
identify a problem in the military because of
individuals who are "by no means functionally
illiterate by usual standards, but are simply not
skilled enough to cope with the difficulty or
complexity of the reading materials and literacy
tasks that their jobs require" (p. 28). The
problem is compounded because of the increasing
complexity of many jobs, both military and
civilian. In addition, in order to move up the
career ladder, an individual must be able to deal
with the literacy demands of the new position.
Promotions may trigger literacy problems (408).
According to McGowan (383) "the problem also
spreads to executives as well though on a less
obvious level" (p. 38). As the needs of business
and industry change there is a need for higher
levels of literacy with fewer slots for those who
cannot cope (383, 385). A relative perspective on
literacy highlights the difficulties adults may
encounter meeting the literacy demands of their
particular context or a new context. We are
beginning to recognize that literacy needs are not
limited to those adults with low levels of
literacy, but are found also in this second group
of adults--those not able to meet the demands of
their particular situation.

Literacy problems can be found in all kinds of
businesses and industries (393). Guthrie (393) and
Miller (409), for example, identify reading as
critical in technological and scientific fields.
Both the volume of reading and the nature of what
needs to be read are of concern. Literacy has been
identified as a particular problem in the fields of
banking, telecommunications, and data processing
(383). The military has encountered serious
problems obtaining recruits able to meet the varied
literacy demands associated with our defense
systems (430).

Literacy in the workplace is viewed at all
levels from a relative perspective. It has been
defined by Mikulecky and Diehl (398) as the
"relationship between the reader, the context, and
what is required to be read. It is a variable
construct that can change from situation to
situation and from person to person" (p. 1). It

has further been suggested that we should be
looking at the demands of the text in work-related
reading, not the skill level of the reader (401).
This relative perspective helps explain the extent
of the literacy difficulties encountered on the
job. In addition, literacy on the job, at any
level, can be literacy for survival. The executive
needs particular literacy abilities and strategies
in order to get and keep his job just as much as
the factory worker does. They both need literacy
to survive.

However, literacy for survival is not the only
definition that is associated with the workplace.
The spokesman (423) for a major corporation
describes the fundamental skills classes provided
for employees who have "problems with reading,
writing, math, and problem-solving" (p. 14). A
goal for the program is identified as the need to
"facilitate learning and assist employees in
becoming proactive learners and workers ....
identifying and developing levels of awareness,
consciousness, and thinking ability, and of
developing models to move the learner into an
active role in the process of living, controlling
his own life and decision-making" (p. 15). This is
literacy for empowerment.

The notion that literacy can provide
opportunities for the individual to grow and
develop also applies to the world of work. Taking
a broad view of literacy and the workplace, Guthrie
and Seifert (394) suggest that "reading enables the
human intelligence to interact with itself. This
supreme accomplishment enables human reason to
becomes more reasonable, a business account to
become more accountable, and science to grow more
scientific. Through reading we create the
environment that shapes our minds and selves" (pp.
498-499). These authors link growth in the
individual through literacy to the marketplace.
Rigg and Kazemek (411), in preparing young adults
in a Job Corps situation, envision literacy as
enlarging the reader's "real world reading" (p.
331) and providing opportunities for students to
"become greater than they are" (p. 333). Although
literacy for survival dominates work-related
programs, these views suggest that literacy in a

work   or   work-related   setting can be literacy for
human development.

Instruction

     In order to plan effective instruction we need
an overview of the purposes and characteristics of
literacy   in   the workplace. A common statement is
that the emphasis of many work-related literacy
tasks   is   on reading-to-do rather than on reading-
to-learn or reading-to-assess (23, 391,   396,   400,
405).   It is suggested that one of the reasons
adults have difficulties when they get into the
workplace is because we prepare them for one kind
of reading in school, primarily reading-to-learn,
yet   we   expect   them   to   perform another kind,
reading-to-do, on the job (396, 400).

     Other discrepencies between literacy in school
and in work have been suggested.   Mikulecky (396)
interviewed and tested high school students, adult
technical students, and workers in a variety of
occupations and   found   that "results suggest that
the students read less often in school than most
workers do on the job, that they read less
competently, face easier materials which they read
to less depth, and that the strategies students
employ may be less effective than those employed by
workers" (p. 1).   He concluded that "very little in
terms   of   literacy   preparation   has   direct
applicability to the workplace" (p. 25).   Mikulecky
and Winchester (399) add that many jobs demand
repetitive reading geared toward action using a
broader variety of materials than are used in
schools. In addition, literacy on the job has a
social component because it involves questioning
and sharing of information with other workers.   A
higher level of proficiency is needed for job-
related materials than for general materials, and a
higher level is needed for training materials than
for materials used while actually performing the
job. While the focus of this present discussion is
not on school training for literacy, these concerns
are germaine to planning work-related programs for
adults.

     Reading on the job, however, may involve more
that reading-to-do or reading to gain specific

information in order to complete a specific task
(405). It is also a thinking activity that
involves problem solving and that is needed for
problem solving. Sticht and Mikulecky (412)
suggest that literacy development for work requires
the use of language and cognitive skills as well as
perceptual skills. Miller (409), in looking at the
reading activity of both technical and managerial
employees in a high-technology industry, found they
were primarily engaged in analytical tasks.
Mikulecky and Winchester (399) found in comparing
the performance of nurses that "it is difficult to
easily characterize the literacy activities of
superior nurses, but literacy for problem-solving
as well as critical thinking and reading come to
mind. The difference between nursing groups was
not so much what they had available as it was in
how they used it" (p. 12). The College Board (390)
confirms this emphasis on problem-solving. In a
dialogue with representatives of business,
"business people pointed out that employees are
expected to be able to reason and develop logical
steps for solving a problem no matter what their
job category may be" (p. 4).

    Because of the practical nature of much work-
related instruction, the emphasis is on linking
instruction and materials to a particular job (386,
416) and to particular materials and tasks required
(388, 389). The stress is on teaching skills and
strategies that apply to the workplace and on
instructing adults in how to apply them to the job
(389, 399, 408). The transfer of skills from the
classroom to the job is not assumed to take place;
transfer is taught. The motivational impact of
this approach for the adult student is obvious and
important (423). This emphasis on transfer
reinforces Harman's (22) third stage of literacy,
the application of skills in meaningful, practical
activities. In addition, the nature of literacy,
and of literacy on the job in particular, suggests
going beyond instruction in basic skills, linking
literacy and thinking (8, 17, 28, 36) and viewing
literacy also as development rather than just as
training.

    Instructional alternatives. The now familiar
issue of decoding or comprehending is also an issue

for those concerned with job-related programs.
Bochtler (417) sums up the problem of many students
who end up in these programs. They "have been
skilled to death" (p. 29). Rigg and Kazemek (411)
believe that programs that stress decoding and
individual skill mastery tended to be the very
kinds of programs that had failed with these
students in the past. Thus, Rigg and Kazemek
stress reading for meaning. This emphasis is not
universally accepted however. Bowman (418), for
example, reports on a successful program developed
for the U.S. Navy that is skill oriented, requiring
mastery of each individual skill and stressing
decoding as a basic set of skills. However, the
widespread acceptance of the use of actual reading
materials from the job or at least the use of
materials developed to simulate job materials
implies that comprehension of a particular text is
the goal, not just the ability to decode a text.
If work-related literacy is action oriented, then
in order to perform the action required the reader
must comprehend the text.

To meet the varied text and task demands on-
the-job, we need to instruct students in a variety
of strategies (410), using a variety of materials.
Miller (409) concluded that "in short, they need a
repertoire of skills and techniques to deal most
efficiently with the great variety in materials and
reading tasks. Clearly, regular school programs or
commercial speed reading courses won't fit.
Neither will the usual packaged programs" (pp. 114-
115). Instructional suggestions include:

1. Analyze the literacy tasks required by the job
    (386, 389, 397, 401, 404, 405, 409). Examine
    the differences between reading-to-do and
    reading-to-learn (400, 405). Examine lists of
    generic skills developed by others (390, 392,
    395, 400, 409). A problem, however, with using
    lists, as Tenopyr (387) points out, is that it
    is difficult to establish a definitive list of
    tasks and skills because the requirements of
    jobs change.

2. Teach reading as a process of reasoning-
    thinking (395). Encourage predictions before
    reading and confirmation or adjustment of the

predictions after reading (410). This might be done using a specific strategy such as the Technical Reading Technique (TRT) with its emphasis on active thinking strategies, metacognitive techniques, and action to be taken as a result of the reading (ibid.).

3. Use literacy skills to solve problems either created by the instructor or the class or actual problems from the job (399, 408).

4. Teach ways of organizing information, establishing a hierarchy of ideas and information, and relating items (399).

5. Instruct in critical reading and thinking (399).

6. Incorporate writing instruction into the reading instruction (407, 408, 409, 411).

7. Analyze and use relevant text structure as a source of information for comprehension (405, 409, 410).

8. Identify and teach pertinent vocabulary (405).

9. Develop job-related reading-to-do tests to match the actual requirements of the job (405, 407). Unfortunately, the commercial tests used are often not appropriate for adults (386) and frequently have been developed for reading-to-learn while the task for workers is reading-to-do (405).

10. Involve the students in the process of identifying needs and posing and solving problems (384).

11. Be prepared to work with students "not only on job-related skills but with their attitudes, feelings and the anxieties of being back 'at school'" (423, p. 14).

12. Devote sufficient time to instruction to insure progress. Instruction provided for a short period of time may yield few gains (386, 405, 433).

<u>Materials.</u> Materials chosen for work-related
programs deal almost exclusively with work-related
information and issues. The emphasis is primarily
on using a variety of materials in instruction,
keyed to the kinds of materials used on the job
(408, 409). Actual job materials can form the
basis for instruction and practice. In addition,
the Language Experience Approach provides a way of
exploring problems that might arise or have arisen
on the job (423). Materials used need not, and
probably should not, be limited to traditional
texts such as books, manuals, and memos but can
include work-related posters, instructions, and
diagrams (ibid.).

<u>Instructors.</u> Again, we see the need for
teachers who can establish a rapport with students
(416) and who are trained to instruct in literacy
and meet the needs of the students (424).
Instructors may be professionals, trained
volunteers, or a combination of the two. It is,
however, common to have a professional teacher or
administrator in charge of the program.

Curriculum and Program Alternatives

In considering options used by others in
developing work-related curriculum, weigh the
impact of the purpose of literacy, the model of
reading, and the role of the adult learner that is
implied or stated. Two basic models have been used
to develop curricula.

The first model emphasizes general academic
skills not necessarily related to a work
environment (422). James (382) compares this
approach, which has been used extensively in the
military, with a currently used functional
approach. The goal of the training in the military
is to improve the worker's performance. The
traditional academic approach of improving general
literacy skills has not worked, according to James,
because there has been little transfer of skills
and little motivation to engage in the task of
learning and applying new literacy skills. The
emphasis on general academic skills fails to take
into account the demands of a particular context.
Because of this, the military has moved to a

functional approach to address the literacy needs
of the job. We are reminded of the difficulties
associated with an absolute approach to literacy.

The second model emphasizes specific work-
related and job-related skills and strategies.
This has been the direction of most work-related
programs. The skills and strategies taught in job
programs are related to the basic mission of a
particular business (412), to a particular
situation (128, 389, 420, 425, 429, 430 432, 433),
to a general vocational curriculum (381, 411, 416),
or to general business related situations or
occupations (388). In any case, the approach is
often a functional one, designed to provide
literacy abilities that will enable the adult to
function in a specific environment.

In developing a work-related curriculum, a
variety of approaches have been taken, none unique
to on the job literacy and all appearing in other
programs. These approaches include competency-
based--perhaps similar to the APL project (384,
412, 424)--, diagnostic-prescriptive (418, 422,
423), and student-developed (406, 411, 419).

Who sponsors work-related programs and what
are some of the program alternatives offered?

1. Government agencies. Literacy programs might
   be offered in conjunction with programs
   developed for the Job Corps (411, 422) or for
   the Job Training Partnership Act (381).

2. Private agencies. The literacy training
   offered may (416) or may not (218) be directly
   related to vocational training. These agencies
   may provide the programs on-site for businesses
   or as part of a community service program
   (429).

3. Private businesses and industries. The role of
   private corporations in the development of
   work-related literacy skills is certainly not
   settled. According to McGowan (383) "while the
   private sector hasn't mounted any serious drive
   to wipe out illiteracy, some companies are
   moving in that direction and others are poised

for a coordinated assault" (p. 40). They may
provide for services indirectly, in such ways
as contributing to community-based reading
programs (383), teacher training programs to
improve instruction in reading and writing
(383), private volunteer literacy organizations
such as Literacy Volunteers of America (384)
and the Coalition for Literacy, or tuition aid
to employees for outside help (392).

In addition, corporations may offer direct
services in-house to employees. The rationale
here is that the company is the one best suited
to improve job-related literacy skills because
the company is in the best position to know the
job demands (392). Whether direct services are
provided may be a matter of self-interest, of
how much the company needs the employee, or it
may be a matter of the social climate of the
times (387). In-house programs can be offered
in conjunction with other groups such as
Literacy Volunteers of America (423) or a local
college (426) or may be offered under the
auspices of the company with an in-house
coordinator and tutors, possibly other
employees (383, 423). The problem is, as
Tenopyr (387) points out, that adult literacy
training on the job is costly "so it is small
wonder that employers are generally
conservative about literacy training for which
the cost/benefits are less clear than they are
for job skill training" (p. 16).

The spokesperson (423) for a major
insurance company summed up one perspective on
the need to support literacy efforts by stating
that "the private sector is the place where
people come for gainful employment, and if 1 in
5 people can't function in basic skills, this
creates a societal problem which we must
address because it extends too deeply into the
core of our society for us to simply say,
'Well, we just don't hire them.'" (p. 11).

4. The military. The military has been faced with
    a declining pool of potential recruits and an
    increasing proportion of recruits with low
    levels of literacy. There has been a shift

from the traditional approach based on an achievement model of literacy in which the concern was for grade level achievement to one based on a functional approach, looking at the specific requirements of the tasks to be done and helping the recruit acquire the literacy skills needed to get that job done (382, 386, 389, 415, 418, 421, 425, 429, 430).

5. Correctional institutions. The population in prisons is characterized by low literacy levels (424, 428). We see in the prison situation a captive audience, at least for some fairly predictable amount of time for some predictable group. Literacy curriculum has had a number of goals for incarcerated adults. The goal might be to enable the student to pass the GED test or to provide literacy skills appropriate to work settings. Some programs have had a broader view of literacy, a concern for developing the individual and his view of life (419). A variety of materials can be provided (417), some dealing with skills, some with concepts, many with both. Literature is included in prisons programs (406, 417, 419). The programs might be part of an Adult Basic Education program or a volunteer program (425). Ryan and Furlong (386) suggest that "prison programs aimed at rehabilitation rather than punishment are perhaps more likely to develop with long term 'social goals' in mind" (pp. 182-183). This may help explain the difference in curriculum and programs.

How do work-related programs address the issues of attendance, retention, and achievement? Attendance is generally not required. In fact, this has been cited by one source as "the secret to our success" (423, p. 14). In some programs such as those in the military, both attendance and completion may be required. In an effort to involve the adult worker, programs may build on the characteristics of adults and their need for active participation (406). Programs may identify situations which inhibit adults from taking full advantage of the instruction offered. For example, because of competing demands on adults' time, programs may be given during work, after hours, or a combination of the two (423).

The need for coordination and cooperation is identified here, as in other areas of literacy needs. Coordination is needed among agencies concerned directly with work-related literacy needs. This might involve coordinated research and programs in work-related programs in general (385), coordination among similar agencies such as prisons (424), or coordination among agencies on the same level of government such as the Federal level (381). There is also a need for these agencies to cooperate with educational institutions in planning instruction, curriculum, and programs (387, 390, 424).

In this area as in other areas there is a need for more research, particularly in identifying the relationship between literacy and success on the job, in defining job related literacy skills in general as well as skills for particular jobs, and in determining the effectiveness of present programs (386, 387).

Summary

Work-related literacy is an area where the immediate practical demands of a situation dictate a certain utilitarian, head-on attack with literacy for survival as a primary goal. However, this goal cannot be allowed to so dominate our total perspective that we forget that adults have a wide range of purposes for literacy. What is needed is a variety of programs offered by a variety of agencies designed to meet the differing requirements of adults at different points in their lives, with on the job literacy focusing, without any apologies, on survival and with other programs providing other alternatives.

Literacy in Postsecondary Institutions

The Extent and Implications of the Problem

The existence on college campuses of students who are unable to cope with the literacy demands and rigors of postsecondary education is not new,

is widespread and may be increasing. Sadler (510)
cites the fact that "college reading programs have
been offered for at least four decades in the
United States" (p. 262). Lederman, Ribaudo, and
Ryzewic (435) found, as the result of a national
survey, that 85% of the postsecondary institutions
responding indicated that poor skill preparation
was a problem for the institution and the
individual, with the extent of the problem
dependent on the standards and selectivity of the
institution. The inability of some students to
meet college-level literacy requirements is
particularly evident in community colleges where,
according to Roueche (507), the problem has existed
for "decades" (p. 21). However, although
"community colleges long have borne the brunt of
adult illiterates in American higher education"
(ibid.), the phenomenon is not limited to community
colleges. Hunter (471) reports on a 1978 study of
four-year colleges that found that "64% of colleges
have remedial reading and/or developmental reading
classes and labs available" (p. 256). In 1982,
Roueche, Baker, and Roueche (508), in studying the
practices of both two- and four-year colleges and
universities, "report with accuracy and confidence
that very few American colleges and universities
have escaped the problem of underprepared students
on their campuses" (pp. 31-32). These authors use
the phrase "millions of underprepared students" (p.
31). In fact, most colleges and universities have
some kind of skill program for the underprepared
and high risk student (507, 508).

It appears that we may have a "growing number
of students whose reading and writing capabilities
would scarcely have qualified them in earlier years
for college study" (448, p. 656). Eurick and
Kraetsch (434) compared reading test results over a
50-year period and found that "on the reading
tests, the 1978 freshmen at the University of
Minnesota scored significantly lower (p .1) than
their 1928 counterparts on vocabulary,
comprehension, and reading rate" (p. 660). The
authors caution against overgeneralization of the
results yet warn us that they "cannot be ignored"
(p. 664). The picture is not, however, universally
viewed as quite that bleak. Muehl (437) looked at
a variety of sources and found that "some hopeful

testing signs may be in the wind, with SAT and   ACT
scores   and   both   Iowa   and   Ohio precollege state
scores showing perhaps a reversal   of   trends" (p.
121).

The   implication   so   far is that the literacy
problem on the college   level   consists   solely   of
underprepared students with low levels of literacy.
This is certainly a significant part of the problem
but   only   a   part   of   it.   We know that there are
students who lack the basic literacy skills   needed
for   postsecondary   education (470,   503).   In
addition, Nist (503) identifies a   second   category
of   students,   those   who   have   not   received
instruction   in   the   advanced   level   skills   and
strategies   needed   for college reading.   These are
students whose literacy abilities may   be   adequate
for many situations but not for this one.   They are
the   students   Holbrook (470) identifies as needing
developmental   help.   We   see   in   the   college
population   the same diversity of needs as in other
populations, a diversity including both adults with
a   low level of literacy   and   those   with   adequate
levels   on   an absolute scale but not on a relative
scale.

Why do we have literacy problems in   colleges?
Remember,   the   issue   of   providing   literacy
instruction in college   is   not   new   although   the
number of students experiencing difficulties may be
increasing.   One reason for this situation might be
a   change   in   the   population   of students, with a
larger proportion coming to college   with   a   wider
range   of backgrounds, preparation, and test scores
(437).   There have   been   other   reasons   proposed,
including   increased   time spent watching television
(434, 455), reduced academic standards in the   high
schools   (434, 455), less motivation on the part of
students   to   learn   (434),   and   changes   in   the
family's   role   in   education   and   in   family life
styles (434).   Identifying and eradicating possible
causes is critical but   beyond   the   scope   of   our
concern.   The   problem   exists   now   and   must be
addressed.

The fact   of   a   large   number   of   unequipped
students   on a campus can have far reaching effects
on   all   aspects   of   college   life,   including

admissions, financial aid, programs and courses
offered, student progress, and faculty conditions,
as well as the cost of providing services (505,
506). The effects on the students can be just as
far reaching, including ability to complete the
general academic program and achievement during and
after it.

As we have already seen, individuals and
institutions respond to those needs which are
viewed as urgent and practical. Colleges and
universities are no different from businesses and
industries, for example, in identifying the need
for literacy for survival. Sadler (510) states
that "although the focus, curriculum, and materials
have changed over the years, the philosophy remains
the same--to eradicate reading deficiencies so that
students can negotiate more effectively the
required courses" (p. 263). This is particularly
important, according to Katz (500), because for
marginally prepared students "to succeed in higher
education, the learner must be able to acquire and
process enormous quantities of information
effectively" (p. 75). In addition, according to
Roueche (507), "as curriculum literacy requirements
escalate at a frightening pace, students are
enrolling today farther and farther behind in those
basic academic skills so critical for success in
college-level courses" (p. 24). Students need help
in literacy skills and strategies in order to
survive.

Literacy for survival in a college or
university, however, does not always mean literacy
on a low level because it is viewed very much from
a relative perspective. Roueche and Comstock
(509), for example, assert that "literacy is the
ability to perform reading, writing, and figuring
tasks consonant with the expectations and needs of
the individual" (p. v). They clearly state two
assumptions. One is that "the expectations and
needs of the individual are socially (and
institutionally) constrained" (ibid.). Basic
skills become those skills basic to the task at
hand and to the expectations of the institution
(512). Thus, on the college level literacy for
survival may mean advanced reading skills and
strategies taught to "good" readers. This is

reminiscent of literacy for survival in business.
The second assumption made by Roueche and Comstock
is that "literacy is a means by which individuals
perceive new alternatives for action" (p. v). They
seem to be suggesting here another purpose for
literacy, literacy for empowerment. Finally,
postsecondary institutions frequently cite the need
for literacy for human development. This goal may
be instead of or, more often, in addition to
literacy for survival. The wording may vary but
the basic goal remains the same: the individual
will grow and develop as a result of literacy.
This goal is certainly not unexpected in
institutions whose mission must include in some
manner the human growth and development of the
student.

      Literacy for human development in colleges can
take a number of different tacks. According to
Smith (458), "instruction in reading and study
strategies relates to larger issues of intellectual
development in college" (p. 5). This is
reminiscent of Scribner's (38) phrase "literacy as
a way of developing minds" (p. 14). Maring and Shea
(436) view the goal of literacy instruction in
college as the development of mature readers,
including the development of an "attitude toward
leisure book reading, time spent in leisure book
reading, and breadth of reading interests" (p.
788). Even when the primary focus of a program is
on enabling students to read course materials,
Baechtold, Culross, and Gray (460) suggest that, in
addition, a well conceived program may "develop
reading habits and interests in world affairs that
continue after the class has ended" (p. 310).
Cooper, Evans, and Robertson (463) believe that the
goal of reading is to "extend our 'tacit awareness'
of the world around us by exploring, testing and
discovering. Polanyi thinks that such a skill
literally becomes a part of the person using it,
ultimately changing that person" (p. 2). Flynn
(464), in describing a reading program designed to
improve performance in college courses, quotes
students' responses. "This semester's work, they
told us, had improved the quality of their lives.
And that, after all, is what it's all about" (p.
67). Interestingly, in this case the students not
the institution cite the goal of literacy for human

development.

Colleges and universities, perhaps more than
other institutions, appear to accept the premise
that there is more than one purpose for literacy
and more than one responsibility that they have in
developing it. Richardson, Martens, and Fisk
(438), in addition to their first purpose of
literacy for survival, identify another, to
"promote larger goals and values of a society" (p.
12). They conclude that "our relational view leads
to the identification of varieties of literacy" (p.
13). This relational view is widely expressed in
the literature on college literacy and has
implications for instruction, curriculum design,
and program development. Cervero's (11) belief
that we cannot achieve a single definition or
standard of literacy is certainly relevant here.
Each college and, to some extent, each academic
classroom will define what are appropriate levels
and kinds of literacy. As we will see, the
emphasis on literacy as training still exists.
However, colleges and universities may be moving
toward literacy as development and toward
Scribner's (38) goal of an ideal literacy that
encompasses all three purposes.

Instruction

Before we can explore instructional
alternatives we need a clear sense of the tasks
associated with college reading, the process of
college reading, and the role of the learner in the
learning process. Only by understanding these
variables can we make the decisions needed for
effective instruction, curriculum, and programs.

First, Chaplin (443) provides a useful
overview of the tasks of college reading.

Reading is essential at the college level.
Students must read with understanding and
apply critical insights to the wide range of
printed sources that accompany academic course
work. College students must be able to
synthesize new knowledge with previous
knowledge and to adjust their thinking
accordingly. To do this, they must be

competent, efficient readers and thinkers.
They must be aware of past experiences which
may help them in understanding present
encounters. (p. 151)

This view of college reading reminds us of
Harman's (22) three stages of literacy attainment.
Harman's notion of literacy as a tool is echoed by
Chaplin's view of it as a means for understanding
and critiquing course material. Harman's second
stage is translated by Chaplin into the general
literacy skills and strategies that students must
attain--skills and strategies we will explore in
depth. Harman's third stage, literacy application,
is similar to Chaplin's view of the role of
literacy in synthesizing knowledge and adjusting
thinking. This application stage is one that is
frequently emphasized in the literature on college
level reading. In fact, the focus on the
application of skills and strategies forms the
basis for many programs. Unfortunately the
application may present problems not only because
students are applying newly mastered basic skills
but because they may also lack the necessary
background information (470) and/or the needed
"underlying cognitive structures" (493, p. 2) to
succeed in college level materials. Chaplin leaves
us with no doubts. Literacy, in all its stages, is
not negotiable for the college student.

Literacy, in fact, appears to relate to the
total college experience. Kennedy (451) believes
that reading is a "higher order thinking skill that
is closely interwoven with writing on the college
level" (p. 131). Whimbey (518) concurs, finding
that reading, writing, and reasoning are all
interrelated. These views certainly place literacy
in good company and suggest implications for
instruction and curriculum. The linking of reading
and thinking has appeared in all areas of adult
literacy but probably no where as strongly as in
college reading. Those who have worked with
college students who are unable to make this
connection can readily appreciate Hovey's (78)
comment that this can present "a serious problem"
(p. 55) to all concerned.

Descriptions and discussions of the process of

college reading are frequently drawn from an
interactive model in which the reader is viewed as
active, involved in the process of reading,
predicting content, sampling text, confirming
hypotheses, and monitoring procedures and progress
(448, 471, 479). Reading is seen as a holistic
process, not as set of subskills to be mastered
(474). In addition, it is not enough for students
to engage in the process of reading; they need to
understand the process (474, 499) and control it,
assuming control from the teacher and emerging as
independent learners (517). Osburn and Maddux
(454) suggest that "perhaps we are 'missing the
boat' by attaching so much importance to specific
skills rather than emphasizing function and control
of reading behavior" (p. 9).

Simpson (439) adds another dimension to our
understanding of college reading by advising us to
consider the learner and to look at learning as an
interactive process, involving the characteristics
of the learner, the tasks, the text, and the
learner's processes and strategies. In addition,
she (457) relates these characteristics to an
interactive model of the reading process, stressing
that the learner must be active, interacting with
text, constructing meaning, and elaborating on that
meaning.

There are two models of instruction for the
learner according to Simpson (439): a content model
in which the teacher decides what to teach and how
to teach, and an andragogical model which
"emphasizes the unique characteristics of the adult
learner" (p. 218). The second model, she believes,
is the one that distinguishes college reading from
elementary school reading. This is familiar
territory, reminding us of the discussion of the
adult learner and of adult literacy practices.
Smith (459) illustrates the impact of student
participation on the process of instruction. If a
student is assigned a task and told what product to
deliver, he will probably do that and no more. A
"student's perception of ownership of a task can
affect choice of learning strategies and depth of
comprehension" (p. 299). Students need to become
part of the decision making process as participants
in an andragogical model of instruction.

Instructional   Alternatives.   In   examining
college literacy, Hunter (471) states that "the
problem   is   not   one   of   inability to decode" (p.
257).   While there is general agreement   on   this,
Nist   (474),   for one, suggests that decoding might
be a problem for some few students, and Kennedy
(451) points out that it might be a problem in some
technical   disciplines.   Generally, however, we are
not concerned with basic decoding skills on the
college level.   What, then, are the problems?

There   has   been research and exploration done
on the characteristics of good and poor college
readers.   These   characteristics can provide some
guidance as to the problems students encounter and
to the development of alternatives for instruction.

Good readers can:

focus on meaning not on individual words (453)
clarify their purpose(s) for reading (481)
identify   and   attend to the important aspects
    of the author's message (481)
engage in self-questioning (481)
organize and manipulate information (447)
monitor their progress and correct failures to
    comprehend (442, 458, 459, 481, 500, 517)

Poor readers may:

be passive readers (474)
have inadequate language comprehension skills
    (471)
be inexperienced with written language (451)
be word-centered   not   meaning-centered when
    reading (453)
have inadequate vocabularies (474)
lack a mature sight vocabulary (451)
lack appropriate or have inadequate prior
    knowledge of the subject (446, 452, 470,
    474)
not relate prior knowledge to text (471)
fail to recognize and use text organizations
    and patterns (446, 449, 450, 451, 471)
have difficulties with inferential, critical
    and evaluative comprehension (451)
be unable to organize their own thoughts (451)
have difficulties with reasoning (493, 494)

have poor comprehension monitoring skills (474)

have limited reading interests (474)

lack flexibility in reading and in reading strategies (474)

not have as a goal the need to learn from text, but rather just to read it and get through it (474)

Osburn and Maddux (453), in discussing college programs, suggest that "perhaps these programs should not only provide instruction in the traditional skills of vocabulary, comprehension and speed, but should also provide instruction in 'knowledge about' and 'control of' the reading process, with emphasis on reading as the transmission of meaning, rather than on reading as the pronunciation of words" (p. 104). Whimbey (518) adds that these programs would also integrate reading, writing, and reasoning, using reasoning as the basis for the integration. Thinking is a part of literacy (8, 17, 28, 35) that cannot be left to chance but needs to be included in instruction (39). The focus in college reading instruction is clearly on meaning (486).

In planning for literacy we need to examine the relationships between reading and writing, the student's goals, and the particular context in which literacy occurs (505). This means that we cannot instruct solely in skills and strategies but must also examine the teacher's requirements, the demands of the text, and the student's purpose in reading (506). The most efficient way to instruct might be to use workbooks, competencies and lists of basic skills. However, in terms of skills and strategies in the academic areas, this may not be the most effective means (474).

Let's consider some suggestions for instruction.

1. Provide opportunities for students to participate in and understand the process of reading though workshops, demonstrations, discussions, and coaching (478, 479).

2. Build on students' motivation and need for

speed by emphasizing that they can read more
productively and efficiently if they develop
comprehension, comprehension strategies, and
flexibility (464, 472).

3. Develop comprehension monitoring strategies
    students may use with any text, such as a
    script to be followed, questions to be asked,
    or a series of steps to be taken (438, 439,
    448, 477, 481, 500, 517).

4. Focus instruction on reasoning, thinking, and
    critical reading and use a variety of
    instructional and learning strategies (463,
    465, 466, 471, 474, 497, 499, 500, 518, 519).
    For example, develop inferencing and critical
    reading skills through written and oral reports
    and class discussions (463, 466) or through
    examining conflicting ideas (465).

5. Integrate cognitive competencies and abilities
    with basic skills instruction (493).

6. Use a problem solving approach that relates
    literacy to course content (472, 515).

7. Emphasize learning strategies such as
    networking, mapping, imagery, analysis of key
    ideas, categorization, and student-generated
    questions rather than isolated skills, and
    focus on problem solving and decision making
    (443, 458, 471, 500).

8. Develop prior knowledge through text
    comprehension strategies (472), direct
    instruction in content (446), visual aids
    (446), news magazines (460), and the reading of
    easier texts (478).

9. Instruct in the recognition and use of text
    structure, employing, for example, diagrams or
    students questions suitable for any text (460,
    477, 500)

10. Suggest ways to organize information and
    synthesize texts, such as a study guide (466),
    a pyramid diagram (483), a structured format
    for note-taking (447), "active reading,

thoughtful text underlining, self-questioning and, most important, thinking during reading" (474, p. 86).

11. Integrate instruction in reading and writing (451, 474, 496, 516) or, possibly, in all the communication areas including, in addition, speaking, listening (499), and thinking (452). Reading can become a model for writing and for the process of writing (460), helping students organize their ideas and understand the organization of other writers (445) and relating critical reading and critical writing (463, 476).

12. Adapt reading strategies to the particular requirements of the text and the subject (471, 472).

13. Encourage vocabulary expansion through the development of meaning, using context and a meaningful framework (474) or a keyword method (456).

14. Address the issues of motivation and attitude by combining basic skills instruction with counseling (511). Ask students what they want to work on and what materials would be helpful (492). Involve students in the decision making process.

15. Use instructional techniques that will facilitate learning such as providing for feedback and practice (517), encouraging group discussion (452, 478, 522), and explaining, modeling, demonstrating, and coaching procedures and their application to new situations (439, 458, 465, 478).

    Materials. The choice of materials for instruction is as critical in college literacy courses as it is in other adult literacy courses. There is particular emphasis in college reading on the application of skills and strategies in a useful and meaningful context both during and after college. Thus, suggestions for choosing and using materials include:

1. Use materials taken directly from college
    courses (443, 448, 470, 474) or materials that
    will be needed after college (515).

2. Provide examples of a variety of materials in
    order to insure that transfer to other
    materials takes place (517). Such materials
    can come from a variety of sources, including
    book lists from the various academic
    departments, a book exchange among students,
    contributions from the faculty, and a book fair
    by the college bookstore (436). Another source
    for materials is the news magazine (460, 466)
    that contains articles related to academic
    majors that are both long enough to be useful
    and short enough to be used in class.

3. Use both long and short selections for
    instruction and practice in comprehending and
    for organizing and relating texts (458, 474).
    The use of a variety of materials has the
    additional benefit of allowing the student to
    acquire flexibility in reading strategies
    (474).

4. Encourage students to self-generate interest in
    materials that may not be inherently
    interesting (475). "If students learn why they
    become interested in things, perhaps they can
    deliberately employ the same techniques with
    material that does not interest them" (p. 117).
    Self-analysis of behavior can be useful in
    developing this ability.

     Assessment. A great deal of testing is done
in college literacy programs to determine need
before instruction and progress after instruction.
A number of cautions have been raised about these
testing procedures.

1. Use tests appropriately, the way the publisher
    intended (468, 487, 504). It is not uncommon,
    for example, for a survey test to be
    incorrectly used as a diagnostic test (504).

2. Be aware of the connections between the test
    used and the view of reading the test
    represents (480). Compare this with the view

of reading that supports the reading program. Is the test testing isolated skills based on a bottom-up model while the instruction is focusing on a holistic, interactive approach to reading? We must relate tests and testing procedures to reading models and assessment research in order to "decide what one wants to measure, in what circumstances,and with what implications for learning" (469, p. 13).

3. When using tests understand what the questions are asking and what skills and strategies they are designed to assess (467).

4. Examine the test manual to determine the technical aspects of the test, the practical elements of administering it, and the use of the results (487).

5. Study the specific tests available (473, 487), the reactions of others to them (469), and evaluations published in journals and reference books (469).

6. Develop informal assessment strategies (469) including "interviews, questioning, observations, self-report measures and diagnostic teaching sessions" (439, p. 217) as well as the retelling orally and in writing of text content (499). Simpson (480) rejects the elementary school model of diagnosis in which a standardized test is given because of the lack of appropriate information obtained. She advocates instead the development of questions and other informal methods to investigate the characteristics of the task, learning strategies employed, characteristics of the text, and characteristics of the learner.

Instructors. College programs tend to be staffed more by professionals and less by volunteers than most other types of adult programs. Many employ full-time professionals, with part-time adjunct faculty seen as an increasingly important source of personnel (514). It is not uncommon for regular academic faculty to teach in these programs, particularly as the need for their services in an academic department has declined.

However, as Roueche (507) warns, it is important
that academic faculty volunteer for reading
programs and not be forced into them. Peer tutors
are also used in these programs and may be
especially useful in helping students understand
the relevance of the skills and strategies being
taught (492, 507).

Because of the large number of college reading
programs Brozo and Stahl (462) state that "never
before has there been a greater need for trained
reading and study skills specialists" (p. 310). In
view of this, it is particularly important that we
examine the qualifications that appear to be
needed. These qualifications cover a wide range of
areas. Brozo and Stahl (462, 484) have compiled a
list of competencies that includes many of those
also identified by others concerned with college
reading programs (468, 497, 510). Brozo and Stahl
list the areas of: training in reading instruction
as well as background in content areas; practical
experience in and theoretical knowledge of
instruction, knowledge of research, measurement,
administration, and counseling; and appropriate
personal characteristics. Other suggested
qualifications include specific training in working
with college students and a willingness to engage
in activities leading to professional growth (468).
In addition, Gruenberg (497) suggests that college
reading instructors should have an attitude of
"academic rigor and an expectation for high level
of student commitment and achievement" (p. 4).
This last quality assumes particular importance in
reconciling the differences between the initial
competency of some high risk students and the
expectations of the institution. It can also be a
source of controversy in programs.

The need for professional training becomes
particularly apparent when we examine the jobs the
instructor in a college literacy program may be
called on to perform. An essential requirement is
the ability to teach courses and provide individual
tutoring (490) commensurate with the demands of the
institution. In addition, an important aspect of
many programs is the ability of the skills
instructor to work with faculty in academic
departments (490, 512) in planning programs and in

overcoming faculty resistance and negative attitudes toward students, their problems, and the skills program itself. There is an increasing trend toward sharing strategies and techniques with all faculty (497) and coordinating efforts to insure that reading instruction is relevant (491) and that skills and strategies are reinforced and applied (478). In many cases reading instructors become consultants to academic faculty (512) and/or team teach courses (498). The role of the skills instructor in the college reflects the extent of the problem presented by the high risk, underprepared student and the commitment of the college toward meeting the problem.

Curriculum and Program Alternatives

In 1978 Chaplin (491) identified future directions for college reading programs. These give us a framework for examining issues and trends in current curriculum and program alternatives. One direction she suggested for programs was that we "must define and articulate our philosophy of reading instruction" (p. 587). This is critical for any literacy program, but seems crucial for a college or university where the commitment must be to furthering knowledge of the process of reading and to applying theory and research in practice. A literacy program in a post-secondary institution should be a testimony to the professional knowledge and commitment of the institution. The model of reading and reading instruction chosen must be one that will serve the needs of college students.

Unfortunately, college programs are widely criticized because of their failure to identify and use appropriate models of reading as the basis for instruction and curriculum development. According to Hayes and Diehl (448) one of the reasons that college literacy programs fail is because they are based on a diagnostic-prescriptive approach emphasizing instruction in separate subskills and the use of isolated words and sets of materials. Nist and Hynd (504), in examining college programs, found that, in fact, programs are emphasizing a diagnostic-prescriptive approach based on faulty tests and are teaching skills instead of strategies. "While the isolated skills approach has diminished somewhat, it remains all too popular" (p. 306). In their review of reading programs in the City University of New York, Soll and McCall (514) found that only three of the seventeen colleges reported courses that were influenced by psycholinguistic models of reading in which the reader constructs meaning based on his prior knowledge and on the characteristics of the text. The bulk of the programs were influenced by a skills model and emphasized the diagnosis and remediation of skills. Finally, Gordon and Flippo (468) in studying colleges in the southeastern United States found a similar situation. In addition, they found that colleges were using tests inappropriately, letting the tests determine the curriculum with a resulting emphasis on diagnostic-prescriptive approaches.

A second direction suggested by Chaplin (491) is to emphasize the "use of sophisticated thought processes that are not characteristic of young children" (p. 587) and that are the hallmark of mature readers. This seems almost self-evident, yet there is concern that we are not moving in this direction. Coleman and Berg (493) find that the instruction provided students "ignores the cognitive structures that would allow them to process, assimilate, and manipulate knowledge at the college level" (p. 2). Prager (477) finds that programs fail to emphasize the thinking processes needed for critical reading. Brittain (489) in a report on the result of a 1982 study of 30 institutions whose programs had been described in professional journals seems to confirm this. The content of reading courses offered dealt overwhelmingly with vocabulary development and reading comprehension. Flexibility, test taking, listening skills, and time management also were high on the list. Thinking, memory, concentration, critical reading, and insights into the language process were indicated by some respondents under "other". These were apparently not priority items.

Pigott (476), citing the concerns expressed and funds expended in the pursuit of college reading improvement, states that "it is difficult to understand why the teaching of reading at the college level is not as sophisticated as the

teaching of writing" (p. 534). It is indeed
difficult to accept that colleges as a whole have
not assumed a leadership role in the application of
theory and research in the field of adult literacy,
using college reading programs as laboratories. A
bottom-up model stressing isolated skills, not
focusing primarily on meaning and the processes
associated with generating meaning, cannot be
appropriate for college students. We need a
clearly articulated model that views reading as a
meaning-gathering, holistic process such as Nist
(474), for example, proposes in theory and Henrichs
(499) describes in practice. The focus must be on
competencies and strategies appropriate to the
college student.

While it is difficult to accept the current
situation at some colleges, in practical terms it
is fairly evident why colleges have stayed with a
school model of instruction, stressing isolated
skills. One reason for this situation may be, as
Gordon and Flippo (468) suggest, that instructors
are so concerned with the daily activities of
teaching that they are not concerned with larger
issues of theory and research and with maintaining
their professional knowledge. Nist (474) sums it
up for us in discussing a holistic approach to
college reading instruction:

> As far as disadvantages are concerned, I
> suppose the major one is that it is a
> tremendous amount of work on the part of the
> instructor, especially the first time the
> course is taught using a holistic approach.
> Collecting materials and deciding what to
> teach and the best way to do it takes time.
> It is much easier to give students a
> standardized reading test and then give a
> 'prescription' for student to follow ...
> easier but not nearly so effective. (p. 87)

Chaplin (491) also suggested that college
reading programs--both developmental and remedial--
should be available and suitable to all students.
Traditionally, reading programs have been offered
to the the high risk student who arrives at college
with poor preparation. Cheek (492) finds that "the
primary goal of college reading programs has become

the remediation of reading and study skill
weaknesses in underachieving undergraduate
students" (p. 556). Because of the constraints of
personnel and finances, institutions often do
identify this as their primary goal. However,
there is a growing acceptance that we should be
offering a range of reading programs for all
students (502) to enable them to meet the
particular demands of college reading. Nist (503)
sees the need for two kinds of programs, remedial
and developmental, with remedial students using
high interest/low vocabulary materials to master
basic skills and developmental students using
materials similar to those used in college courses
to master and apply content area skills. In 1984 a
professional journal in the field dropped the words
"& Remedial" from its title and became the JOURNAL
OF DEVELOPMENTAL EDUCATION. An explanation in
Volume 8, Issue 1, 1984 in that journal stated, "we
believe that the emerging field of developmental
education has matured to the extent that
remediation is now a concern--but not the ONLY
concern of most developmental educators."

Chaplin (491) provided us with yet another
direction for the future when she suggested that
"reading is a necessary concomitant to all academic
instruction and must be woven carefully into the
curriculum fabric" (p. 587). She goes on to
suggest that "reading instruction at the college
level must be relevant to students' academic
experiences and reflect an understanding of the
demands that are made on students in the wider
academic community" (p. 588). This direction
points us away from isolated courses or labs that
focus on individual skills and toward learning
experiences that have a direct application for the
student so "students can cope successfully with the
reading tasks demanded of them in college and in
their lives outside of college" (514, p. xv).

In practice, one reason that programs are
deemed ineffective is because they fail to provide
for the relevant application of skills and
strategies in the academic subject areas (448,
509). Hunter (471), for example, found that "many
programs in four year colleges have failed because
they give practice and instruction that is not tied

closely to the reading demands of academic courses"
(p. 256). One result of recognizing this failure
has been an increasing movement toward the
integration of both remedial basic skills
instruction and developmental instruction into the
mainstream of the college (490, 492). In
developing a delivery system that will insure this
integration, we need to examine two areas: how to
structure the students' experiences to insure
transfer of skills and how to structure faculty
responsibility to insure that the experiences
happen.

Probably the predominant delivery model (435)
in colleges is a separate course or lab experience
that may use actual college texts as the
instructional materials or as application and
practice materials. Brittain and Brittain (461),
however, question whether in general these separate
courses view reading as a holistic process even
though they may at some point use college texts. A
second model utilizes skill courses that are
offered as adjuncts to academic courses,
incorporating instruction in both basic skills and
content area subject matter (501). These courses
require close coordination between the skills
instructor and the academic instructor. A third
possible approach incorporates skills and strategy
instruction in the academic course, with the skills
instructor and the academic instructor either team
teaching or cooperating on the content and
approaches used (489). The latter two
alternatives, because of the integration of skills,
strategies, and content, lend themselves to a
holistic view of reading with the pursuit of
meaning as the goal.

All of these models require, as Granschow
(496) points out, that faculty in all disciplines
are involved in the process if we are to "seek new
solutions to the academic problems of
nontraditional students" (p. 26). The key to
insuring that the learning experience is successful
appears to be the cooperation and coordination
between the skills instructor and the academic
faculty. Yet the academic faculty often resist
this cooperation. According to Hunter (471),
"professors see reading skills as something

unrelated to their academic discipline" (p. 257).
She stresses that all faculty must address the
problem and "become familiar with the reading and
learning strategies important to their specific
disciplines" (ibid.). In most instances, from a
practical perspective, it will be the
responsibility of the skills instructor to take the
initiative and assume a leadership role. In fact,
this has already been identified as a major
responsibility of reading instructors.

A second and closely related question is how
to insure faculty responsibility in carrying out
cooperative programs. Generally the responsibility
is assumed by the department in charge of the
skills instruction. Frequently a separate skills
department or center is established and charged
with the responsibility of insuring in some way
that skills instruction takes place (468, 470, 489,
497). Roueche, Baker, and Roueche (508) in a
nationwide survey found that large institutions
generally offered basic skills instruction as part
of a separate department and smaller institutions
offered it as part of the traditional academic
department. The concern with the first arrangement
is that it might not foster sharing of ideas
between reading faculty and academic faculty and
may fail to take the academic teacher's
requirements and text demands into account in the
instruction (506). Again, the responsibility falls
on the reading instructor and this is where care
must be taken in the hiring and training of such
instructors. The advantage to this arrangement is
the possibility of greater expertise and often more
enthusiasm in planning reading curriculum and
offering instruction than may occur in a
traditional academic department.

We have already explored the range of
definitions and purposes of literacy in terms of
the college student. While the emphasis is
certainly on literacy for survival it has not been
limited to the survival of the low level student
but has encompassed the survival of all students in
a college environment. In addition, either clearly
stated or implied, we find literacy for human
development a part of many programs. The
recognition and acceptance of these purposes for

literacy have undoubtedly had two important
effects: they have accelerated a trend toward
making literacy instruction available to all
students and they have succeeded in moving services
from the laboratory and the learning center to the
regular classroom. The result has been an array of
curriculum and program models designed to address
multiple purposes for literacy and literacy
development.

The variety of curriculum alternatives that
have been designed and put into practice is
encouraging, suggesting that colleges are
addressing the needs of students and institutions
in particular contexts. The following programs,
all focusing on reading but in a variety of ways
and in combination with a range of other
competencies, offer possibilities that might be
adapted to different institutions. In examining
these alternatives, we need to keep in mind Nist
and Hynd's (504) statement that "the teacher and
the approach used are the primary elements in
providing a comprehensive program to help deficient
college students become readers" (p. 309).
However, we must also offer curriculum models that
will meet their needs and encourage them to join
programs and stay with them until they are able to
function successfully in the larger college
environment. Consider the following alternatives:

1. Reading and Writing:

    A program of "total immersion" (451, p. 135)
    uses "reading and writing as avenues for
    acquiring disciplinary content" (ibid.). A
    basic course, offered by a teacher of writing,
    stresses the interrelationship of the two with
    an extension and application of the process in
    the various content courses.

    A reading/writing course for high-risk
    freshmen, team taught by a reading specialist
    and a writing specialist, integrates reading
    and writing, using novels as well as teacher-
    and student-generated writing for the course
    material (516).

    A course for college honors students in the

development of writing skills stresses
critical reading as a way of understanding the
process of reading and writing (476).

Communication and reasoning skills are
incorporated into various academic courses by
faculty who are trained by other faculty in
the departments of reading, writing, English,
speech, and education (494).

Basic reading, writing and study skills are
offered in courses that are paired with
academic courses. A reading instructor, a
writing instructor, the academic faculty, and
a student tutor cooperate in planning and
teaching the paired courses (496).

Critical reading and analytical writing are
combined either on an individual tutorial
basis or as part of an English course with an
emphasis on transferring the skills to any
content course and with the ultimate goal of
changing the individual (463). Student
reading journals provide a vehicle for
analyzing, thinking about, and reacting to
text.

2. Reading, Reasoning and Problem Solving:

Occupational reading and problem solving are
integrated into a content course taught by an
academic faculty member in a community college
(515). Instructional modules are designed to
enable the student to improve reading skills
and to use technical manuals "to solve
problems on the job" (p. 97).

Critical reading and analytical reasoning are
developed in a separate course based on a
problem solving approach using verbal and
mathematical materials (518, 519).

A basic skills course is employs 12 cognitive
competencies that emphasize the process of
acquiring and using the basic skills (493).

A credit course, designed as a laboratory for
a research project, stresses "learning to

learn" strategies and methods, including comprehension monitoring and incorporates basic skills instruction (517). Generally, the participants are high risk students. Instruction is based on content materials and utilizes a mix of large and small group instruction and discussion.

3. Reading Related to Content:

A skills course is offered as an adjunct to academic courses, emphasizing skills applicable to the particular content (498). It is jointly planned and taught by academic faculty and skills instructors. In addition, the program offers individualized help and a precollege program providing intensive content knowledge and skills instruction.

A lab program is based on a "holistic, content-based approach" (504, p. 306) to reading. The emphasis is on teaching process and strategies, not skills. A combination of small group instruction and individual tutoring is provided.

A total learning support program is integrated into the college curriculum. The stress is on "reading as a process rather than as a set of skills" (490, p. 3). Literature and academic texts are used in class for instruction.

4. Reading and Counseling:

Basic skills training and counseling in a learning center are combined in a one-on-one therapy approach in order to effect a "change in personality variables through skills training" (511, p. 646). The skills therapist combines knowledge of counseling techniques with competency in basic skills instruction.

It is difficult and somewhat misleading to place these programs into strict categories because in practice they are not narrowly conceived. Many address issues related to instruction in academic content and content area skills and strategies even though they have not been listed under Reading

Related to Content. Issues related to instruction in thinking and learning likewise appear in many programs. Indeed, the strength of college programs may well be in the broad approach taken to curriculum design illustrating the trend identified by Brittain (489) "toward programs that are concerned with improvement of reading in the content areas and, broadly, with the improvement of learning in college" (p. 3). In addition, consider how the various components involved in planning vary according to the needs and background of the institution, the students, and, probably, the faculty. Courses are offered to students identified by an institution as benefiting from instruction, and they range from high risk students and those lacking in basic skills to honors students. Materials used vary from content materials to those written by teachers and by students. As Brittain asserts (489), "programs need to be situationally tailored" (p. 8).

Chaplin (491) has provided an additional direction and challenge. We must make "courses dynamic, challenging and necessary for student success" (p. 586). Instruction in literacy must include an emphasis on reasoning, problem solving, and comprehension monitoring. Students need to acquire strategies, not focus on mastering skills; they need to understand reading as a holistic process, not as a set of isolated skills. The emphasis must be on the application of skills and strategies within the content area and, in the long run, on the improvement of learning in college (489). In addition, there must be "the perception that basic skills instruction has a positive value and appropriate place in college" (497, p. 3). Finally, colleges and universities must become leaders in developing reading research and theory as well as in applying this knowledge in appropriate programs for college students.

Literacy programs for college students have been faced with the same problems of recruitment, retention, and achievement that have plagued other adult programs. College students view reading instruction as something they left behind when they arrived at college. Unfortunately, this resistance is highlighted and compounded by the elementary

school models and inappropriate instruction offered
in some programs. Cross's (30, 48) dispositional
barrier to learning created by dislike of school is
certainly evident in many instances. However,
Simpson (439) provides encouraging news, suggesting
that "the field of college reading is presently
going through a process of trying to define and
wean itself from the ever-present elementary and
clinical model of reading" (p. 213).

In addition to the need for appropriate
instruction, consider the impact on students of
offering skills courses for credit vs. no credit.
The granting of institutional credit seems to
provide motivation for students and also enables
them to apply the course toward the total needed to
obtain financial aid. The granting of graduation
credit, in addition, moves the student toward
completion of a degree. Non-credit courses,
understandably, receive low priority from students
(498). Attaching credit to remedial and
developmental courses is one way to address
problems raised by both institutional and
dispositional barriers in recruitment, retention,
and achievement. The advantages of granting credit
must, however, be balanced against the issue of
dilution of the academic degree by allowing non-
traditional courses to be awarded academic credits.
In practice, Gruenberg (497) found that courses
generally were offered for either graduation credit
or institutional credit rather than no credit.

Another question that is particular to college
programs is whether enrollment and attendance in
separate courses should be required for high risk
students. In required courses recruitment is
certainly not a problem but meaningful retention
and achievement may be. Mandatory courses are
reminiscent of the elementary school model that, as
we have seen, adults find unsatisfactory.
Voluntary programs have the advantage of putting
the adult in control, of allowing him to overcome
for himself some of the dispositional barriers
associated with having to take a course in an area
he may have thought he had left behind. Roueche,
Baker, and Roueche (508) found that, in practice,
basic skills courses are generally not mandatory.
Unfortunately, they also found that of the students

who were deficient in basic skills, fewer than one-half volunteered for courses. Friedlander (495) identified the same problem with voluntary courses. He found that students may cite the inconvenience of the time the course is offered or their own lack of time. Frequently, however, they do not perceive the need for supportive help.

This issue is a knotty one that has continually plagued college reading courses. Friedlander (495) proposes a solution to overcome both the problems of volunteering and the stigma of requiring enrollment. He advocates "integrating remediation into college-level courses" (p. 62). This solution, of course, also addresses the problems raised by the credit/no credit issue and insures application of skills and strategies.

Overall, how successful have college programs been? Palmer (455) found that courses in reading and writing, while improving reading speed and the ability to write cohesive essays, had little impact on reading comprehension and the mechanics of writing. He identifies the need for "significant improvement in the ability of colleges to upgrade student reading and writing skills" (p. 28). This need for improvement is echoed throughout the literature. The success of college programs has been "marginal at best" (507, p. 21). Their history has been "bleak" (448, p. 656). "As they currently operate, most college skills programs are ineffective" (ibid., p. 660).

Why? A variety of reasons have been suggested. Programs are often too brief to allow students to learn to apply reading and thinking skills and strategies to content materials (448, 498). There is a disturbing lack of emphasis on critical literacy demanding the highest levels of thinking as well as a lack of emphasis on independence and self-direction (506). These are serious concerns that address the heart of literacy development.

There have been a number of investigations into the characteristics of successful programs. Roueche (507), for example, identifies features contributing to success as including: strong administrative support, mandatory counseling and placement, structured courses, awarding of credit, flexible completion strategies, multiple learning systems, volunteer instructors, use of peer tutors, monitoring of student behaviors, interfacing with subsequent courses, and program evaluation. Brittain (489) identifies somewhat similar features of successful reading programs and adds affective variables such as "attention to enhancing students' self-concepts" (p. 8). In discussing these features, she cautions that "the actual extent to which they contribute to program success is uncertain due to the paucity of systematic evaluative data" (p. 9).

A somewhat broader view of successful programs looks beyond the specific characteristics. Gruenberg (497) concludes that the specifics of a program, such as the issue of credit vs no credit or the location of the course in a separate department or in an academic department are not as important as the "commitment and capacity for serving the needs and character of the institution while also providing a positive medium for developmental students to build new competencies upon existing strengths" (p. 4).

Summary

The need for college literacy programs exists; colleges have documented the varieties of difficulties students experience in meeting the demands of college reading. The mechanisms are available to solve the problems. Hayes and Diehl (448) provide us with a framework to use in the process of decision making in planning and executing college programs. They suggest that:

> Guided by sound principles of instruction firmly grounded in prose learning research, we can reform college skills programs to provide instruction that capitalizes on students' strengths, fosters their sense of responsibility for self-improvement, and promotes independent learning. Successful college study demands nothing less. (p. 660)

Literacy Around the World

The Extent and Implications of the Problem

In examining issues of literacy and illiteracy worldwide, we are faced with an unsettling reality. Many concerns have been raised about the extent of illiteracy throughout the world; many efforts have been made to alleviate the problem; however, much remains to be done. In 1979, M'Bow (523), Director-General of UNESCO, stated that the percentage of the world's population over 15 years of age classified as illiterate was 32.4% in 1960 and was predicted to be 28.9% in 1980 and 25.7% in 1990. In absolute numbers, because of an increase in the world's population, M'Bow estimated that the number of illiterates worldwide would increase from about 800 million to 884 million in 1990. He concluded that "despite the efforts that have been made, the situation is more worrying than ever" (p. 398). Although it is difficult to obtain definitive statistics, M'Bow's figures reflect a fairly general consensus that the problem is one of substantial proportions (528, 569). The participants in an international seminar held in Berlin in 1983, for example, estimated that there were "close on one billion adult illiterates in the world" (521, p. 11). In addition to sheer numbers, consider the different kinds of countries facing the problems posed by illiteracy and low levels of literacy. We may think first of countries like Mali (575) where 95% of the women are illiterate or Ethiopia (568) with a 90% overall illiteracy rate, not recognizing that in Canada there is "a problem of enormous dimensions" (543, p. 9) in regards to the number of functionally illiterate adults. Problems of illiteracy and low levels of literacy are found in third world countries, underdeveloped, developing, and developed countries.

Who are the illiterate and the functionally illiterate? The categories are predictable: the poor (521, 523, 528, 536), women (521, 523, 528), residents of rural areas (528), those in trouble with the law (559). Fisher (520) warns us that "the 'have-nots' in terms of literacy are also worse off in terms of life expectancy, infant mortality, educational provision, communications, nutrition,

health services, food production, and income; their
industry is less developed, their agriculture is
less productive" (p. 161). He concludes that
"illiteracy must not be viewed as a problem in
isolation" (ibid.). The implications of this
conclusion for curriculum development are
compelling.

The problems of illiteracy and low levels of
literacy around the world have certainly not been
ignored. There have been many programs initiated on
a variety of levels, sponsored by many organizations
including all levels of government as well as
private agencies. M'Bow (523) cites encouraging
examples of countries with effective programs.
Lazarus (531) identifies the "great advances" in
both elementary school and adult education programs
dealing with literacy in many countries throughout
the world. Noor (533) finds that the "interest in,
and commitment to, promoting literacy is not
declining in the developing world. Rather, it is
gaining momentum and can be seen in the plans of
many developing countries and international
agencies" (p. 165). He provides examples from
India, Afghanistan, Bangladesh, and Saudi Arabia.
In addition, we find Great Britain (525, 585), the
United States (585), and Canada (543) cited as
countries addressing problems of illiteracy and low
levels of literacy. However, as Lange (524)
concludes, "despite the many efforts to promote
literacy around the world, the problem of illiteracy
continues to fester" (p. 278). There is a caution
expressed. One reason may be that programs, while
well meant, may not be addressing the issues of
literacy and illiteracy effectively (544). Lange
(524) urges us to review programs with a view to
identifying "the successes that might be transferred
from one program to another" (p. 279).

With illiteracy occurring in such large
percentages of the population and affecting such a
substantial number of people, it might seem that
literacy efforts would center exclusively on
literacy for survival, literacy to achieve a minimum
standard according to the particular society's
literacy requirements. There is no question that
survival is an accepted, important purpose for
literacy. A program in Honduras (548), for example,

emphasizes skills that are immediately applicable and that link literacy and health education. The National Literacy Campaign in Ethiopia (568) has a similar emphasis. The aim there is to teach reading, writing, and mathematics, relating these basic skills to everyday concerns. The problems of acquiring basic literacy are so extensive that few countries can afford not to make literacy for survival an immediate goal.

There is another purpose, however, that is cited frequently in the literature on worldwide literacy, cited with a fervor not always seen elsewhere. Gayfer, Hall, Kidd, and Shrivastava (522) in examining literacy in various parts of the world suggest that literacy arouses in the individual "critical awareness of social reality, enabling him or her to understand, master and transform the reality" (p. 7). Literacy is "a means by which millions of individuals can transform both themselves and their societies" (521, p. 11). When a society is in the process of change or when change is viewed as desirable and/or useful, literacy for empowerment may become an important goal. In fact, Lange (524) believes that "perhaps the most vital sign of literacy is when it heightens the individual's awareness and control over living conditions" (p. 281).

Much of the concept of literacy for empowerment, particularly in developing countries, has come from the writings of Freire (15, 16, 136, 561) and his notion of literacy as a resource for transforming reality and planning actions. Hirshon (563), in describing the Nicaraguan Literacy Crusade, identified it with Freire's idea that control of "the word" gave the reader the ability to change the social order. "The literacy crusade was one expression of the Nicaraguan revolution's determination to give power to the people, to make them actors in their own social destiny. And it also taught them to read" (p. xii). The priorities here are clearly established. In fact, literacy for empowerment has political implications, probably nowhere more clearly seen than in many of the developing countries (521). We must consider that "revolutionary ... non-revolutionary ... and highly pluralistic political systems and societies may each

in their own way be making valiant efforts to
promote their kind of literacy" (ibid., p. 17).
Deiner (560) points out that it is, in fact, this
political involvement and the partisan nature of the
Nicaraguan Crusade that made the crusade
controversial.

The third purpose for literacy, literacy for
human development, is also frequently cited as a
goal. Interestingly and understandably, it is
generally linked to one or both of the other two
purposes. Power (528), for example, identifies a
clear connection between literacy and power as well
as between literacy and quality of life. Lazarus
(531) cites the same two broad purposes for literacy
stating that "literacy is not only a means of
personal development but of enabling the new
literates to participate more effectively in the
qualitative transformation of their environment" (p.
68). The participants in a regional conference held
in Viet Nam under the auspices of UNESCO stated that
literacy programs should "help learners not only to
read and write but also to improve their earning
capacities and the ability to overcome the social
and economic problems of daily life" (587, p. 6).
In addition, they held that literacy must "include
knowledge, skills and attitudes conducive to the
enhancement of quality of life" (p. 5). Here we see
literacy for survival, literacy for empowerment, and
literacy for human development.

In these statements of purpose we find the
notion of literacy as a "relative concept" (525, p.
13), a concept we have seen before. In fact,
Malmquist (525) points out that "there is a
continuous evolution ongoing everywhere as regards
definitions of what is meant by literacy" (p. 12).
Definitions of literacy change from country to
country and from one period of time to another. The
implication is clear. We must link instruction, the
development of curriculum, and a delivery system to
a specific context, taking into account the concept
of literacy as relative and changing.

The advantages to societies and to individuals
that are associated with raising literacy levels are
obvious. One set of advantages for both the group
and the individual includes: social and economic

progress (531, 533, 543, 569, 590), improved health
practices (528, 533, 569), and increased political
awareness and participation (525, 531, 533, 590). A
second set of advantages pertains more to the
individual, although certainly society would
ultimately benefit.   Here we see the link between
literacy and increased self-esteem, independence,
and privacy (569) and "the liberation of a mind from
the bondage of dependence" (533, p. 163). As Noor
(533) points out, an understanding of these purposes
and related benefits "is critical in determining the
structure, content, method, effect and ultimate use
of literacy programmes in a neo-literate society."
(p. 163).

Instruction

     In planning literacy instruction in both
developing and developed countries, we need to
examine two broad areas: the choice of the language
to use in instruction and the impact of cultural
constraints on adult literacy achievement.   In
practical terms, one of the first and most immediate
questions is what language should be used for
instruction and for the development of written
literacy (521, 524, 532, 533, 587). This question
arises in any country in which one or more languages
is in common use in addition to a national, official
language. Examples include such diverse countries
as Ethiopia with "about ninety languages spoken by
different nationalities" (568, p. 193) plus Amharic,
the official language; and Canada with two
predominant languages, French and English spoken in
at least part of the country and with adults who are
unable to speak either of these languages (543).
Lange (524) provides the examples of the USSR with
"over 122 national languages" (p. 279), China with
"many dialects" (ibid.), and Africa with a wide
variety of languages and dialects. The question of
the choice of the language of instruction is a
particularly knotty issue because of political,
social and, sometimes, religious connotations and
undercurrents.

     The choice of the language to be used must be
related to the student's ease in using the language
in terms of both knowledge of it and familiarity
with the information and concepts it expresses. The

use of a local, native language certainly enables the student to begin literacy instruction immediately without the complication of learning another language. In addition, the native language relates to and often expresses the native, familiar culture, while the national language may relate to a culture that is unfamiliar, removed from the adult student. This unfamiliar culture, however, is often part of the content and structure of the text--part of the prior knowledge the student is expected to have in order to read the text. The discrepancy between the prior knowledge held by the adult and the prior knowledge assumed by a text written in a national or official language can be a source of difficulty for many students. Obah (534) identifies this as a "culture-concept gap" (p. 131) that can occur at any level of literacy. For this reason, according to Richmond, (538) "the development of materials in the native language is therefore mandatory" (p. 41) and such materials "must be produced within the parameters of the culture to which the materials are directed" (p. 41). Ease of use has certainly produced strong support for the use of a local, native language for instruction and for the development of materials (523, 532, 538), although the number of local languages that can be included is often subject to practical contraints (524).

A persuasive argument for the use of both local and official languages was offered by the participants in a regional conference held under the auspices of UNESCO (536). They concluded that while it is essential to recognize local needs there may be situations in which the national context must prevail and the national, official language should be used rather than the local language. They suggested using the indigenous language to enable people to "become aware of their own roots, their values and world view" (pp. 19-20) and the state language "for enabling people to participate in modern life, to draw the benefits of development, and to play their role in the nation" (p. 20). For example, a national literacy campaign in Indonesia stressed the use of Latin characters and Arabic numerals to teach the national Indonesian language in order "to develop a sense of national union and national unity" (573, p. 213).

In planning instruction and programs, it is also important to examine the cultural constraints or barriers that have an impact on literacy. Deckert (529), in discussing Iran, suggests seven constraints. They are not, however, necessarily limited to Iran and can provide guidance in identifying potential cultural barriers to the attainment of literacy. The barriers include: time-consuming routines such as endless bargaining and afternoon breaks which leave the adult with little free time for literacy instruction; "family solidarity which may inhibit the pursuit of individual reading" (p. 745); intergroup rivalry which leads to suppression of information in newspapers and books; authoritarian control which inhibits critical reading, writing, and thinking; an emphasis on rote memorization which limits the number of books read; the confined role of women which emphasizes traditional activities generally not including literacy; and a Quranic world view which "may ultimately engender an outlook that stands in sharp tension with open inquiry into the view of other books" (p. 748). Obviously, not all of these constraints apply to all countries. However, Deckert's point that we must examine the cultural features that explain reading behavior and attitude is well taken.

Instructional alternatives. Although the literature on literacy around the world deals with the questions of how to deliver services in some detail and provides guidance in developing curriculum, it fails to provide many specific suggestions for instruction. However, many of the same issues appear here as appear in the literature on literacy in other populations. We see the same concern with the need to emphasize meaning, to put literacy into a meaningful context, to develop active, independent learners, and to provide opportunities for the application of literacy. Consider these suggestions:

1. Integrate literacy and content, providing specific information about a topic (522). This insures motivation and interest as well as the opportunity to use and apply literacy. It also reflects a consideration of illiteracy as a problem in a context (520).

2. Teach phonics and syllabication through language
    experience, using the student's own words and
    experiences (563).

3. Relate vocabulary to the experience of the adult
    and teach it as part of a larger concept (538).
    Vocabulary should not be taught or learned in
    isolation, using lists of words.

4. Utilize group discussion as a way of involving
    students and developing information and
    concepts. This approach was formulated in depth
    by Freire (532) and applied, as we will see, in
    programs in a number of countries.

5. Provide instruction for the student that will
    "help him to get skills and knowledge he wants--
    and let him go" (580, p. 6). The aim is
    independence for the student. This implies that
    the student must become involved in developing
    instructional goals, materials, and self-
    evaluation strategies.

6. Provide for post-literacy experiences in which
    adults can use their literacy skills and receive
    additional instruction if needed and desired
    (522, 524, 533, 583, 584).

   Materials. The questions of the kinds of
literacy materials to be used and who should develop
them are as pressing here as they are in any
discussion of literacy instruction. In fact, the
problem is compounded in many areas because of the
dearth of readily available commercial materials.
Because literacy in various countries has been
linked to particular political points of view and
because of the frequently expressed emphasis on
literacy for empowerment, Bogaert's (535) reference
to the well-known quote from McLuhan and Fiore, "The
Medium is the Message" (p. 3), is timely. Bogaert
reminds us that "literacy materials contain a
message presented through a medium" (p. 2). He
suggests that we need to be concerned both with what
the materials say, linking it to the purpose for
acquiring and using literacy, and with "the methods
and the language through which the message can be
most adequately expressed" (p. 14). Again, the
question of whether to use a native language or the

official language assumes importance and has
numerous implications regarding content.

We need a variety of materials that will
motivate various groups of adults at various stages
in the literacy process (541) to begin and complete
programs (536), to insure success along the way
(551), and to develop themselves as self-motivated
readers (539, 542). In looking at the problem of
materials development over a continuum of
experiences, the suggestion to use both native and
national languages (536) is an appealing one. This
strategy provides a way to begin the process of
literacy acquisition and to reinforce and utilize
the knowledge, culture, and experiences of the
adult. In addition, this strategy can extend the
world of the adult through the introduction of the
written materials of a different language and
culture. Such an approach has an additional
advantage of affording the variations in form and
content that Wendell (542) suggests are critical to
the four stages of literature ranging from familiar
content and free text to unknown content and
translated, formal text. Finally, materials need to
be developed that will reflect the current and
future needs, concerns, and problems of the
potential readers (533), thus linking literacy to a
context. Again, the use of both native and national
languages can help accomplish this aim.

The practical question of who should develop
materials is of major concern here. In addition to
the use of materials from the student's own
environment, consider the following alternatives:

1. Students can create their own instructional
    materials through the use of language experience
    stories (537, 563, 581). This "encourages the
    development of indigenous materials by the
    students themselves" (585, p. 106). In
    addition, the newly literate can create
    materials to insure that the skills acquired are
    reinforced and used (537). These materials can
    also be used to instruct others.

2. Other adults can develop materials that include
    a recognition of the impact of national policy,
    learners' needs, individualization of materials

and teaching, and choice of language (539). These can take a variety of forms. For beginning materials, for example, local citizens can be provided training in the art of writing down their thoughts and experiences and in creating appropriate materials in native languages (542). Folk songs and tales might also form the basis of the materials (535).

3. Teachers and students can develop materials cooperatively (535), providing a way for students to participate in the process of acquiring and using literacy and insuring relevance of both the "medium and the message."

In evaluating materials (535) look at the view of the adult that is implied or stated in the text. Consider also such questions as whether the learner is participating in the learning process, what the purpose of the material is, how the material is intended to be used in instruction, and how instruction is to be provided. These questions provide insights into the suitability of the materials and their function in the total instructional process.

Finally, we must also plan for ways of insuring wide distribution of available materials (541), particularly in hard to reach areas. Strategies might include the use of minilibraries, the establishment of village "learning groups", and the rotation of books between schools (549).

Instructors. Because of the difficulties of delivering services to widespread and often remote areas and because of the disproportionate size of the population needing instruction compared to the size of the population trained to provide it, it is not feasible in many countries to plan on a staff composed solely of professionals (522). As a result, volunteers are widely used. The phrase "each one teach one" is based on two premises: if you can read you can teach others, and the educated have an obligation to teach the uneducated. Programs in Cuba (576) and Nicaragua (545) were based on extensive use of volunteers. In Indonesia, because of local circumstances, the phrase became "each one teach ten" (573). Who are the volunteers?

They might be production workers who are trained to
teach   (522, 590), members of the community (533),
people chosen by their peers (548), or even middle-
and primary-school students (533, 590).

The practical emphasis on the use of volunteers
does not mean that professionals are not included in
planning and providing instruction and programs.
They are. The participation of professional
teachers was deemed "essential" in Nicaragua (545,
p. 704), and many programs encourage the
participation of professionals at some point in the
process.

There is a growing recognition of the need for
training for administrators (552) and instructors in
working with adults (530, 554, 587), in
understanding and fostering the learning process,
and in acquiring and transmitting competency in
content or subject matter (533). In addition to
training, instructors need "a willingness to work in
difficult and unpredictable circumstances" (533, p.
176).

Curriculum and Program Alternatives

A major issue that has been addressed in
curriculum and program development around the world
is whether the program will identify and reach a
selected population or whether it will utilize a
mass approach designed to reach all adults in need
of literacy training and development (533). The
decision to initiate and implement a mass campaign
involves further questions regarding what agencies
should be involved on the national level and what
the role of the local agencies should be.

In selective literacy programs specific groups
are targeted, such as women or farmers, because of
their needs, sometimes because of their ages, and
often because of the priorities of the sponsoring
agencies. These selective programs are frequently
but not always developed by private, voluntary
agencies. On a large scale the Experimental World
Literacy Program (525, 569, 586), under the auspices
of UNESCO, eventually worked with 55 countries
stressing the development of selective literacy
programs. Specific literacy needs, requirements,

and abilities were identified in order to plan
instruction, curriculum, materials, and programs for
specific groups within a particular context (544,
586). According to Noor (533) selective campaigns
are in general effective but expensive--"much too
expensive for mass implementation" (p. 168).

The mass literacy campaign has often been
identified with revolutionary political situations
(521, 546) and with situations in which there is a
strong national commitment to developing literacy
(524, 533), as in Great Britain (581), or where
there is an authoritarian government, as in China
(524, 533). Because of its scope, a mass literacy
campaign requires "intensive use of available
economic resources (533, p. 168). Noor (533), in
1982, asserted that "the commitment to forge ahead
with mass literacy campaigns is growing among the
leaders of the developing world" (p. 166). In 1983,
the participants in an international conference
(521) "agreed that the time is now ripe in many
countries for sustained national programmes, if
possible on a mass scale. If we are to make a major
impact on the promotion of universal literacy by the
end of this century, nothing less should be
considered" (p. 19).

The mass campaign and the selective literacy
approach are not necessarily mutually exclusive. A
mass campaign can be phased in by establishing
priority groups and piloting and testing
alternatives (533). Possibilities include targeting
specific groups within a national campaign or
following up a national campaign by targeting
selected groups. In China (521), Pakistan (566) and
Ethiopia (530, 568), for example, women have
frequently been selected for special consideration.

A mass campaign can mean not only reaching all
those who lack appropriate literacy skills but also
involving all those who can contribute. This might
include utilizing the resources of a number of
national government agencies. In Indonesia (573)
one agency, the National Planning Board, coordinated
the literacy program with other development
programs. In a program for farmers in India (557),
three national government agencies, concerned with
education, agriculture, and communication, combined

their efforts. Mass campaigns can also involve
other agencies. Valdehusa (541) in defining a mass
campaign suggests that there is a need "to involve
all sectors--academic, business, government, civic,
and professional--within the framework of a grand
strategy" (p. 634). A mass literacy campaign in the
United Kingdom, for example, included both a
government agency and the British Broadcasting
Corporation (562, 567, 581). These liaisons remind
us of the trend toward partnerships in Adult Basic
Literacy programs in the United States.

Within mass campaigns there is ample room and,
in fact, need for local input. In view of the
relationship between literacy and its context, local
input seems critical in the development of
curriculum and programs within a national framework
(579). Local authorities may identify and meet
local needs within the guidelines established by
central policy making and planning (533, 573, 590).
Local literacy programs, for example, were developed
for each of six language groups in Northern Ghana
all within a national setting (550). Thomas (585)
suggests that because there is no one method for
providing literacy instruction, instructional
methodology can best be decided on the local level.

In the development of curriculum and programs
to deliver services, we see the same threads running
through program descriptions that have been apparent
in the literacy programs for the other populations
we have considered. Four examples will be
considered: the first illustrates the evolution of a
program in one country, the second illustrates the
adaptation of the ideas of one man in various
countries, the third illustrates the now-familiar
links between literacy and content, and the fourth
illustrates a recurrent emphasis in the literature
on post-literacy development.

First, Ouane (575) describes the evolution of
literacy instruction in Mali, an agricultural
country in East Africa with a high rate of
illiteracy. Early efforts at reducing this rate
included instruction conducted in an official
language unfamiliar to the adults and using
inappropriate content and methods based on
children's education. As a result of the failures

of this program another one was begun under the
auspices of the Experimental World Literacy
Programme, using four languages, linking literacy to
work, and emphasizing post-literacy experiences
designed to develop and enhance the adult's ability
to "take decisions in a continuous process of
improvement and greater control of the environment"
(p. 244). The use of rural newspapers and the radio
was highlighted as a way of extending literacy,
"enriching" (p. 253) knowledge, and creating "a
literate environment" (ibid.). There was a
recognition of the need to involve both local and
national agencies if the emphasis on raising
literacy levels and developing post-literacy
experiences was to continue.

Second, the possibilities for the spread and
adaptation of literacy efforts internationally are
illustrated by the network of programs influenced by
Paulo Freire (569). He has written extensively (15,
16, 136, 561) and has had a significant effect on
the development of instruction, curriculum, and
programs in many parts of the world. According to
Freire instruction must involve the learner in an
active role in the learning process. Reading is
more than decoding; it is meaning. It relates to
and extends beyond experience and develops in a
particular context. The purpose of literacy is to
enable critical thinking, problem-solving, and
political action, thus empowering the individual.
Freire's ideas have often been associated with mass
literacy campaigns in countries where empowerment
and political action have been identified as
positive goals, such as Cuba (554, 565, 569, 572,
576), Honduras (548), and Nicaragua (545, 555, 560,
563, 573).

The curriculum developed in Nicaragua
illustrates Freire's use of generative themes as the
basis for literacy development. First, photographs
are used to encourage group discussion of a topic
significant to the group. Then a text is read,
words are decoded, and new words are developed based
on the phonemes taught. Instruction is provided by
volunteers in convenient locations such as the
adults' homes, fields, and factories. In the
beginning, teachers from other countries were
involved in providing short, intensive training

periods for the volunteers and developed text books
in which "lessons were based on recent Nicaraguan
history and the incidents of the Nicaraguan
Revolution" (560, p. 124).

In Honduras "the activities center on the
literacy circles. Groups of campesinos meet daily,
after work, to discuss their problems and search for
solutions; at the same time they learn to read and
write" (548, p. 72) using the strategies developed
by Freire. Local conditions and problems are
incorporated into the program through the use of
problem cards, tape recorders, and instant photos.

A program (589) was developed in a remote
tribal village in India that combined the goals of
enabling adults to acquire functional literacy
skills, improve health, and gain control over their
lives and destinies. Local leaders ran the program,
but Freire's influence on the instructional methods
and the content of materials that were developed to
address local issues is evident and acknowledged.

In Mexico (571), a literacy training program is
provided in both native languages and in Spanish,
and is based on the concepts of Freire. Small local
groups use relevant words and concepts to form the
basis for the instruction. In addition, this
program employs current technology. Television is
used in conjunction with a workbook for both
instruction and practice, and a toll-free telephone
number is available in the event that assistance is
required. The program tailors instruction and
curriculum to meet the needs of a particular
audience. For example, Indian women receive
training in literacy as well as in health and
primary education.

Elements of Freire's concepts have been
included in these various programs but have been
changed and adapted to meet local needs and to
utilize the resources available. Such
incorporations and/or adaptations need not be
limited however to developing and revolutionary
countries. Dalglish (559), for example, suggests
that if programs in the prison system in Great
Britain are to succeed they must incorporate
Freire's ideas.

Third, the link between literacy and content that is a feature of many programs in the United States ranging from adult basic literacy to work-related and college programs is also evident in international programs, although most of them emphasize basic levels of literacy. Literacy may be linked to whatever content is needed by the participants (569), such as work skills in Indonesia (573) and Tanzania (521), agriculture in India (557), or health in Honduras (548), Mexico (571), and India (589). A mass campaign in Ethiopia (568) was designed to "teach participants reading, writing and numeracy and to help them to relate what they are learning to the everyday concerns of health, agriculture, family living and political consciousness, and to revive the diversified cultures of the nationalities" (p. 194).

Finally, we find in many programs an emphasis on the need for post-literacy experiences that reinforce and apply literacy, an emphasis that echoes Harman's (22) third stage of literacy, that of literacy application. We have already seen the need for literacy application with other populations. Lazarus (531) states emphatically that "if complementary post-literacy planning is not part of the initial literacy strategy, then the retention of literacy is at stake" (p. 68). Her emphasis is on creating a "literate environment" that includes "content and structure being geared to local/national conditions" (p. 69). A literate environment can take the form of insuring that appropriate reading materials are available and that there are opportunities to use skills to become "agents of change" (p. 68). In discussing post-literacy in Mali, Ouane (575), who also advocates a "literate environment", states that "post-literacy instruction enables the adults to practise the capacities they have acquired in the literacy phase and to increase their knowledge, learning at the same time to take decisions in a continuous process of improvement and greater control of the environment. It is a motivation phase that prepares them for lifelong education" (p. 244). The efforts of various countries to create a literate environment are reminiscent of the efforts of Rigg and Kazamek (411) to create a "literate environment" in a Job Corps situation.

Consider what some countries have done to provide post-literacy experiences. In Mali (575) appropriate and useful reading materials have been produced that are written equivalents of the traditional oral literature. The mass media has been involved in motivating adults to continue the process of education. In Tanzania (521) a variety of services have been provided including courses, rural libraries, newspapers, radio program, and movies, all designed to encourage the use of literacy skills. The application of skills has been related to work, politics, and the development of the community through programs in history, politics, and leadership abilities, using Swahili as well as English. In Great Britain (583, 584) post-literacy activities began with the production of suitable reading materials for low-levels readers and then added periodicals and textbooks at various reading levels. Traveling libraries encourage the use of the materials. Adult education centers and the media have contributed to the development of special interest programs. The involvement of the adults themselves in developing materials is seen as a way of encouraging post-literacy activities (537, 584). The national program in Morocco (564) won the IRA Literacy Award for 1985. One of the reasons the program was cited for excellence was its inclusion of a follow-up stage to insure retention of skills.

The problems associated with recruitment, retention, and achievement are, unfortunately, present here as in other literacy programs. "In many cases, only a few of those who enroll will actually complete the entire sequence of classes" (569, p. 1). Again, we see Cross's (30, 48) barriers to learning at work.

Developing programs that provide instruction and content appropriate to the particular adult is one important way of overcoming the dispositional barriers associated with discouragement due to slow, uneven progress and with questions having to do with the usefulness of the task. These barriers reinforce the need not only to relate literacy to content and context but also to involve the adult in the process and to provide for post-literacy activities and opportunities. The active participation of adults in planning and implementing

programs can have a positive effect on recruitment
and retention by motivating them (588) and allowing
them to explore possibilities for acquiring and
using literacy (574). "A literacy programme must
become the programme of the people themselves" (573,
p, 219). Ownership of the program through
involvement is as important in Indonesia (ibid.) as
it is in the United States.

Location is critical in meeting the situational
barrier of transportation to the program and the
dispositional barrier of negative or uncertain
attitudes toward school and studying. Programs have
frequently been located in formal education settings
with school-like programs. Noor (533), in
discussing developing countries, found there was a
need for separate facilities because of the
reluctance of adults to attend classes in schools
meant for children. Lazarus (531) cites the high
dropout rate in these formal education programs in
both developing and developed countries.

There is a trend both abroad and in the United
States toward moving out into the community to
provide classes where they are needed and where it
is convenient for the adult. In Ethiopia (568), for
example, "the planners of the campaign suggested
that 'every site is a learning place' and specified
the following places: schools, urban dweller's
association centres, factory workshops, business
places, military camps, prisons, private homes,
offices, churchyards, mosque courtyards, youth
centres, state farms, assembly halls, verandas, or
simply under the shade of trees" (p. 195). This
list probably covers most locations and certainly
gives a flavor to the phrase "moving out into the
community." The need to move out into the community
to provide services is echoed in a wide variety of
programs in all parts of the world from Cuba (554)
and China (590) to Scotland (580) and Canada (585).

A fairly recent trend in providing services
that may help in addressing Cross's barriers has
been the use of the mass media. Mass media has been
used for recruitment, for example, in India (573)
and Great Britain (562, 567, 581) as well as for
instruction in Mexico (571) where the instruction is
supplemented with a workbook and in Pakistan (591)

where the program is often aired in community
viewing centers. In Jamaica (524) taped lessons,
suitable for audio cassettes, have been developed in
addition to instruction developed for radio and
television. The use of radio and television
programming can motivate adults and address issues
of concern to them, with adult-oriented rather than
child-oriented content and with a format free from
the possible negative connotations of traditional
school.

Can literacy programs improve literacy rates?
According to Rivera (577), "until recently ...
literacy was primarily a sphere of action rather
than analysis" (p. 24) with only a cursory emphasis
on program evaluation. Certainly programs cite
statistics to prove that they are effective (521),
but they may cite formative and not summative data
(573). Questions of program evaluation are
complicated in many countries because of the
difficulties of "keeping and collecting data" (568,
p. 198). Such difficulties suggest that we must be
uncertain about overall results. Noor (533)
expresses the common concern that we do not know
whether mass campaigns have succeeded in producing
literate adults who have applied and used skills, or
have even retained skills. There is a need for
extensive research into formulating workable methods
for program evaluation in developing as well as
developed countries and for involving universities,
professional associations, and government in this
enterprise (577).

There is a widespread and growing conviction
that if literacy programs are to be successful there
is a need for a total national commitment (9, 521,
524, 525, 543, 551, 553) or possibly "a total
mobilization" (546, p. 7). Bogaert (535) suggests
that when "active promotion ends" (p. 1) progress
made in literacy programs slows and "interest wanes"
(ibid.). To overcome this, a program must be part
of a total effort that requires:

a sustained, substantial effort (566)
cooperation among agencies (531, 551, 553, 574,
588, 591)
cooperation between national and local levels of
government and communities (548)

involvement of private agencies including, for
example, social service agencies, universities,
churches (531, 574, 585)

In fact, such an effort must transcend the
national level to include international cooperation
and "the recognition of common interests in literacy
which extend beyond ideological or political
differences" (521, p. 35). M'Bow (523) asserts
that:

> The struggle against illiteracy must be waged on
> a worldwide scale. After so many years of
> hesitation and often isolated efforts, it calls
> for a wide-ranging campaign. And only an
> energetic movement of solidarity throughout the
> world will make possible effective support for
> the efforts of the countries concerned. (p. 399)

These efforts can take a variety of forms.
Malmquist (525) suggests that cross-national studies
be done of different methods of reading instruction.
There might be an exchange of consultants or a
sharing of ideas and information at conferences and
meetings (521). In very practical terms, "it is in
the recruitment and training of personnel, and in
the production of reading materials where there is
probably the most scope for a transfer of techniques
and ideas between one country and another" (ibid.,
p. 29).

It must be recognized that national literacy
programs and international cooperative efforts cost
money--money that may be difficult to raise and that
may represent a substantial portion of a national
budget placing a constraint on programs (521). In
the decision-making process, according to Rivera
(577), most programs now look at short-term economic
costs and benefits. Instead we should be looking at
the long-run educational benefits and their
"payoffs" (p. 25). Adult basic education studies,
according to Rivera, "indicate significant economic
gains for participants over their lifetimes and,
therefore, for society, despite what appear to be
major initial economic expenditures" (ibid.).

Summary

Scribner's (38) goal of an ideal literacy encompassing the three major purposes is alive and well in many parts of the world. Her commitment to the use of a "diversity of educational approaches" (p. 18) can also be seen in these countries where programs have been and are being transformed to meet changing needs. The emphasis traditionally has been on identifying and meeting practical needs and urgencies, but there is also an emerging recognition of the need to develop programs that will identify and meet a wider spectrum of needs and that are based on the research and theory related to instruction in general and to reading instruction in particular. Even under difficult circumstances that may strain national resources countries have made major commitments toward the planning and carrying out of literacy services. It may be that we can learn from each other.

A Final View

At this point, after examining these various groups of adults, certain common threads and conclusions become clear. No matter what the need or how the adult might be categorized we recognize that we need to:

consider the three major purposes of survival, empowerment, and human development when designing and developing programs.

view literacy as a relative concept in which literacy needs and purposes are determined according to each adult's situation.

provide varieties of programs for adults at different levels and stages both in terms of literacy needs and purposes as well as the demands of their particular situations.

include options and alternatives within programs to enable each adult to achieve his current primary purpose for literacy and also to begin to achieve other purposes.

Although there are unanswered questions in
the fields of adult learning and reading theory,
we have sufficient knowledge to formulate suitable
programs for adults. We need to:

> treat the adult as an adult, overcoming the
> barriers to learning that the adult may
> experience and confirming the relationship
> between teacher and student as that of adult
> to adult. This suggests that we need to
> rethink how we deliver services to adults.
> For example, programs need to be in locations
> that are convenient for the learners, not
> necessarily the teachers. The time frame in
> which they are offered should be flexible.
> Teachers, both professional and volunteer,
> may require training in adult learning theory
> in order to plan and implement programs in
> adult literacy. The elementary school model
> of instruction is not appropriate for adults.

> involve the adult in the decision making
> process. This suggests that adults
> participate in determining what they need to
> learn as well as how and when they will learn
> it, choosing materials to be used, and
> identifying situations in which the literacy
> may be useful.

> stress reading as meaning, not reading as
> decoding. Decoding, thus, becomes a means
> not an end in the process of acquiring
> strategies for reading and writing. This
> suggests that reading materials must be
> meaningful and important to the reader as
> well as of sufficient variety to enable
> transfer and application of skills and
> strategies. It also suggests that the skills
> and strategies learned are useful in
> meaningful situations, regardless of the
> purpose for literacy. The goal of literacy
> instruction must be to enable adults to
> become independent, understanding and
> monitoring the process of reading,
> comprehending text, and applying strategies
> to new situations.

The waste of human potential of even one adult who, because of literacy difficulties, fails to fulfill his own and society's expectations, is so great that we cannot continue as a society or as individuals to let that adult flounder, regardless of his literacy level. The waste is compounded manyfold by the numbers of adults encountering some difficulty or shortfall. We, as a society, have learned to do many things and, in fact, have performed incredible feats. We can certainly provide adults with opportunities to acquire the literacy abilities they need and want whether these abilities are used for survival, empowerment, human development or some combination of the three. The cost may be substantial; we know that the need is substantial.

ADULT LITERACY: A BIBLIOGRAPHY

An Overview: Literacy and Illiteracy

Historical Perspectives

1. Clifford, Geraldine Joncich. "Buch and Lesen: Historical Perspectives on Literacy and Schooling." REVIEW OF EDUCATIONAL RESEARCH 54 (Winter 1984): 472-500.

   Clifford examines three aspects of literacy: definitions, purposes, and populations. Literacy has been defined and viewed in terms of achievement, function and, more recently, thinking. The implications for instructional materials and strategies of the changing definitions are explored in a historical context. The uses and values of literacy in social, cultural, political, and economic contexts are examined in terms of a movement toward universal literacy.

2. Cook, Wanda Dauksza. ADULT LITERACY EDUCATION IN THE UNITED STATES. Newark, Delaware: International Reading Assn., 1977.

   Cook traces the history of adult literacy education in the United States from 1900 to the mid 1970s with a view toward learning from the past in order to provide more effective instruction and services now and in the future. She examines definitions of literacy and illiteracy as well as past and present programs and approaches. The concept of literacy includes grade level achievement, but it is more than that. It also involves life related tasks, such as those included in the Adult Performance Level Study. The way to

achieve literacy can take a variety of forms.
In any program, a diagnostic-prescriptive
approach is suggested, teacher training is
essential, and provision must be made for the
attitude and motivation of the student.

3. Graff, Harvey J., ed.   LITERACY AND SOCIAL
    DEVELOPMENT IN THE WEST: A READER. New
    York: Cambridge University Press, 1981.

    This collection of essays examines the
    relationship of literacy to social, economic,
    cultural, and political factors at various
    points in history and in various countries and
    cultures.   Literacy, contrary to popular
    belief, has not always empowered and enabled
    the individual nor has its advancement always
    been encouraged by such factors.   The
    relationship is a complex one raising
    questions about our current approaches to
    literacy education and our efforts to extend
    it.

4. Kaestle, Carl F. "The History of Literacy and
    the History of Readers." REVIEW OF RESEARCH
    IN EDUCATION, VOL. 12. Edited by Edmund W.
    Gordon.   Washington, D.C.: American
    Educational Research Assn., 1985, pp. 11-53.

    Kaestle examines chronologically the history
    of literacy and related issues from 1600 to
    the present time in Europe and in the United
    States. Definitions of literacy and illiteracy
    are explored, as are uses and theories of
    literacy.   The article provides a broad
    background and overview of the topic as well
    as an extensive bibliography.

5. Resnick, Daniel P., ed.   LITERACY IN
    HISTORICAL PERSPECTIVE. Washington, D.C.,
    1983. 170pp. (ED 237 942)

    This collection of papers presented at the
    Literacy in Historical Perspective Conference,
    Washington, D.C., July, 1980, includes
    descriptions and analyses of historical
    changes in the definitions and contexts of
    literacy.   The topics cover a range of

historical periods and a variety of countries.

6. _____, and Lauren B. Resnick. "The
   Nature   of   Literacy: An   Historical
   Exploration." HARVARD EDUCATIONAL REVIEW 47
   (August 1977): 370-385.

   Resnick and Resnick trace the historical
   changes that have occurred in our definitions
   of literacy, in the resulting requirements and
   standards for it, and in methods of acquiring
   it. The authors document that there has been
   an   increase   in   both   expectation   and
   performance, with the United States currently
   having the highest and most widely applied
   requirements in history. In order to enable
   all our population to meet these standards,
   the authors suggest that new forms of pedagogy
   that focus on comprehension rather than on
   "back to basics" will need to be developed and
   applied.

Definitions and Purposes

7. Ahmann, Stanley. "The Exploration of Survival
   Levels of Achievement by Means of Assessment
   Techniques." READING AND CAREER EDUCATION.
   Edited by Duane M. Nielsen and Howard F.
   Hjelm.   Newark, Delaware: International
   Reading Assn., 1975, pp. 39-42.

   Ahmann   provides   three   definitions   of
   functional literacy: one from the Right to
   Read Advisory Council, a second from UNESCO,
   and a third from the National Assessment of
   Educational   Progress.   The   first   two
   definitions emphasize "essential knowledge and
   skills" (p. 39). The last is the broadest,
   including as well as basic skills such skills
   as: manual-perceptual,   decision-making,
   interpersonal, and employment-seeking.   The
   author examines issues related to assessing
   these   skills   and developing an index of
   functional literacy in view of the "lack of a
   well-accepted   definition   of   functional
   literacy" (p. 42).

8. Aronowitz, Stanley.   "Toward   Redefining

Literacy." SOCIAL POLICY 12 (October 1981):
53-55.

Aronowitz examines the "back to basics"
movement in terms of its historical context
and its effects. He concludes that it is on
"very shaky ground" (p. 54). Literacy in the
United States is not declining; rather, the
literacy demands of the workplace are
increasing. The back to basics approach does
not meet current literacy demands which
require critical thinking as well as basic
reading skills. Functional literacy is not
the answer. Literacy must be linked to the
development of critical thinking to reach that
population that has been "historically
excluded from the benefits of <u>critical
literacy</u>" (p. 55).

9.   Bhola, Harbans S. "Why Literacy Can't Wait:
     Issues for the 1980s." CONVERGENCE 14
     (1981): 6-23.

     Bhola asserts that nonformal education has
become an accepted means of delivering
education services to adults, but that
literacy education has not been linked closely
with nonformal education. There is a
prevailing notion that adults can gain
information and skills without being literate.
Once adults begin to gain this information and
develop skills, they recognize the need for
literacy and become motivated to achieve it.
The author examines the effects of literacy on
the individual, the family, the community, and
society, and concludes that "when not
deliberately abused literacy is positive and
potent. Literacy cannot wait" (p. 16). After
examining other alternatives, he proposes mass
literacy campaigns in order to provide people,
particularly in the Third World, with an
opportunity to participate in the life of
their country.

10. Bormuth, John R. "Reading Literacy: Its
     Definition and Assessment." READING
     RESEARCH QUARTERLY IX (1973-1974): 7-66.
     (Also published in TOWARD A LITERATE

SOCIETY.   Edited by John B. Carrol and
Jeanne S. Chall.   New York: McGraw-Hill,
1975.)

Rather than limiting the discussion to other
people's definitions of literacy and means of
measuring it, Bormuth provides guidelines,
parameters, and limitations to consider in
developing definitions of literacy and
appropriate measurement techniques.   He
examines various models of literacy and ways
of   measuring   literacy   performance   and
concludes that we need a model that "permits
us to jointly identify a criterion of literacy
and readability" (p. 65).

11. Cervero, Ronald M. "Is a Common Definition of
     Adult Literacy Possible?" ADULT EDUCATION
     QUARTERLY 36 (Fall 1985): 50-54.

In   examining   current   definitions   of
literacy, Cervero traces a change in
perspective from an absolute to a relative
view.   In the former, the definition is based
on grade level achievement; in the latter, the
definition   centers   on   the   needs   of   a
particular individual or group in a particular
context.   Both   points   of view prevail, the
former in the definition used by the U.S.
Census,   the   latter   in   definitions   of
functional literacy and literacy of the Adult
Performance Level competencies. Literacy as
defined in the Adult Education Act encompasses
both views.   In the reauthorization of the Act
"funding   guidelines   defined   the   target
population not only as those with less than a
high school diploma, but also those who lacked
the   skills   to   function   productively   in
American society" (p. 51).

Cervero links definitions to values. Since
one   value   system   does   not   exist   in   our
pluralistic   society,   one   operational
definition of literacy is not possible.   He
cites   studies   showing   that   "once   a
relativistic approach to defining literacy is
accepted, a common operational definition is
not attainable" (p. 52).   He concludes that "a

common definition of literacy would limit the
range of choices available to adult learners"
(p. 54).

12. Chall, Jeanne S. "New Views on Developing
    Basic Skills with Adults." Paper presented
    at the National Adult Literacy Conference,
    January 19-20, 1984, Washington, D.C. 31pp.
    (ED 240 299)

    Chall sees a change both in adult students
    and in the reading demands that are made on
    them. Such changes demand a broad range of
    programs--from adult basic literacy to
    functional literacy to courses that aim for
    reading proficiency in highly technical areas.
    She discusses five reading stages in some
    depth, provides text to illustrate them, and
    asserts that the stages of development are the
    same for adults as for children although
    "there is a need for a somewhat different
    emphasis depending upon maturity, and
    different text content" (p. 10). She cites
    the need both for further research and for
    increasingly higher levels of literacy to meet
    the demands of the workplace.

13. Crane, John M. "Adult Literacy--a Continuing
    Need." ADULT EDUCATION (London) 56
    (September 1983): 147-152.

    Crane examines definitions and dimensions of
    adult literacy in both Britain and in North
    America. He points out that while there is
    substantial agreement that illiteracy can be
    defined only in context, a quantitative
    definition is usually provided. Although we
    may recognize the importance of context,
    definitions do not commonly identify a
    particular context but instead identify age or
    grade level. It is not that the individual
    cannot read effectively in a particular
    situation, but that he can't read on a certain
    grade or age level. Crane examines reasons
    for illiteracy in Britain and proposes that
    illiterates are "the untaught, the ill-taught
    and, sadly, the unteachable" (p. 149). Why is
    literacy important? There are a variety of

reasons that have been stressed by different
writers at different times: individuals need
to be literate to function in their social
setting; society needs skilled workers;
"democracy needs a literate, informed
electorate" (p. 150); workers need
opportunities to grasp power. In a broad
sense, literacy is required in order to read
and study the past as a way of anticipating
and understanding the future.

14. Fitzgerald, Gisela G. "Functional Literacy:
     Right or Obligation?" JOURNAL OF READING 28
     (December 1984): 196-199.

     Fitzgerald examines the issue of whether it
     is an adult's right or his/her obligation to
     learn to read. She accepts the definition of
     functional literacy used by the U.S.
     Department of Education and others as the
     "ability of an individual to use reading
     skills in everyday life situations--reading
     street signs, reading and comprehending
     written directions, labels, applications, and
     work-oriented information" (p. 196). She
     points out the "staggering" (p. 198) financial
     obligations to society caused by individuals
     who cannot read at this level. She also
     points out that education for school children
     is compulsory; we do not have a right to
     accept or reject it. "Society as well as the
     illiterate adult must recognize that
     voluntarism in basic adult education has
     contributed to putting the United States at
     risk" (p. 199). The author concludes that the
     adult illiterate does not have the right to
     remain illiterate.

15. Freire, Paulo. "The Adult Literacy Process as
     Cultural Action for Freedom." HARVARD
     EDUCATIONAL REVIEW 40 (May 1970): 205-225.

     Freire advocates an active view of literacy
     in which the acquisition of literacy enables
     the individual to examine himself and the
     society in which he lives and take appropriate
     action. Within this context Freire examines
     the implications of many of the current

methods and philosophies of teaching adults
literacy skills. Rather than a one way
process in which the teacher chooses what to
teach and provides all instruction, Freire
advocates a dialogue between teacher and
student with the student "reflecting
critically on the process of reading and
writing itself, and on the profound
significance of language" (p. 212). Students
write their own texts, using their own words
and concepts, and in the course of this
process become empowered.

16. _____. EDUCATION FOR CRITICAL
    CONSCIOUSNESS. New York: Seabury Press,
    1973.

    In the first of the two essays Freire
outlines his political and social views and
relates them to the Brazilian experience. He
stresses the need "to create an educational
process encouraging critical attitudes" (p.
33). The student must be an active, inquiring
participant in the process. He describes a
literacy program designed to develop this kind
of student. Examples of "situations"
discussed by the students give a flavor of the
program. In the second essay Freire examines
the concept of communication and details the
need for dialogue between teacher and student
as equals.

17. Greene, Maxime. "Literacy for What?" PHI
    DELTA KAPPAN 63 (January 1982): 326-329.

    Greene views literacy as "an opening, a
becoming, never a fixed end" (p. 326). She
links literacy to empowerment of the
individual, to critical reflectiveness, to
conceptual thinking, and to the ability to
examine one's world with "wider and more
diverse perspectives" (p. 329). Literacy
cannot be achieved through emphasizing basic
skills or competencies. Rather she would
emphasize "open doors and open possibilities"
(ibid.), working from the perspective of the
student not the system.

18. Guthrie, John T. "Being Literate."   JOURNAL
     OF READING 22 (February 1979): 450-452.

     Guthrie's definition of literacy goes beyond
     decoding and word meaning, beyond functional
     or survival reading and its attendant skills,
     to literacy that enables and empowers the
     individual to "explore himself or herself, to
     discover other people, to find respite, or to
     be startled" (p. 451).

19. _____. "Functional Reading: One or
     Many."   JOURNAL OF READING 22 (April 1979):
     648-650.

     In this article, Guthrie explores the
     question of what is functional reading and
     concludes, after providing examples, that
     there are many functions for reading related
     to the "beliefs, interests, and cultural
     expectations of a person" (p. 650). A person
     may be literate in one kind of reading and
     illiterate in another. He may read financial
     materials, for example, and not religious
     materials. He may choose not to read at all.
     Guthrie reminds us that functional literacy is
     related to context.

20. _____. "Equilibrium of Literacy."
     JOURNAL OF READING 26 (April 1983): 668-670.

     Guthrie defines literacy as "primarily a
     social exchange" (p. 668) with the reader's
     level of literacy defined by the situation and
     by the expectations of others. Literacy is
     the equilibrium of the demands of the
     situation and the achievement of the
     individual. A traditional view of literacy
     holds that there is one level of literacy for
     everyone. Not so, according to Guthrie. We
     must look at both the competencies of the
     individual and the demands of the situations
     they must meet in determining the number of
     illiterates we have and in planning programs.

21. _____, and Irwin S. Kirsch.   "The
     Emergent Perspective on Literacy."   PHI
     DELTA KAPPAN 65 (January 1984): 351-355.

Guthrie and Kirsch examine the traditional view of literacy. It is a feature of the person that is acquired through education; it is unitary in that literacy takes only one form; it is a binary state in that a person is literate or is not literate. By this definition, illiteracy can be eradicated with proper education and training. Once a literate person, always a literate person. The authors challenge this notion, putting literacy squarely into a social context and asserting that different situations have different literacy demands. A student may meet the demands in high school, but not in college. This difference in demands helps explain the many college programs for teaching reading and study skills. Similarly, the literacy demands of the workplace may be different from those of school. The purposes for reading and the kinds of materials read have an impact on the literacy demands made on the reader. We cannot characterize an individual as literate or not literate. The authors, in the course of the discussion, review a number of current studies on literacy requirements. They conclude that "literacy was learned best when the social context, purpose, and content of the reading in classrooms were similar to those of the environments in which students would ultimately function" (p. 355). The emerging perspective on literacy focuses on social interaction in which reading instruction and materials relate to the demands of the student's environment and his purposes in becoming literate.

22. Harman, David. "Illiteracy: An Overview." HARVARD EDUCATIONAL REVIEW 40 (May 1970): 226-243.

Harman defines three stages of literacy. In the first stage, literacy is conceptualized and recognized as a tool. In the second stage, literacy is attained through the acquisition of reading and writing skills. In the third stage, the skills are applied in a meaningful way by the learner. Harman

examines the extent of illiteracy in the world
and in the United States and concludes that
because of "lack of testing, reliance upon
grade-completion criteria, and inadequate
definitions of functional literacy" (p. 230),
we have underestimated the extent of the
problem. He examines programs and
methodologies here and abroad and finds a lack
of coordination, planning, and evaluation. He
makes a number of suggestions for designing
literacy programs that can be adapted to
specific situations and populations and that
can become the basis for continuing adult
education.

23. Harste, Jerome C., and Larry J. Mikulecky.
     "The Context of Literacy in Our Society."
     BECOMING READERS IN A COMPLEX SOCIETY.
     Eighty-third Yearbook of the National
     Society for the Study of Education. Edited
     by Alan C. Purves and Olive Niles. Chicago:
     The University of Chicago Press, 1984, pp.
     47-78.

     Harste and Mikulecky examine the complex
role of language in the development of thought
and in communication between and among people.
Reading is put squarely into this framework--a
framework that is both psychological and
sociological. In examining the history of
literacy they point out that in 1900 literacy
was for the elite few. Today it is necessary
for functioning in the everyday world. The
authors make some useful distinctions between
school reading and on-the-job reading. The
purpose of school reading is to ascertain
facts and answer questions; the purpose of on-
the-job reading is to accomplish tasks and
solve problems at the same time involving more
social interaction in the reading task.
Technology, rather than eliminating the need
for literacy, has redefined literacy.
Educating for literacy is not a question of
preparation in the basic skills of reading and
writing but of preparation for meeting the
needs of the world in which the person
functions.

24. Heath, Shirley Brice. "The Functions and Uses
     of Literacy." JOURNAL OF COMMUNICATION 30
     (Winter 1980): 123-133.

         Heath   paints   a   fascinating   picture of
     literacy, of "its functions (what literacy can
     do for individuals) and its uses (what
     individuals can do with literacy skills)" (p.
     123). She presents varied definitions of
     literacy, looks at literacy from an historical
     perspective,   and   examines   literacy   in
     different societies. Her description of the
     community uses of reading and the relevance of
     context   based   on   a   study   of   an all-black
     working class community in the Southeastern
     United States is particularly revealing. She
     concludes that reading should not be taught
     exclusively in schools, does not require a
     strict adherence to a skill sequence, should
     incorporate all the life skills of the reader,
     and should include all the varied meanings of
     literacy for various groups and individuals.
     Heath goes beyond a school definition of
     literacy and looks at literacy from a
     community perspective.

25. Hirsch,   E.D.,   Jr.   "Cultural Literacy."
     NATIONAL ADULT LITERACY CONFERENCE. January
     19-20, 1984, Washington, D.C.: National
     Institute of Education, the Far West
     Laboratory and The Network Inc.

         According to Hirsch, literacy requires more
     than   decoding   and   linguistic   skills.   It
     requires a "system of information" (p. 9), a
     set   of   words,   and   relevant background
     information. It is incumbent on the schools
     to   decide   what is required and to teach it.
     Once we define cultural literacy for our
     society and determine the relevant information
     the reader needs, then the level of adult
     literacy will rise because the reader will
     have the prior knowledge needed for higher
     level thinking and reading skills.

26. Hunter, Carman St. John.   "Literacy   for
     Empowerment and Social Change." VISIBLE
     LANGUAGE XVI (Spring 1982): 137-143.

Hunter views literacy as more than a set of technical competencies. "Literacy is closely related to self-reliance and a sense of personal power over conditions that affect one's life" (p. 138). Competency-based education is not the way to help adults achieve this state. Rather, educational programs should consider what the learner wants to learn, why he wants to acquire literacy, and how literacy will enable him to become an agent, to control his life. Hunter concludes that "the transmission of knowledge, skills, and attitudes that result in immediately measurable behavioral changes is too narrow a goal for education" (p. 142).

27. Kazemek, Francis E. EPISTEMOLOGY AND ADULT LITERACY: AN EXPERIENTIALIST, PRAGMATIC PERSPECTIVE. November 1983. 20pp. (ED 236 326)

Kazemek examines literacy from a philosophical perspective, reviewing the thinking of a number of philosophers on notions of universal knowledge and truth as compared to a pragmatic view of knowledge and truth. The author concludes that adult literacy must be viewed within the context of a particular individual in a particular culture and society.

28. _____. ADULT LITERACY EDUCATION: AN ETHICAL ENDEAVOR. 1984. 18pp. (ED 239 043)

Kazemek supports the notion that adult literacy education is, in fact, an ethical endeavor. The author examines the principles of John Dewey, particularly his "faith in the individual for intelligent and responsible action" (p. 6) and relates them to examples that illustrate those principles. Implications from Dewey for adult literacy education include learning about the adults to be taught by living and working with them and developing "community-based programs ... based upon local needs and themes which emerge from individuals in the community" (p. 14). Literacy is viewed as a means to an end enabling individuals to take action in their world.

29. Kirsch, Irwin, and John T. Guthrie. "The Concept and Measurement of Functional Literacy." READING RESEARCH QUARTERLY XIII (1977-1978): 485-507.

Kirsch and Guthrie review various definitions of literacy, functional literacy, and functional competency and explore the issues of skill definition, means of measurement, and estimations of population size raised by the definitions. They offer general suggestions for the development and use of measures that will yield information about high school requirements, work-related requirements, and the demands of functional reading materials.

30. Lehr, Fran. "Adult Literacy." JOURNAL OF READING 27 (November 1983): 176-179.

Lehr comments on the lack of a consistent definition of literacy. We often, in fact, use different terms interchangeably, such as literacy, functional literacy, and competency. Literacy can be defined as the number of years in school completed, the ability to read material necessary for survival, or the ability to read particular materials sufficiently to function in a particular environment. The differences in definitions give rise to differences in assessing abilities and levels of literacy. Lehr also examines the issue of how to attract and keep students in literacy programs. She cites the barriers to participation identified by Cross: situational, dispositional, and institutional. All have an impact on the structure of programs.

31. Levine, Kenneth. "Functional Literacy: Fond Illusions and False Economies." HARVARD EDUCATIONAL REVIEW 52 (August 1982): 249-266.

Levine attacks the notion of functional

literacy as misleading both to individuals and
to society. Functional literacy promises that
some undefined and varying level of literacy
will "directly result in a set of universally
desired outcomes, such as employment, personal
and economic growth, job advancement, and
social integration" (p. 250). According to
the author, this rarely happens. He reviews
the history of the term and concept with
particular emphasis on the role of UNESCO in
studying and recommending solutions to the
problems of world illiteracy. He highlights
projects and results, emphasizing changing
reasons for literacy. The difficulties in
giving the term functional literacy a
precision that can carry over to various
situations are discussed. Levine includes
problems in identifying materials as well as
using age or grade level designations. Many
of these difficulties have arisen because the
term has been defined by reading experts,
psychologists and school teachers in terms of
the individual. Instead, Levine suggests
looking at literacy as a social practice in
various cultural and political contexts.
Included in the concept of illiteracy are not
only readers but also writers who fail to
transmit ideas and information effectively.
Each individual determines his own degree of
literacy and literacy needs and relates them
to different kinds of information and
materials.

32. Miller, Harry G., and Freddy L. Shapiro.
    ADULT LITERACY AND NATIONAL DEVELOPMENT.
    1982. 26pp. (ED 224 918)

    Miller and Shapiro examine a variety of
adult literacy issues in light of economic,
political and social concerns. The evidence
here for determining relationships such as
cause and effect is not definitive,
particularly in developing countries. They
assert that "adult literacy is measured by the
demand society places on its citizens" (p. 3).
Standards for literacy must meet changing
demands within the society. Functional
literacy is related to other skills needed to

move ahead in a society, such as family
planning and the adoption of work habits. In
developing countries, a total approach to
literacy is often advocated. Reasons for
developing literacy are discussed as well as
the role of a variety of organizations. The
authors raise a number of pertinent questions.
Should the focus of literacy campaigns be on
the masses or on a selected few? How should
adult literacy programs relate to educational
institutions? Should programs provide for
post-literacy training?

33. Murphy, Richard R. "Assessment of Adult
    Reading Competence." READING AND CAREER
    EDUCATION. Edited by Duane M. Nielsen and
    Howard F. Hjelm. Newark, Delaware:
    International Reading Assn., 1975, pp. 50-
    61.

    Murphy identifies ways of determining the
    reading competencies adults need to function
    in society and the difficulties in
    establishing them definitively. On the basis
    of a national assessment of reading
    activities, it seems clear that competency in
    reading work-related materials is important.
    The author also reports on representative
    reading tasks developed by the Test
    Development Division of Educational Testing
    Service as well as on results of the National
    Survey of Adult Functional Reading Performance
    which used these tasks to devise items.
    Difficulties in using the results to establish
    standards for functional reading competence
    are discussed.

34. Northcutt, Norvell W. "Functional Literacy
    for Adults." READING AND CAREER EDUCATION.
    Edited by Duane M. Nielsen and Howard F.
    Hjelm. Newark, Delaware: International
    Reading Assn., 1975, pp. 43-49.

    Northcutt proposes a definition of
    functional literacy based on the Adult
    Performance Level study. Three conclusions
    came from that study: literacy is meaningful
    only within a specific cultural context;

literacy is the application of a set of skills
to a set of general knowledge; and literacy is
directly related to success in adult life. He
also describes the tentative results of a
national survey on occupational knowledge and
consumer economics. This essay is
particularly interesting because it shows work
in progress on a major study that has since
been completed and widely publicized.

35. Oxenham, John. LITERACY: WRITING, READING AND
    SOCIAL ORGANIZATION. Boston: Routledge and
    Kegan Paul, 1980.

    Oxenham examines the development and
    implications of literacy within a historical
    context. He links literacy in the individual
    to the development of reasoning and thinking.
    Literacy enables the individual, and society,
    to deal with vast amounts of information and
    complex problems. Because of the growing
    pressures of society we have created a demand
    for universal literacy.

36. Peck, Cynthia Van Norden, and Martin Kling.
    "Adult Literacy in the Seventies: Its
    Definition and Measurement." JOURNAL OF
    READING 20 (May 1977): 677-682.

    Peck and Kling examine the emerging view
    that literacy is relative not absolute. They
    trace the recent history of attempts to define
    literacy and conclude that because of
    variations in definitions there are variations
    as well in estimates of the extent of
    illiteracy. "The figures change as the
    definitions change" (p. 678). The authors
    examine in some detail current efforts to
    define and measure literacy in terms of "real-
    life reading skills" (p. 679) using criterion-
    referenced testing. They raise questions
    about this approach but accept the premise
    that in defining and assessing literacy "the
    focus on literacy as a problem peculiar to a
    given population or subpopulation seems to be
    a critical one, for individuals and their
    needs differ from area to area, rural to
    urban" (p. 682).

37. Robinson, Jay L.   "The   Users   and   Uses   of
     Literacy."   LITERACY FOR LIFE: THE DEMAND
     FOR READING AND WRITING. Edited by Richard
     W. Bailey and Robin Melanie Fosheim. New
     York: The Modern Language Assn. of America,
     1983, pp. 3-18.

     Robinson   provides   a useful overview of the
     articles in this volume and summarizes many of
     the major issues. He examines definitions of
     literacy   ranging   from literacy as a survival
     skill to literacy as a cognitive means of
     finding new meanings.   He looks at ways of
     providing access to it and of engaging schools
     and colleges in the process.

38. Scribner, Sylvia.   "Literacy   in   Three
     Metaphors."   AMERICAN JOURNAL OF EDUCATION
     93 (November 1984): 6-21.

     Scribner   suggests that   the   definitional
     controversy   over   the   term "literacy" has
     significant implications for the measurement
     and   evaluation   of the problem as well as for
     program development.   She   proposes   that
     because literacy must take place within a
     social context, the definition of literacy
     must   account   for   the   demands   of   that
     particular context. "We may lack consensus on
     how best to define literacy because we have
     differing   views   about   literacy's   social
     purposes and value" (p. 8).   The author
     examines   the   social   implications   of   three
     views of literacy: literacy as adaptation,
     literacy as power, and literacy as a state of
     grace. These are not necessarily mutually
     exclusive and, in fact, may all be part of the
     "multiple meanings and varieties of literacy"
     (p. 18).   Scribner   includes   examples   from
     Third World countries in order that we might
     see ourselves more clearly by   examining
     others.

39. _____, and Michael Cole.   "Literacy
     without Schooling: Testing for Intellectual
     Effects."   HARVARD   EDUCATIONAL   REVIEW 48
     (November 1978): 448-461.

The relationship between literacy and intellectual development is examined in the context of relevant literature and the authors' work with the Vai people of Liberia. Two theories and their resulting educational implications are explored: literacy as development and literacy as practice. Literacy as development holds that higher order thinking abilities develop from the concrete to the abstract and are effected by the development of literacy skills. The authors raise questions about this approach and suggest that the act of engaging in literacy activities--the practice of literacy itself--promotes particular skills related to the activity. Adult illiterates cannot be assumed to lack the ability to think abstractly because they have not developed the ability to read. "Reading and writing activities need to be tailored to desired outcomes" (p. 460). If we want to encourage analytic ability, we need to include that in the instruction provided. In all areas, the authors stress the need for further research.

40. _____. THE PSYCHOLOGY OF LITERACY. Cambridge, Massachusetts: Harvard University Press, 1981.

The authors report on their studies of literacy in the Vai tribe of Liberia. There they found that it was not a simple matter of the members being literate or non-literate, but rather of having various kinds of literacy in different situations and for different purposes. English was learned in school and used to obtain information and to get and keep jobs. Vai script was learned outside of school to communicate with other tribal members and to transmit local culture and history. Arabic was learned for religious reasons and to transmit the Islamic culture. Different individuals from different groups were considered literate in different languages, using their literacy for different purposes. Literacy is thus viewed by the authors as existing within a social or religious context.

41. Thimmesch, Nick, ed. ALITERACY: PEOPLE WHO
     CAN READ BUT WON'T. Washington, D.C.:
     American Enterprise Institute for Public
     Policy Research, 1984.

     This volume presents the proceedings of a
     conference held in 1982 and is charged with
     exploring problems and solutions associated
     with the growing phenomenon of aliteracy. The
     papers and discussions examine reasons why
     some people who can read do not, implications
     of this development for individuals and for
     society, and alternative courses of action to
     remedy it. A variety of perspectives are
     represented, from the academic view of reading
     as a holistic, thinking process to the impact
     of reading daily newspapers and to the notion
     that literacy and the exercise of literacy is
     a "power question" (p. 50). One of the
     contributors, Marsha Levine, concluded that "I
     found the definitions of literacy, illiteracy,
     and aliteracy blurred together, at times
     indistinguishable, in the sense that one
     creates the other" (pp. 58-59).

42. Weber, Rose-Marie. "Adult Illiteracy in the
     United States." TOWARD A LITERATE SOCIETY.
     Edited by John B. Carrol and Jeanne S.
     Chall. New York: McGraw-Hill, 1975, pp.
     147-164.

     Although the statistics on the extent of
     illiteracy are somewhat dated, the discussion
     of how to define and describe illiteracy is
     relevant and useful. Weber examines the aims
     of literacy instruction and takes issue with
     those who see literacy merely as a means of
     achieving higher level jobs. In contrast she
     focuses on broader educational objectives such
     as literacy in relation to thinking, making
     decisions, reflecting, and initiating change.
     Within this framework, she examines federal
     programs and highlights their shortcomings,
     reviews research on adults' learning to read,
     examines methods and materials, and raises
     questions concerning teacher preparation and
     testing. Weber provides us with a broad
     overview of issues and questions related to

adult illiteracy.

Adults as Learners: Implications for Instruction and Curriculum

43. Adam, Felix, and George F. Aker, eds. FACTORS IN ADULT LEARNING AND INSTRUCTION. THEORY, INNOVATION, AND PRACTICE IN ANDRAGOGY. No. 1. Tallahassee, Florida: Florida State University, International Institute of Andragogy, June 1982. 67pp. (ED 228 461)

    This monograph contains two papers originally published in 1971 by Collie Verner and Catherine V. Davison that investigate the psychological and physiological factors of adult learning. They provide a useful overview of issues, problems, and strategies in learning and instruction, although the citations and references are somewhat dated.

44. Beder, Hal. "The Relationship of Knowledge Sought to Appropriate Teacher Behavior in Adult Education." LIFELONG LEARNING 9 (September 1985): 14-15, 27-28.

    Beder suggests that adult educators should not be forced to choose either a pedagogical approach or an andragogical approach. In some situations formal/segmented pedagogy is appropriate while in others problem oriented andragogy is more effective. The difference is in the nature of the knowledge to be learned. Beder explores the implications of this notion for instruction.

45. Beder, Harold W., and Gordon G. Darkenwald. "Differences Between Teaching Adults and Pre-Adults: Some Propositions and Findings." ADULT EDUCATION 32 (1982): 142-155.

    Beder and Darkenwald, using an interview technique, investigated issues related to working with adults from the perspective of how teachers who instruct both adults and pre-adults actually teach each group. The results showed that there are differences in teaching behavior and that these differences are

generally related to the teachers' perceptions
of differences in the two groups of students
in terms of motivation, task orientation,
self-direction, and pragmatism. Teachers
working with adults tended to be less
structured and controlling and more open to
incorporating student experiences and feedback
than those working with younger students. The
authors caution that "the findings do not,
however, demonstrate that teachers employ
pedagogical techniques with pre-adults and
andragogical techniques with adults" (p. 153).
Rather, teachers seemed to use learner-
centered techniques with adults to the extent
that they perceived the adults as motivated
and self-directed.

46.   Brockett, Ralph. "Self-Directed Learning and
       the Hard-to-Reach Adult" LIFELONG LEARNING
       6 (April 1983): 16-18.

       Brockett examines literature on the adult
learner and proposes that we need a broad
perspective on learning, the situations in
which it occurs, and the ways in which adults
can participate in it. Learning for adults
can happen outside of classrooms and is not
dependent on books. Self directed learning is
a powerful activity. Brockett suggests that
in working with hard-to-reach adults we should
not limit our efforts to traditional
educational settings, but should work in the
broader community. The teacher must strike a
delicate balance between intervening and
letting the adult learner assume
responsibility for his learning.

47.   Conti, Gary J. THE COLLABORATIVE MODE IN
       ADULT EDUCATION: A LITERATURE REVIEW.
       Unpublished doctoral dissertation, Northern
       Illinois University, 1978. 25pp. (ED 229
       534)

       Conti reviews the literature related to
Blaney's three modes of developing adult
education curriculum. In the Institutional
Mode, someone other than the learner plans the
curriculum. In the Individual Mode, the

learner is in charge of the curriculum. In
the Shared-Membership Mode "the learner and
teacher cooperatively determine the ends,
means, and evaluation of learning" (p. 1).
This last mode, according to the author, has
the most promise for effective implementation
of adult learning theory.

48. Cross, K. Patricia. ADULTS AS LEARNERS. San
    Francisco: Jossey-Bass, 1981.

    The focus of this book is on theory and
    research. Cross examines a wide range of
    current thought dealing with the questions of
    who the participants are in adult learning,
    why they participate, how they learn, and what
    they want to learn. The discussion is
    detailed and useful. Many of the examples
    relate to adults returning to a college
    setting, but the conclusions are widely
    applicable. The discussion of barriers to
    learning, for example, can be translated into
    many settings. The problems of situational
    barriers (other responsibilities, cost, child
    care, transportation), institutional barriers
    (amount of time required, schedule of classes,
    red tape), and dispositional barriers (age of
    adult, attitude toward school and studying)
    are as relevant to the adult basic education
    program as well as they are to the college
    skill center. Cross looks at learning
    theories, at the role of andragogy in adult
    education, and at problems of distinguishing
    the learning needs of adults from those of
    children. The questions Cross raises are
    important; her conclusions and suggestions are
    thought-provoking. A particularly useful
    bibliography is included.

49. Darkenwald, Gordon G., and Sharan B. Merrian.
    "Adults as Learners." ADULT EDUCATION:
    FOUNDATIONS OF PRACTICE. New York: Harper &
    Row, 1982, pp. 75-116.

    The authors review and compare major
    theorists and researchers in two critical
    areas: characteristics of adulthood and the
    adult learning process. What is crucial in

their opinion is that the instructor understand the concept of "adulthood in conjunction with the learning process" (p. 75).

50. Davenport, Joseph, and Judith Davenport. "A Chronology and Analysis of the Andragogy Debate." ADULT EDUCATION QUARTERLY 35 (Spring 1985): 152-159.

Davenport and Davenport present a history of the changing definitions of the term "andragogy" and of the writers and theorists who have explored the issues and implications related to it. The authors suggest that there is a need for more empirical research to confirm whether andragogy is a method of instruction or a theory.

51. _____, and Judith Davenport. "Andragogical-Pedagogical Orientations of Adult Learners: Research Results and Practice Recommendations." LIFELONG LEARNING 9 (September 1985): 6-8.

Davenport and Davenport examine the history of andragogy from 1833 to the present, give Malcolm Knowles credit for "reintroducing and popularizing" (p. 8) the term and detail his assumptions about adult learning. The implications of both andragogy and pedagogy are explored in terms of the learning process, the design of curriculum, and instructional techniques. Recent research on the effectiveness of these two basic approaches is presented. Although many questions have not been answered by the research and andragogy "is still a considerable distance from being a fully-developed theory" (p. 8), the authors provide suggestions to teachers that utilize one approach or the other or a combination of approaches.

52. ERIC Clearinghouse on Adult, Career, and Vocational Education. GUIDELINES FOR WORKING WITH ADULT LEARNERS. Overview: ERIC Fact Sheet No. 25. Columbus, Ohio, 1982. 4pp. (ED 237 811)

This fact sheet provides guidance in understanding adult characteristics and their application to developing adult educational programs, designing instruction, and motivating students.

53. Gerstein, Martin, and Michele Papen-Daniel. UNDERSTANDING ADULTHOOD. A REVIEW AND ANALYSIS OF THE WORKS OF THREE LEADING AUTHORITIES ON THE STAGES AND CRISES IN ADULT DEVELOPMENT. California Personnel and Guidance Assn. Monograph No. 15. Fullerton, California, January 1981. 38pp. (ED 219 616)

The authors examine the contributions of Erikson, Levinson, and Sheehy to a theory of adult development that links predictable, sequential changes to age thus providing a theoretical background for educators of adults.

54. Jarvis, Peter. ADULT AND CONTINUING EDUCATION: THEORY AND PRACTICE. New York: Nichols Publishing, 1983.

Jarvis reviews types of adult education and theories of adult learning. He relates these considerations to various theoretical and practical approaches to teaching adults and developing curriculum for them. The discussion of teacher-centered and individual student-centered methods is detailed and clear and includes a variety of strategies, methods, and teaching aids. A final chapter describes the history of adult education in the United Kingdom.

55. Kidd, J.R. HOW ADULTS LEARN. New York: Association Press, 1977.

In determining how adults learn, Kidd examines the learner and his characteristics, capabilities, and development in some depth. He looks at various theories and practices of learning, drawing from a variety of backgrounds and citing a number of examples. He explores the learning environment, the role

of the learner, and the place of the teacher
in the learning situation. The goal of
learning, he concludes, is for the learner to
become self-directed, managing his own
learning.

56.   Knowles, Malcolm S. THE MODERN PRACTICE OF
      ADULT EDUCATION: FROM PEDAGOGY TO ANDRAGOGY.
      Chicago: Follett Publishing Co., 1980.

      Knowles establishes a dialogue with the
      reader as a model for his belief that the role
      of the educator of adults is to establish a
      "climate of mutual inquiry" (p. 13). His
      concept of andragogy forms the foundation for
      his view on adult learning and adult education
      programs. Andragogy is based on the
      assumption that adults are self-directed
      learners, have life experience to apply to
      learning, are motivated to learn within their
      social roles, and are performance-centered
      rather than subject-centered, preferring
      immediate application of learning to postponed
      application. Knowles acknowledges that there
      are situations in which adults may learn
      better using a pedagogical approach. He views
      pedagogy and andragogy as being on a
      continuum, but with the latter more
      appropriate for adults. Within this context
      the author examines the roles and features of
      adult education programs and applies this
      information in very practical ways to the
      organization and administration of programs as
      well as to the development and execution of
      learning activities.

57.   Knox, Alan B. ADULT DEVELOPMENT AND LEARNING.
      San Francisco: Jossey-Bass, 1977.

      This comprehensive guide to adult learning
      provides a theoretical and practical framework
      for understanding adult development and the
      context in which it occurs as well as for
      planning appropriate adult education programs.
      Although the focus of the book is not
      primarily on program planning and curriculum
      development, and certainly not on the
      development of basic literacy skills, there is

much valuable information on these subjects.

58. Lasker, Harry, and James Moore. "Current Studies of Adult Development: Implications for Education." ADULT DEVELOPMENT AND APPROACHES TO LEARNING. U.S. Department of Education, Office of Educational Research and Improvement. Washington, D.C.: U.S. Government Printing Office, September 1980, pp. 3-41.

Lasker and Moore detail the major theories of adult development and relate their implications to adult education programs and programming. They divide adult development theories into two general groups both of which "assume that there are qualitative changes in the ways adults understand and act, and that certain aspects of these changes occur in progressive sequences" (p. 3). Phasic theories relate these changes to age periods. Stage theories view them as developmental changes, not correlated with age, that reflect the psychological development of the individual. The authors present a clear, detailed but concise comparison of the two approaches and discuss the major theorists within each approach. Implications for education are suggested, as is the need for further research in this area.

59. Long, Huey B. THEORETICAL FOUNDATIONS OF ADULT EDUCATION: BORROWING FROM OTHER DISCIPLINES. THEORY, INNOVATION, AND PRACTICE IN ANDRAGOGY. No. 3. Tallahassee, Florida: Florida State University, International Institute of Andragogy, December 1982. 23pp. (ED 228 463)

The author provides a general theoretical background as well as specific examples on the contribution of other disciplines to the understanding and functioning of adult education, particularly in the areas of learning and instruction, participation and persistence, program planning, and research. Citations are included that can be pursued for further study in this area.

60. McKenzie, Leon. "The Issue of Andragogy."
     ADULT EDUCATION XXVII (Summer 1977): 225-
     229.

     McKenzie examines andragogy from the
     perspective of philosophy. He discusses the
     classical approach that holds that adults and
     children are essentially the same and that
     therefore their education ought to be
     essentially the same. The phenomenological
     approach holds that they are existentially
     different, with existentially different
     educational needs. The author identifies the
     need for a more complete and scholarly
     examination of the philosophical issues
     related to the concept of andragogy.

61. Merriam, Sharan B. ADULT DEVELOPMENT:
     IMPLICATIONS FOR ADULT EDUCATION. Columbus,
     Ohio: ERIC Clearinghouse on Adult, Career,
     and Vocational Education, 1984. 48pp. (ED
     246 309)

     Merriam presents a variety of models of
     adult development and relates them to issues
     in adult education. The field of adult
     development is relatively new but is one
     teachers need to become familiar with "if
     adult educators are to serve their clients
     effectively" (p. 25). The author examines the
     connections between adult development and
     program development, administration,
     instruction, and counseling. In the area of
     instruction, for example, she relates the
     adult's need for self-direction to the role of
     the teacher and to the use of contract
     learning.

62. Newton, Eunice Shaed. "Andragogy:
     Understanding the Adult as a Learner."
     READING AND THE ADULT LEARNER. Edited by
     Laura S. Johnson. Newark, Delaware:
     International Reading Assn., 1980, pp. 3-6.

     Newton summarizes the theories of Knowles
     and Kidd, concluding that the adult learner is
     "an autonomous, experience laden, goal
     seeking, 'now' oriented, problem centered

individual" (p. 4). In view of this, she suggests the use of the language experience approach in teaching reading to adults.

63. Rachal, John. "The Andragogy-Pedagogy Debate: Another Voice in the Fray." LIFELONG LEARNING 6 (May 1983): 14-15.

Rachal examines the linguistic dimensions of the andragogy-pedagogy debate and proposes that "self-directed and teacher-directed seem much more serviceable terms" (p. 15). The philosophical dimensions are difficult because the two approaches are not opposed but rather are on a continuum. Learning situations are probably never completely teacher- or self-directed. The adult educator must attempt to synthesize the two approaches to provide the best learning situation for particular students while, at the same time, maintaining educational standards.

64. Rada, Heath. "An Interview with Malcolm Knowles." JOURNAL OF DEVELOPMENTAL AND REMEDIAL EDUCATION 4 (Fall 1980): 2-4.

Knowles provides a psychological definition of an adult as one who perceives himself as responsible for his own life and as self-directed in his learning. He advocates beginning with instruction in "those learnings at the lowest level of complexity...and those in areas with which the learner is unfamiliar" (p.3). When the adult has the basic skills and the content he can become a self-directed learner. Knowles also discusses seven procedures to be used in working with adults including, for example, learning contracts and self-assessment. Education for adults must become "life-centered rather than subject-centered" (p. 4). An example of the former is the APL approach in which basic skill instruction is related to life problems.

65. Simpson, Edwin L. "Adult Learning Theory: A State of the Art." ADULT DEVELOPMENT AND APPROACHES TO LEARNING. U.S. Department of Education, Office of Educational Research

and Improvement.   Washington, D.C.: U.S.
Government Printing Office, September 1980,
pp. 43-74.

Simpson's focus is on integrating theory and
practice in adult education. He reviews
learning theory and studies of adult learning
as the basis for suggesting a variety of
approaches to adult education. This monograph
takes a broad perspective, providing the
reader with specifics and principles from four
major areas: behaviorism, cognitivism,
psychoanalytic theory, and self theory.   The
theories are related to conditions in which
learning can occur and discussed in terms of
how they interact with the adult's personal
style and orientation as he moves toward
independence in learning.   Suggestions for
needed research are made.

66. Wager, Walter. INSTRUCTIONAL TECHNOLOGY AND
     THE ADULT LEARNER. THEORY, INNOVATION, AND
     PRACTICE IN ANDRAGOGY. No. 2. Tallahassee,
     Florida: Florida State   University,
     International   Institute   of   Andragogy,
     October 1982. 66pp. (ED 228 464)

     Wager analyzes the theory of adult learning
     from the prespective of andragogy, relates it
     to instruction, and provides specific
     applications for those who teach adults. Much
     of the information can be applied to
     instruction in a variety of literacy settings.
     A Spanish translation is included.

67. Yonge, George D. "Andragogy and Pedagogy: Two
     Ways of Accompaniment."   ADULT EDUCATION
     QUARTERLY 35 (Spring 1985): 160-167.

     Yonge rejects the notion that it is the
     elements of teaching and learning that
     characterize andragogy and pedagogy. Rather,
     he suggests that it is the situation in which
     the learning takes place that is the critical
     element.   Andragogy is a situation that
     involves an adult-adult relationship and
     pedagogy is one that involves an adult-child
     relationship.   The aims are also different.

The purpose of andragogy is to assist the adult to become a more competent adult; the purpose of pedagogy is to assist the child to become an adult. The author analyzes the implications of these differences and presents the findings of others in the field.

The Teacher of Adults

68. Berdeaux, Jack, and Jill Borden. THE ADULT LEARNER. A HANDBOOK FOR VOLUNTEER AND NEW ADULT EDUCATION TEACHERS. Phoenix, Arizona: Phoenix Union High School District, April 1984. 25pp. (ED 253 735)

    Berdeaux and Borden identify topics related to the instruction of undereducated adults that are of concern to teachers and volunteers. They discuss differences in learning between children and adults as well as characteristics of adults. The aim in setting up an instructional situation is to create a positive, supportive environment. To do this, the instructor must understand the adult learner. This handbook is designed to assist him in accomplishing this end.

69. Grabowski, Stanley M. TRAINING TEACHERS OF ADULTS: MODELS AND INNOVATIVE PROGRAMS. Publications in Continuing Education, No. 46. Syracuse, New York: Syracuse University, October 1976.

    Because of the paucity of institutional programs that train teachers to work with adults, the responsibility for the training often falls on the adult education program. This publication is a practical resource for developing inservice programs for teachers of adults. It defines the objectives of such programs, examines the knowledge, skills and attitudes the teachers should possess, provides a very useful set of teacher competencies, and identifies the characteristics and criteria for inservice programs. A wide variety of models are discussed, with specific examples of innovative and interesting programs.

70. Hansford, Sandra G., ed. LEARNING NEVER ENDS.
     A HANDBOOK FOR PART-TIME TEACHERS OF ADULT
     BASIC EDUCATION. Jacksonville: University
     of North Florida, 1983. 104pp. (ED 244
     149)

         This monograph is designed for the beginner
     as well as the experienced teacher of adult
     basic education students. Two sections are
     included, one for the trainer of teachers and
     the other for the teachers to use in
     practicing the suggestions and learning
     activities. The focus is on combining
     theories of adult development with practical
     applications in classroom instruction. A
     variety of topics are discussed--all related
     to the key words "Affordability,
     Accessibility, and Relevance" (p. 11).
     Fundamental to the handbook is the notion that
     basic skills instruction must be integrated
     with students' higher level needs.

71. Levine, S. Joseph et al. TEACHING ADULTS!!
     TRAINING MATERIALS FOR ADULT EDUCATION STAFF
     DEVELOPMENT. East Lansing, Michigan:
     Michigan State University, Department of
     Adult and Continuing Education, 1981.
     183pp. (ED 213 824)

         This document is useful for training
     teachers in any adult setting. Twelve modules
     are presented covering a wide variety of
     topics relevant to adult learning from how
     learning takes place and how we can facilitate
     it to involving the learner and evaluating the
     learning. Specific details, worksheets,
     transparencies, and handouts are provided.

72. Lindsay, Michael. "Teacher Education for
     Adult Educators." JOURNAL OF TEACHER
     EDUCATION XXXIV (May-June 1983): 50-53.

         Lindsay identifies a growing adult education
     population. His concern is with the lack of
     research available to provide guidance in
     formulating instructional procedures. There
     is also a critical need to prepare teachers to
     work with this particular population. In

order to meet this constellation of needs, he
makes five recommendations. We must review
the literature to identify validated
instructional strategies. We must conduct
experimental and field research to validate
current practices. We must develop and refine
a theory of adult cognitive development. We
must generate a theory of adult instruction.
Finally, we must develop a model of teacher
education based on these notions.

73. Wickett, R.E.Y. THE APPLICATION OF THE
    LEARNING PROJECT INTERVIEW AS A METHOD OF
    COMMUNICATING PRINCIPLES OF LEARNING THEORY
    TO FACILITATORS OF ADULT LEARNING. 1982.
    15pp. (ED 224 865)

    Wickett outlines a procedure for involving
    adults in the learning process by
    reconstructing and analyzing, in workshops and
    through group discussions, learning projects
    they themselves have undertaken. Some
    specific guidance is given in leading the
    activity.

Adult Basic Literacy

The Extent and Implications of the Problem

74. Beris, Carole. A COMPARISON OF THE
READABILITY OF SELECTED INSTRUCTIONS,
PUBLICATIONS AND FORMS COMMONLY USED BY
ADULTS AND THE MINIMUM LITERACY LEVEL AS
DEFINED BY THE UNITED STATES OFFICE OF
EDUCATION. Master's Thesis, Kean College of
New Jersey, April 1982. 64pp. (ED 217 372)

Beris used the Fry Readability graph to
analyze 23 forms, instructions, and
publications in general use and found that
five were at the fifth through eighth grade
level, five were at the tenth through twelfth
grade level and thirteen were at the college
level. She concluded that there is a wide
discrepancy between the reading level required
and the reading level of many of the users of
the documents.

75. Brod, Rodney L., and John M. McQuistos.
"American Indian Adult Education and
Literacy: Some Findings of the First
National Survey and Their Implications for
Educational Policy." Paper presented at the
Meeting of the Pacific Sociological Assn.,
April 1982, San Diego, California. 38pp.
(ED 225 765)

This report provides data to support the
conclusion that although Eastern Indians
perform at a higher level of literacy than
Western Indians, both groups perform at a
level that leaves them out of the mainstream
for jobs and prevents them from "participating
in the quality of life and reaping the
benefits of late twentieth century life in the

181

United States" (p. 16). The authors use terms
such as "devastating" (p. 16), "tragically
low" (p. 17), and "grave" (ibid.) in
describing the results and implications of the
study. An important part of the report is the
section on recommendations. The authors
suggest there is a need to continue research
studies, evaluate and revise the Indian
education delivery system, provide education
in the traditional language, offer instruction
and background in both cultures (traditional
Indian and Western), critically evaluate and
change the adult education system, increase
levels of support and search out funding
sources for Indian education, examine civil
rights and enforce laws, and promote self-
determination in Indian education. The scope
of the problem and of the recommendations
provide food for thought in terms of American
Indians as well as of other specific
populations.

76.   Copperman, Paul. "The Decline of Literacy."
      JOURNAL OF COMMUNICATION 30 (Winter 1980):
      113-122.

      Copperman examines a variety of statistics
related to reading achievement and concludes
that there was an increase in achievement
until the mid-1960s. Since then, there has
been a "sharp and steady decline" (p.119) with
serious consequences for adult literacy and a
subsequent impact on many aspects of adult
life, including, for example, occupational
levels and criminal activity.

77.   Fingeret, Arlene. "Through the Looking Glass:
      Literacy as Perceived by Illiterate Adults."
      Paper presented as the Annual Meeting of the
      American Educational Research Assn., March
      19-23, 1982, New York. 14pp. (ED 222 698)

      Fingeret presents a unique and vivid picture
of literacy--unique because it comes from the
illiterate adults interviewed for a study and
vivid because it includes many direct quotes
from the interviews. Illiterate adults who
live in a literate society recognize the

practical advantages of reading and writing
for independent living. On the other hand,
illiterate adults who live surrounded by other
illiterate adults view literacy with mixed
feelings. Literacy can lead to independence,
but at the same time it can lead to possible
alienation from existing social groups.

78. Hovey, Sheryl.   FUNCTIONAL   ILLITERACY.
    Columbia, Missouri: University of Missouri,
    School of Journalism, Freedom of Information
    Center, November 1982. 9pp. (ED 224 030)

    Hovey takes a broad look at functional
    illiteracy, examining numbers, definitions,
    and costs to society. In addition, she looks
    at who the functionally illiterate are,
    delving into areas such as income, employment,
    public assistance, race and ethnic background,
    age, and incarceration. Causes of the problem
    and present attempts to solve it are also
    examined. Many questions are raised; few
    solutions are offered or conclusions reached.
    Adult Basic Educations programs are viewed as
    a viable solution, but problems of poor
    attendance and high attrition must be solved.
    Many of the remedies suggested are
    preventative and include for example beginning
    to deal with problems of literacy in
    elementary and secondary schools.

79. Hunter, Carman St. John.   "Adult Illiteracy in
    the United States."   NAPCAE EXCHANGE 3
    (Summer 1980): 2-4.

    Hunter asserts that literacy levels in the
    United States have never been higher than they
    are today. The problem we are facing as a
    society is that we now require "competence far
    beyond simply literacy" (p. 2). In fact, we
    cannot determine a list of functional literacy
    skills.   Rather, each individual must
    determine for himself what the skills are that
    he needs to fulfill his own objectives. The
    author identifies four groups of adults with
    the "greatest literacy-related disadvantages"
    (p. 3), links their needs to possible delivery
    systems, and urges the development not just of

functional literacy but of human competence as well.

80. _____, and David Harman. ADULT ILLITERACY IN THE UNITED STATES. A REPORT TO THE FORD FOUNDATION. New York: McGraw-Hill, 1979.

Hunter and Harman have provided us with a comprehensive, readable overview of the topic of adult illiteracy, looking at definitions, causes, numbers, populations, programs, and possibilities. Specific suggestions are provided, all relating to a central recommendation for "the establishment of new, pluralistic, community-based initiatives whose specific objective will be to serve the most disadvantaged hard-core poor, the bulk of whom never enroll in any existing program" (p. 133). The book contains a comprehensive annotated bibliography.

81. Johnson, James N. ADULTS IN CRISIS: ILLITERACY IN AMERICA. San Francisco, California: Far West Laboratory for Educational Research and Development; Andover, Massachusetts: Network of Innovative Schools, Inc., March 1985. 30pp. (ED 254 755)

Johnson identifies illiteracy as a major social problem that stems from a variety of causes. The impact of illiteracy falls mainly on the poor and minorities creating social, political, and economic problems for them and for society. He suggests the need for an total commitment to the problem of illiteracy, working on all aspects of it from recruitment of the illiterate to research on strategies and sufficient funding to support it. Specifically, the effort requires a broad definition of literacy, a delivery system geared to meet the needs of the clients, and coordination among agencies with more community involvement. Teachers need adequate and appropriate staff development with more professionals involved in instruction. Program evaluation must be detailed and

helpful. We need to upgrade programs and
provide opportunities for continued research.
All of this requires sufficient funding,
particularly from the Federal government.

82. Kozol, Jonathan.   PRISONERS OF SILENCE:
    BREAKING THE BONDS OF ADULT ILLITERACY IN
    THE UNITED STATES.   New York: Continuum,
    1980.

    Kozol examines the extent of the problem of
    illiteracy in the United States and estimates
    that, even though figures vary, about 25
    million people lack the literacy skills needed
    to function in today's society.   He also
    describes what it means to be illiterate in
    human   terms--the   fear,   anxiety,   self-
    protection, deception and humiliation, as well
    as the economic effects. The adult illiterate
    is not only kept out of the job market but he
    is also kept silent, unable to express his
    frustration and hopelessness. Kozol advocates
    a massive campaign with a bold program.   He
    calls for dialogue between teacher and learner
    using   volunteers.   He wants a "shared
    endeavor" with a National Literacy Commission
    and with local groups taking leadership roles.
    An "all-out" effort is needed to break the
    bonds of silence.

83. _____.   ILLITERATE AMERICA.   New York:
    Anchor Press/Doubleday, 1985.

    Kozol identifies 60 million Americans as
    illiterate (25 million) or semi-literate (35
    million).   While the first category has
    probably decreased in size over the past few
    years,   the   second has increased, partly
    because of the increased literacy demands of
    our society.   Kozol traces the effects of
    these low levels of literacy on this large
    group and on their children as well as on
    society. Current programs, on the whole, are
    clearly not solving the problems of
    illiteracy. Kozol makes many suggestions for
    recruitment of students, recruitment and
    training of teachers and volunteers, structure
    of programs, and instructional methods.   He

advocates integrating reading, writing, and
thinking and using language experience as well
as meaningful and motivating words and
concepts.

84. Lehr, Fran. "A Portrait of the American as
     Reader." JOURNAL OF READING 29 (November
     1985): 170-172.

     Lehr examines a variety of studies and
surveys to determine the amount of reading
being done, who is doing the reading, and what
is being read. She concludes that "the
picture of reading in the United States
appears bright--with several dark areas" (p.
171). She cites the statistics showing that
Americans spend more time with television and
radios than with books. She also decries the
findings that reading tends to be utilitarian
rather than for pleasure. Finally, she
identifies a potential area of concern in the
decline in young readers.

85. Lumsden, D. Barry. "Why Johnny's Grandparents
     Can't Read." EDUCATIONAL GERONTOLOGY 4
     (1979): 297-305.

     Johnny's grandparents can't read because of
"those great social and economic upheavals
that accompanied the turn of the century and
continued on through the depression years"
(pp. 297-298). The tragedy of adult
illiteracy is still with us. The author
examines the all-out approach taken in Cuba
that resulted in the eradication of
illiteracy. He compares this approach to that
taken in UNESCO programs and to approaches
taken in the United States and suggests that
successful programs must deal with content and
concerns that are important to the adult
student. A cognitive approach is important
but the author also stresses the need for
developing the affective aspects of reading
and learning. In working with the elderly, we
must seek them out and go to them when
providing services. Data is provided to show
that the problem is far from solved. Johnny
also may not be able to read. We need a

national effort reaching into all schools and homes.

86. Mark, Jorie Lester. "On Current Literacy Efforts." LIFELONG LEARNING 6 (April 1983): 25-26.

Mark identifies the dimensions of illiteracy in the United States: the growing number of illiterates and the substantial cost to society, and the changing technological and social demands for literacy. He identifies national programs that have been developed to help teachers and tutors work with adults and describes a recent effort, the Coalition for Literacy.

87. _____. "In Pursuit of Adult Literacy." LIFELONG LEARNING 8 (May 1985): 4-5.

Citing the "alarming" (p. 4) statistics that show that 27 million adults are not literate enough to function in the United States today and that 47 million more function only with difficulty, Mark explores the implications of adult illiteracy in human and societal terms stressing the effect of illiterate parents on their children. The solution requires "locally built partnerships between all segments of the community, including business and industry, labor, community and welfare groups, the arts, communications, and all segments of education, including public and private schools, colleges and vocational-technical institutions" (p. 5). He provides examples of current efforts to further these kinds of cooperative ventures.

88. McEvoy, George F., and Cynthia S. Vincent. "Who Reads and Why?" JOURNAL OF COMMUNICATION 30 (Winter 1980): 134-140.

McEvoy and Vincent report the results of a study conducted in 1978 using a random sample of 1450 adults to determine patterns of adult reading in the United States. A profile of heavy readers and the kinds of materials read is presented. The authors suggest that three

factors appear to influence the amount and
kind of reading. These include the presence
of basic reading skills, the association of
pleasure with reading, and the ability to
integrate reading into an already active life.
The findings suggest that not all who can read
do, and that those who do read read a variety
of materials.

89. McGrail, Janet. ADULT ILLITERATES AND ADULT
     LITERACY PROGRAMS. A SUMMARY OF DESCRIPTIVE
     DATA. San Francisco, California: Far West
     Laboratory for Educational Research and
     Development; Andover, Massachusetts: Network
     of Innovative Schools, Inc., 1984. 29pp.
     (ED 254 756)

     McGrail presents data on two aspects of the
     current illiteracy problem in the United
     States. She provides numbers and
     characteristics of five main groups of
     illiterates: the elderly, minorities, the
     poor, the unemployed, and Southern and rural
     residents. She also examines the various
     categories of literacy programs: state
     administered under the Adult Education Act,
     volunteer, community based, correctional,
     military, business and industry, Federal
     occupational training, and college and
     university.

90. Micklos, John Jr. "Reading and Literacy--
     Alive and Well." READING HORIZONS 22
     (December 1982): 116-119.

     Micklos looks at the statistics available on
     literacy levels, educational attainment, the
     prevalence and amount of on-the-job and
     recreational reading, the total book sales and
     the kinds of books sold, and concludes that
     "literacy is not on its deathbed--it is well"
     (p. 118). He cites statistics, research
     studies, and surveys to support this
     conclusion.

91. Monteith, Mary K. "How Well Does the Average
     American Read? Some Facts, Figures and
     Opinions." JOURNAL OF READING 23 (February

1980): 460-464.

Monteith reviews selected ERIC/RCS documents
(1970-1979) that address the question of adult
reading ability. The answers provided are
"partial" (p. 460) and certainly
contradictory, ranging from "poorly" (p. 463)
and "worse" (ibid.) to "OK" (ibid.) and "fine"
(ibid.). The issues examined are useful in
defining and understanding the extent and
implications of adult reading problems. The
author reviews information on the questions of
what the average adult reading level is, what
the average American needs to read, what he
can read, and what he does read.

92. Negin, Gary A., and Dee Krugler. "Essential
    Literacy Skills for Functioning in an Urban
    Community." JOURNAL OF READING 24 (November
    1980): 109-115.

    Negin and Krugler identify the written
    materials an adult needs to be able to read in
    order to function effectively in an urban
    community. The materials encountered are
    those of everyday life such as medicine
    labels, bank statement, job applications, and
    street and traffic signs. The materials are
    analyzed to determine reading level,
    vocabulary, and functional skills required.
    The authors conclude "that the minimal level
    of literacy that Milwaukee demands of its
    adults is very high....In addition, literacy
    demands will probably increase in the future
    as society becomes more complex" (p. 113).
    Detailed information obtained from the
    analysis of different kinds of reading
    materials is included in the article.

93. Sticht, Thomas G. "Strategies for Adult
    Literacy Development." Paper presented at
    the National Adult Literacy Conference,
    January 19-20, 1984, Washington, D.C. 10pp.
    (ED 240 300)

    In reviewing the Adult Literacy Initiative
    Sticht suggests that adults view literacy as
    the means to an end, not as an end in itself.

Adults have an obligation to become literate in order to obtain both personal and national freedom. We must stress continuous development of literacy, not literacy to a particular point. He also discusses other adult literacy issues in the United States, ranging from the need to develop general assessment and instructional strategies, to problems of particular groups, such as ESL students and students in business and industry. In addition, he suggests that we need to identify differences in literacy development between the United States and other countries as well as differences between adults and children in order to fully understand our own literacy problems.

94.   Ulmer, Curtis, and James Dorland.   "Modern Adult Basic Education: An   Overview." OUTLOOK FOR THE 80'S: ADULT   LITERACY. Edited by Lorraine Y. Mercier. Washington, D.C.: U.S. Department of Education, Basic Skills Improvement Program, September 1981, pp. 1-21.

The authors provide a brief history of literacy education before and after 1964. They use that year as a dividing line because the Economic Opportunity Act of 1964 made illiteracy a national concern and paved the way for the development of adult education professionals. Ulmer and Dorland describe characteristics, attitudes, and needs of the adult illiterate. The impact of legislation and the development of adult literacy materials and curriculum are discussed. Current programs are examined and proposals made for the future. The authors foresee that literacy programs will become more social and political. There may well be a new administrative level of education developed that will serve the need of these particular adult students.

95.   U.S., Congress, House Committee on Education and Labor. ILLITERACY AND THE SCOPE OF THE PROBLEM IN THIS COUNTRY. HEARING BEFORE THE SUBCOMMITTEE ON POSTSECONDARY EDUCATION,

97th Cong., 2d sess., September 21, 1982.
87pp. (ED 244 145)

The verbal and prepared statements, letters,
and supplemental materials included here
provide a vivid picture of the problems and
programs associated with adolescent and adult
illiteracy. A variety of individuals and
organizations are represented testifying to
the growing and unanswered problem of adult
reading difficulties.

96. U.S., Congress, House Committee on Education
and Labor. OVERSIGHT HEARING ON ADULT
ILLITERACY. HEARING BEFORE THE SUBCOMMITTEE
ON POSTSECONDARY EDUCATION, 97th Cong., 2d
sess., December 2, 1982. 38pp. (ED 242
918)

Representatives of the private sector
testified on the extent of adult illiteracy,
its attendant problems and possible solutions.
One topic of interest was the role of the
Federal government and that of local
organizations. Suggestions included, for
example, that of Peter Waite, National
Director of the Laubach Literacy Action, for
community-based projects, for public, private,
and nonprofit partnerships, and for "massive
utilization of volunteers" (p. 4).

97. U.S., Congress, Senate Committee on Labor and
Human Resources. REAUTHORIZATION OF THE
ADULT EDUCATION ACT, 1984. HEARING BEFORE
THE SUBCOMMITTEE ON EDUCATION, ARTS AND
HUMANITIES ON THE PROPOSED AMENDMENTS TO
PUBLIC LAW 97-377, 98th Cong., 2d sess.,
March 20, 1984. 86pp. (ED 247 459)

The testimony included in this document
gives evidence of the scope and impact of
adult illiteracy in various parts of the
United States and includes brief statements on
some programs. Issues addressed include the
impact of the federal government on literacy
programs, and the role of the states in
determining and controlling programs and
coordinating services.

98. U.S., Department of Education. "On Literacy."
     CLEARINGHOUSE ON ADULT EDUCATION, Division
     of Adult Education Services, Washington,
     D.C., June 1983.

     This document provides a brief overview of
     current statistics on literacy, including the
     extent of functional illiteracy in the United
     States, the relationship of literacy to
     schooling, to earnings, and to employment, and
     the extent and composition of Adult Basic
     Education Programs.

99. U.S., Department of Education. "Special
     Issue: Adult Literacy." CLEARINGHOUSE ON
     ADULT EDUCATION, Division of Adult Education
     Services, Washington, D.C., January 1984.

     This issue is a compendium of current
     articles from newspapers, periodicals, and
     journals on the extent and implications of
     adult illiteracy in the United States as well
     as suggestions for alleviating the problem.
     It provides a unique combination of articles
     for the layman and reviews and reports for the
     professional. What emerges for the reader is
     a vivid picture of the adult illiterate, his
     place in our society, and a sense of possible
     routes to follow in overcoming this tremendous
     problem.

100. Wick, Tom. "The Pursuit of Universal
     Literacy." JOURNAL OF COMMUNICATION 30
     (Winter 1980): 107-112.

     Wick documents the historical changes in the
     definitions and uses of literacy from the time
     of Plato. Modern America has failed to
     achieve the goal of universal literacy,
     particularly for certain groups such as non-
     whites and males. The author explores the
     implications of this in terms of socio-
     economic class, occupation, and family
     structure.

Instruction: An Overview

101. Cranney, A. Garr. "The Literature of Adult

Reading: Selected References." JOURNAL OF READING 26 (January 1983): 323-331.

Cranney cites a rapid expansion in the literature on adult reading, noting, however, that the literature is dispersed and not always easily available. In this article he provides a list of selected, often annotated, references of works he considers both useful and accessible to the reader. Over 75 items covering major areas in the field of adult literacy and representing a variety of sources of information have been included.

102. _____. "Two Decades of Adult Reading Programs: Growth, Problems, and Prospects." JOURNAL OF READING 26 (February 1983): 416-422.

Cranney asserts that there has been substantial growth in the number of reading programs for adults in a variety of settings ranging from basic literacy to credit-bearing college courses. The number of non-school courses has increased, as has the number of commercial programs available to adults. One problem in the field that is being slowly solved is that of teacher training. However, the problems of lack of professional standards and of professional pay remain areas of concern. Cranney examines tests and materials and finds the first "limited" (p. 418) and the second "increased in quantity and somewhat in quality" (p. 421). Computer Assisted Instruction is not a replacement for "the compassionate attention and sympathetic understanding of skilled teachers" (p. 419), although it can perform a valuable service. He also examines program evaluation and the scope and sources of literature and finds both to be growth areas.

103. Fingeret, Arlene. ADULT LITERACY EDUCATION: CURRENT AND FUTURE DIRECTIONS. Columbus, Ohio: ERIC Clearinghouse on Adult, Career, and Vocational Education, 1984. 68pp. (ED 246 308)

In this paper Fingeret provides a guide to understanding not only topics and concepts relevant to the field of adult literacy instruction, but also the relationships among and between them. She reviews issues related to the variety of definitions of literacy and concludes that literacy is not a finished product but changes over time and with new situations and circumstances. The author presents reading models for the adult, reminding us of the paucity of research in the area and of the dangers of applying the results of studies conducted with children to adult students. She examines various perceptions of the adult illiterate and the impact of these perceptions on program development. A variety of program models and program components (planning and evaluation, instructors, instructional approaches and the curriculum, instructional methods and materials) are discussed. The reader is cautioned not to look for the best model or program but rather to investigate "which approach appears to meet the needs of which persons in particular circumstances" (p. 37).

104. Godbey, Gordon C., and Iran C. Mohsenin. DETERMINING MAINTENANCE OF ACHIEVEMENT FROM ABE PROGRAMS. University Park, Pennsylvania: Pennsylvania State University, Division of Education Policy Studies, June 1982. 68pp. (ED 229 564)

Godbey and Mohsenin report on a study conducted with former students in ABE classes (in 1974, 1976, and 1978) to determine the extent of maintenance and use of the acquired literacy skills. The authors found that they were maintained and used, generally through daily reading of all or part of a newspaper. Because of this, they concluded that it is cost-effective to recruit undereducated adults and teach literacy skills. Copies of the questionaire and interview script used are included.

105. Gold, Patricia Cohen, and Pamela L. Horn. "Achievement in Reading, Verbal Language,

Listening Comprehension and Locus of Control of Adult Illiterates in a Volunteer Tutorial Project." PERCEPTUAL AND MOTOR SKILLS 54 (1982): 1243-1250.

Gold and and Horn describe a study that analyzed achievement gains in youths and adults reading below the fifth grade level who were tutored for 34 hours by trained volunteers. The results were compared to gains in a similar group who did not receive tutoring. The findings confirmed that the subjects made significant gains in general reading and in discrete reading subskills but not in the other areas tested. The authors conclude that adults can improve reading abilities through tutoring and that trained volunteers can be used for this purpose. They suggest the need for more extensive tutoring to obtain more growth in achievement and the need for more research in this area.

106. Jones, Edward V. READING INSTRUCTION FOR THE ADULT ILLITERATE. Chicago: American Library Assn., 1981.

Jones gives us a broad perspective on the topic of illiteracy in the United States. He places the issues and concerns related to instruction and instructional programs clearly within the context of describing and defining adult illiteracy and adult learning. The author traces the changing definitions of literacy and illiteracy as they relate to changing societal demands and changing estimates of the extent of the problem. The cost of illiteracy to society, to the individual, and to the family is outlined, in both personal and financial terms. Programs and projects are reviewed with the warning that "as programs grow and the number of minimally educated persons diminishes, the extent of functional literacy competence needed to cope with modern living continues to increase" (p. 24). A profile of development stages in adulthood, adult learning patterns, and the social environment of adult illiteracy provides a useful framework for planning appropriate reading instruction.

With this information as a background Jones presents a program of reading instruction which based on a view of reading as a language-thinking process. He proposes teaching adults using a language experience approach as a basis, with reading subskills taught "to the learner only as he requires them to improve his reading ability--not in a manner which tries to insist that he learn in a particular way" (p. 70). Jones advocates setting up a program with the student and teacher working collaboratively to design the instruction and choose the materials. Detailed help is provided the teacher in the areas of the language experience approach, assisted reading, word identification, reading to learn, and writing as an aid to reading. In addition, the topic of diagnosis and assessment is explored with emphasis on informal instruments. Specific tests are identified and rated in four areas.

107. Karnes, Frances A., Clyde N. Gunn, and Beverly Bill Maddox, eds. ISSUES AND TRENDS IN ADULT BASIC EDUCATION: FOCUS ON READING. Jackson, Mississippi: University Press of Mississippi, 1980.

This book contains a collection of articles from a variety of journals--some from the field of reading and others from the field of adult education. Although the articles are somewhat dated, they do provide an overview of factors and issues involved in adult learning, teaching adults to read, diagnosis and evaluation of adult reading, methods of instruction, and innovative programs.

108. Kazemek, Francis E., and Pat Rigg. ADULT LITERACY. Newark, Delaware: International Reading Assn., 1984.

This annotated bibliography includes professional journal articles and books that focus on adult literacy. Topics included

are: the state of adult literacy nationally
and internationally, current philosophical
assumptions about literacy, research on the
nature of literacy and illiteracy, and
teaching (the adult learner, instructional
strategies, evaluation, and classroom
resources).

109. Lindsey, Jimmy D., and Leasa T. Jarman.
     "Adult Basic Education: Six Years After
     Kavale and Lindsey's Literature Review."
     JOURNAL OF READING 27 (April 1984): 609-
     613.

     Lindsey and Jarman address the problem
     raised by Kavale and Lindsey in 1977 of the
     limited effectiveness of ABE programs in
     promoting adult literacy. The current
     authors provide insight into changes taking
     place in the focus of quantitative and
     qualitative descriptors of programs, the
     extent and use of empirical data to study
     program designs and evaluations, research on
     reading strategies and instructional
     implications. While "significant progress
     has been made in ABE's research efforts since
     1977" (p. 612), Lindsey and Jarman identify a
     number of areas where further research is
     needed.

110. Lyman, Helen Huguenor. READING AND THE ADULT
     NEW READER. Chicago, Illinois: American
     Library Assn., 1976.

     Lyman recognizes the responsibility of
     libraries to provide services in response to
     needs. She also recognizes that by ignoring
     certain materials, libraries "impose limited
     services and resources" (p. 3). A changing
     focus of library services is the response to
     populations that have not been traditionally
     served. One of these groups is the adult new
     reader, the reader who is in the process of
     developing more mature reading skills. The
     author explores the extent of literacy
     problems and the heritage, values, and
     reading interests of a variety of readers of
     different ethnic and cultural backgrounds

often found in the category of "new reader."
She also examines the role and evaluation of
reading materials for the adult new reader.
In all of this, Lyman takes a broad view of
literacy. "Men and women of all ages can
read for amusement, instruction, and, most of
all, in order to live" (p. 13).

111. Newman, Anabel P.   ADULT BASIC EDUCATION:
     READING. Boston: Allyn and Bacon, 1980.

     This book is designed to be useful to both
     the professional teacher and the volunteer.
     It provides a brief overview of
     characteristics of adults and reading theory
     as an introduction to the practical matters
     of diagnosing and assessing students,
     establishing goals and objectives, planning
     strategies, programs and resources,
     integrating learning, and evaluating
     progress. Newman's aim is to provide
     "instruction that is meaningful, effective,
     and flexible" (p. 185). Numerous specific
     examples, suggestions, and aids are provided.

112. Phillips, Kathleen, et al.   RESEARCH AND
     DEVELOPMENT AGENDA. San Francisco,
     California: Far West Laboratory for
     Educational Research and Development;
     Andover, Massachusetts: Network of
     Innovative Schools, Inc., 1985. 33pp. (ED
     254 757)

     The research and development agenda of the
     National Adult Literacy Project is presented
     in this paper. The items were collated from
     other papers in the project and provide an
     overview of areas where we need additional
     knowledge. The areas identified include:
     attributes of adult beginning readers,
     diagnosis and assessment, staff training,
     impact of literacy programs on students'
     lives, teacher characteristics and
     methodologies, technology, and literacy
     development in other countries.

113. Smith, Edwin H., and McKinely Martin. "Do
     Adult Literacy Programs Make a Difference?"

LITERACY FOR DIVERSE LEARNERS. Edited by
Jerry L. Johns. Newark, Delaware:
International Reading Assn., 1975, pp. 87-
92.

The answer to the question posed by the
authors is generally "yes." Smith and Martin
review a number of studies done in New York,
Florida, Mississippi, and Missouri that
indicate an improvement in literacy skills.
The need to include "respectable evaluational
measures" (p. 91) is stressed as is the need
to insure relevancy of programs and to
provide motivation for students to enroll and
to succeed.

Instruction and Literacy Acquisition: Theory and Research

114. Amoroso, Henry C., Jr.   "On Becoming
      Literate: Personal Perspectives." Paper
      presented at the Annual Meeting of the
      American Educational Research Assn., April
      23-27, 1984, New Orleans, Louisiana. 15pp.
      (ED 248 410)

      Amoroso reports on interviews with adults
      who were learning to read. The purpose of
      the interviews was to identify motives for
      learning to read, concepts of the nature of
      the learning process, and perceptions of the
      role of teacher and student. Excerpts from
      the interviews are included in the paper and
      provide insights into these areas. A picture
      begins to emerge of the anxieties and
      uncertainties the adult illiterate
      experiences while attempting to become
      literate as well as the need he exhibits for
      understanding, approval, and respect. The
      importance of the student's growth in
      understanding about himself and his views of
      literacy is also evident in the interviews.

115. Boraks, Nancy, et al. ETHNOGRAPHIC RESEARCH
      ON READING INSTRUCTIONAL STRATEGIES FOR
      ADULT BEGINNING READERS. Richmond,
      Virginia: Virginia Commonwealth University,

1982. 161pp. (ED 239 072)

This research was designed to investigate instructional strategies for teaching adult students word recognition cues. The authors identify specific differences in learning-to-read behavior between adults and children in addition to four roadblocks for adults in the process of learning-to-read. Based on this information the strategies studied included phonemic cues, segmenting, phonemic/syntactic cues, variable vowel /e/, spelling clusters, and semantic cues. Two strategies were studied in depth: segmenting and variable vowel /e/. After receiving intensive inservice training, 90 percent of the teachers in the program felt that segmenting complemented their existing program and 57 percent believed that instruction in the use of the variable vowel /e/ was useful.

The authors also found that the existence of certain conditions promoted the acceptance of the use of a strategy by the adult student. These included, for example, factors such as the simplicity of the strategy and its use by peers, modeling by a teacher committed to the strategy, and knowledge of the fact that the strategy is a strategy and can be applied in many instances. They found too that the existence of certain conditions encouraged teachers to adopt particular instructional strategies. Again, simplicity and peer use were important as was the ability to incorporate the strategy into teaching style and current curriculum. In the case of both teacher and student, the need to avoid failure and risk and to succeed was critical.

116. _____, and Sally Schumacker. ETHNOGRAPHIC RESEARCH ON WORD RECOGNITION STRATEGIES OF ADULT BEGINNING READERS: TECHNICAL REPORT. Richmond, Virginia: Virginia Commonwealth University, 1981. 264pp. (ED 219 552)

Boraks and Schumacker describe and analyze

the reading behavior of members of adult
basic education classes in Richmond. The
sample used is small; a detailed analysis is
presented of seven students and a general
description given of seven more. The
findings, however, are interesting and
relevant to those teaching reading to adults.
Students who had a meaning approach to
reading and could actively manipulate vowels
and consonants tended to make progress.
Students who viewed reading as word calling
made less progress. It appeared important in
terms of student retention and progress to
have the teachers model the process of
learning and reading and take into account
student's learning styles. The authors do
more for us, however, than analyze reading
behavior. In addition, they present a vivid
picture of the students in the study and
share with us their backgrounds, their goals,
their reactions.

117. Charnely, A.H. and J.A. Jones. THE CONCEPT
     OF SUCCESS IN ADULT LITERACY. Cambridge,
     England: Huntington Publishers Limited,
     1979.

Charnely and Jones take a broad view of
literacy, seeing it as something that occurs
within a particular context and that relates
both to the demands of the written material
and to the needs and motivations of the
reading student. "Only a child can learn to
read; an adult learns to read something and
to some end" (p. 18). The student must not
be limited by behavioral objectives but must
be allowed to follow his own ends.

With this background, the authors
interviewed students who participated in the
Adult Literacy Campaign in England from 1974
to 1978. The students identified the kinds
of successes that were important to them.
Affective personal achievement was identified
as the most important, with affective social,
socio-economic, cognitive, and enactive
identified in decreasing order. The most
important achievement for students was their

new ability to feel confident and at ease
within themselves. Receiving tuition for
attending classes and using reading and
writing skills for daily tasks were
identified as the least important goals. The
book has implications for the recruitment and
motivation of students as well as for
planning instruction and programs.

118. Ferguson, Charles A. COGNITIVE EFFECTS OF
     LITERACY: LINGUISTIC AWARENESS IN ADULT
     NON-READERS. FINAL REPORT. Stanford
     California: Stanford University, Department
     of Linguistics, March 1981. 22pp. (ED 222
     857)

     The author reports on a project that
     examined possible relationships between
     linguistic awareness, level of literacy, and
     language background (monolingual vs.
     bilingual). Because of the limited size of
     the sample and the difficulties in finding
     participants who were non-literate, the
     author raises cautions about accepting the
     results as definitive. The results obtained
     did seem to indicate, however, that awareness
     of segmentation and the concept of "word"
     correlated with reading level, but not with
     language background. The report raises more
     questions than it answers--questions related,
     for example, to the directionality of the
     relationship between metalinguistic awareness
     and literacy level, to how adults define a
     word, and to the connection between dual
     language background and problems in acquiring
     literacy. These are matters of concern to
     the theorist, the researcher and, ultimately,
     to the teacher.

119. Gambrell, Linda B., and Betty S. Heathington.
     "Adult Disabled Readers' Metacognitive
     Awareness About Reading Tasks and
     Strategies." JOURNAL OF READING BEHAVIOR
     XIII (1981): 215-222.

     Gambrell and Heathington compared the
     metacognitive awareness of task and strategy
     variables of adult good readers and adult

disabled readers (below fifth grade level). There has been relatively little research done, according to the authors, in the area of adult disabled readers in general, and very little on how they perceive the reading process.

Task variables were identified as the reader's awareness of the role of motivation, prior knowledge, and the structure of text. Adult poor readers were aware of the role of motivation and interest as well prior knowledge in the task of reading. The authors suggest that this indicates the possible effectiveness of the language experience approach as an instructional strategy. Adult poor readers were not aware of the significance of text structure or organization in comprehending paragraphs and stories.

Strategy variables were identified as purposes for reading, reading mode, reading skills, and ways of resolving comprehension failure. The authors used the word "dramatic" to characterize the findings here. Adult poor readers viewed reading as a decoding, not a comprehending process. On every count, these students "reported fewer strategies, more misconceptions about strategies, and were not as sensitive to how and when to use specific reading strategies" (p. 220). The authors conclude that teachers must teach adults about the process of reading as well as provide instruction in appropriate comprehension and metacognitive strategies.

120. Gillis, M.K. "Influence of Background Experience and Interest on Instructional Level of Adult Beginning Readers." Paper presented at the Annual Meeting of the College Reading Assn., October 29-31, 1981, Louisville, Kentucky. 14pp. (ED 209 649)

Gillis examined the instructional levels of adult beginning reading texts using narrative, familiar content, and unfamiliar content materials. The author found significant differences among the three sets of materials, with unfamiliar content material having the lowest instructional level. This suggests the need to examine materials carefully in order to choose appropriate ones. The conclusion is particularly significant, since teachers in the study incorrectly chose materials for nearly half the students.

121.   _____. EFFECT OF BACKGROUND INFORMATION ON A.B.E. READERS' COMPREHENSION. FINAL REPORT. Austin: Texas Education Agency, Division of Adult Programs, February 1983. 11pp. (ED 226 200)

A study was conducted to determine the effect on comprehension of providing ABE students with background information before reading a selection. The background information consisted of pronounciation of new words, discussion about meaning, additional information about word meaning from the teacher, and a map that showed where the action of the selection would take place. Those readers who had access to the background information had better comprehension and gained more information than readers who did not have the information. The implication for teachers of adults is clear. We must prepare students for reading whether they are learning reading skills or acquiring content knowledge.

122.   Kirsch, Irwin S., and John T. Guthrie. "Adult Reading Practices for Work and Leisure." ADULT EDUCATION QUARTERLY 34 (Summer 1984): 213-232.

Kirsch and Guthrie report the findings of a study conducted with 99 adults from different occupations to determine the impact of occupation and setting on contents, materials, and uses for reading. A Reading Activity Inventory was developed and used in interviews. The results indicated that the complexity of reading demands that we

consider more than time spent reading and the
occupation of the reader. For example, time
spent reading brief documents and reference
material was consistently high for
occupational reading and low for leisure
reading regardless of occupation but the
content read differed for the various
occupational groups. The authors suggest
that knowledge of adult reading practices has
implications in motivating adult students,
developing and administering adult reading
tests, and planning literacy programs that
will provide efficient and relevant
instruction enabling individuals to "perform
tasks associated with a variety of social,
personal, and occupational contexts" (p.
231).

123. Longnion, Bonnie.   "Reading Strategies of
      Adult   Readers: Implications   for
      Instruction." LIFELONG LEARNING RESEARCH
      CONFERENCE PROCEEDINGS.   College Park,
      Maryland: University of Maryland Department
      of Agriculture and Extension Education,
      1982.   272pp.   (ED 215 198)

      Longnion reports on a study conducted to
      "examine the reading strategies of adult
      readers as they proceed through the text" (p.
      148) using ABE students, high risk college
      freshmen, and college seniors. Although some
      differences were found among the three
      groups, a number of significant similarities
      were identified.   All groups used
      graphophonic, syntactic, and semantic cue
      systems in reading and "readers at all levels
      need assistance from a teacher when a
      selection does not match his/her background
      of knowledge and experiences, language
      patterns, and ability to decode the words in
      the text" (p. 151).

      The author makes a number of suggestions
      for instruction in working with adults.
      These include using language experience,
      providing direct instruction, using familiar,
      relevant text for practice, providing needed
      background information, and selecting text

longer than a few sentences or paragraphs.

124.   Malicky, Grace, and Charles A. Norman.
       "Reading Strategies of Adult Illiterates."
       JOURNAL OF READING 25 (May 1982): 731-735.

       Malicky and Norman, recognizing the
       "paucity of information on how adult
       illiterates read" (p. 731), studied
       differences between children and adults who
       were learning to read. They found
       differences in the use of strategies at
       different points in the process that have
       implications for instruction. For example,
       adult students who relied heavily on graphic
       cues were aided in using their prior
       knowledge of language as a cue by a program
       that stressed the interactive, communicative
       nature of reading. Among other things the
       authors conclude that it is probably
       unrealistic to expect even, continuous gain
       in reading ability from adults. In fact, it
       may be beneficial to have periods of no-gain.
       The study found that differences do exist in
       the way adults and children learn to read
       which suggests the need for additional study
       in this area.

125.   Mikulecky, Larry J., Nancy Leavitt Shanklin,
       and David C. Caverly. ADULT READING
       HABITS, ATTITUDES, AND MOTIVATIONS: A
       CROSS-SECTIONAL STUDY. Bloomington,
       Indiana: Indiana University, School of
       Education, 1979.

       This study was undertaken for a number of
       reasons. There was a dearth of information
       in the area of adult reading habits,
       attitudes, and motivations that could be used
       to develop programs for them. In addition
       the information could further be used to
       insure that adults provided literacy role
       models for children and to examine the
       question of "aliteracy"--the phenomenon in
       which a person who can read does not. This
       study compares present findings to previous
       research identifying changes, for example, in
       job-related reading demands and in the kinds

and sources of help adults will seek when
they encounter reading difficulties. The
results of the study encourage providing a
variety of services and analyzing the
potential population in order to insure that
the services reach the adults who need them.

126. Schnell, Thomas R. "Teaching Educationally
     Disadvantaged Adults to Read: A Pilot
     Study." LITERACY FOR DIVERSE LEARNERS.
     Edited by Jerry L. Johns. Newark,
     Delaware: International Reading Assn.,
     1975, pp. 100-104.

     Schnell describes a study conducted to
     determine if intensive teaching of reading
     skills could improve the reading abilities of
     semiliterate adults and, if so, what
     materials would seem to be effective. The
     results indicated that reading skills could
     be improved through instruction. The group
     using "materials chosen for their utility in
     daily activities" (p. 102) without regard for
     reading level showed significantly higher
     gains than the group using high-interest
     materials at an appropriate reading level.
     Schnell concludes that the learner's
     motivation and interest in the materials is
     critical and that "no specially developed
     instructional materials are necessary" (p.
     104).

127. Schumacher, Sally. "Adult Development and
     Adult Beginning Reading Behaviors: An
     Exploratory Study." Paper presented at the
     Annual Meeting of the American Educational
     Research Assn., April, 1983, Montreal,
     Canada. 11pp. (ED 230 704)

     Schumacher reports on an study that found
     no pattern of relationship in 14 adults
     between age and developmental phase and
     motivation in learning to read. The dominant
     motivation appeared to be anxiety and
     frustration which occurred at all ages.
     Knowledge of adult developmental phases
     appeared important for the teacher because
     when "learning-to-read was an integral part

of a developmental task of an adult, the
adult showed progressive reading behaviors"
(p. 4). Because of the wide variations in
adults, the author suggests the use of both
individual and group instruction.

128. Sticht, Thomas G. EVALUATION OF THE "READING
      POTENTIAL" CONCEPT FOR MARGINALLY LITERATE
      ADULTS.   Alexandria, Virginia: Human
      Resources Research Organization, April
      1982.

      Sticht examines the assumptions made about
      adult illiterates in the traditionally brief
      reading programs provided for them. The
      expected substantial gain in reading level is
      often not achieved. Adults are expected to
      have oral language capabilities higher than
      those of grade school children. Thus adults
      have greater "reading potential" and will
      make more and faster progress than the grade
      school children in closing the "gap" between
      oral and written language capabilities.
      Sticht, in studying marginally literate men
      (MLM), found that in fact "the oral language
      skills of the MLM did not exceed those of the
      children" (p. 22). The expected greater
      "reading potential" did not exist. Nor did
      he find the expected substantial gain in
      general reading after brief, concentrated
      instruction in general literacy. He did
      find, however, that "marginally literate
      adults in a job-related reading program made
      twice the gain in job-related reading that
      they did in general reading, suggesting that
      more rapid learning of particular types of
      reading will occur when training is
      specifically focused on that type of reading
      rather than on 'general' literacy" (p. 23).

129. Whyte, Joan. "Language and Reading: A Study
      of Adult Literacy Students in Northern
      Ireland." JOURNAL OF READING 24 (April
      1981): 595-598.

      Whyte compared a group of adult male
      literacy students with a similar group of
      normal readers to determine whether

differences existed in linguistic and
cognitive functions. She found that the
literacy students obtained lower scores on
task that "required some kind of operation on
the material plus the production of language.
They seemed less able to integrate on a
verbal level when it involved synthesis,
selection, inference, memory plus verbal
expression about matters which they had not
experienced in concrete form" (p. 597). Does
lack of reading skill result in difficulties
with higher order thinking and language use
or do these difficulties cause poor reading
skills? We do not know at this point.

130. _____. "Does Comprehension Depend on
        Reading Age?" Paper presented at the
        Annual Meeting of the Reading Assn. of
        Ireland, September 1981. 14pp. (ED 211
        926)

        Whyte found, after studying the
        comprehension level of adult literacy
        students in Ireland, that comprehension does
        not depend on reading age (or reading level).
        The author concluded that these results
        confirmed that reading is an interactive
        process, in which prior knowledge is a
        critical variable both for reading words and
        for comprehending. Students were able to
        answer difficult questions correctly because
        of the impact of prior knowledge. This
        conclusion has implications for teachers in
        choosing appropriate materials and in
        teaching students strategies to use prior
        knowledge.

Instruction: Content and Methodology

131. Amoroso, Henry C. "Organic Primers for Basic
        Literacy Instruction." JOURNAL OF READING
        28 (February 1985): 398-401.

        Amoroso describes the organic primer
        approach as one that combines the "central
        concepts of Freire's (1972) generative word
        approach with psycholinguistic notions about

the reading process" (p. 398). The author
points out the similarities between this
approach and the one used in the Cuban
literacy campaign. The organic primer
includes active stories with an eclectic
content using natural and predictable
language. The emphasis is on using meaning
and syntax to read words, not on mastering a
set of sequential subskills. Directions are
provided for the construction and use of
organic primers.

132. Boraks, Nancy, and Judy Richardson.
    "Teaching the Adult Beginning Reader:
    Designing Research Based Reading
    Instructional Strategies." Paper presented
    at the Annual Meeting of the College
    Reading Assn., October 29-31, 1981,
    Louisville, Kentucky. 20pp. (ED 216 329)

    Boraks and Richardson base their
    suggestions for instruction on the assumption
    that teachers need to broaden the social
    context of the adult learner, to enable the
    adult to become an active learner, and to
    focus on reading as meaning not as word
    calling or decoding. The authors advocate
    eight principles for instruction and provide
    a theoretical and research base and specific
    instructional suggestions for each one. The
    eight principles include teaching time
    management, providing appropriate materials,
    enlarging the adults social/cultural
    environment, encouraging individual
    approaches to word recognition, focusing on
    the organization of written materials, using
    a language-experienced based program,
    learning words in context, and beginning with
    concrete materials and moving to more
    abstract.

133. Cassidy, Jack, and Timothy Shanahan.
    "Survival Skills: Some Considerations."
    JOURNAL OF READING 23 (November 1979): 136-
    140.

    Cassidy and Shanahan illustrate the
    similarity in demands between traditional

reading skills taught in elementary school and those taught in survival reading courses for adults. Since appropriate materials are critical in survival reading, the authors suggest criteria for selecting functional materials. They do not, however, neglect reading for enjoyment.

134. Colvin, Ruth J., and Jane Root. TUTOR: TECHNIQUES USED IN THE TEACHING OF READING. Syracuse, New York: Literacy Volunteers of America, 1984.

Colvin and Root present material designed to enable the inexperienced tutor to work in the area of adult basic literacy. They provide guidance in developing reading through the Language Experience Approach, reading words through phonics, the sight approach, and the use of context, developing comprehension, planning lessons, and using materials.

135. Escoe, Adrienne S. "The Communication Experience Approach to Learning Basic Skills." Paper presented at the Annual Meeting of the College Reading Assn., October 26-29, 1977, Cincinnati, Ohio. 8pp. (ED 157 034)

The Communication Experience Approach is very similar to the Language Experience Approach, except that the former recognizes and responds to the individual's social needs. The student identifies a purpose for communicating which becomes the means of developing a social skill. Speaking, writing, reading, and listening are integral parts of the process. The communication product is revised and then used in a real situation. A sample lesson plan and examples of CEA situations are included.

136. Freire, Paulo. "The Importance of the Act of Reading." JOURNAL OF EDUCATION 165 (Winter 1983): 5-11.

Freire explores the relationship between

reading and world knowledge, between reading
and comprehension, and between reading and
decoding. He personalizes this exploration
by examining his own childhood and his growth
in literacy. He views literacy as dynamic,
an interaction between the word and the
world. He also provides some general
conclusions about adult reading--for example,
that reading is a great deal more than
decoding. Reading instruction cannot rely on
students "mechanically memorizing vowel
sounds" (p. 10) and cannot reduce "learning
to read and write merely to learning words,
syllables, or letters" (ibid.). The words
used in literacy instruction must come from
the students' experience. "Reading always
involves critical perception, interpretation,
and re-writing what is read" (p. 11).

137.   Harrison, David, Barbara Little, and Graham
       Mallett. READING DEVELOPMENT: A RESOURCE
       BOOK FOR ADULT BASIC EDUCATION. Victoria,
       British Columbia, Canada: Ministry of
       Education, Province of British Columbia,
       1982.

       This handbook provides guidance for
       developmental reading instruction beyond the
       level of basic literacy yet still within the
       scope of adult basic education. The authors
       include a brief theoretical overview of
       reading and of adult learning, proposing that
       reading is a holistic process, that the
       reader's background information is of
       "overwhelming" (p. 5) importance, and that
       instructional materials "should parallel the
       kind of reading that adults do in normal
       living" (p. 6). Specific techniques and
       strategies are provided, with examples and
       materials, for developing lessons in
       comprehension, vocabulary, reading rate,
       reading to learn, reading for special
       purposes, and reading for enjoyment. An
       annotated bibliography of student materials
       is included. Much of the handbook can be
       adapted to instruction in basic literacy,
       using appropriate materials.

138. Hoffman, Lee McGraw. "ABE Reading
     Instructions: Give Them Something to Read."
     COMMUNITY COLLEGE REVIEW 8 (Summer 1980):
     32-37.

     Hoffman decries the lack of substantial and
     conclusive research in the area of ABE,
     particularly as regards program effectiveness
     in teaching adults to read. The author
     examines research in the areas of teacher
     training, direct vs. indirect instruction,
     materials and methods, and processes in adult
     reading. Implications for instruction are
     suggested, such as: using teacher- or
     student-made materials, planning time use
     effectively so students are reading not
     merely engaging in reading-related tasks,
     allowing the student to improve in reading by
     reading material that will enable him to
     reach a goal. She suggests a "radical
     prescription" (p. 36): "find what the learner
     wants to read and provide it" (ibid.).

139. Kazemek, Francis E. WRITING IN THE ADULT
     LITERACY PROGRAM: A THEORETICAL BASE.
     1983. 16pp. (ED 243 123)

     Kazemek builds a case for including writing
     in adult literacy instruction because of the
     interaction between reading and writing in
     the development of meaning. The act of
     writing has implications for the development
     of adult literacy skills. The writer becomes
     cognizant of the role of the author's purpose
     and the impact of reaction of the intended
     audience as he himself writes. In defining
     and developing the concept of writing,
     Kazemek broadens the definition of functional
     literacy. "Reading a poem for wonder and joy
     is just as valid a function as reading an
     employment application" (p. 11). In fact,
     instruction should begin with reading and
     writing poems then "move out from poetry to
     other functions of reading and writing" (p.
     12). This approach would allow adults to
     analyze, raise questions, and become involved
     cognitively and affectively in the acts of
     reading and writing.

140.   _____. "'I wauted to be a Tencra to
        help penp to 1_____': Writing for Adult
        Beginning Learners." JOURNAL OF READING 27
        (April 1984): 614-619.

        Kazemek investigates the variety of writing
        activities found in adult programs and finds
        they generally involve writing for functional
        purposes.   She advocates writing as a means
        of   "learning,   knowing,   exploring,   and
        'composing   the   mind'"   (p.   615).   Writing
        enables the writer to think like a reader.
        It is a natural part of reading.   She
        includes comments on a program she and her
        colleagues   developed   as   well as samples of
        students'   written   stories,   poems,   and
        functional lists.   Suggestions are made to
        the teacher on structuring lessons.

141.   _____.   "Functional Literacy Is Not
        Enough: Adult Literacy as a Developmental
        Process." JOURNAL OF READING 28 (January
        1985): 332-335.

        In   the   context   of   advocating the use of
        reading   and   writing   poetry   and   language
        experience   stories,   Kazemek comments on the
        differences   between   literacy   training   and
        literacy   development.   Literacy   training
        results in the manipulation of the surface
        structure of written language, in "survival"
        skills, not in the development of the ability
        to "express and create as well as to analyze
        and   communicate" (p.   335), which is the
        hallmark of literacy development.   Literacy
        cannot be acquired in a short amount of time.

142.   Koenke, Karl.   "Teaching Adults to Read:
        Exhortations, Explanations, and Examples."
        JOURNAL OF READING 22 (March 1979): 552-
        555.

        Koenke reviews ERIC/RCS documents on issues
        and examples related to teaching adults to
        read.   Issues discussed include, for example,
        characteristics   of   ideal programs, teaching
        strategies, materials and methods, and the
        relation of curriculum development to adult

characteristics. The author concludes, on
the basis of the variety of suggestions made
in the literature, that "the profession can
continue to expect varying types of ABE
programs in the future because there are
different groups of people who want to read
different types of materials for different
purposes" (p. 552).

143. Lamorella, Rose Marie, John Tracy, Anne Marie
     Bernazza Haase, and Garrett Murphy.
     "Teaching the Functionally Illiterate
     Adult: A Primer." READING HORIZONS 23
     (Winter 1983): 89-94.

     The authors discuss theory and research
     related to adult learning, adult reading,
     testing and diagnosis, and materials and
     instructional strategies. In each area,
     implications for teachers are explicit. In
     remediation the method ought to be one of
     teaching sequential skills, based on a
     diagnostic/prescriptive approach, and using a
     variety of commercial materials. The
     interaction between teacher and student is
     important both in student learning and
     retention of the student in the program.

144. Mocker, Donald W. "Cooperative Learning
     Process: Shared Learning Experience in
     Teaching Adults to Read." READING AND THE
     ADULT LEARNER. Edited by Laura S. Johnson.
     Newark, Delaware: International Reading
     Assn., 1980, pp. 35-40.

     Mocker uses as the basis for his proposal
     the fact that there are differences between
     adults and children, He points particularly
     to the differences in background information
     of adults and children and the differences in
     purpose. Adults generally have specific
     needs and plans for applying new knowledge.
     He draws on Knowles' notion of andragogy in
     suggesting a modification of the directed
     reading lesson and the directed reading-
     thinking activity. In cooperative learning,
     the student selects his own material and
     determines his own purpose for reading it.

Mocker involves the student in the reading
lesson through problem solving and
predicting. Role playing encourages
interaction between students. Transfer of
skills to real life situations is critical.

145.   Rigg, Pat. "Petra: Learning to Read at 45."
       Paper presented at the Annual Meeting of
       the Teachers of English to Speakers of
       Other Languages, March 16-19, 1983,
       Toronto, Canada. 22pp. (ED 249 761)
       (Also published in JOURNAL OF EDUCATION 167
       (1985): 129-151.)

       Rigg vividly describes Petra's motivation
       to learn to read as well as her firm
       conviction that reading was getting "the
       letters right" (p. 12). This view of reading
       conflicted with the psycholinguistic view
       held by both the author and the tutor which
       was that reading was building meaning. Rigg
       documents the continuous adjustment that was
       made to accommodate both views of reading
       while respecting the adult status and
       integrity of the student. The author
       highlights missed opportunities for the
       student and for the tutor relating to themes
       and stereotypes of women and Mexican
       immigrants.

146.   Sharpe, Connie, and Leonore Ganschow.
       "Teaching an Adult to Read: A Case Study."
       JOURNAL OF DEVELOPMENTAL & REMEDIAL
       EDUCATION 5 (Spring 1983): 22-23, 26.

       Sharpe and Ganschow believe that while
       "most adult basic education programs are
       centered on the use of various materials with
       emphasis on specific skills" (p. 22), this
       approach is not appropriate for all adult
       students. In fact, for students who have had
       this type of instruction for a number of
       years and have met with little success,
       another method may be needed. The program
       the authors developed was based on a
       psycholinguistic approach to literacy that
       involved total language skills, used
       materials important to the students,

interrelated all communication skills, and stressed guessing and using errors for instructional purposes. The emphasis was firmly on the meaning of the written material. The authors provide a detailed diary of the course of instruction and evidence for gains made in both test scores and student attitude.

147. Singh, Judy, Nirbhay N. Singh, and Neville M. Blampied. "Using Repeated Reading to Increase the Reading Proficiency of Adult Learners." LIFELONG LEARNING 8 (October 1984): 8-11.

The authors suggest a reading approach based on the theory of automatic information processing proposed by LaBerge and Samuels. Repeated reading of material allows the reader to attain automaticity in word recognition skills and thus to devote his attention to comprehension. Singh, Singh, and Blampied advocate extending the Language Experience Approach with repeated listening and reading of the student's material and suitable commercial materials. Evidence is cited showing the effectiveness of this technique with children, but only one study is available documenting its usefulness with adults. The authors point out the need for further research.

148. Thistlethwaite, Linda. "Teaching Reading to the ABE Student Who Cannot Read." LIFELONG LEARNING 7 (September 1983): 5-7, 28.

Thistlethwaite presents a brief, easily understood, comprehensive explanation of three current reading theories: bottom-up, top-down, and interactive. She favors the last alternative and provides a number of suggestions for strategies that will enable the beginning adult reader to focus on comprehension, while using decoding skills as needed in the process. She suggests assisted reading, language experience approach, integration of listening and discussion with reading, reading through writing, daily reading activities, and reading aloud to adults. In all of these activities, the stress is on the adult as an independent learner and on approaching the task through comprehension rather than through phonics and small sequential skills.

149. _____. "The Adult Disabled Reader--An Independent Learner?" LIFELONG LEARNING 7 (November 1983): 16-17, 28.

Thistlethwaite examines characteristics of adult learners that are relevant to reading and proposes appropriate instructional and learning strategies. Adults are capable of self-direction in learning, but adult disabled readers (below fifth grade reading level) may have barriers to assuming self-direction. Such barriers might include lack of goals, fear and insecurity, lack of confidence and of motivation, failure to understand "why" they are doing a task, and lack of understanding of the critical role of meaning in reading. The author makes suggestions in each area for instructional strategies. The emphasis is on a comprehension-based model of reading using appropriate techniques such as knowledge of the reading process, comprehension monitoring, and sustained silent reading.

150. Ulmer, Curtis. "Responsive Teaching in Adult Basic Education." NEW DIRECTIONS FOR CONTINUING EDUCATION 6 (1980): 9-15.

Teachers of adults face a dual challenge. Adult students must be encouraged to persist in an educational program and they must be taught educational content. Teachers, in order to accomplish these tasks, need to have knowledge of content, of learners, and of methods, particularly those relevant to adults. A specific example for teaching reading is included, based on the premise that "learning to read reflects basic thought association patterns" (p. 13). Guidelines are also provided that include teaching basic associations of time, space, and amount;

using the sentence as the basis of instruction and moving quickly to the paragraph; and teaching students to print.

Instruction: Word Recognition and Functional Reading

151. Afflerback, Peter P., Richard L. Allington, and Sean A. Walmsley. "A Basic Vocabulary of U.S. Federal Social Program Applications and Forms." JOURNAL OF READING 23 (JANUARY 1980): 332-336.

The list of words provided in this article was compiled from a study of six health and income support forms used frequently by the aged but not all limited to use by the elderly. The authors found that the forms required knowledge of a "difficult and extensive unfamiliar vocabulary" (p. 335) with few words appearing on all the forms. The authors suggest the need for instruction in these words in literacy programs, alternative ways of obtaining needed information, and revision of required forms.

152. Bunner, Linda G. "The Remediation of a Graphophonic Decoding Deficit in an Adult." JOURNAL OF READING 27 (November 1983): 145-151.

Bunner describes a tutoring experience with an adult who had a wide experiential background and good oral language skills, but had difficulty decoding words. He was able to predict content in written text but could not read critical words. The program developed for him included oral reading, "look alike" words, key words, and self-monitoring strategies. The author also points out the importance of a supportive, task oriented classroom atmosphere.

153. Hansen, Cheryl L., and Phil Feinburg. "Which Words Shall They Learn?" Paper presented at the Annual Meeting of the Far West Regional Conference of the International Reading Assn., April 1-3, 1982, Portland,

Oregon. 19pp. (ED 216 314)

Using a wide variety of sources (publishers lists, curriculum guides, and teachers' rankings) the authors developed six lists of high utility sight words categorized according to intent or meaning. Hansen and Feinburg include the lists in the monograph. Rank ordering of words within the lists is also indicated as a way of helping teachers plan which words to include in instruction.

154. Joynes, Yvonne D., Sandra McCormick, and William L. Heward. "Teaching Reading Disabled Students to Read and Complete Employment Applications." JOURNAL OF READING 23 (May 1980): 709-714.

Joynes, McCormick, and Heward report on a program developed for readers age 15-18 in a correctional institution. The article provides copies of materials used and complete instructions for developing a nine step training program. Each item in the example provided is discussed and practiced, along with appropriate variations in words and wording. The authors suggest that the program can be used with older disabled readers.

155. McWilliams, Lana J. "Riding and Reading." JOURNAL OF READING 22 (January 1979): 337-339.

McWilliams provides a list of over 125 common highway signs that a driver should be able to read in order to insure safety on the roads. Many of these signs are clearly beyond the skills of "less able readers, those unfamiliar with the language and terminology, or even those who can read well enough, but too slowly to be able to see the words as a car travels quickly past" (p. 338). She suggests the list be used in adult literacy classes.

156. Meyer, Valerie. "Prime-O-Tec: A Successful Strategy for Adult Disabled Readers."

JOURNAL OF READING 25 (March 1982): 512-515.

Meyer reports on research conducted to determine the effectiveness of a multisensory technique for teaching decoding and comprehension to adults. The student listens to material recorded on a tape, follows the written text with his finger, and reads along with the recording. "The listening, seeing, saying, and touching must all be in unison" (p. 512). A group of 20 adults were included in the study, equally divided between a control group and an experimental group. The results indicated that the method was useful for developing sight vocabulary but not for improving reading comprehension. The author indicates the need for further research in the field of reading instruction for the adult basic education student.

157. Wangberg, Elaine G., Bruce Thompson, and Justin E. Levitov. "First Steps Toward an Adult Basic Word List." JOURNAL OF READING 28 (December 1984): 244-247.

The authors compiled a list of words used frequently by 22 illiterate adults in the composition on a microcomputer of language experience stories. The lesson was interactive, with the microcomputer program randomly generating questions and comments as the student wrote the story in response to a list of topics. The word list was developed both as a spelling aid to the students and as a resource for teachers in planning instruction.

Instruction: Vocabulary and Comprehension

158. Holland, V. Melissa, and Janice C. Redish. STRATEGIES FOR UNDERSTANDING FORMS AND OTHER PUBLIC DOCUMENTS. Document Design Project, Technical Report No. 13. Washington, D.C.: American Institute for Research; Pittsburgh, Pennsylvania: Carnegie-Melon University; New York, New York: Siegel and Gale, Inc., September

1981. 29pp. (ED 213 028)

The authors examined forms from the perspective of discourse analysis and have identified text characteristics that appear in most forms. They relate the reading of forms to the reader's prior knowledge. Three levels of reading skill for forms are discussed and a model of functional reading is proposed. Holland and Redish analyze a typical form and highlight the problems readers may have comprehending and completing it. General suggestions are made for instruction, with the promise of more to come after further study.

159. Johnston, Suzanne. ADULT READING LABORATORY. BUILDING COMPREHENSION IN ADULT EDUCATION STUDENTS. Oakland Adult Reading Laboratory, 1980. 16pp. (ED 219 501)

Johnston describes an individualized method of teaching reading to adults that focuses on the comprehension and organizational skills they lack. She stresses critical reading, organizational patterns, and features of the text. The students in this program showed an improvement in comprehension, motivation, and attitude.

160. Keefe, Don, Valerie Meyer, and Claire Lindberg. "Adult Disabled Readers: Instructional Strategies to Improve Comprehension." READING WORLD 21 (May 1982): 320-325.

The authors review a research study they conducted that found that adult disabled readers generally viewed reading as a process of decoding or word reading, not as one of obtaining meaning. The 15% who were classified as "meaning makers" "made significantly greater gains in Adult Basic Education (ABE) programs than did their counterparts" (p. 320). The article provides specific suggestions including questions for a reading interview, a series of activities used to confirm for the adult student that

reading is a meaning-based process, and items
for informally assessing students' approaches
to reading.

Materials: Selection, Preparation, Examples, and Readability

161. Abram, Marie J. "Readability: Its Use in
     Adult Education." LIFELONG LEARNING: THE
     ADULT YEARS 4 (January 1981): 8-9, 30-31.

     Abram stresses the need to match the
     readability level of a text with the reader's
     skill level in order to promote reading as a
     method of instruction, to increase learning,
     and to reduce the time needed to read a
     selection. She describes the history of
     readability formulas, discusses ways of
     rewriting text, and suggests means of
     determining individual and group reading
     levels (reading tests, cloze tests, and self-
     assessment).

162. The Adult Learning Association. RESOURCE
     GUIDE. Waterville, Washington, 1982.

     This guide contains an extensive annotated
     bibliography of materials for adult students
     in adult basic education, GED preparation,
     ESL, and job/college preparation, as well as
     materials for professionals.

163. Armstrong, Audrey A., and Sally P. Hunt,
     comps.; Nan Hawkins Witcher and Susanne
     Nolan, anns. THE NEW VITAL BIBLIOGRAPHY. A
     Basic Collection of Books and Learning
     Materials for an Adult Literacy Program.
     Bloomington, Indiana: Monroe County Public
     Library, 1983.

     This is a useful and practical source of
     information for those concerned with teaching
     reading in adult literacy programs.
     Annotated references are provided for
     professional materials (professional reading
     for tutors, adult literacy curriculum guides,
     and training programs); instructional
     materials (language arts, GED preparation,

mathematics, ESL materials, games, word
cards, and periodicals); life management
skills; reading for information; reading for
pleasure; and easy reading materials for
adults.

164.   Atwood, Beth S.   READABILITY: DEFINING THE
        PROBLEMS, FINDING SOLUTIONS. A Connecticut
        ABE Staff Development Project Resource
        Unit.   West Hartford, Connecticut: Capitol
        Region Education Council, June 1977.   17pp.
        (ED 226 323)

        Atwood discusses problems associated with
        readability formulas and examines the
        elements which are not included in the
        formulas but which affect readability, such
        as prior knowledge, language, style,
        organization of information, and visual
        format.   The Fry formula for adult
        readability is reviewed.

165.   Bhola, H.S. WRITING FOR NEW READERS: A BOOK
        ON FOLLOW-UP BOOKS. Workshop. Bonn, West
        Germany: German   Foundation   for
        International Development, 1981.   192pp.
        (ED 239 821)

        Bhola addresses the issue of suitable
        materials for new adult readers, particularly
        in developing countries.   Based on the
        premise that reading materials should support
        lifelong learning and promote communication,
        the author provides guidance for policy
        makers, publishers and writers. He includes
        suggestions for training writers how to write
        such materials.

166.   Carey, Susan.   "15 Nonfiction Books for
        Developing Adult Readers."   JOURNAL OF
        READING 27 (MARCH 1984): 520-522.

        Carey provides a list of nonfiction books
        for the adult reader who has a fourth to
        tenth grade reading level.   The categories
        included are biography, education, science,
        self development, and psychology.

167. Carmen, Florence W. "Selection and Use of
      Materials in Adult Basic Education Literacy
      Instruction."   NEW   DIRECTIONS   FOR
      CONTINUING EDUCATION 17 (March 1983): 85-
      93.

      Carmen relates the effectiveness of
      materials to the "features of the instructor
      and the social environment" (p. 86). In
      fact, training for teachers of adults in
      methodology is held to be less important than
      developing the teachers' abilities to
      challenge, motivate, and allow students to
      become independent and to assume
      responsibility for their own learning.
      Within this context, the author provides
      guidelines for choosing materials. For
      example, the materials should be self-
      instructional, with questions that can be
      checked by reader. In addition they should
      have content, format, and language suitable
      for adults. Creative writing is seen as a
      way of improving language and self-concept.
      A short, annotated bibliography for teachers
      and for students is included.

168. Cranney, A. Garr. BIBLE REFERENCES BY
      COMPUTER FOR ADULT READING TEACHERS. 1981.
      14pp. (ED 214 114)

      Cranney accepts the basic premise of
      separation of church and state, but also
      recognizes that adults often express an
      interest in and need to learn to read the
      Bible, particularly in church-supported
      settings. He identifies Bible passages that
      can be used by reading teachers. A reference
      list is included.

169. Ellowitch, Azi. WHAT'S ON YOUR MIND? READING
      AND LANGUAGE ACTIVITIES FOR ADULT BASIC
      EDUCATION EMPHASIZING THEMES FROM THE WORLD
      OF WORK. Philadelphia, Pennsylvania: La
      Salle College, June 1983. 183pp. (ED 244
      110)

      The material and suggestions in this manual
      are for adults who are unemployed and

presumed to be members of minority groups.
The readings are job-related in some way and
are followed by questions or activities for
comprehension, vocabulary or grammar, and
writing.

170.   Holcomb, Carol Ann. "Reading Difficulty of
       Informational Materials from a Health
       Maintenance Organization." JOURNAL OF
       READING 25 (November 1981): 130-133.

       Holcomb provides an example of the
       practical application of a readability
       formula (the Flesch Reading Ease formula) to
       the problem of identifying potential
       difficulties in widely available reading
       materials. A random selection of materials
       distributed by a health organization was
       evaluated according to the formula and found
       to be too difficult for most of the program's
       enrollees. The suggestions made by the
       author, such as simplifying vocabulary and
       sentence structure and writing at levels
       appropriate for the specific audience,
       illustrate some uses of readability formulas.

171.   Jefferson County Adult Reading Program.
       ATTITUDES   APPLICATION   ACTIONS:
       EMPLOYABILITY SKILLS FOR THE ADULT LITERACY
       STUDENT. Kentucky Department of Education,
       no date.

       This booklet provides an outline for
       developing work-related skills and includes
       examples of materials and activities.

172.   Jefferson County Adult Reading Program.
       GUIDE TO THE SELECTION OF ADULT LITERACY
       MATERIALS: ANALYZE BEFORE YOU BUY.
       Kentucky Department of Education, no date.

       This document includes descriptions and
       critiques of six basal reading series for
       adults, supplementary materials from six
       publishers, and three reading tests.
       Criteria for evaluating reading materials are
       suggested and references are given for
       further study of readability formulas.

Bibliographies for student and teacher
resources, as well as publishers addresses
are included. Finally, eight common
instructional approaches are described
briefly, with advantages and disadvantages
listed.

173. Kennedy, Katherine, and Ellen Sarkisian.
GAMES AND BUTTERFLIES. A RESOURCE BOOK FOR
TEACHERS OF ADULT BASIC EDUCATION.
ESPECIALLY THOSE WHO TEACH ENGLISH AS A
SECOND LANGUAGE. Syracuse, New York: New
Readers Press, 1979.

This collection of games and teaching
techniques is described by the authors as an
"addition to our teaching" (p. 3) enabling
students to practice and master skills. The
games are divided into four categories:
getting to know people, listening and
speaking, reading, and writing. Each of the
last three have activities on three levels:
words, sentences and more than sentences. In
many instances the format of the game may be
familiar to the elementary or secondary
teacher but the examples given are
appropriate to adults. The activities
require few materials and are easily adapted
to various groups.

174. Korpl, Barbara, comp. MATERIALS FOR TEACHING
ADULT FUNCTIONAL LITERACY IN NORTH DAKOTA.
ANNOTATED BIBLIOGRAPHY. Dickerson, North
Dakota: Dickerson Public School District,
April 1979. 171pp. (ED 199 479)

This extensive bibliography includes not
only a wide variety of informational and
training materials for the professional, but
also materials for the student in developing
coping skills. Special sections are included
for working with adults and for teaching
English as a second language.

175. Lawson, V.K. THINKING IS A BASIC SKILL:
CREATING HUMANITIES MATERIALS FOR THE ADULT
NEW READER. Syracuse, New York: Literacy
Volunteers of America, Inc., 1981. 65pp.

(213 822)

Based on the premise that adults reading
below the fifth grade level need stimulating,
relevant materials, Lawson describes in
detail how to develop reading materials based
on the humanities in order to bring these
adults closer to the political and cultural
mainstream. He suggests a collaboration of
librarians, literacy program personnel
(learners, tutors and staff), and humanists.
The author provides guidelines and timetables
for creating, writing, editing, publishing,
and funding the project. The samples of
original and edited materials are especially
useful.

176. _____, B.J. MacDonald, and Margaret
      Williams. READ ALL ABOUT IT! TUTOR ADULTS
      WITH DAILY NEWSPAPER. TUTOR HANDBOOK.
      Syracuse, New York: Literacy Volunteers of
      America, Inc., 1984. (ED 244 518)

This handbook is designed to enable tutors
to use all parts of the newspaper to teach
reading and critical thinking skills. The
material is keyed to the Adult Performance
skill levels. Sample lesson plans are
included. (See also entry 212.)

177. Literacy Volunteers of America, Inc.
      BIBLIOGRAPHY OF ADULT AND TEENAGE READING
      MATERIALS, ESL, AND THE HUMANITIES.
      Syracuse, New York: Author, 1980.

This bibliography contains basic reading
books for adults organized according to the
Adult Performance Level categories and listed
with reading levels. In addition,
information is provided on books in the
humanities that are appropriate for adult
literacy students. A list of publishers is
also included.

178. Manning, Diane Thompson. "Everyday Materials
      Improve Adults' Reading." JOURNAL OF
      READING 21 (May 1978): 721-724.

Manning asserts that adults need materials that insure "immediate and practical application of reading skills" (p. 721) and that "foster active student participation" (ibid.). The use of common, everyday reading matter such as newspapers, information materials, and magazines, can achieve these aims. The author describes in some detail a program using these materials.

179. Newman, Anabel P., and George W. Eyster. "Checklist for Evaluating Adult Basic Education Reading Material." JOURNAL OF READING 24 (May 1981): 701-706.

The checklist included in this article was prepared by the Committee for Basic Education and Reading of the IRA. It includes ratings on: appeal, relevance, purpose, process, human relations, evaluation, function, format, teacher directions, and content. Using the checklist, it is possible to assign a numerical rating to reading material. The article also includes instructions on determining the readability level of material using Robert Gunning's Fog Index.

180. O'Brien, Roberta Luther, comp. BOOKS FOR ADULT NEW READERS. Cleveland, Ohio: Project LEARN, August 1982. 386pp. (ED 224 878)

This annotated bibliography contains a wealth of suggestions for materials useful in developing skills, acquiring knowledge, and reading for pleasure. The APL subject areas were used as a basis for compiling the non-fiction section. O'Brien has made the criteria for selection clear and applicable to a wide range of readers. The emphasis is on materials that are directly relevant to adults.

181. Quarg, Patrice. SMOKE SIGNALS: AN ADULT NATIVE AMERICAN READING AND WRITING SKILLS WORKBOOK. Phoenix: Affiliation of Arizona Indian Centers, Inc., 1981. 116pp. (ED 227 990)

This workbook is designed to help students
pass the reading and writing sections of the
General Educational Development (GED) exam.
It illustrates how a variety of reading and
writing skills can be integrated into content
that is relevant and particular to a group of
adults. The materials in this case are
Southwest Indian myths, legends, poems, and
history.

182. Rigg, Pat, and Francis E. Kazemek. "For
    Adults Only: Reading Materials for Adult
    Literacy Students." JOURNAL OF READING 28
    (May 1985): 726-731.

    Rigg and Kazemek recognize the recent
    growth in the number of commercial materials
    available for use in adult basic literacy
    instruction. At the same time, they are
    critical of many of these materials because
    of their frequent focus on "cracking the
    code" (p. 727) and their lack of emphasis on
    reading as a "meaning-building process"
    (ibid.). The authors identify six criteria
    to use in the selection of adult literacy
    materials. They must be meaningful and
    complete, have literary merit, be readily
    available and inexpensive, and "promote the
    integration of...students' developed language
    abilities, reading and writing" (p. 728).
    Rigg and Kazemek provide numerous examples of
    the use of country music, religious writing,
    and poetry in adult literacy classes. They
    also suggest such instructional strategies as
    the language experience approach, students'
    own writings, rereading, and the cloze
    technique.

183. Shaw, Marilyn Baron, and Mary Roark.
    EVERYDAY EVERYWHERE MATERIALS AS TEACHING
    RESOURCES IN ADULT BASIC EDUCATION.
    Blacksburg, Virginia: Virginia Polytechnic
    Institute and State University, 1977.

    Shaw and Roark identify "found" materials
    from the world of the student and present
    exercises and activities designed for maximum
    involvement of the student. The focus is on

relating learning activities to adult coping skills. This is a useful resource for teachers, providing ideas, examples, and sources of materials.

184. Short, J. Rodney, and Bev Dickerson. THE NEWSPAPER: AN ALTERNATIVE TEXTBOOK. Belmont, California: Pitman Learning, Inc., 1980.

Short and Dickerson advocate using the newspaper as a textbook for a variety of reasons. The topics covered are motivating to the adult reader. Newspaper articles "provide raw, unfiltered data" (p. 2) that requires active processing on the part of the reader. Newspapers are current, inexpensive, and accessible. The authors analyze each section of newspapers and suggest learning activities for intermediate grades, middle or junior high school grades, and high school and adult classes, including English as Second Language classes.

185. Weibel, Marguerite Crowley. "Use the Public Library with Adult Literacy Students." JOURNAL OF READING 27 (October 1983): 62-65.

Weibel's message is simple. Adult literacy students need interesting, challenging material to read and adult collections in the library contain that material. What is needed to bring the two together is a knowledgeable librarian. The author suggests and illustrates that there is much material available that can be used to advance literacy skills, including poetry, art and photography books, song lyrics, cartoons, and explanatory books.

Assessment: Issues and Methods

186. Anders, Patricia L. "Test Review: Tests of Functional Literacy." JOURNAL OF READING 24 (April 1981): 612-619.

Anders reviews five tests of functional

literacy for students ranging in age from 10
years to adult. The tests are:
Reading/Everyday Activities in Life (R/EAL);
Performance Assessment in Reading (PAIR);
Senior High Assessment of Reading Performance
(SHARP); Life Skills (Reading); and Minimal
Essentials Test (MET). The discussion of
each test covers the major areas of
information needed by the professional and in
each case Anders provides a critical review
of the test.

Possibly because of the questions raised by
the review, Anders goes on to consider two
major issues: the definition of functional
literacy and ways of measuring it. She
questions whether functional literacy is
solely a set of competencies and skills for
living. She poses the need for a more
holistic way of measuring functional
literacy, perhaps using an ongoing profile of
the student functioning in a literacy
environment.

187. Anderson, Beverly L.   GUIDE TO ADULT
      FUNCTIONAL LITERACY ASSESSMENT USING
      EXISTING TESTS.   Portland, Oregon:
      Northwest Regional Education Laboratory,
      June 1981. 113pp. (ED 210 317)

      Assessment of adult functional literacy is
      complicated because of the varying
      definitions of functional literacy. She
      identifies three categories of literacy
      skills: generic or basic literacy, everyday
      literacy, and on-the-job literacy. Before
      choosing a testing method the examiner must
      decide on the kind of literacy to be
      assessed, the purpose of the testing, the
      uses and users of the test results, the
      examinee characteristics, and the logistics
      of the testing situation. This monograph is
      a useful resource, providing information on
      reviewing tests, matching learning objectives
      and tests, and analyzing case studies. In
      addition, lists of tests are provided, as
      well as suggestions for scoring writing
      samples.

188. Bowmar, Barbara, et al. ADULT BASIC LITERACY
      ASSESSMENT   KIT.   Victoria,   British
      Columbia: British Columbia Department of
      Education, 1981. 553 pp. (ED 221 652)

      The purpose of this kit to provide a
      resource   for   adult   educators   in   the
      construction and use of tests, checklists and
      questionaires to   assess   adult   literacy
      skills. The assessment kit contains items
      keyed to the Adult Basic Literacy Curriculum
      and to the APL competencies. There is a
      discussion of the rationale, purpose, and
      follow-up instruction for each of ten skill
      areas, including reading. Samples items are
      also   included as is information on the
      validity and reliability of the items.

189. Boyd, Robert D., and Larry G. Martin.   "A
      Methodology   for   the   Analysis of the
      Psychological Profiles of Low   Literate
      Adults."   ADULT EDUCATION QUARTERLY 34
      (Winter 1984): 85-96.

      Boyd   and   Martin   identify   psychosocial
      problems as being major factors in the
      learning difficulties of adults. They review
      the literature dealing specifically with
      psychosocial problems of low literate adults,
      including conditions such as negative self-
      concept; fear of failure, school, and change;
      mistrust; and lack of initiative.   The
      authors believe that it is critical that
      teachers recognize and understand these
      factors. The Self-Description Questionnaire
      draws heavily on Erickson's Ego Stage and is
      designed   to   help   teachers   understand
      individuals and the barriers to their
      learning. The authors propose that the scale
      is useful both for recruitment of adult
      students and for instruction.   They also
      advocate that teacher training sessions be
      held before using the scale.

190. Fisher, Donald L.   "Functional Literacy
      Tests: A Model of Question-Answering and an
      Analysis of Error."   READING RESEARCH
      QUARTERLY XVI (No. 3, 1981): 418-448.

Fisher presents his model of the question-
answering process that he uses to analyze
errors made by respondents on a test of
functional literacy developed by the
Educational Testing Service. The model is
presented in some detail with examples and
the errors made are analyzed and classified.
He suggests that it is possible that "many of
the errors are indeed the consequence of
information processing failures" (p. 444)
that may be unrelated to "level of
functioning" (ibid.). He states further that
we are including successful individuals in
the category of functional illiterates
because of process oriented errors or
carelessness. This failure to exclude
process oriented variables from definitions
of functional literacy has an effect on our
estimates of the extent of the problem and
the remediation required. The model of
question-answering and the examples are
useful in helping teachers focus on the
process and variables involved in test-
taking.

191.   Fox, Barbara J., and Arlene Fingeret. "Test
        Review: Reading Evaluation Adult Diagnosis
        (Revised)." JOURNAL OF READING 28
        (December 1984): 258-261.

        The Reading Evaluation Adult Diagnosis
        (READ) is an oral reading test developed by
        the Literacy Volunteers of America for use by
        volunteer tutors in diagnosing students'
        abilities and in planning programs in related
        LVA instructional materials. Fox and
        Fingeret review the content and format of the
        test and evaluate it. They find that as a
        diagnostic tool it is "oriented to a subskill
        approach to testing and teaching" (p. 259),
        lacks adequate technical data to support all
        aspects of the test, and contains some
        confusing instructions. They suggest that
        the test is probably most useful in
        conjunction with LVA instructional materials.

192.   Leigh, Robert K., et al. GIFT. GOOD IDEAS
        FOR TEACHING. ASSESSING THE ADULT LEARNER.

Tuscaloosa: Alabama   University,   1980.
119pp.   (ED 252 710)

This guide provides detailed information on
the assessment of adult reading readiness and
decoding skills within the larger context of
looking at abilities in language, critical
thinking, problem solving, and mathematics.
A range of competency levels are considered
from beginners to those students preparing
for the GED. Information is also included on
writing instructional objectives, choosing
materials, planning lessons and techniques,
and identifying interests and attitudes.

193. O'Donnell, Michael P., and Margo Wood. "The
London Procedure: A Screening/Diagnostic
Guide   for   Adult   Learning   Problems."
JOURNAL OF READING 27 (February 1984): 443-
447.

The London Procedure was developed to
identify strengths and weaknesses of adult
basic education students. The definition of
adult learning problems is broad according to
this   procedure   and   includes   physical,
psychological, and emotional difficulties.
The London Procedure measures visual and
auditory acuity as well as visual and
auditory perceptions (including encoding and
decoding). O'Donnell and Wood observe that
"analysis   of   the   tests   reveals,
unfortunately, that they are based on an
earlier   measure   founded   on   unproven
assumptions, lacking a strong rationale, and
weak in content validity" (p. 443). The
authors recommend "diagnosing reading needs
and   prescribing   appropriate instruction"
(p.447),   not   "identifying   obscure,
perceptually based possible causes of
learning problems" (ibid.).

194. Torres, Rosalie T., and Delwyn L. Harnisch.
"Functional Literacy Testing in the United
States: Measurement Issues and Theoretical
and   Practical   Implications."   Paper
presented at the Annual Meeting of the
American Educational Research Assn., April

11-15, 1983, Montreal, Quebec. 21pp. (ED 230 622)

Torres and Harnisch provide us with a review of major studies that have attempted to measure literacy in the United States and a detailed analysis of the content, criterion-related, and construct validity of tests measuring literacy. Their examination of validity issues is both revealing and, at the same time, discouraging for serious questions are raised in each of the areas considered.

In addition, the authors identify issues that must be addressed. There can be no one definition of functional literacy, because "any definition must be made within the contexts of specific groups, their goals, and the skills required to meet these goals" (p. 13). We will need "highly specific tests" (ibid.) developed for each group. Then, we can determine validity based on "the appropriateness of the test for specific purposes" (ibid.). In the meantime, they suggest careful use of the tests we now have. Suggestions include exploring patterns of responses to determine whether the group has received appropriate instruction and examining the type of error made to determine whether it is the result of a knowledge deficit or a processing error.

195.   Vacca, JoAnne L., and Casandra Sparks.   "The Evaluation of Adults Seeking Improvement in Reading."   READING WORLD 20 (March 1981): 197-200.

Vacca and Sparks proceed from the assumption that teacher and student in an adult education setting will work and plan cooperatively in the areas of goal selection, instruction, and evaluation. Tests are threatening to students, particularly adult students. Because of this the authors advocate using formal tests only when required and then only with complete explanation. They prefer continuous, informal evaluation in order to provide immediate feedback to the student. This can take many forms from discussion and observation to paper and pencil activities. Accurate record keeping is critical for measuring progress.

Teacher Training: Programs, Problems and Potentials.

196. Armstrong, Audrey A., and Sally P. Hunt. VITAL GUIDELINES. TUTOR TRAINING FOR AN ADULT LITERACY PROGRAM. Bloomington, Indiana: Monroe County Public Library, 1982. 63pp. (ED 244 104)

   This manual contains numerous practical resources for training the volunteer tutor, including reading objectives, an interest inventory, guidelines for selecting and writing adult materials, and a list of 220 Dolch basic sight words. Armstrong and Hunt also discuss the use of the language experience approach, the impact of learning disabilities on adult readers, and tutor training guidelines.

197. Blaine, Nancy. PROJECT B.E.S.T. BETTER EDUCATIONAL SERVICES THROUGH TESTING. FINAL PROJECT REPORT: 1981-82. El Dorado, Kansas: Butler County Community College. 1982. 33pp. (ED 229 631)

   This report describes a teacher training project designed to enable adult educators to evaluate learning disabled adults and plan appropriate programs for them based on an individual education program (IEP). The training sessions provided the participants with information about adult learning disabilities. Much stress is placed on the identification and remediation of auditory and visual perceptual problems, thus limiting the approach.

198. Brown, Barbara E. "The Identification of Volunteer Literacy Tutors' Training Needs." LIFELONG LEARNING RESEARCH CONFERENCE

PROCEEDINGS. February 12-13, 1982, College Park, Maryland. 272pp. (ED 215 198)

Brown describes the process used to develop the Tutor Self-Assessment Inventory. The most important competencies for beginning volunteer tutors were identified from the literature, from experts, and from the tutors. The competencies include the areas of adult psychology, interpersonal relationships, personal and administrative responsibilities, reading skills and instructional methods, assessment, and implementation of instruction. The inventory can be used as a basis for offering inservice workshops, for determining the tutor's readiness to teach, and for deciding if further training is needed.

199. Burnett, Richard W., and Thomas R. Schnell. "A Look at the Future: Teachers in Non-Traditional Adult Reading Programs." READING HORIZONS 24 (Fall 1983): 33-38.

Non-traditional reading programs for adults outside a school setting appear to be growing in number and in importance. We do not, however, routinely provide training for teachers in this field. Burnett and Schnell identify some of the differences between school programs and non-traditional adult programs. In the latter, we do not have the luxury of time to educate. Rather, instruction must be direct and oriented toward an immediate goal. The focus is on training the reader to comprehend specific kinds of texts for specific purposes. The authors identify a number of teacher competencies that would be applicable to a non-traditional adult setting.

200. Eno, Rebecca A. PROJECT LEAP. "SOMETHING STOPS YOU AND MAKES YOU THINK": AN ADAPTATION. FINAL REPORT. Philadelphia, Pennsylvania: Center for Literacy Inc., 1981. 136pp. (ED 221 680)

In order to expand recruitment and improve

training of volunteer tutors, the Center for
Adult Literacy instituted a number of
programs including telephone procedures for
after hours calls, mass media tutor
recruitment announcements, and a brochure
with a response sheet. Workshops for tutors
were given in ESL and basic literacy.
Details, forms, handbooks, and outlines are
included.

201. Indianapolis Public Schools. PROJECT UPDATE.
     FINAL REPORT. Indianapolis Indiana, June
     30, 1982. 89pp. (ED 222 684)

     This report describes a wide variety of
     projects designed to disseminate information
     to ABE teachers and to provide inservice
     training. Details are provided; sample
     materials are included. This document can
     serve as a resource for those concerned with
     staff development.

202. International Reading Assn. "Survey of
     Certification Requirements for Adult Basic
     Education Teachers of Reading." JOURNAL OF
     READING 23 (May 1980): 730-736.

     The Basic Education and Reading Committee
     of the IRA surveyed the 50 states, the
     District of Columbia, and New York City to
     determine certification requirements for
     teachers of adult basic reading. The survey
     provides interesting information on
     credentials. Although 69% of the respondents
     indicated some certification requirement, 91%
     indicated no special requirement in reading
     beyond that required of any ABE teacher. The
     list indicating preference of qualifications
     for hiring is also interesting, particularly
     for those looking for positions.
     Demonstrated competency and graduate courses
     in teaching reading topped the list.

203. James, Waynne B. "The Care and Feeding of
     Instructors of Adult Literacy and Basic
     Education." OUTLOOK FOR THE 80'S. Edited
     by Lorraine Y. Mercier. Washington, D.C.:
     U.S. Department of Education, Basic Skills

Improvement Program, September 1981.

James addresses a number of critical issues related to the recruitment, selection, and training of adult literacy instructors. The guidelines proposed are firmly related to the need for the instructor to understand the adult learner and provide for a wide variety of needs. The instructor must be an educator, counselor, and administrator. Most importantly, the instructor must be a friend, a humanist. The author provides guidance in a variety of areas: an overview of the needs of the adult learners, a list of competencies for the adult literacy educator, sources for finding instructors, and suggestions for interviewing and selecting them. A particularly useful section of the monograph provides details on current innovative training programs for adult literacy educators. Sources for obtaining information on these programs, as well as a useful bibliography in the area of training instructors, are included.

204. Jones, Edward V., and Jean H. Lowe. "Teacher Evaluation and Staff Development in Adult Basic Education (ABE)." NEW DIRECTIONS FOR CONTINUING EDUCATION 15 (September 1982): 59-71.

Jones and Lowe link teacher evaluation to improving teacher performance rather than to rating teachers for administrative purposes. Based on this premise, teacher evaluation is seen as one integrated phase of staff development. A useful and interesting review of the literature is provided to support this view. Three strategies are discussed in detail: the use of a biased questionaire (sample questions are included), peer observation, and staff meeting case study.

205. Kreitlow, Burton W. "Teaching the Adult of the '80's." Paper presented at the Annual Meeting of the Michigan Reading Assn., March 8-10, 1981. 15pp. (ED 207 009)

Kreitlow provides a variety of statistical data to demonstrate the parameters of adult education and the needs of low literate adults in particular. Students' low self esteem and their need for success are critical elements that teachers must recognize in working with this population. The author identifies capabilities needed by ABE teachers including: assessing, teaching skills directly and successfully, choosing appropriate materials, working with students' expressed needs, and organizing a learning-to-read curriculum. Beyond these capabilities and overriding them all, is the need for ABE teachers to understand and respect adults, their particular needs, and the constraints they live under. To do this, Kreitlow exhorts teachers to be learners themselves.

206. McAlister, Ellen D., and A.C. Bickley. HANDBOOK FOR THE TEACHING OF BEGINNING ADULT LEARNERS AND/OR ADULTS WITH LEARNING PROBLEMS. A PRODUCT FORMULATED FOR STAFF DEVELOPMENT OF ADULT EDUCATORS, VOLUNTEER TUTORS AND INSTRUCTIONAL AIDES. South Carolina: Darlington County School District, 1983. 184pp. (ED 244 112)

This handbook covers a range of topics relating to adult basic education including applying adult learning theory; assessing perceptual abilities, verbal intelligence, and reading and math achievement; and supplementing the Laubach reading instructional method.

207. Meyer, Valerie. "The Adult Literacy Initiative in the U.S.: A Concern and a Challenge." JOURNAL OF READING 28 (May 1985): 706-708.

Meyer expresses concern about the use of volunteers in adult literacy programs and identifies as a challenge the role of reading professionals in the Adult Literacy Initiative. Volunteers are needed but they require training to understand instructional

strategies and student learning problems.
The training is expensive to provide in terms
of time and money, particularly if tutors
drop out of a program. Volunteers need to be
motivated to stay with a program even in the
face of slow student progress. The kinds of
support that professionals can provide are
varied and essential. Meyer offers
suggestions for professional reading teachers
in the areas of gaining knowledge about
current efforts, training tutors, and
coordinating resources.

208.   Portage Township Schools. ADULT EDUCATION
       RESOURCE CENTER. FINAL REPORT. Portage,
       Indiana, June 30, 1982. 91pp. (ED 222
       679)

       This report documents the dissemination
       activities of a regional center for adult
       education. Based on the premises that
       teachers need to interact with teachers from
       different localities and that staff
       development takes time and should be
       conducted within the context of adult
       education, the center provides workshops,
       information on projects and materials, and
       serves as a network within the region. The
       report is particularly useful for suggestions
       on staff development.

209.   Rogers, Joy J. "Maintaining Volunteer
       Participation in Adult Literacy Programs."
       LIFELONG LEARNING 8 (November 1984): 22-24.

       According to Rogers, a trained volunteer
       tutor is a valuable resource. Yet literacy
       organizations traditionally lose volunteers,
       even after expending time, money and effort
       to train them. In an effort to overcome this
       problem, the author makes a number of
       suggestions, many of them involving relating
       the act of tutoring and the outcome of the
       process to individual students and their
       specific needs.

210.   Rose, Harold, et al. COMPETENCY BASED ADULT
       EDUCATION AND LEARNING DISABILITIES

DEVELOPMENT/TRAINING   PROGRAM   FOR   ABE
PERSONNEL.   FINAL   REPORT: 1979-80.
Kentucky: Morehead State University, July
1980. 105pp. (ED 195 753)

The   authors   present   a   comprehensive
description   of   a   preservice   and inservice
training program that includes   workshops   on
developing   an   understanding   of   adult
learning disabilities and an ability   to
diagnose   these   problems.   In   addition,
information is provided on   competency   based
education,   disadvantaged   adults,   and
paraprofessional programs.   Materials   and
forms are included.

211. Williams, David C. "Toward an Ergonomics of
     Adult Basic Education Instructor and Staff
     Development."   Paper   presented   at   the
     Annual Meeting of the American Educational
     Research Assn., April 12, 1983, Montreal,
     Canada. 11pp. (ED 228 444)

     Williams studied the   variables   associated
     with job satisfaction to see if more frequent
     participation   in   staff development programs
     for   ABE   teachers   was   related   to   job
     satisfaction.   The   results   were   mixed
     depending on the amount of the   participation
     and   how   useful   it   had   been.   Williams
     concluded that   increased   participation   was
     not   a   guarantee   of   job   satisfaction   for
     everyone. We should assess the needs of ABE
     teachers,   not   assume we know what they need
     and want.

212. Williams, Margaret, et al.   READ   ALL   ABOUT
     IT! TUTOR ADULTS WITH DAILY NEWSPAPER.
     LEADER HANDBOOK.   Syracuse,   New   York:
     Literacy Volunteers of America, 1984. (ED
     244 519).

     This handbook enables a leader to conduct a
     training   workshop   for   inexperienced
     volunteers   in   using   the newspaper to teach
     reading   and   critical   thinking   skills.
     Detailed   information   is   provided   on
     materials,   presentation   techniques   and

schedules, and outlines and plans for tutors. (See also entry 176.)

213. Wood, Margo, et al. "The Design and Validation of a Process-Oriented Staff Development Program in Adult Literacy." Paper presented at the Annual Meeting of the American Educational Research Assn., April 11-14, 1983, Montreal, Canada. 18pp. (ED 228 451)

This program, developed at the University of Southern Maine Reading Academy, is based on the premise that "learning to read involves progression through several distinct, sequential stages" (p. 2). The model, incorporating these stages, details of reading progress, student entry characteristics, reader level, major instructional goals, and instructional approaches to be used. An important feature of the program is the preservice and inservice process-oriented, diagnostic/ prescriptive training given to the tutors. In the implementation of the program, the process-oriented model was translated into specific, observable tutor behaviors in the form of a checklist. The training provided was important because it appeared to insure that the tutors would carry out the program.

Curriculum: Issues and Alternatives

214. Belz, Elaine. "Educational Therapy: A Model for the Treatment of Functionally Illiterate Adults." ADULT EDUCATION QUARTERLY 35 (Winter 1984): 96-104.

This article is based on the assumption that "if the treatment of reading problems is to be effective, the dynamic interaction between affective and cognitive domains must be addressed" (p. 97). Belz describes a curriculum based on exploration, experimentation, reflection, and working that is designed to deal with the personal and social problems of the adult.

215. Bhola,   H.S.   CURRICULUM   DEVELOPMENT   FOR
      FUNCTIONAL LITERACY AND NONFORMAL EDUCATION
      PROGRAMS. Workshop. Bonn, West Germany:
      Germany   Foundation   for   International
      Development, 1979. 279pp. (ED 239 819)

      This monograph provides a broad framework
      for issues relating to curriculum development
      and functional literacy, ranging from the
      relation of the curriculum to national policy
      to issues and techniques for training
      teachers. Delivery systems are identified
      and international projects are examined.
      Issues in curriculum analysis and evaluation
      are presented and discussed.

216. British Columbia Department of Education.
      NATIVE LITERACY AND LIFE SKILLS CURRICULUM
      GUIDELINES. A RESOURCE BOOK FOR ADULT
      BASIC EDUCATION. Victoria, British
      Columbia, Curriculum Development Branch,
      1984. 347pp. (ED 250 471)

      This resource book was developed to teach
      basic literacy skills as well as pre-
      employment skills, life skills, computational
      skills and personal cultural awareness to
      Native Americans. The manual provides
      information on native education as a
      framework for the instructional program. The
      language experience approach and commercial
      materials are suggested as vehicles for
      fulfilling the instructional objectives.
      Much detail is provided in developing lessons
      and choosing materials. The curriculum is
      designed to incorporate basic skill
      instruction with needed life competencies
      while at the same time building on the native
      culture.

217. Dickinson, Gary, et al. ADULT BASIC LITERACY
      CURRICULUM AND RESOURCE GUIDE. Victoria:
      British Columbia Department of Education,
      1980. 461pp. (ED 221 653) Also see Bowmar
      under assessment.

      The authors defined an integrated approach
      as occurring "when basic skills 'and general

knowledge are learned at the same time" (p.
8). This document is a detailed and thorough
compendium of curriculum and resources to
support this approach. Nine basic skill
areas are defined, illustrated and discussed.
Reading is defined as "both a language
process and a cognitive or thinking process"
(p. 47). The approach suggested reflects
this orientation. The general knowledge
areas are drawn from the APL competencies,
although the authors recognize that they may
have to be changed or adapted for particular
communities and students. The information
provided is exceptionally detailed, with
annotated bibliographies of materials, page
references within the materials, special
features etc.

218.   Ellowitch, Azi.   CURRICULUM IN EMPLOYMENT:
        WOMEN AND THE WORLD OF WORK. Philadelphia,
        Pennsylvania: Lutheran Settlement House
        Women's Program, 1983.

This handbook describes the setting for the
literacy program and the rationale for the
curriculum and the instruction. It also
includes materials developed by the staff for
the program. Literacy instruction is offered
at the settlement house in a multi-racial,
multi-cultural location as part of a multi-
service approach to meeting community needs.
The goals of the literacy program include
identifying and using the knowledge and
experience of the students, enabling students
to understand and control their lives, and
providing for growth in "students' skills to
critically think, make informed and realistic
decisions and act responsibly on those
decisions in their lives" (p. 4). The
material that was developed was designed to
reflect the problems and concerns of the
students and includes, for example, text on
parenting, unemployment and education.
Instruction is based on "reflective dialog"
in which both students and teachers are
partners in the process of learning. The
dialog methodology was developed from the
ideas of Freire and involved students in

developing vocabulary, concepts and critical thinking.

219. ERIC Clearinghouse on Adult, Career and Vocational Education. COMPETENCY EDUCATION FOR ADULT LITERACY. ERIC Overview. Fact Sheet No. 10. Columbus, Ohio, 1982. 4pp. (ED 237 798)

This brief fact sheet defines competency based education and discusses ways in which it overcomes problems of traditional adult education. Common components of most competency-based programs include identified competencies, a formal assessment system, functional literacy subject matter that integrates basic skills and life skills, and certification of mastery of competencies. A brief overview is also provided of research findings in this area.

220. Fischer, Joan Keller. COMPETENCIES FOR ADULT BASIC EDUCATION AND DIPLOMA PROGRAMS: A SUMMARY OF STUDIES AND CROSS-REFERENCE OF RESULTS. Washington, D.C., 1980. 51pp. (ED 222 644) (Also published in APL REVISITED: ITS USES AND ADAPTATION IN STATES. Washington, D.C.: U.S. Department of Education, Office of Educational Research and Improvement, September 1980.)

Fischer has examined 12 studies related to competencies for adult basic education and diploma programs. Six of these studies draw on or validate the APL competencies, the other six present different orientations. The studies are compared and the competencies are listed and cross-referenced. The project is a useful source of information for planning or reviewing literacy programs.

221. Greenfield, Leni, and Flynn Nogueira. "Reading Should be Functional: The APL Approach." READING AND THE ADULT LEARNER. Edited by Laura S. Johnson. Newark, Delaware: International Reading Assn., 1980, pp. 30-34.

Greenfield and Nogueira explain the APL
approach in terms of specifics for the
teaching of reading. This may mean, for
example, reading the label on cans for
consumer economics. They provide examples of
how to teach adults functional reading by
building on prior experiences and knowledge.
They also offer suggestions for developing
materials using community resources.

222.   Griffith, William S., and Ronald M. Cervero.
       "The Adult Performance Level Program: A
       Serious and Deliberate Examination." ADULT
       EDUCATION 4 (Summer 1977): 209-224.

       The authors examine the claims of the
       developers of the Adult Performance Level
       Program (APL), the theoretical soundness of
       the approach taken, and the technical
       constructs of the APL tests, as well as the
       role of the Department of Education in the
       development and promotion of the program.
       The questions they raise are serious ones;
       the issues they examine might be applicable
       to many ABE literacy programs.

223.   Haney, Walt, and Lloyd David. "The APL
       Study: Science, Dissemination, and the
       Nature of Adult Education." APL REVISITED:
       ITS USES AND ADAPTATION IN STATES.
       Washington, D.C.: U.S. Department of
       Education, Office of Educational Research
       and Improvement, September 1980.

       Haney and David review the history of
       competency-based education and of the APL
       project in particular. They examine in some
       detail the various criticisms that have been
       made of the project and conclude that "if we
       are to judge the APL study as a scientific
       inquiry, these criticisms are, we think,
       essentially correct" (p. 66). Why then has
       the APL study has such a wide-spread impact
       on adult literacy training? Partly, the
       authors suggest, because of the enthusiasm
       and promotion of the U.S. Office of
       Education. In addition, the approach is
       appealing to adults who want to use literacy

skills as the means to an end, improving
general living conditions and obtaining
employment. Finally, the commercial
materials developed seem to overcome some of
the technical problems associated with the
APL test.

224. Kazemek, Francis E. AN EXAMINATION OF THE
     ADULT PERFORMANCE LEVEL PROJECT AND ITS
     EFFECTS UPON ADULT LITERACY EDUCATION IN
     THE UNITED STATES. 1983. 26pp. (ED 236
     576) (Also published in LIFELONG LEARNING
     9 (October 1985): 24-28.)

     After reviewing the APL project, Kazemek
     examines the concept of "functional
     competency" and the assumptions and methods
     of the project. The author concludes that
     the "APL project not only presents a
     reductive view of functional competency, but
     also embodies a noxious view of the
     relationship between the individual and
     society" (p. 21). In addition "the validity
     and reliability of the APL tests and data are
     suspect" (p. 14). Political and social
     objections are raised about the project. No
     attempt has been made in the APL project to
     "deal with the moral and ethical aspects of
     adult literacy" (p. 16).

225. Northcutt, Norvell. ADULT FUNCTIONAL
     COMPETENCY: A SUMMARY. Austin: The
     University of Texas, 1975.

     This widely quoted study proposed a general
     theory of adult functional competency.
     First, the study identified general knowledge
     areas, or the content of adult literacy,
     which included consumer economics,
     occupational knowledge, community resources,
     health, and government and law. Then, four
     needed skill areas were identified:
     communication, computation, problem solving,
     and interpersonal relations. The notion of
     functional competency is based on the
     particular demands of a particular context,
     the two-dimensional construct of knowledge
     and skills, the dynamic interaction between

the individual capabilities and the demands
of society, and the association of success
for the individual with the acquisition of
functional competency. APL competency
objectives were specified which related to
the general knowledge areas. Three APL
levels were established based on income,
education, and job status. Although, it has
certainly not been without its critics, this
study has provided us with a concrete,
specific starting point for working with
adults as well as for establishing and
examining programs.

226. Rigg, Pat, and Francis E. Kasemek. "Adult
Illiteracy in the USA: Problem and
Solutions." CONVERGENCE 16 (1983): 24-31.

The extent of the problem of illiteracy
depends on how the term is defined. The
authors present a number of different
definitions with resulting different
estimates. "Regardless of whether there is a
'crisis,' the problem of illiteracy does
exist" (p. 24). Rigg and Kasemek examine
three approaches to meeting the literacy
problem. The first approach, in which adult
reading skills are diagnosed and remediated,
often using a compentency-based program,
fails to enroll and retain students because
the adults' needs and goals are not
considered by the teachers. The second
approach, in which literacy is viewed as a
community program with political goals, may
provide an appropriate context, but fails
because of ineffective instruction. The
authors propose a third approach. This is
based on a dialogue between student and
teacher, with both involved in determining
what the adult wants and needs to learn. It
uses instructional strategies based on a
understanding of the reading process, with
comprehension and meaning at the heart of
that process. "Phonic drills or word lists
typify the materials that literacy
instructors should reject" (p. 28). Finally,
the approach includes writing activities as
thinking activities, not as filling out

forms.

227. Shelton, Elaine.   "Competency-Based   Adult
      Education: The Past, Present and Future."
      Keynote address at the National Competency-
      Based Adult Education Conference, , November
      29, 1983, New York. 25pp. (ED 248 353)

      Shelton describes competency-based adult
      education, particularly the Adult Performance
      Level   project,   and   its   historical
      relationship to the development of functional
      literacy.   She   also   describes   current
      projects such as the National Adult Literacy
      Project, The Adult Literacy Skills Required
      for Training in the Work Place Project, and
      the Coalition for Literacy.   Each effort
      takes a different direction, but all focus on
      developing   and   sharing   information
      programming ideas, delivery systems, and
      instructional techniques. Foremost as a goal
      is the need to share and disseminate
      information.   Within this context, Shelton
      advocates   competency-based   programs   as
      effective ways of developing literacy, as
      demonstrated in a wide variety of current
      programs.

228. Singh, Sohan. LEARNING TO READ AND READING
      TO LEARN: AN APPROACH TO A SYSTEM OF
      LITERACY INSTRUCTION.   Amersham, England:
      Hutton Educational Publication Ltd.   in
      cooperation   with   the   International
      Institute for Adult Literacy Methods,
      Tehran, Iran, 1976.

      Singh presents an integrated approach to
      literacy in which the program is built around
      an economic, social, or even recreational
      theme.   He   identifies and includes in his
      program two stages: learning to read and
      reading to learn. This is especially useful,
      since one of the problems with literacy
      programs is that students do not apply their
      newly acquired skills. He discusses how to
      develop subject matter content, how   to
      present and sequence it, and how to integrate
      reading and writing. The numerous examples,

generally drawn from a literacy program in
India, are helpful. In addition, there is a
detailed discussion of developing literacy in
mathematics.

229. Ulmer, Curtis. "Adult Competency Based
     Instruction." COMMUNITY COLLEGE REVIEW 8
     (Spring 1981): 51-56.

     Competency based adult education (CBAE) is
     a process not a curriculum in which the
     emphasis is on the learner and his goals and
     on the "development of self in terms of
     performance in the 'real world'" (p. 51).
     Ulmer describes the extent of the problem of
     functional literacy within the context of
     functional competency in the United States.
     He examines the issues of measurement, adult
     learning, and the role of teachers in
     relation to CBAE. The author views CBAE as a
     way of meeting the learning needs of adults
     by learning through doing.

230. U.S., Department of Education. COMPETENCY-
     BASED ADULT ED NETWORK. Division of Adult
     Education Services, Washington, D.C.,
     December 1984.

     This document describes the Competency-
     Based Adult Education Network and provides a
     number of references for resources in the
     areas of: staff development, adult reading,
     vocational education, curriculum development,
     employability, research, and
     assessment/testing.

231. U.S. Department of Education. ERIC RESUMÉS
     ON COMPETENCY-BASED ADULT EDUCATION.
     Division of Adult Education Services,
     Washington, D.C., December 1985.

     This ERIC search contains a substantial
     number of references in the area of
     competency-based adult basic education as
     well as in the areas of external degree
     programs, related business/industry programs,
     and adult vocational education. The resumés
     are drawn from both RESOURCES IN EDUCATION

and CURRENT INDEX TO JOURNALS IN EDUCATION.

Computers: Uses in Developing Literacy

232. Alessi, Stephen M., Martin Siegel, Dorothy
     Silver, and Hank Barnes. "Effectiveness of
     a Computer-Based Reading Comprehension
     Program for Adults."   EDUCATIONAL
     TECHNOLOGY SYSTEMS 11 (1982-83): 43-57.

     The authors discuss the design and
     evaluation of a computer-based reading
     comprehension program used with pre-GED
     disadvantaged adults in a correctional
     institution. The design of the program is
     explained clearly with useful examples. The
     emphasis of the program is on providing
     feedback and information to the student while
     enabling him to practice a variety of
     comprehension skills and strategies. Only
     two skills were taught and evaluated at the
     time of this article. Positive results were
     obtained in teaching students to find
     information and paraphrase text. The authors
     raise questions about the formats used,
     particularly in teaching and evaluating
     paraphrasing, and urge others to "test and
     improve their programs until they succeed in
     teaching what they are intending to teach"
     (p. 57).

233. Blanchard, Jay S.   "U.S. Armed Services
     Computer Assisted Literacy Efforts."
     JOURNAL OF READING 28 (December 1984): 262-
     265.

     Blanchard cites two approaches used by the
     Armed Forces, one to improve general literacy
     and the other to improve on-the-job literacy.
     "Neither has greatly improved the vast
     majority of the young adult population's
     communication and computational skills" (p.
     262). The computer-based efforts described
     in some detail in the article are seen as
     having the potential to make a difference. A
     variety of approaches are discussed
     including, for example, developing vocabulary
     through games, problem-solving using

functional literacy skills, and improving
literal comprehension through generating
text. The author points out that these
programs have "immediate application for
nonmilitary settings" (p. 263).

234. Buckley, Elizabeth, and Peter Johnston.
      PILOT PROJECT IN COMPUTER ASSISTED
      INSTRUCTION FOR ADULT BASIC EDUCATION
      STUDENTS. ADULT LEARNING CENTERS, THE
      ADULT PROGRAM, 1982-83. Great Neck, New
      York: Great Neck Public Schools, 1983.
      35pp. (ED 230 738)

      Buckley and Johnston report on a study of
      the cognitive and affective results of
      computer-assisted instruction as a
      supplementary tool in adult basic education
      classes. The results confirmed previous
      findings. The authors cite the "dramatic
      cognitive growth" (p. 26) and the affective
      changes that were "perhaps even more
      significant" (p. 27). Reading and
      mathematics skills improved significantly,
      students become more positive, self-directed
      learners, and attendance became more regular.

235. Geller, Daniel M., and Mark Shugell. "The
      Impact of Computer-Assisted Instruction on
      Disadvantaged Young Adults in a Non-
      Traditional Educational Environment."
      Paper presented at the Annual Meeting of
      the American Educational Research Assn.,
      April 11-14, 1983, Montreal, Canada. 29pp.
      (ED 229 501)

      Disadvantaged young adults in a Job Corps
      Comprehensive Computer Program were studied
      to determine the effects on reading and
      mathematics achievement of supplementary
      instruction using CAI. The control group did
      not receive CAI but both groups did receive
      the same basic instruction using Job Corp
      paper-and-pencil materials. The experimental
      group showed substantially greater gain in
      reading over the control group. The CAI
      group also had a shorter stay in the Job Corp
      and a lower dropout rate. The authors

discuss the problems and difficulties encountered in the study and point out that it would be unwise to make too many generalizations based on the results.

236. Glidden, William C., et al. "The Coast Guard's CAI Approach to Basic Math and Reading Skills." Paper presented at the National Adult Education Conference, November 6-10, 1984, Louisville, Kentucky. 22pp. (ED 249 365)

This paper contains a description a computer assisted instructional program that was developed by the Navy to increase the basic skill level of recruits and reduce attrition rate. The materials used were designed to meet particular individual needs. Instruction is provided on an individual as well as on a group basis. A review of initial data indicates that the program appears successful.

237. Golub, Lester S. "A Computer Assisted Literacy Development Program." READING AND THE ADULT LEARNER. Edited by Laura S. Johnson. Newark, Delaware: International Reading Assn., 1980, pp. 47-54.

Golub reviews the advantages of using computers in a literacy program for such purposes as monitoring student progress, actively involving the student in the process of learning, and individualizing instruction. He describes a two phase program that teaches reading skills using job oriented materials and provides career information. The evaluation of the program indicated growth in reading skills, acquisition of career information, and a positive attitude toward using the computer.

238. Paul, Daniel M., comp. HANDBOOK FOR THE IDENTIFICATION AND ASSESSMENT OF COMPUTER COURSEWARE FOR THE ADULT LEARNER. Shenandoah, Pennsylvania: Shenandoah Valley School District, June 1982. 75pp. (ED 228 457)

This document provides guidelines for
evaluating computer software for ABE or GED
courses, suggested sources for acquiring
software, and evaluations of specific
courseware including some reading programs.
The appendixes containing annotated lists of
catalogs, directories, magazines, journals,
newsletters, and resource centers are
particularly helpful.

239. _____, and Jonathan D. Kantrowitz.
      MICROCOMPUTERS/ADULT BASIC EDUCATION: A
      PROJECT DIRECTED AT IMPLEMENTING CAI FOR
      ADULT LEARNERS AND IDENTIFYING COURSEWARE
      FOR GED/ABE PROGRAMS. REPORT NO. 1.
      IMPLEMENTING COMPUTER ASSISTED INSTRUCTION
      IN ADULT BASIC EDUCATION PROGRAMMING:
      OBSERVATIONS IN A RURAL SETTING. REPORT
      NO. 2. SELECTED COURSEWARE FOR GED/ABE
      PROGRAMMING. Shenandoah, Pennsylvania:
      Shenandoah Valley School District, 1983.
      189pp. (ED 240 326)

      The authors provide theoretical and
      research-based background to computer
      assisted instruction. They also present an
      overview of a specific project developed for
      GED/ABE students. Details are included on
      the courseware used in the program and
      student/teacher reaction to it. In addition,
      the report contains information on courseware
      suitable for adults in a number of
      instructional areas, including reading
      skills.

240. Smith, Shirley C. USING CBI TO DEVELOP JOB-
      RELATED READING AND STUDY SKILLS: THE PREST
      CURRICULUM FOR NAVY RECRUITS.
      Philadelphia, Pennsylvania: Research for
      Better Schools, Inc., March 1981. 9pp.
      (ED 228 991)

      Smith describes a program developed for
      Navy recruits who do not have the reading and
      study skills required to complete basic
      training and perform in subsequent military
      assignments. The curriculum was specifically
      oriented toward enabling the recruit to

succeed in a task using job-related
materials. The results of study of the
programs indicated that the "greatest
emphasis should be placed on word analysis,
literal comprehension, and study skills" (p.
5) and that computer instruction was
successful and highly motivating. An added
benefit was that instructors needed a minimal
amount of training.

241. University of Southwestern Louisiana.
HOMEBASED COMPUTER ASSISTED ADULT EDUCATION
PROJECT--PHASE II. FINAL PROJECT REPORT,
SEPTEMBER 1, 1981 THROUGH AUGUST 31, 1982.
Lafayette, Louisiana, 1982. 75pp. (ED 220
654)

This report describes a delivery system for
an ABE/GED curriculum using computer-assisted
and computer-managed instruction in which
software and a curriculum guide were
developed for adults to use in an out-reach
program. The material, at the time of the
writing of this report, had not been field
tested. However, adults in a normal adult
education program had been able to use CAI
programs satisfactorily and had positive
attitudes toward CAI instruction.

242. Wood, Bruce. "Computers and Reading at the
Secondary School, College and Adult
Levels." JOURNAL OF READING 28 (May 1985):
750-752.

Wood examines two aspects of the use of
computers in reading instruction: first, new
approaches and second, new computer and
program capabilities. The discussion
includes the use of software not developed
primarily for reading improvement, such as
word processing and language games, and
examples of a teacher-developed program for
pre- and post-organizers as well as an
interactive program using glosses. The
recent expanded capabilities of computer
instruction, such as interactive text and
information retrieval systems, has allowed
the development of programs that show promise

for computer-assisted instruction.

Program Planning: Issues in Recruitment/Retention of Students and Delivery of Services

243. Axam, John A. "The Library's Role in Eradicating Illiteracy." CATHOLIC LIBRARY WORLD 55 (October 1983): 122-123.

Axam asserts that "if the public library is serious about its educational role, then like institutions engaged in more formal education, it must assume the responsibility for providing avenues of personal development for each major segment of its clientele" (p. 122). One major segment is the functionally illiterate. The author provides a general outline for determining and developing the library's role in meeting the problem of illiteracy. He includes suggestions on identifying the extent of illiteracy in the community and efforts at alleviating the problem, analyzing the library's resources, and choosing the most appropriate services either for teachers or for students.

244. Bhola, H.S., and Joginder K. Bhola. PLANNING AND ORGANIZATION OF LITERACY CAMPAIGNS, PROGRAMS AND PROJECTS. Bonn, West Germany: German Foundation for International Development, 1984. 207pp. (ED 240 302)

The authors take a broad view of the variables involved in the development of literacy programs including: policy and planning, administrative and instructional delivery systems, technical support, social mobilization, curriculum and materials development, and evaluation. Each area is explored in terms of examining possible delivery systems for adult literacy programs. Particular attention is paid to the needs for planning within the context of the Third World, though Bhola and Bhola present an overview that is applicable to many situations. As the authors suggest, "theory ... is the most practical thing .... Theory is the sure-footed mule on whose back we can

carry experience from one setting to another.
To transport the experience of literacy
workers from India or Tanzania or Cuba to our
particular setting, we must use the vehicle
of theory" (p. 194).

245. Crandall, David P., et al. GUIDEBOOK FOR
     EFFECTIVE LITERACY PRACTICE. 1983-1984.
     San Francisco, California: Far West
     Laboratory for Educational Research and
     Development; Andover, Massachusetts:
     Network of Innovative Schools, Inc., 1984.
     477pp. (ED 253 776)

     This guidebook provides a comprehensive,
     detailed analysis of effective programs in
     the National Adult Literacy Project. It
     examines eight programs in depth, looking at
     student recruitment, orientation, counseling,
     diagnostic testing, instructional methods and
     materials, assessment, follow-up, and program
     evaluation. Each program appears to have one
     of the following three basic philosophies
     that influences all aspects of it: a job-
     skills or academic orientation does not
     stress personal development of the student; a
     human development orientation that is
     concerned with "the student's self-esteem and
     life problems as well as their academic or
     vocational accomplishments" (pp. 24-25); or
     an empowerment orientation concerned with the
     development of a student's control over his
     own learning and his own life. The authors
     found that programs with a clear "commitment
     to integrate and systematically plan,
     implement, and evaluate the educational
     process--those that create a coherent system
     of adult literacy instruction are the ones
     that are most successful" (p. 5-1).

246. Darkenwald, Gordon G. "Continuing Education
     and the Hard-to-Reach Adult." NEW
     DIRECTIONS IN EDUCATION 8 (1980): 1-10.

     Darkenwald identifies the "hard-to-reach"
     as any population that an agency wishes to
     recruit but can't. Frequently this includes
     the "elderly, the disadvantaged, blue-collar

workers, the handicapped, the geographically
isolated, and many other identifiable groups
and subgroups within the general population"
(p. 1). The discussion of the various
barriers to participation by these adults is
particularly useful, as is the discussion of
models of participation. Implications for
recruitment and retention of adult students
are suggested.

247. Development Associates. AN ASSESSMENT OF THE
     STATE-ADMINISTERED PROGRAM OF THE ADULT
     EDUCATION ACT. FINAL REPORT. Washington,
     D.C.: U.S. Department of Education, Office
     of Program Evaluation, July 14, 1980.

     This report deals with a study designed to
     examine programs and to identify "impact
     measures" (p. 1) that could be studied over
     time. Information that can be considered in
     developing, designing, and maintaining
     programs is provided in the areas of target
     population, program purpose, benefits to
     participants, student outreach and retention,
     characteristics of instructional settings,
     teacher selection and training, auxiliary
     services, the roles of the states, and the
     relations between the Federal, State and
     Local levels. (See entry 268 for summary of
     report.)

248. Eggert, John D. "Concerns in Establishing
     and Maintaining a Community Based Adult
     Literacy Project." Paper presented at the
     National Adult Literacy Conference, January
     19-20, 1984, Washington, D.C. 28pp. (ED
     240 295)

     Eggert suggests that underlying any
     discussion of establishing and maintaining a
     literacy project must be the recognition that
     there may be an "unavoidable tension between
     the needs of an individual and the goals of
     the group or organization intending to serve
     that individual" (p.1). Within this context,
     he discusses three areas of concern--the
     clients, the means of serving them, and the
     degree of stability or change desired in the

program. This discussion of the dilemmas
facing professionals and volunteers can focus
our thinking about issues and our efforts to
deal with the problems raised. In every
case, the emphasis is on thoughtful, informed
decision making.

249. Fingeret, Arlene.   "Oral   Subculture
     Membership: A   Non-Deficit   Approach to
     Illiterate Adults."   LIFELONG   LEARNING
     RESEARCH CONFERENCE PROCEEDINGS. February
     17-18, 1983, College   Park, Maryland:
     Maryland University. 235pp. (ED 226 228)

     The   rich oral tradition of illiterate
     adults is described and examined in some
     detail.   Oral skills enable them to create
     and function within a supportive social
     network.   Common   sense,   or "concrete,
     specific   knowledge-in-context,"   often
     developed and   passed   on   through   the
     collaborative efforts of members of the
     network, enables the illiterate adult to
     assess the   world and   make decisions.
     Fingeret suggests that there is a need to
     help these students see the relationship
     between oral and written language in a way
     that is not alien to them. Programmed texts,
     for example, might be considered alien. She
     advocates home tutoring and community-based
     programs as ways of keying into the social
     networks.   Publicity must be carefully
     planned so it does not give the impression
     that the program is for adults who are
     incompetent or unable to cope.

250. _____.   "Social   Network: A   New
     Perspective on Independence and Illiterate
     Adults."   ADULT   EDUCATION   QUARTERLY 33
     (Spring 1983): 133-146.

     Fingeret studied the social structures that
     adult illiterates create and the relationship
     of the structures to the concepts of
     dependence and independence. She found that
     illiterate adults create social networks that
     involve them and require that they be
     contributing members. These adults do not

necessarily see themselves as dependent. The
numerous examples and quotes included give a
picture of the contributions a non-reader can
make to others in a group. The author
contends that in planning literacy programs
for these adults we tend to ignore such
realities. This may imply, for example, that
we should be using existing social groups as
a way of forming literacy classes.

251. Fitzgerald, Gisela G. "Can the Hard-to-Reach
     Adults Become Literate?" LIFELONG LEARNING
     7 (February 1984): 4-5, 27.

     The answer Fitzgerald gives to the question
     she raises is at best conditional. In
     identifying the characteristics of hard-to-
     reach adults, she examines the literature and
     reports on a study in which 100 adults from a
     midwestern slum area were interviewed. The
     author clearly points out the variables
     identified by most studies as well as the
     conflicting results obtained in the various
     studies. Unanswered questions are raised
     about different aspects of the problem, such
     as sources of motivation of the adults and
     appropriate staffing of the centers. There
     are indications that programs fare better in
     reaching the illiterate if they are community
     based and are in touch with the social,
     economic and psychological needs of the
     adults. Fitzgerald has identified a critical
     area and has raised important questions to
     consider in establishing and evaluating
     programs.

252. Glustrom, Merrill. "Educational Needs and
     Motivations of Non High School Graduate
     Adults Not Participating in Programs of
     Adult Basic Education." LIFELONG LEARNING
     6 (April 1983): 19-21.

     Glustrom briefly reviews the history of
     Adult Basic Education legislation as well as
     studies of ABE programs and participants. He
     points out the shortcomings of some of these
     studies. The article reports in detail on
     the Wisconsin Educational Needs Assessment,

1981, and the author's follow-up on that study. The Wisconsin study found that younger adults were more likely than older adults to participate in ABE programs. Adults who think they are functioning successfully without a high school diploma are not likely to enroll in ABE. Potential students who have unmet social and economic needs because of the poverty of their lives are not likely to attend ABE. The follow-up study essentially validated these results.

The author makes some general suggestions. He advocates focusing ABE programs on two groups not likely to participate, the elderly and the poor. In addition, he supports and strengthens the suggestion of the original study that we have a national commitment to meeting the fundamental social, economic, and psychological needs of the target population if ABE is to be totally effective.

253. Heathington, Betty S., Judith A. Boser, and Thomas Salter. "Characteristics of Adult Beginning Readers who Persisted in a Volunteer Tutoring Program." LIFELONG LEARNING 7 (February 1984): 20-22, 28.

Because of the high rate of attrition in adult literacy programs and the resulting adverse affect on reading achievement, the authors investigated characteristics that appeared significant for retention of students. They reviewed research in the field and analyzed data from an adult tutoring program. Students who persisted were older, had less prior schooling, were more likely female, and had school children at home. Entry level reading ability did not appear to be a factor. The authors point out features of their particular program that may account for these results. For example, since the program allows tutor and tutee to meet anywhere at any convenient time, mothers with children may find this a workable format. They also discuss contrary findings from other studies and raise important issues for literacy programs. For example, should

we target specific groups who seem more
likely to persist and benefit or should we
try to encourage everyone? Generally,
programs must respond to and meet specific
needs. The challenge for the administrator
is to identify them and plan accordingly.

254.   Irish, Gladys H. "Reaching the Least
        Educated Adult." NEW DIRECTIONS FOR
        CONTINUING EDUCATION 8 (1980): 39-53.

        Irish addresses two related issues in
        reaching the least educated adult:
        recruitment and retention. She describes
        three programs that have dealt effectively
        with recruitment and discusses in detail how
        to use mass media, referrals, and recruiters
        to enroll students in a program. Innovative
        programming alternatives for retaining
        students are suggested.

255.   Jefferson County Adult Reading Program. "IF
        ONLY THEY CAN BE REACHED..." STRATEGIES
        FOR LITERACY PROGRAM RECRUITMENT. Kentucky
        Department of Education, 1983. 28pp. (ED
        235 323)

        This booklet provides useful suggestions
        for organizing a recruitment campaign,
        developing fact sheets, and using the media.
        The emphasis is on the practical, with
        examples and samples included.

256.   _____. ORGANIZING A SUCCESSFUL ADULT
        LITERACY PROGRAM. Kentucky Department of
        Education, 1983. 107pp. (ED 235 320)

        This handbook contains a wealth of
        practical suggestions, forms, handouts,
        lists, job descriptions, etc. The topics
        covered include organizing a program, staff
        development and training, student recruitment
        and retention, instructional design, and
        accountability and evaluation. A
        bibliography for teachers is also included.

257.   Jones, Paul L., and John R. Petry.
        "Attitudes of Adult Basic Education

Students toward Education and Their Teachers." THE CLEARINGHOUSE 57 (January 1984): 213-216.

Using a rating scale, the authors studied the attitudes of students in Adult Basic Education classes in Tennessee toward their teachers. The study analyzed the significance of teacher empathy, teacher attitude, anticipated value of education, teacher competence, and curriculum relevance according to sex, age, income, race, and time in program. The results were generally positive and are presented in some detail. Of particular interest was the finding that adults under 30 constituted the largest group, tended to stay in the program no more than one year, and displayed somewhat less favorable views of the program. The authors conclude that we must be sure we are meeting their needs because we have only one chance with this group.

258. Kozol, Jonathan. "Fight Illiteracy with Volunteer Youth." JOURNAL OF EXPERIENTIAL EDUCATION 5 (Summer 1982): 17-21.

Kozol recognizes the serious, unmet problem of adult illiteracy in the United States. Since current programs have not been able to meet this need, he proposes a different approach. We need to tap an vast reservoir of talent--high school and college age students. Kozol proposes that volunteer youths who have had a minimum of training in basic phonics live within the community with the target population in order to build a sense of "common cause" (p. 18). Instruction should be through the development of oral histories that can be edited and duplicated to form the basis for the growth of literacy. The author forsees that financial support can be obtained from business and industry for this type of program.

259. Lawson, Virginia K., and Jonathan McKallip, eds. MANAGEMENT HANDBOOK FOR VOLUNTEER PROGRAMS. Syracuse, New York: Literacy

Volunteers of America, Inc., 1984.

This handbook details techniques and strategies developed by the Literacy Volunteers of America for planning and managing volunteer programs. The editors include information on developing and conducting community needs assessments, organizing programs, recruiting and training tutors and students, and identifying potential resources for financial stability.

260.   Long, Jerry. "Recruiting and Retaining the Prospective Adult Basic and Secondary Education Student." LIFELONG LEARNING 7 (October 1983): 12-13, 24-25.

Recruitment and retention are two critical areas in Adult Basic Education programs. Long identifies potential clients here as frequently having "very adverse attitudes toward further education" (p. 12). After reviewing theory and research in the area of participation and motivation, Long proposes the following four motivational orientations and suggests that recruitment advertising be based on them: social contact/community service/external expectations; professional advancement; escape-social stimulation; and cognitive interest. He identifies particular audiences for specific motivational orientations. These same orientations should be considered in planning programs to insure retention of students.

261.   Lyman, Helen Huguenor. LITERACY AND THE NATION'S LIBRARIES. Chicago, Illinois: American Library Assn., 1977.

Lyman addresses the issue of the nature and scope of the illiteracy problem in the United States. The practical suggestions she makes for involving libraries in the solution to the problem are useful in planning and developing adult literacy programs. These suggestions include, for example, conducting community needs assessments, training tutors, and disseminating information to other literacy centers.

262. Madeira, Eugene L.   REACHING THE LEAST
     EDUCATED. 130 LOCAL ABE DIRECTORS TELL
     HOW.   PENNSYLVANIA'S   HANDBOOK   ON
     RECRUITMENT. Lancaster, Pennsylvania: ELM
     Consultants, 1980. 141pp. (ED 237 661)

     This guide provides information on twelve
     techniques for recruitment of ABE students,
     ranging from utilizing the media in various
     ways to using the adult student as a
     recruiter of other students.   Details and
     examples of the strategies are provided.

263. McDermott, Peter.   "Conversational Asides:
     The Social Context of an Adult Literacy
     Class."   JOURNAL OF READING BEHAVIOR XIV
     (No. 4, 1982): 460-473.

     McDermott identifies social context as a
     significant factor in the effectiveness of
     learning activities. This is as true for
     adults as for children and adolescents. His
     study investigates social contexts in an
     adult literacy class by analyzing
     conversational asides. He identifies three
     distinct social contexts: the waiting context
     in which students are waiting for the teacher
     to arrive; the entry context in which the
     teacher conducts the preliminaries; and the
     instructional context. A wealth of examples
     illustrate the conventions observed and the
     functions performed in each context. The
     results reveal that students at a low level
     of literacy and a high level of anxiety
     seemed to come to school lacking the self-
     direction often associated with adult
     learners. This has implications for the
     teacher's role in the various social
     contexts.

264. Mezirow, Jack, Gordon D. Darkenwald, and Alan
     B. Knox.   LAST GAMBLE ON EDUCATION:
     DYNAMICS OF ADULT BASIC EDUCATION.
     Washington, D. C.: Adult Education Assn. of
     the U.S.A., 1975.

This book reports on a study done through the Center for Adult Education at Teachers College, Columbia University. The authors used field observations in six major cities as well as an extensive national survey to "develop a dependable, comprehensive, and analytical description of significant patterns of program organization and classroom interaction in addition to presenting in an organized fashion the perspectives of those involved" (p. v). The description of the classroom interaction they found is discouraging and depressing: the loneliness of the adult student, the emphasis on attendance for administrative purposes, and the instructional emphasis on present-recite/test-correct.

The authors identify the adult basic education student and the reasons why he, or more likely she, is in the program. In addition, they cite the critical need to understand the student's goals and time perspective as well as the benchmarks the student uses to measure progress. The description and analysis includes a discussion of the roles of teachers, counselors, directors, and the community.

This study represents what was observed in a study in a point in time. It can serve as a frame of reference for establishing, examining, judging and altering programs today.

265. O'Malley, Paulette F., and Ann Marie Bernazza Haase. "Retaining the Returning Adult in a Reading Program." READING HORIZONS 21 (1981): 200-205.

Adults return to school to upgrade their reading skills for a variety of economic, social and personal reasons. They all, however, take a risk in returning to school when they expose their reading problems and deficiencies. They also risk not being able to overcome these problems and thereby achieve their goals. Such anxieties and

pressures contribute to a high attrition rate
in adult reading classes. The authors
advocate an open-entrance/open-exit program
to enable adults to enter when it is
convenient and to leave when they have
reached a goal. They provide suggestions to
make this plan workable, as well as for
overcoming some of the other reasons for the
attrition problem. We must provide direct
instruction using relevant materials. We
must respect the individual, recognizing his
life experience and his anxieties. We must
create an atmosphere of success, trust, and
involvement. Appropriate instruction will
help retain the adult student.

266. Patterson, Oliver, and Lewis L. Pulling.
     "Critical Issues in Adult Literacy."
     OUTLOOK FOR THE 80'S: Adult Literacy.
     Edited by Lorraine Y. Mercier. Washington,
     D.C.: U.S. Department of Education, Basic
     Skills Improvement Program, September 1981,
     pp. 23-48.

     Patterson and Pulling view the adult
     illiterate as an invisible member of society.
     They provide a broad definition of illiteracy
     that encompasses "human as well as work
     needs" (p. 27). Within this context, the
     authors examine six major issues related to
     adult illiteracy. The issues include:
     recruitment and retention of students, goals
     of community-based organization,
     instructional objectives and evaluation,
     identifying populations to be served,
     minimizing failure, and mobilizing community
     resources. The discussion is detailed, with
     examples, charts, lists, suggestions, and
     questions.

267. Phillips, Kathleen J., et al. AFFECTIVE
     ASPECTS OF ADULT LITERACY PROGRAMS: A LOOK
     AT THE TYPES OF SUPPORT SYSTEMS, TEACHER
     BEHAVIOR AND MATERIALS THAT CHARACTERIZE
     EFFECTIVE LITERACY PROGRAMS. San
     Francisco, California: Far West Laboratory
     for Educational Research and Development;
     Andover, Massachusetts: Network of

Innovative Schools, Inc., 1985. 35pp. (ED 254 758)

Information from 400 adult literacy programs was analyzed. From this group 15 programs were chosen for a field study to determine the affective aspects of programs that effected the success of the programs. Peer support was found to be an important variable for adult learners while teacher support was identified as crucial to program effectiveness. Teachers not only instruct but they also counsel students, often informally. The attitude of respect for the adult student, for his background and his experience, was found to be important in student and program success.

268. U. S., Department of Education. EXECUTIVE SUMMARY. ASSESSMENT OF THE STATE-ADMINISTERED PROGRAM OF THE ADULT EDUCATION ACT. Office of Program Evaluation, Washington, D.C., September 1980.

This report presents the conclusions of a core study and two substudies that were designed to examine programs and to identify "impact measures" (p. 2) to be used in long-term studies. See the final report of the assessment (247) for the topics included.

269. Waite, Peter A. "The Role of Volunteers in Adult Literacy Programs." Paper presented at the National Adult Literacy Conference, January 19-20, 1984, Washington, D.C. 14pp. (ED 240 294)

Waite asserts that literacy programs must be community-based, coordinated with other local agencies, and use large numbers of trained volunteers. He concludes that we need a national commitment to programs using volunteers with an emphasis on the local level.

270. Way, Max W. USING BILLBOARD POSTERS TO PROMOTE ADULT BASIC EDUCATION PUBLIC AWARENESS AND RECRUITMENT IN OHIO.

Piketon, Ohio: Scioto Valley Local School District, November 1982. 12pp. (ED 233 237)

This monograph describes and evaluates a statewide campaign to promote adult basic education which featured Johnny Cash and used billboards to spread the message. The response to this recruitment approach was positive for both ABE directors and the public. The author recommends the use of public figures or themes as a recruitment device.

271. Weibel, Marguerite Crowley. THE LIBRARY LITERACY CONNECTION. USING LIBRARY RESOURCES WITH ADULT BASIC EDUCATION STUDENTS. Columbus, Ohio: Public Library of Columbus and Franklin County, August 1984. 56pp. (ED 247 464)

Weibel addresses a number of issues involved in making the connection between the library and the literacy student. She examines criteria for selecting and evaluating books for students as well as for determining resources within the total library collection. Reading skills and needs are identified and related to books available in a library. The question of motivation to use a library's collection is also addressed. The appendixes contain useful, specific information for libraries interested in working with ABE programs and students.

Program Alternatives: Field-Based Solutions and Program Evaluation

272. Akenson, James E. "The Southern Literacy Campaign 1910-1935: Lessons for Adult Learning in an Information Society." Paper presented at the National Adult Education Conference, November 1984, Louisville, Kentucky. 42pp. (ED 252 726)

Akenson examines the history of the Southern Literacy Campaign in order to draw relevant lessons for literacy programs today.

He specifically compares the campaign in
Alabama in 1910-1935 to the current campaign
in Tennessee. In both instances neither the
resources available nor the enthusiasm of
their supports were sufficient to meet the
problem. In order to solve the extensive
problems of illiteracy, a strong central
commitment must be made by educational
institutions.

273. Baker, George A. III. "Serving Undereducated
Adults: Community as Learning Center." NEW
DIRECTIONS FOR CONTINUING EDUCATION 20
(December 1983): 31-42.

The author describes an outreach program
originated and carried out by a community
college. Interdisciplinary teams form the
basis for the individualized, competency-
based mastery learning program of basic
skills. Recruitment is aimed at adults and
out-of-school youths. Instruction is provided
at various sites in the community. In order
to meet the needs of the students, the
program is offered with flexible time units
in which students determine the frequency and
length of sessions. Mobile vans are used to
transport materials, audiovisual equipment,
and personnel to the students. The aim of
the program is to provide "nontraditional
delivery of critical services to those who
typically receive little from the community
but who can benefit from learning" (p. 42).

274. Bhola, H.S. EVALUATING FUNCTIONAL LITERACY.
Amersham, England: Hulton Educational
Publications Ltd. in cooperation with the
International Institute for Adult Literacy
Methods, 1979.

Bhola describes a variety of evaluation
techniques but focuses on one, the 3-S
(situation specific strategy). He addresses
issues related to statistical measures, test
development and selection, and use of test
data as well as the politics of program
evaluation.

275. _____. "Evaluation Planning of Post-
     Literacy Programs." Paper presented at the
     National Seminar on Strategies for Post-
     Literacy, Follow-up and Continuing
     Education in Rural and Urban Context,
     September 24-30 1982, Hyderabad, India.
     30pp. (ED 221 672)

     Bhola advocates that "evaluation planning
     should be part of program planning" (p. 6).
     He provides guidance in developing questions
     in five broad areas that can be used to plan,
     implement, and evaluate adult post-literacy
     programs. Such programs, as described by the
     author, are needed to insure both the
     retention and the extension of newly acquired
     literacy skills.

276. _____. EVALUATION PLANNING, EVALUATION
     MANAGEMENT, AND UTILIZATION OF EVALUATION
     RESULTS WITHIN ADULT LITERACY CAMPAIGNS,
     PROGRAM AND PROJECTS (with Implications for
     Adult Basic Education and Nonformal
     Education Programs in General). A Working
     Paper. Bonn, West Germany: German
     Foundation for International Development,
     November 1982. (ED 221 759)

     Bhola provides detailed rationale and
     suggestions for the internal evaluation of
     literacy systems. He outlines steps to take
     for setting up an evaluation agenda,
     procedures to follow, and criteria to
     establish. He also provides a series of
     questions to ask in the evaluation of
     literacy programs as well as a list of
     statistical indicators that can be used.

277. Ciavarella, Michael A., ed. COMMUNITY
     EDUCATION EXPANSION AND OUTREACH LINKAGES:
     IMPACT ON ADULT EDUCATION. Shippensburg,
     Pennsylvania: Shippensburg State College,
     1981. 184pp. (ED 219 499)

     The seven essays in this volume cover a
     wide range of topics, all related to
     developing and improving programs of adult
     basic education through linkages to the

community. Areas discussed include linking
ABE to the student's career path in business
and industry, involving the staff of the ABE
program with advocacy of the program, using a
community advisory council in assessing
needs, reaching the elderly and those in
rural areas, and recruiting students. The
importance of establishing a plan is
underscored in a number of ways, with
particular stress on the plan's impact on
marketing and funding.

278.   Cincinnati Public Schools. HOMEBOUND/CLUSTER
       - A.B.E./SPECIAL DEMONSTRATION PROJECT-309.
       Cincinnati, Ohio, June 1979. 82pp. (ED
       220 607)

       This manual describes and illustrates a
       delivery model in which ABE is brought into
       local communities, using a variety of sites,
       and in which the students are instructed in
       small groups of two to eight. All aspects of
       the project are detailed: recruiting and
       instructing students, training teachers,
       scheduling, administering, and managing the
       project. Suggestions are also made for
       adapting the project to smaller cities.

279.   Couvert, Roger. THE EVALUATION OF LITERACY
       PROGRAMMES: A PRACTICAL GUIDE. Paris:
       United Nations Educational, Scientific and
       Cultural Organization, 1979.

       The author addresses two aspects of program
       evaluation--internal and external--and makes
       a clear and useful a distinction between
       them. Couvert provides information for
       professionals with different levels of
       expertise and different purposes in
       conducting evaluations. This is not a manual
       intended to instruct the novice in program
       evaluation, but rather a reference for those
       requiring more assistance and sources of
       information on the topic.

280.   Eberle, Anne, and Sandra Robinson. THE ADULT
       ILLITERATE SPEAKS OUT: PERSONAL
       PERSPECTIVES ON LEARNING TO READ AND WRITE.

Washington, D.C.: The National Institute of
Education, U.S. Department of Education,
September 1980.

This monograph discusses four topics: what
it is like to be illiterate, what it is like
to decide to be literate, what the process of
acquiring literacy is like, and how a
particular state-wide program addresses those
needs. Eberle and Robinson flesh out the
statistics, the statements, the theories of
literacy and illiteracy with a wealth of
quotes from adults who live their lives with
limited literacy skills. We move into their
world and experience it. The authors
describe the Vermont Adult Basic Education
Program that uses tutors and literacy
volunteers in a home or other familiar
setting to develop literacy skills. The
instruction is one-to-one or in small groups
and relates the acquisition of literacy
skills to real life.

281. Graham, Janet Roth. ADULT BASIC EDUCATION
LINKAGE PROJECT. FINAL REPORT.
Pittsburgh, Pennsylvania: Allegheny
Intermediate Unit, 1980. 52pp. (ED 204
638)

This project was designed to link ABE, ESL
and GED programs to community groups and
businesses in order to attract students. The
development of a variety of outreach efforts
is described.

282. Grede, John, and Jack Friedlander. ADULT
BASIC EDUCATION IN COMMUNITY COLLEGES.
Junior College Resource Review. Los
Angeles, California: ERIC Clearinghouse for
Junior Colleges, August 1981. 6pp. (ED
207 649)

Grede and Friedlander review the extent of
adult illiteracy in the United States and
examine current efforts in the field. They
identify problems in teacher training,
effectiveness of instruction, and funding.
They suggest that the community college can

meet these problems and can "provide sound
ABE programs" (p. 5). However, they caution
that a college needs to consider its total
mission and its other programs before
undertaking this commitment.

283. Harris, Joan E. "The Design & Administrative
Management of Literacy Training Programs in
South Carolina." Paper presented at the
National Adult Literacy Conference, January
19-20, 1984, Washington, D.C. 28pp. (ED
240 293)

Harris describes the structure of the adult
literacy program in South Carolina and the
experience gained from it in that state. The
focus of the program is on meeting local
needs and on developing support, funding, and
leadership for programs within local
communities. The author discusses a variety
of issues and illustrates how programs in the
state have been structured to meet local and
individual needs.

284. Heaney, Thomas W. "'Hanging On' or 'Gaining
Ground': Educating Marginal Adults." NEW
DIRECTIONS FOR CONTINUING EDUCATION 20
(December 1983): 53-63.

Heaney describes a community-based program
for Hispanic adults in which the City
Colleges of Chicago act as a "conduit for
state and federal adult education funds" (p.
54). The colleges provided the money and the
program provided the curriculum. The program
seemed successful because the curriculum was
"infused with the day-to-day life of the
students" (ibid.) and because of the high
level of community control. However, this
approach did not follow the traditional adult
education model. In the resulting conflict
between the program leaders and the
administration of the colleges, funding was
discontinued. The author raises significant
issues relating to how to manage programs,
attract and maintain students, and retain an
institutional base. He examines differences
between adult education and schooling, and

reminds us of the need to emphasize the "proactive role of the adult learner in shaping his or her own learning" (p. 63).

285. Hooks, William Michael, and Floride Nelson. THE ADULT LITERACY LEAGUE AND THE CENTER FOR ADULT LITERACY. 1982. 10pp. (ED 227 923)

The authors describe a delivery model in which an adult literacy program and a community college work together to recruit and train volunteer teachers to teach a developmental reading course to adults. Some detail on the relationship between the two agencies is provided.

286. Horrell, Sallie. BEARS AND BUTTERFLIES: THE LITERACY VOLUNTEERS OF GLOUCESTER. PROJECT POWER 1982-1983. Richmond: Virginia State Department of Education, Adult Education Service, 1983. 25pp. (ED 244 075)

The literacy program in Gloucester County, Virginia includes both Adult Basic Education students and English as a Second Language students. Horrell describes the establishment of the Literacy Volunteers of Gloucester and the extensive use of these volunteers.

287. Johnen, Elizabeth T. "Challenging Adults to Read Effectively." Paper presented at the Annual Meeting of the Far West Regional Conference of the International Reading Assn., March 17019, 1983, Spokane/Seattle, Washington. 25pp. (ED 233 310)

The literacy program in a rural Oregon area that is described in this paper is designed to provide assessment, materials, and individualized instruction to adults with low level reading skills. Johnen outlines the steps to be taken in setting up such a program and provides examples and suggestions. The program was developed by the reading staff of a community college basic education program.

288. Kadavy, Rhonda, ed.   REDUCING FUNCTIONAL
      ILLITERACY: A NATIONAL GUIDE TO FACILITIES
      AND SERVICES. Lincoln, Nebraska: Contact
      Literacy Center, June 1985.

           This   directory provides information on
      national organizations concerned with the
      issues related to functional illiteracy as
      well   a   comprehensive   list   of   names,
      addresses, and services for local adult basic
      education, community and volunteer groups,
      and correctional programs in each of the
      states.   In addition, lists of names and
      addresses are included for   sources   of
      assistance   from   national   and   local
      organizations   and   state   education
      departments.

289. Kessler, Caren. BLUE RIDGE TECHNICAL COLLEGE
      ADULT   READING   PROJECT.   Flat Rock, North
      Carolina: Blue Ridge Technical College, June
      1981. 41pp. (ED 214 145)

           Frustrated by problems of attracting and
      retaining students and volunteer tutors
      within the confines of a college reading
      center, Blue Ridge Technical College obtained
      funds to start an outreach program in which
      centers were established throughout the area.
      Kessler describes the project in some detail,
      including   staffing,   materials, publicity,
      tutor training, management, and results
      obtained.   Copies are included of working
      documents, materials, and resources. A very
      complete picture is presented of how a local
      effort met a local problem.   Much of the
      information can be used in a variety of
      settings. The discussion of publicity, for
      example, details how a crucial problem in
      recruitment of adults who cannot read was
      solved with thoroughness and creativity.

290. Kinnamon, Sue E.   "Commercial Television and
      Adult Reading."   READING AND THE ADULT
      LEARNER.   Edited by Laura S. Johnson.
      Newark, Delaware: International Reading
      Assn., 1980, pp. 41-46.

Kinnamon reports on a survey designed to determine the extent and kinds of programming for instruction in reading on commercial television channels. Although the survey is somewhat dated, the results obtained reveal some of the alternatives that have been offered. The author, in general, cites the lack of suitable programing for teaching adults to read. She raises the question of whether there is, in fact, not a need for such programming or whether there is a need that is not being met.

291. Klem, Lynn. "A Competency-Based Adult Reading Management System." LIFELONG LEARNING RESEARCH CONFERENCE PROCEEDINGS. February 12-13, 1982, College Park, Maryland. 272pp. (ED 215 198)

Klem describes a program developed by adult educators in New Jersey based on a commitment to competency-based education. The program provides "each adult student with a personalized educational program based on his or her own goals" (p. 136). To achieve this, a system was developed that includes an interest assessment, competency assessment tests, a list of skills needed for adult reading, an inventory of competency-based adult reading materials, and functional word lists.

292. _____. THE SOUL OF A NEW SYSTEM. NEW JERSEY ADULT READING PROJECT. F.Y. '80-F.Y. '84. FINAL REPORT. Glassboro, New Jersey: Glassboro State College, Office of Adult Continuing Education, 1984. 16pp. (ED 247 410)

The New Jersey Adult Reading Project was developed to enable adults to achieve the literacy skills necessary to function in specific areas in today's world. To accomplish this, adult educators developed a competency-based management system that includes assessment tests, needed reading skills, a computer-based prescriptive program, and a student recordkeeping system.

Klem describes the program and outlines the results of pre- and post-tests showing the success of the project.

293. Louisiana State Department of Education. LIBRARIES: A DISCOVERY FOR ADULT LEARNERS. FINAL REPORT. Baton Rouge, Louisiana, 1983. 100pp. (ED 245 074)

This monograph reports on a project designed to insure and enhance cooperation between public libraries and adult education programs. The report details the activities of all parish libraries and particularly the intensive pilot programs in four systems. It demonstrates the variety of cooperative activities that can take place, including, for example, the sharing of book lists, information on adult learners, and publicity.

294. Mangum, Garth L. "Adult Literacy in Utah: Even a Leader has Unmet Needs." Paper presented at the National Adult Literacy Conference, January 19-20, 1984, Washington, D.C.. 44pp. (ED 240 287)

Mangum describes the six programs available in Utah to adults with inadequate basic skills. He concludes that even in a state that places a high premium on education and that has a high rate of literacy, the resources available for adult literacy training are limited. There are many more adults in need of training than can be accommodated in the available programs. The author relates literacy training to jobs and includes the list of necessary basic skills for the work force developed by the Center for Public Resources.

295. Mattleman, Marciene S. MAYOR'S COMMISSION ON LITERACY IN PHILADELPHIA. FINAL NARRATIVE/REPORT. Philadelphia, Pennsylvania: Mayor's Commission on Literacy, August 23, 1984. 18pp. (ED 246 263)

The program developed by the Mayor's

Commission on Literacy in Philadelphia has a number of components and involves the cooperation of different agencies in the delivery of services. It also utilizes volunteer tutors and provides resources, information, training, and support to existing programs.

296. McCullough, K. Owen. "Adult Basic Education Instructional Strategies: Their Design and Improvement." OUTLOOK FOR THE 80'S: ADULT LITERACY. Edited by Lorraine Y. Mercier. Washington, D.C.: U.S. Department of Education, Basic Skills Improvement Program, September 1981, pp. 49-71.

McCullough describes a variety of models for adult basic education, including GED-oriented ABE programs, the Adult Reading Academies, and Adult Basic Skills Centers. He describes problems, strengths, and trends for the models and provides names and locations of centers. The increasing importance of the lay person in eradicating illiteracy as well as the varieties of programs are identified as current trends. The author addresses important issues for those concerned with adult basic education. He lists ideal characteristics of instructors, stressing their roles as counselors and helpers, as well as their focus on process more than content. Characteristics of adult learners are identified and learning theory is related to adult basic education.

297. Micklos, John. "Literacy in the United States: What is the Status? What's Being Done?" READING TODAY 3 (October/November 1985): 6-7.

Micklos examines the range of estimates on the extent of illiteracy resulting from differing definitions of illiteracy and concludes that "everyone would like to reduce the illiteracy rate, whatever it may be" (p. 6). He presents an overview of the efforts of the federal government, the business

sector, newspapers, and a variety of literacy
programs.   Micklos   includes   names   and
addresses to contact for further information.

298.   Mulcrone,   Patricia.   "Adult Basic Education:
       A Racetrack Setting." LIFELONG LEARNING   5
       (February 1982): 7.

       The   article   is   short.   The   message is
       clear. If we are to meet the needs of adult
       students we must go to them, not expect them
       to   come   to us.   Mulcrone describes   the
       services   and   incentives offered in teaching
       literacy to non-English and English speaking
       students in a racetrack setting. The program
       is   jointly   sponsored   by the   racetrack
       management and a local community college.

299.   Newman,   Anabel,   and   Ruth   E.   Huffman.
       COLLECTION,   EVALUATION,   DISSEMINATION
       SYSTEM (CEDS). An Index of 309/310 Adult
       Basic   Education   Projects, Indiana 1976-
       1981. Final Report. Bloomington, Indiana:
       Indiana University, School of Education,
       1982. 39pp. (ED 222 680)

       Newman and Huffman describe what can be
       done on a state-wide level to collect,
       evaluate,   and disseminate information to ABE
       teachers. Successful adult basic education
       special   projects   were   identified   and
       information about them disseminated.   The
       instruments used to evaluate the projects are
       included and discussed. Dissemination took
       place through a computer   network, hands-on
       experience, or workshops.

300.   Nickse, Ruth S. THE COLLEGE WORK-STUDY ADULT
       LITERACY   PROJECT.   National Assn. of
       Student   Employment   Administrators,
       September 1984. 44pp. (ED 251 660)

       Nickse   reports   on   the results of a
       questionnaire distributed to 19 colleges and
       universities who engaged in literacy training
       using   college   students as part of the
       National Adult Literacy Initiative. On the
       basis of the 18 questionnaires returned,

Nickse describes the role of the colleges and collaborating agencies in recruiting and training tutors and tutees. Both of these groups appeared to have benefited from the experience.

301. Northwest Regional Educational Laboratory. HOW TO ESTABLISH A BRANCH LITERACY COUNCIL IN A RURAL AREA. Special Experimental Demonstration Project. Portland, Oregon, 1981. 32pp. (ED 215 183)

This manual provides guidelines and suggestions for establishing and organizing a literacy council. Help is given in many areas: planning publicity, attracting students, getting and training volunteers, establishing relationships with other agencies, and presenting workshops to tutors to name a few. The suggestions are presented chronologically to aid the reader in the process of establishing the council. Specific forms and samples of materials are provided.

302. Outman, Bob, et al. ALLEN ISD-COMMUNITY EDUCATION ADULT "RIGHT TO READ" PROGRAM. COLLIN COUNTY ADULT LITERACY COUNCIL. SPECIAL PROJECT REPORT. Collin County, Texas: Allen Independent School District, July 12, 1984. 159pp. (ED 246 243)

This document provides an overview of the establishment and administration of an adult right-to-read program and includes numerous sample documents and plans used in the program. Many aspects of the program are detailed, including tutor recruitment and training, recruitment of students, and instruction and materials as well as administrative matters.

303. Patterson, Patsy A. HOW TO OPERATE AN INDIVIDUALIZED LEARNING CENTER. A HANDBOOK FOR TEACHERS OF ADULT BASIC EDUCATION. Cleveland, Ohio: Cleveland Public Schools, September 1979. 79pp. (ED 220 606)

Patterson recognizes the difficulties beginning teachers have in adapting instruction to meet the varied needs of adults. She provides guidance in establishing and running a learning center, testing, prescribing instruction, using programmed learning and group instruction, record keeping, and using aides.

304. Pennsylvania State Department of Education. RECRUITING VOLUNTEERS FOR OUR CAUSE. THE TALC PROGRAM (TUTORING ADULTS THROUGH LITERACY COUNCILS). Division of Adult Education and Training Programs, Harrisburg, Pennsylvania, June 1983. 56pp. (ED 241 808)

This document describes how college education departments can become involved in promoting literacy education through literacy councils and through the encouragement of student participation in literacy programs. In particular it details the ways in which a campaign to promote such a program was organized and led by one college. The paper provides details on the campaign, a symposium for participants, and the number of volunteer tutors recruited and colleges enlisted.

305. Quickel, Rosemary L., and James E. Wise. HORRY COUNTY READING CRUSADE. Final Evaluation Report, 1981-82. Conway, South Carolina: Horry County Board of Education, June 7, 1982. 27pp. (ED 221 315)

The authors describe a program, jointly sponsored by the local school district and the Literacy Council, designed to raise the literacy level in the local area. Details are provided on the establishment and administration of the program, the role and training of volunteer and peer tutors, and the total community effort behind the crusade.

306. Samuels, Frank, and Lester Gierach. "The Design and Implementation of an Urban Adult Basic Education Program." Paper presented

at the National Adult Education Conference, December 1, 1983, Philadelphia, Pennsylvania. 36pp. (ED 237 657)

Samuels and Gierach describe an extension program in adult basic education operated by an urban technical college in cooperation with local agencies. The program incorporated a flexible time plan, instruction based on survival skills, the use of local personnel as instructors and local, influential people as recruiters, adult and cultural characteristics in planning instruction, and the involvement of students.

307. U.S., Department of Education. CATALOG OF ADULT EDUCATION PROJECTS. Fiscal Year 1982, Office of Vocational and Adult Education, Clearinghouse on Adult Education, Washington, D.C., 1982. 442pp. (ED 228 379)

This catalog provides abstracts of 255 projects related to adult education. Many of the projects are concerned with literacy instruction. Other projects of interest include program evaluation, student assessment and testing, staff development, and tutoring alternatives. A description is provided, target audience identified, contact person named, funding information and an evaluation of the project included. The document is a useful resource for identifying program alternatives to consider, programs to visit, and strategies currently in use.

308. U.S., Department of Education. CATALOG OF ADULT EDUCATION PROJECTS. Fiscal Year 1983, Office of Vocational and Adult Education, Clearinghouse on Adult Education, Washington, D.C., 1983. 380pp. (ED 235 370)

This catalog reviews 243 projects in the area of adult education. See entry 307.

309. U.S., Department of Education. DIRECTORY OF ADULT-SERVING PROGRAMS DEPARTMENT OF

EDUCATION. Division of Adult Education
Services, Washington, D.C., February 1983.

This directory provides information on 29
programs in the Department of Education that
deal directly with adult education or provide
support to adult education programs. In
addition to the program title, information is
provided on the purpose, authorizing
legislation, funds, eligible applicants and
contact person. A number of the programs
have either a primary or secondary focus on
adult literacy.

310. U.S., Department of Education. ADULT
EDUCATION PROGRAMS THAT WORK. Newsclip VI
and Newsclip VII. Division of Adult
Education, Office of Vocational and Adult
Education, Washington, D.C., April 1984 and
August 1984.

These two compilations of news articles
from around the country provide a vivid
overview of the variety of approaches and
delivery systems being used to meet the
challenge of raising literacy levels. Rather
than focusing on statistics, these articles
focus on people and programs.

311. U.S., Department of Education. ADULT
LITERACY: PROGRAMS THAT WORK. National
Diffusion Network and the Division of Adult
Education Services, Washington, D.C.,
Spring 1984.

This catalogue describes 22 exemplary
programs in the area of adult illiteracy. In
each case, a description of the program is
provided as well as the target audience,
evidence of effectiveness, implementation
requirements, financial requirements,
services available and the name of the
contact person.

312. U.S., Department of Education. CATALOG OF
ADULT EDUCATION PROJECTS. Fiscal Year
1984, Division of Adult Education, Office
of Vocational and Adult Education,

Clearinghouse on Adult Education, Washington, D.C., 1984. 529pp. (ED 250 496)

This catalog describes 382 projects in 19 areas of adult education. Over 180 products from the projects are listed. In each case, a description of the program is provided as well as the target audience, evidence of effectiveness, implementation requirements, financial requirements, services available and the name of the contact person.

313. U.S., Department of Education. CATALOG OF ADULT EDUCATION PROJECTS. Fiscal Year 1985, Division of Adult Education, Office of Vocational and Adult Education, Clearinghouse on Adult Education, Washington, D.C., 1984. 190pp. (ED 251 675)

This catalog includes 400 projects in 18 areas of adult education. The products of over 200 projects are indicated. See entry 312.

314. U.S., Department of Education. SECTION 310 COMPETENCY-BASED ADULT EDUCATION PROJECTS. Fiscal Year 1985, Division of Adult Education, Washington, D.C., January 1985.

This catalog includes a number of competency-based adult education projects designed to improve literacy skills. Included for each project is the name of the contact person, funding, project description, and product.

315. U.S., Department of Education. VOLUNTEER Section 310 Special Projects. Fiscal Year 1985, Division of Adult Education, Washington, D.C., January 1985.

This catalog provides information on 40 programs utilizing volunteers. Approximately 75% of the programs described are directly related to the development of literacy. Information is provided on the funding,

contact   person,   program   description,   and
product.

316.   U.S., Department of Education.   ADOPTING   NDN
        PROJECTS: A   GUIDE   FOR   ADULT   EDUCATION
        PROGRAMS.   Division   of   Adult   Education,
        Washington, D.C., April 1985.

        This   catalogue describes 22 adult programs
        including   a   number   focusing   on   the
        development   of literacy skills.   Information
        is also provided on procedures for adopting a
        National Diffusion Network (NDN) program.

317.   U.S., Department of Health,   Education,   and
        Welfare.   ADULT   LITERACY   PROGRAM: A
        COMPILATION   OF   READING   ACADEMY   PROGRAM
        EXPERIENCES.   Office of Education.   Edited
        by Andres R.   Montez.   Washington,   D.C.,
        1980.

        This   practical   document   details   the
        operational procedures of the Right   to   Read
        Reading Academies.   Topics   of   concern to
        administrators   of   adult   literacy   programs
        include   working   with volunteers, recruiting
        and retaining students, developing staff   and
        materials,   keeping   records,   evaluating
        programs, and teaching English as   a   Foreign
        Language.   The   information is detailed and
        many original forms are included.

318.   Vachon, Claude.   REGIONAL,   RURAL   HOME   ABE
        PROGRAM   SPELLS   IMPACT.   April   4, 1981.
        12pp.   (ED 214 747)

        Vachon describes a program designed to meet
        the needs of hard-core functional illiterates
        in a rural area.   An   in-home   instructional
        program,   using   "strong   linkages with human
        services agencies   and   institutions   at   the
        local,   district,   and county levels" (p. 10)
        was developed.   Staff development is   a   high
        priority,   as is outreach to find and attract
        students.

319.   Vines, Diane Welch.   "Secretary's   Initiative
        on Adult Literacy."   Paper presented at the

National Adult Education Conference, December 2, 1983, Philadelphia, Pennsylvania. 15pp. (ED 239 037)

Vines describes the National Adult Literacy Initiative that is based on a joint effort by public, private, voluntary, and military agencies to meet the problems of illiteracy. She addresses issues of funding, recruitment of students, involvement of a wide variety of volunteer tutors, dissemination of information about model programs, and the maintenance and expansion of information networks.

320. Wolf, Evelyn, and Catherine Kavanagh. "Adult Illiteracy: A Public Library Responds." CATHOLIC LIBRARY WORLD 55 (October 1983): 125-128.

Wolf and Kavanagh describe a program in the Queens Borough Public Library, New York, New York that was designed to meet the needs of functionally illiterate adults living in a large metropolitan area. Literacy Volunteers is an "integral part" (p. 126) of the program. The article discusses the recruitment, training, and retention of the large group of volunteers needed for the success of the program. Another critical element in the success is the requirement that the library staff does not actively recruit students. Rather, students must make the first overture to the program in order to be admitted.

Legislation and Literacy

321. Delker, Paul V. "State of the Art in Adult Basic Education." NATIONAL ADULT LITERACY CONFERENCE. January 19-20, 1984, Washington, D.C.: National Institute of Education, Far West Laboratory and The Network, Inc.

Delker reports on adult basic education programs supported by the State-administered program under the Adult Basic Education Act,

Public Law 91-230. He reviews the purposes
of the act and highlights the focus of adult
basic skills training as a means to an end,
not an end in itself. He summarizes the
assessment of these programs prepared by
Development Associates, Inc.

322.   Ellis, Jeanine.   A HISTORY AND ANALYSIS OF
       THE ADULT EDUCATION ACT. October 21, 1984.
       21pp. (ED 252 658)

Ellis traces the history of the Economic
Opportunity Act and the Adult Education Act
beginning in 1964, examining purposes,
procedures and strategies. The changing
roles and responsibilities of local, state
and federal agencies are identified, with the
current (1984) emphasis on state agencies
assuming more responsibility in tailoring ABE
programs to meet particular needs.

323.   Haase, Ann Marie Bernazza. LAW AND POLICY IN
       EDUCATING UNDER-EDUCATED ADULTS.   Paper
       presented at the Annual Meeting of the
       International Reading Assn., April 27-May
       1, 1981, New Orleans, Louisiana. 9pp. (ED
       205 943)

Haase relates employment and literacy,
describes the difficulties experienced under
CETA by those not able to take advantage of
services, and proposes that training for
employment must be linked to training for
literacy. She urges policy makers to
consider this when developing legislation.

324.   Taylor, Paul G.   "The Adult Education Act
       Issues   and   Perspectives   on
       Reauthorization."   LIFELONG LEARNING 7
       (September 1983): 10-11, 26-27.

Taylor provides a summary of reports on the
history of ABE, beginning with the Economic
Opportunity Act of 1964, as well as an
overview of assessments that have been
conducted. Finally, issues are identified in
the areas of congressional, federal
administrative, state/local/operational, and

structural that the author believes must be
addressed in any discussion of future federal
policy in ABE. This article is the first in
a series. (See entries 325 and 326.)

325. _____. "Legislating Basic Education for
Adults: Responding to the Issues."
LIFELONG LEARNING 7 (October 1983): 7-9.

Taylor presents a questionnaire designed to
elicit educators' opinions on issues related
to legislation for adult basic education. He
asks readers to respond in order to present
politicians with field-generated data related
to critical issues. This article is the
second in a series. (See entries 324 and
326.)

326. _____. "Report of a National Survey of
Issues in Federal Legislating of Basic
Education for Adults." LIFELONG LEARNING 7
(April 1984): 13-16, 18-19, 31.

Taylor provides both the questions in the
survey and the results. These results should
be considered as in progress, though they
indicate strong support for "a federal
policy-making role in basic education of
adults" (p. 19) particularly in the area of
funding. Respondents saw the local level as
the primary source of determining services
and service delivery, followed by state and
federal levels chosen in that order.
Uncertainties were also identified such as to
who should participate in programs and
whether personnel in programs should be
certified. This article is the third in a
series. (See entries 324 and 325.)

327. U.S., Congress, Senate Committee on Labor and
Human Resources. ADULT EDUCATION ACT
AMENDMENTS OF 1984: REPORT TO ACCOMPANY S.
2496, 98th Cong., 2d sess., June 6, 1984.
26pp. (ED 250 521)

This Congressional report provides
information on the background to the
amendments (the results of the needs

assessment and the legislative history) and presents an analysis of the changes.

328.   U.S., Department of Education, ON THE STATE-ADMINISTERED ADULT EDUCATION PROGRAM PUBLIC LAW 91-230, AS AMENDED. Division of Adult Education Services, Office of Vocational and Adult Education, Washington, D.C., August 1983.

This monograph provides background information on the history and purposes of the Adult Education Act. The purposes include enabling adults to acquire basic skills, to complete their education to at least the secondary level, and to obtain training to become "employable, productive and responsible citizens" (p. 2). The state-administered program, as well as the two national discretionary programs, are described. Program accomplishments for 1981 are outlined and limited statistics since 1966 are provided.

329.   U.S., Department of Education. ANALYSIS OF THE CARL D. PERKINS VOCATIONAL EDUCATION ACT (PUBLIC LAW 98-524) AS IT APPLIES TO ADULT EDUCATION. Division of Adult Education Services, Office of Vocational and Adult Education, Washington, D.C., January 25, 1984.

This document analyzes those parts of the Vocational Education Act that allow for linkages in identifying clients, funding, and developing curriculum between vocational education and adult education.

330.   U.S., Department of Education. THE ADULT EDUCATION ACT. Division of Adult Education, Office of Vocational and Adult Education, Washington, D.C., October 1984.

This is the Adult Education Act, Public Law 91-230, and its amendments through October 19, 1984. The legislative history including Public Laws and dates is included.

Literacy and the Older Adult

The Extent and Implications of the Problem

331. Allington, Richard L., and Sean A. Walmsley.
"Functional Competence in Reading among the
Urban Aged." JOURNAL OF READING 23 (March
1980): 494-497.

Using two of the Adult Performance Level
content area measures, Allington and Walmsley
assessed the functional competence in reading
of volunteers 60 years and older from a
senior citizen center. The results were
"bleak" (p. 496). The subjects scored
substantially lower than other groups tested
on the same measures. The authors add that
they feel the results, for a variety of
reasons, underestimate the low level of
functioning of the urban elderly.
Suggestions are made for overcoming the
problem.

332. Courtenay, Bradley C., Robert T. Stevenson,
and Maretta P. Suhart. "Functional
Literacy Among the Elderly: Where We
Are(n't)." EDUCATIONAL GERONTOLOGY 8
(July-August 1982): 339-352.

The authors examine various definitions of
literacy and functional literacy and conclude
that it is difficult to measure literacy when
we have such varying definitions. There are
few studies dealing with literacy in the
elderly. To compound the problem, many of
the studies have used tests designed for
children to measure literacy in adults.
Studies examined in this article include:
U.S. Bureau of Census studies, studies using

293

educational attainment, the Adult Functional
Reading Study, The Survival Literacy Study,
and The Adult Performance Level Study. The
authors conclude that there is no definition
or measure of functional literacy for the
elderly, a group comprising a large portion
of the population unable to meet the literacy
demands of society. In addition, "there is
evidence to raise the question of age bias in
many, if not all, of the estimates examined"
(p. 349). However, the authors caution that
we cannot ignore present problems of the
elderly while we develop appropriate
research. We must use what we have to meet
current needs.

333. Kasworm, Carol E. "The Illiterate Elderly."
Paper presented at the White House
Conference on Aging, November 30-December
3, 1981, Washington, D.C., and at the
Annual Meeting of the Adult Education Assn.
of the U.S.A., October 29-November 2, 1981,
Anaheim, California. 35pp. (ED 215 282)

Kasworm identifies the elderly as the
largest group of functional illiterates and
as the group participating the least in
literacy programs. The author reviews
research and theory, describes this
population, explores implications of
illiteracy in the elderly, identifies needs,
and examines problems in recruitment and
participation.

334. Wass, Hannelore, and Stephen F. Olejnick.
"An Analysis and Evaluation of Research and
Cognition Among Older Adults." Paper
presented at the Annual Meeting of the
American Educational Research Assn., April
14, 1983, Montreal, Canada. 25pp. (ED 228
441)

The authors review research studies on
aging published within the past twenty years
in journals and psychological handbooks.
They raise questions about the design and the
emphasis of many of the studies. They
conclude from this analysis that we do not

have answers to questions about the decline
in learning or remembering written prose
associated with aging. The review raises
issues to be considered by those planning
research and by those reading the published
results of studies.

Instruction and Literacy Acquisition: Theory and Research

335. Check, John F., and Sharon Toellner.
     "Reading Patterns of Adults." READING
     IMPROVEMENT 21 (Summer 1984): 82-88.

     Check and Toellner relate the kinds of
     reading done by adults to the requirements of
     their age and status in life. They identify
     adult learning characteristics, such as
     independence, life experiences and roles, as
     affecting reading habits. Reading interests
     and purposes also vary according to age, sex,
     occupation, education level, and income
     level. The authors studied the attitude
     toward reading, reading habits, types of
     materials read, leisure activities, and
     purpose for reading for adults 70 years and
     older in nursing homes and in regular homes.
     They found that older adults, whether in a
     nursing home or a regular home, read less
     than younger adults. However, all
     participants in the study, even in the 90+
     group, did some reading. Most reading was
     done in newspapers and magazines, not books.
     The older adults read for an understanding of
     current events, for relaxation and enjoyment,
     and finally, for spiritual satisfaction. The
     authors note the contributions of reading to
     the health and mental well being of older
     adults.

336. Courtenay, Bradley C., et al. "Assessing the
     Educational Needs of Undereducated Older
     Adults: A Case for the Service Provider."
     Paper presented at the Annual Scientific
     Meeting of the Gerontological Society of
     America, November 19-23, 1982, Boston,
     Massachusetts. 25pp. (ED 226 176)

The authors of this study of undereducated
elderly conclude from their findings that
this population has widely diverse reading
interests. Professionals do not always
understand or agree on the literacy needs of
this group, but the health professionals who
are in regular contact with the elderly have
accurate perceptions of their needs. Since
the elderly did not identify ABE as a
priority, it is suggested that ABE be
integrated into health education classes.

337. Ernst, Nora S., and Sharon Baggett.
PROCEEDINGS FROM ADVANCED TRAINING FOR
NURSING HOME INSERVICE COORDINATORS. THINK
IT OLDER PROJECT. Dallas, Texas: Texas
University, Gerontology Services
Administration, June 1981. 134pp. (ED 236
417)

This document is designed to enable the
nursing home inservice instructor to provide
workshops on adult learning. The focus of
the project is on understanding the needs of
the elderly, providing ways for them to
participate in their learning, and creating
an atmosphere and using strategies conducive
to learning. Specific examples and materials
are included.

338. Heilsel, Marsel, and Gordon Larson.
"Literacy and Social Milieu: Reading
Behavior of the Black Elderly." ADULT
EDUCATION QUARTERLY 34 (Winter 1984): 63-
70.

Heilsel and Larson report on the results of
a study investigating the "literacy behavior"
of a group of 132 black elderly in an urban
area. Based on existing literature it would
seem that this group would have a high degree
of total illiteracy. This was not what the
authors found. Rather, the subjects had
acquired, for the most part, the literacy
skills they needed for their particular
social environment. "Literacy demands and
abilities can only be assessed within a given
social context" (p. 69). That particular

social context must form the basis for
planning for and executing literacy programs.

339. Kingston, Albert J., Jr. "Reading and the
      Aged: A Statement of the Problem."
      EDUCATIONAL GERONTOLOGY 4 (1979): 205-207.

      Kingston relates the reading behavior of
      the elderly to their previous reading
      behavior, education, and socio-economic
      status. Even though they have more leisure,
      the elderly do not seem to read more than
      they did previously. This may be due to the
      lack of appropriate materials and to the lack
      of special programs for the elderly designed
      to develop an interest in reading as a means
      of improving the quality of life.

340. Murray, Martha S. "Older Adults and Reading,
      The Effect of Residential Lifestyles."
      LIFELONG LEARNING: THE ADULT YEARS 4
      (January 1981): 17, 31.

      Murray compared the reading preferences of
      older adults living in an apartment complex
      for the elderly to those of older adults
      living in a nursing home. The purpose of the
      study was to determine if the place of
      residence influences reading preferences.
      Differences were identified in the areas of
      access to reading materials and purpose for
      reading. A need was cited for condensed,
      large print books and for newsletters
      suitable for the elderly.

341. Ribovich, Jerilyn K., and Lawrence Erickson.
      "A Study of Lifelong Reading with
      Implications for Instructional Programs."
      JOURNAL OF READING 24 (October 1980): 20-
      26.

      The authors investigated reading patterns
      of the elderly to determine interests and
      habits as well as changes over the life of
      the reader. In spite of the limitations of
      the sample used, the study suggests that
      reading interests are varied and magazines
      seem more popular than books. Reading habits

over the lifespan vary, generally due both to
past experiences and current circumstances.

342. Rigg, Pat, and Francis Kazemek.   "Literacy
      and   Elders: What We Know and What We Need
      to   Know."   EDUCATIONAL   GERONTOLOGY   9
      (September-December 1983): 417-424. (Also
      available from ERIC. ED 221 834)

      Rigg and   Kazemek lament the   paucity of
research on reading needs and patterns of the
elderly.   The lack of appropriate research
results in reading programs that are poorly
designed and often ill-conceived. Programs
for the elderly should not be extensions of
the   educational   system. Elderly should not
be treated as children or as young adults.
Research is cited to show that the elderly do
not   need to meet the APL competencies, but
rather need reading, for example, to provide
mental stimulation and form a basis for
social contacts. The elderly must have input
in planning literacy programs and choosing
materials.   We have only recently come to
view their reading needs as a concern but in
order to meet them we must develop research
proposals to identify the interests of the
elderly as well as the effects of societal
expectations.

343. Robinson, Richard D., and Ann Marie Bernazza
      Haase.   "The   Reading   Process and the
      Elderly."   EDUCATIONAL   GERONTOLOGY   4
      (1979): 223-228.

      Robinson and Haase review the limited
research on current reading patterns of the
elderly.   They cite the benefits of reading
programs that can provide an opportunity for
the discussion of present reading and prior
experiences as well as for the promotion of
social interaction. A specific list of
research needs is included.

344. Walmsley, Sean A., Kathleen M. Scott, and
      Richard   Lehrer.   "Effects of Document
      Simplification on the Reading Comprehension
      of the Elderly."   JOURNAL OF READING

BEHAVIOR XIII (1981): 237-248.

The authors identify a discrepency between
the typical elderly adult reading level of
about 8th grade and the readability level of
health-related documents of 9th grade or
higher. However, since readability does not
necessarily indicate comprehensibility,
Walmsley, Scott and Lehrer studied the effect
of simplifying a document on its
comprehension by elderly readers. They found
that simplification had little effect on
comprehension, suggesting that the source of
difficulty must lie outside of the document.
There is a need to "focus more broadly on
factors associated with their use of social
service documents" (pp. 246-247) rather than
just looking at the document itself.

345.   Wolf, Ronald E. "What is Reading Good For?
       Perspectives from Senior Citizens."
       READING AND THE ADULT LEARNER. Edited by
       Laura S. Johnson. Newark, Delaware:
       International Reading Assn., 1980, pp. 13-
       15.

       Wolf reports on a study conducted with
       retirement home residents to determine
       purposes and functions of reading for the
       elderly. Reading appeared to fulfill two
       categories of needs: one category related to
       the interests and needs of the inner person,
       enabling him to cope with life and the other
       category related to the social needs of the
       individual, enabling him to communicate with
       life.

Instruction: Alternatives,   Materials,   and
Instructors

346.   DeSanti, R.J. "Cue System Utilization Among
       Older Readers." EDUCATIONAL GERONTOLOGY 4
       (1979): 271-277.

       DeSanti reports on a study designed to
       investigate the cue systems used by older
       readers with expository and narrative texts.
       The readers tended to use word level cues,

regardless of the text. The author concludes
that the reading process is essentially the
same regardless of demands made by various
content materials. Automatic decoding is not
essential for comprehension, since the
subjects were able to comprehend in spite of
errors. Interestingly, "strong concern for
accurate decoding was related to poor
comprehending" (p. 276). The study has
implications for planning instructional
programs for older readers. We need to be
concerned with comprehension and with reading
as a meaning-gathering task.

347. Glynn, Shawn M., and K. Denise Muth. "Text-
      Learning Capabilities of Older Adults."
      EDUCATIONAL GERONTOLOGY 4 (1979): 253-269.

      Glynn and Muth examine the information-
      processing capabilities of older adults and
      their memory for text information. They
      relate these areas to instructional
      strategies that can be used before reading a
      text and those that are suitable for use
      during reading. The discussion relates
      theory to practice and raises important
      research issues.

348. Haase, Ann Marie Bernazza, Richard D.
      Robinson, and Ruth Beach. "Teaching the
      Aged Reader: Issues and Strategies."
      EDUCATIONAL GERONTOLOGY 4 (1979): 229-237.

      The authors examine the elderly, both as
      learners and as readers, reviewing their
      cognitive functioning, motivation, and
      perceptions of the reading task. We have
      little information on effective teaching
      strategies for elderly readers. However, two
      studies are reported, both viewing reading
      programs as opportunities for socialization
      and for meaningful activity. Some specific
      suggestions are made for instruction at
      various levels of literacy.

349. Kasworm, Carol, and Bradley C. Courtenay.
      "Functional Literacy in Older Adults:
      Proactive Approaches to Research and

Teaching." Paper presented at the National
Adult Education Conference, November 14,
1982, San Antonio, Texas. 30pp. (ED 229
559).

The authors review data documenting the
high level of functional illiteracy in the
elderly and the low level of participation
among members of that group in literacy
programs. The results of two research
projects are discussed and suggestions are
made as a result of these findings. Reading
materials and subject matter must be relevant
and based on expressed concerns of the
elderly. Classes should be held in
facilities for the elderly when appropriate.
A number of research needs are discussed.

350.   Scales, Alice M., and Shirley A. Biggs.   "A
       Survey of Reading Habits with Suggested
       Instructional Strategies: Elderly Adults."
       Paper presented at the Annual Meeting of
       the International Reading Assn., May 2-6,
       1983, Anaheim, California. 19pp. (ED 233
       332)

       Scales and Biggs report on a study
conducted with 49 elderly adults that
demonstrated that the subjects were
physically able to read and could attend to
the task, had the time to read, and wanted
instruction in various aspects of reading.
The authors describe a program designed to
meet these identified requirements. The need
to include a motivational element is stressed
as is the need to share reading experiences.

Curriculum and Program Alternatives

351.   Gentile, Lance M., and Merna McMillan.
       "Reading: A Means of Renewal for the Aged."
       EDUCATIONAL GERONTOLOGY 4 (1979): 215-222.

       Gentile and McMillan describe a program for
the elderly that is designed not to increase
their functional literacy but rather to
increase the quality of their life by
developing old and new interests. The

authors explore problems encountered in the
program by the reading professionals and
aides and by the elderly themselves. The
article is concerned with all elderly, not
just those who are reading on a low level. A
bibliography of books and magazines on a
variety of reading levels that might be of
interest to the elderly is included.

352. Lehr, Fran. "Reading Programs for the Older
      Adult." JOURNAL OF READING 28 (December
      1984): 276-278.

      Lehr reviews recent literature in order to
      identify reading needs of the elderly and
      programs that have been developed to meet
      those needs. The needs are diverse and the
      program responses must also be diverse. The
      author asserts that we must go beyond
      assuming that the older readers require
      functional reading skills ar.d look instead at
      ways of bringing readers together and
      involving them in the planning of the program
      and the materials to be used.

353. Lovelace, Terry. "Reading Activities to
      Enhance the Lives of Nursing Home
      Patients." EDUCATIONAL GERONTOLOGY 4
      (1979): 239-243. (Revised article also
      published in READING AND THE ADULT LEARNER.
      Edited by Laura S. Johnson. Newark,
      Delaware: International Reading Assn.,
      1980, pp. 7-12.)

      Lovelace describes a program developed for
      older patients in a nursing home. The
      participants were given copies of a story
      that was read aloud to them. They were then
      encouraged to participate in a discussion of
      the story. The author suggests that group
      reading sessions may be a way to "enhance the
      lives of the elderly" (p. 243).

354. Spore, Melissa. EXTENDING BASIC EDUCATION TO
      THE ELDERLY: A GUIDE TO PROGRAM
      DEVELOPMENT. Albany: New York State
      Education Department, Bureau of Community
      and Continuing Education Program Services,

1980. 66pp. (ED 207 639)

Spore cites the discrepency between the
large number of elderly who lack literacy
skills and the small number who are enrolled
in literacy programs. The problem is
compounded for those elderly who are not
proficient in English. The author examines
needs, characteristics, and learning patterns
of the target population. She looks at
principles of teaching adults, testing and
instruction in ABE and ESL. Descriptions are
provided for a wide variety of programs, and
help is given in planning and executing
appropriate programs. This document provides
a theoretical and practical overview for
those concerned with programs for the
elderly.

355. U.S., Department of Education. EDUCATION FOR
      OLDER PERSONS: ILLUSTRATIVE LOCAL PROJECT
      PROFILES AND STATE LEVEL AGREEMENTS.
      Administration on Aging and Office of
      Vocational and Adult Education, Washington,
      D.C., Spring 1984.

This document provides information on
projects for the elderly, including program
objectives, description, administrators,
background, funding/status, area served,
persons served, staff requirements, admission
standards, materials/information, contacts,
date verified, and keyword terms used in AOA
and ERIC. The projects cover a range of
areas, with only a few dealing directly with
basic literacy development. However, those
included illustrate a variety of program
models. The section on state agreements
reproduces the memorandum of understanding
between departments of aging and departments
of education in seven states.

Literacy and the Speaker of English as a Second Language

The Extent and Implications of the Problem

356. Stupp, Emma Gonzalez, and Jennifer Gage, comps. ADULT BASIC EDUCATION FOR NON-ENGLISH SPEAKERS: A Bibliography. Rosslyn, Virginia: InterAmerica Research Associates and Arlington, Virginia: National Clearinghouse for Bilingual Education, 1981. 46pp. (ED 214 382)

This annotated bibliography contains 51 references on a variety of topics, including such areas as: examining and planning programs, identifying vocational interests and vocabulary, and teaching preliterate adults.

357. Wallerstein, Nina. "Literacy and Minority Language Groups." Paper presented at the National Adult Literacy Conference, January 19-20, 1984, Washington, D.C. 23pp. (ED 240 298)

Wallerstein views a functional definition of literacy as too narrow to meet the needs of ESL students (and perhaps all students). Literacy involves self-image. It involves critical thinking as well as problem-posing and problem-solving. She advocates "community literacy" in which literacy takes place within and with the help of the entire community. The author discusses the community, social, and cultural demands placed on ESL literacy students. The teacher must take these demands into account in developing literacy programs. In addition,

the outside world should be included in the
community literacy program. General
suggestions are made for curriculum
development and instructional strategies.

Instruction and Literacy Acquisition: Theory and Research

358. Chang, Frederick R. READING AND LISTENING
     PROCESSES IN BILINGUALS. San Diego,
     California: Navy Personnel Research and
     Development Center, November 1984.

     Because of the declining size of the pool
     of available Native English-speaking (NES)
     recruits, the Navy will need to increase its
     use of bilingual personnel. Chang reports on
     a study conducted to determine the
     difficulties speakers of English as a second
     language (ESL) have with comprehension,
     vocabulary, and decoding. A comparison of
     scores of NES and ESL students on the Gates-
     MacGinitie Reading test showed almost
     identical performance in decoding. The
     comprehension difference between the two
     groups could not be fully explained by the
     difference in vocabulary knowledge. Areas
     for further research are identified.

359. _____, and Cosette M. Lare. TEXT
     COMPREHENSION PROCESSES IN BILINGUALS. San
     Diego, California: Navy Personnel Research
     and Development Center, August 1985.

     Chang and Lare report on two experiments
     that compared the cognitive performance of
     recruits who were speakers of English as a
     second language (ESL) to that of those who
     were Native English speakers (NES). The two
     groups "differ widely in their ability to
     integrate information across sentences into
     paragraphs" (p. vii). The authors recommend
     instruction in high-level comprehension
     skills and continued research in the area.

360. Wilson, Marilyn. "Developmental Patterns of
     Reading Proficiency in Adult ESL Students:
     Implications for ESL Classrooms." Revised

version of a paper presented at the Annual
Meeting of the Teachers of English to
Speakers of Other Languages, March 1983,
Toronto, Ontario. 21pp. (ED 248 709)

Wilson examined the changes in oral reading
and retelling abilities over a four-month
period of seven low-intermediate level
students of English as a second language.
She reports the finding that literacy
acquisition is similar in both the second
language and the first language. Learning
modes of students are important. To become
literate in English it is not essential for a
student to be totally proficient in English.
Teachers should not allow poor readers to
rely too heavily on graphic and syntactic
information in their reading. Students must
use all sources of information, including
prior knowledge, to obtain meaning. The
Language Experience Approach is suggested as
one alternative.

Instruction: Alternatives, Materials, and Instructors

361. Andersson, Billie V., and John G. Barnitz.
"Cross-Cultural Schemata and Reading
Comprehension Instruction." JOURNAL OF
READING 28 (November 1984): 102-108.

Andersson and Barnitz review the critical
role of background knowledge in reading
comprehension for both adults and children.
They specifically examine the role of prior
knowledge of text structure, cultural
content, and linguistic differences and
complexities for readers from various
cultures. They assert that this is a
neglected area in ESL instruction. The
authors provide a number of guidelines for
comprehension instruction designed to meet
these difficulties. The strategies suggested
include, for example, the provision of
background knowledge by the teacher, the use
of the Language Experience Approach, the
Directed Reading-Thinking Activity and the
Experience-Text-Relationship method, the

development of vocabulary, and language
instruction. Andersson and Barnitz observe
that "these guidelines are also relevant to
teaching content material to any student" (p.
106).

362. Bright Jeffery P., et al. AN ESL LITERACY
      RESOURCE GUIDE. A HANDBOOK FOR ESL/ADULT
      EDUCATORS IN ILLINOIS. Arlington Heights,
      Illinois: Illinois Statewide English as a
      Second Language/Adult Education Service
      Center, November 1982. 57pp. (ED 223 871)

      This comprehensive guide places ESL
      literacy training within the context of
      current views on literacy. The authors
      examine assumptions about the ESL illiterate
      adult, define goals, and consider instruction
      within the framework of three stages of ESL
      literacy (pre-literacy, beginning literacy,
      and initial reading). Suggestions for
      strategies, materials, and lessons are
      provided as well as for program planning and
      assessment of skills.

363. Cohen, Judy, et al. A READING AND WRITING
      PROGRAM USING LANGUAGE-EXPERIENCE
      METHODOLOGY AMONG ADULT ESL STUDENTS IN A
      BASIC EDUCATION PROGRAM. Volunteer Tutor
      Manual. Salt Lake City, Utah: Guadalupe
      Educational Programs, Inc., November 1981.
      210pp. (ED 213 915)

      This manual presents detailed instructions
      in using the language-experience approach to
      develop English literacy in adult ESL
      students. Steps and strategies are outlined,
      sample lesson plans are provided, and forms
      are included for applying language-experience
      to reading one's own language, reading the
      language of others, and teaching language
      skills. (See also entry 371.)

364. Graham, Janet Roth. BILINGUAL ADULT BASIC
      EDUCATION PROJECT. FINAL REPORT.
      Pittsburgh, Pennsylvania: Allegheny
      Intermediate Unit. August 1980. 294pp.
      (ED 195 724)

This comprehensive report documents the instruction provided to bilingual adults based on the Adult Performance Level life-coping skills. Copies of the products developed in English, Spanish, Vietnamese, Lao, and Cambodian are included.

365. Longfield, Diane M. "Teaching English as a Second Language (ESL) to Adults: State-of-the-Art." Paper presented at the National Adult Literacy Conference, January 19-20, 1984, Washington, D.C. 43pp. (ED 240 297)

Longfield believes that it is incumbent on us as a society to develop reading and writing literacy skills in all non-native Americans. She identifies the cultural, social, linguistic, and educational problems that contribute to our difficulties in doing this. The author describes the qualities and characteristics needed in ESL literacy teachers who "must practically walk on water" (p. 17).

Rather than teaching oral English first and then reading and writing, Longfield recommends that they can be taught together, with one reinforcing the other. She suggests a number of practical instructional strategies to accomplish this, including Language Experience, strip stories, One-Word approach, the cloze technique, and snap reading. Suggestions are also made for the administration and development of delivery systems and outreach programs.

366. Paul, Michael. "Reading after Survival Literacy: Language Immersion and an Idea from Confucius." JOURNAL OF READING 29 (February 1986): 423-427.

Instruction in this literacy program for adult refugees is based on the premise that literacy training for survival is not enough. The goal must be for "lifelong literacy: that is, the ability to receive and encode information and ideas in print" (p. 423). Paul advocates using "culturally relevant

paragraphs and stories, instead of isolated
words and sentences out of context" (ibid.).
The author relates the instruction provided
to a model of reading that requires the use
of prior knowledge, prediction and
confirmation of the prediction. Thinking
skills are of primary importance. Strategies
include the use of: prior knowledge, text
structure in reading and writing, writing to
resolve uncertainties, cloze passages to
teach grammar and to foster predictions,
words in context to teach vocabulary, and
inferential and evaluative questions. In
addition, the classes are viewed as
"nonthreatening places to interact with the
new culture" (p. 427) and as places where the
students can pose and solve problems raised
by new experiences. These can also form the
basis for the content of lessons.

367. Pratt, Sidney. "ESL/Literacy: A Beginning."
TESL TALK 13 (Summer 1982): 96-103.

Pratt identifies four kinds of ESL/literacy
students: the complete illiterate, the semi-
literate (who has mastered a few sight
words), the functional literate (who has
functional skills in his native language but
does not use them extensively), and the non-
Roman alphabetic (who is in one of the above
categories but is not familiar with the Roman
alphabet). Reading materials must be
relevant and use the oral language of the
students. Language experience is one
possible approach suggested. Pratt urges
teachers to share their materials and
successful strategies in order to develop a
body of knowledge and resources in this
field.

368. Reyes, Elizabeth R., et al. THE ADULT
ENGLISH AS A SECOND LANGUAGE DIAGNOSTIC
READING TEST. Burlingame, California:
Assn. of California School Administrators,
Foundation for Educational Administration,
1981. 141pp. (ED 240 830)

This individual or group diagnostic test

was developed for adult education or community college programs in order to identify reading strengths and weaknesses and to provide instructional suggestions. The test uses both a cloze format and a maze format (multiple answer cloze) to diagnose reading errors. The focus of the test is on the semantic appropriateness or inappropriateness of the student's responses. A reading profile is developed to be used for planning strategy lessons.

369. Savage, K. Lynn. "Teaching Strategies for Developing Literacy Skills in Non-Native Speakers of English." Paper presented at the National Adult Literacy Conference, January 19-20, 1984, Washington, D.C. 35pp. (ED 240 296)

Savage presents suggestions for working with four categories of students: preliterate, illiterate, semiliterate and non-Roman alphabetic. The suggestions are specific, often illustrated, and relate to the three approaches the author advocates: synthetic (focus on patterns), analytic (focus on meaning), and pre-reading. In all cases, speaking precedes reading and writing, content must be relevant, and lessons should be short, incorporating a variety of approaches.

370. Sherman, Nancy J. "Reading in English: Insights from Adult ESL Students." LIFELONG LEARNING RESEARCH CONFERENCE PROCEEDINGS. Compiled by Gene C. Whaples and William M. Rivera. February 12-13, 1982, College Park, Maryland. 272pp. (ED 215 198)

Sherman studied adult ESL students from four language backgrounds who were reading English at an intermediate level. She found that students whose oral reading was relatively error free were not necessarily comprehending, and those with more oral reading errors seemed to comprehend. The author asserts that adult ESL students "must" develop general language competency, vocabulary and sight words. Because of the usefulness of the psycholinguistic model of reading in analyzing reading behavior, she raises the question of its possible appropriateness in curriculum planning and in instruction. Sherman cites the scarcity of research in English reading by adult speakers of other languages. She suggests that there may be reading behaviors that are common to all adults regardless of language background.

Curriculum and Program Alternatives

371. Cohen, Judy, et al. A READING AND WRITING PROGRAM USING LANGUAGE-EXPERIENCE METHODOLOGY AMONG ADULT ESL STUDENTS IN A BASIC EDUCATION PROGRAM. Administrators/Instructors Manual. Volunteer Tutor Manual. Salt Lake City, Utah: Guadalupe Educational Programs, Inc., November 1981. 173pp. 210pp. (ED 213 914, ED 213 915)

The first manual describes the language-experience approach, provides guidance to tutors in using it to test and teach adult ESL students, and suggests ways for administrators to replicate the model. The second manual provides detailed instruction on teaching strategies for using the Language Experience Approach with a wide variety of language abilities. (See also entry 363.)

372. Craige, Tito. LIGHT A CANDLE: A LITERACY PROGRAM WITH HAITIAN FARMWORKERS. Raleigh, North Carolina: Migrant and Seasonal Farmworkers Assn., Inc., 1983. 64pp. (ED 231 225)

Craige places literacy within a social context. He describes Haiti, its culture, economics, politics and social life, and discusses why the Haitians emigrate to the United States and what their life here is like. Problems for the teacher and the learner are related both to the student's background and to his current needs. The

author involves the reader in the drama of
the Haitian farmworker's life and in his joy
at becoming literate.

373. Crystal, Catherine, ed. PERSPECTIVES IN ESL
     LITERACY: THE   NEIGHBORHOOD   CENTERS
     EXPERIENCE.   AN   ENGLISH   AS   A   SECOND
     LANGUAGE   CURRICULUM   GUIDE   SUPPLEMENT.
     Oakland, California: Oakland Unified School
     District, June 1982. 112pp. (ED 244 113)

     This guide details the curriculum and the
     program developed by the Oakland Neighborhood
     Centers for nonliterate ESL students. It
     contains background information on the
     emotional, social, physical, and conceptual
     difficulties of these students, many of which
     are common to all literacy students. It also
     provides specific suggestions for assessment,
     classroom organization, needed competencies
     and skills, and instructional techniques and
     plans.

374. Eno, Rebecca A. PROJECT LEAP. "SOMETHING
     STOPS   YOU   AND   MAKES   YOU   THINK":   AN
     ADAPTATION.   FINAL REPORT. Philadelphia,
     Pennsylvania: Center for Literacy, Inc.,
     1981. 136pp. (ED 221 648)

     Eno describes the efforts of an urban
     literacy center to recruit, train, and retain
     volunteers for a tutorial program in literacy
     and English as a Second Language. The
     monograph includes backup documents for all
     aspects of the program including, for
     example, the outline for the tutor training
     workshops, training handbooks, and workshop
     evaluations.

375. Maryland   University.   ABE/ESOL   NEEDS
     ASSESSMENT REPORT. Catonsville, Maryland:
     Center for Educational Research and
     Development, 1981. 58pp. (ED 222 642)

     The need for workshops and classes in
     assisting teachers in assessment and
     instruction as well as in using new
     methodologies within ABE/ESOL programs was

documented in a needs assessment. There was also a need for information on sources for resource materials as well as for person-to-person contact between a university resource center and teachers in the field. The survey instruments used in the needs assessment are included. This monograph provides direction for teacher training within a geographical area as well as within one program.

376.   Massoglia, Elinor Tripato. "Promoting Literacy Through The Adult School Program." LITERACY FOR DIVERSE LEARNERS. Edited by Jerry L. Johns. Newark, Delaware: International Reading Assn., 1975, pp. 105-119.

Massoglia identifies five tasks essential to the establishment, maintenance, and "organizational renewal" (p. 107) to meet future needs of programs offering bilingual literacy education in existing adult programs. The tasks are based on the author's view of the adult learner as a person who is active and in control of his own learning, utilizes his experiences and prior knowledge, and needs to learn how to learn.

377.   Miller, Janet M. ABE/ESL VOLUNTEER PROGRAM ORGANIZATIONAL HANDBOOK. Seattle, Washington: Washington Literacy, 1983. 62pp. (ED 232 039)

This handbook for volunteer coordinators focuses on the daily operations of a volunteer tutorial program as well as on the development of effective volunteers. The handbook includes annotated lists of sources and references and copies of materials used in the program.

378.   U.S., Department of Education. ENGLISH AS A SECOND LANGUAGE: SPECIAL PROJECTS SERVING ADULT LEARNERS. Division of Adult Education, Office of Vocational and Adult Education, Washington, D.C. December 1984.

This group of ESL projects and related products was funded under Section 310 of the Adult Education Act. Included are the resumes of reports available from the Educational Resources Information Center (ERIC) as published in RESOURCES IN EDUCATION. The projects cover a wide range of topics--many of them dealing with some aspect of literacy development.

379. U.S., Department of Education. CATALOG OF ADULT EDUCATION PROJECTS. ENGLISH AS A SECOND LANGUAGE. Fiscal Year 1985, Division of Adult Education, Washington, D.C., no date.

This catalog contains listings of programs related to English as a Second Language, including a number that focus on literacy training. The listings include program title, funding, contact person, program description, and product.

Literacy in the Workplace

The Extent and Implications of the Problem

380. Baxter, Milton B., Jerry L. Young, and Nancy A. Schubert. "Reading: A Vocational Skill." THE CLEARINGHOUSE 56 (November 1982): 115-117.

The authors report on a survey conducted in urban and rural schools in Mississippi that identified reading and understanding as the most needed skill for employability. Baxter, Young and Schubert conclude that "the key to preparing students for vocations in a period of rapid technological change is to make them proficient in the skills on which future learning is based--the ability to read, a true vocational skill" (p. 117).

381. Butler, Erik Payne, et al. THE LITERACY-EMPLOYMENT EQUATION. EDUCATION FOR TOMORROW'S JOBS. A POLICY OPTIONS MONOGRAPH. San Francisco, California: Far West Laboratory for Educational Research and Development, 1985. 35pp. (ED 253 773)

Citing the relationship between literacy and the ability to function in the workplace, the authors examine connections between literacy training and preparing for successful employment. Suggestions are made on the local level to relate training in programs funded under the Job Training Partnership Act to the development of literacy skills. On the federal level the need for agency coordination and financial commitment to training efforts is stressed.

382.   James, James J. "Basic Skills Education in
       the Military: A Summary." INNOVATIONS IN
       BASIC SKILLS EDUCATION FOR MILITARY
       PERSONNEL. Proceedings of Division of
       Military Psychology Symposium, 88th Annual
       Convention of the American Psychological
       Assn., Washington, D.C.: Office of the
       Assistant Secretary of Defense, September
       1980, pp, 53-55.

       James compares two approaches to basic
       skills education: an academic approach and a
       functional approach. The first approach has
       not worked with military personnel. There
       has been little transfer of general literacy
       skills, little motivation to enter and
       succeed in programs, and no appropriate
       instrument to measure and communicate
       whatever success was attained. The
       functional approach is designed to meet
       specific job-related literacy needs of the
       military.

383.   McGowan, William. "Corporations Aim to Wipe
       Out Illiteracy." BUSINESS AND SOCIETY
       REVIEW (Winter 1983): 37-40.

       McGowan paints a disturbing picture of the
       extent of illiteracy problems in the
       workplace and the effect these problems have
       on both corporations and on workers. The
       author provides a brief overview of some
       corporate efforts to deal with their own
       particular situations.

384.   Moore, Allen B. "Relating Literacy
       Development to Career Development.
       Literacy: Meeting the Challenge." Paper
       presented at the National Right to Read
       Conference, May 27-29, 1978, Washington,
       D.C.. 20 pp. (ED 211 937)

       Moore uses the Adult Performance Level
       (APL) matrix of literacy skills and content
       areas to demonstrate that the development of
       such skills fosters career goals. He
       examines the problems in six selected
       literacy and employment training programs and

proposes a program designed to meet these
problems. He identifies such things as: the
need to involve adults in the planning, the
requirement that general and specific
employment needs be included in any program,
and the importance of moving the adult out
into the work world through visits, a
placement service, and assistance for further
job-related education. Literacy education is
linked in a variety of ways to career
development.

385. O'Donnell, Holly. "Striving for Functional
     Literacy in the Job Market." JOURNAL OF
     READING 29 (OCTOBER 1985): 74-76.

     O'Donnell reviews current literature on
     literacy characteristics of those in the
     workforce, citing examples of insufficient
     literacy skills that limit the individual and
     reduce the level of job performance and
     safety. She also examines efforts in
     business and industry to improve worker's
     literacy skills. As the author points out,
     literacy requirements change and what might
     be a sufficient level of literacy today may
     be insufficient in the future. In order to
     meet the changing needs we will need "a well
     coordinated attack on adult illiteracy" (p.
     74).

386. Ryan, T.A. and William Furlong. "Literacy
     Programs in Industry, the Armed Forces, and
     Penal Institutions." TOWARD A LITERATE
     SOCIETY. Edited by John B. Carroll and
     Jeanne S. Chall. New York: McGraw-Hill,
     1975, pp. 165-189.

     Ryan and Furlong examine in some depth
     programs that have been offered in industry,
     the armed forces, and penal institutions that
     have been directed toward increasing the
     literacy and employability of minorities and
     the poor. Important questions are raised
     about instruction, assessment and
     measurement, long-term benefits to
     individuals, effects on employment, and
     research issues. The results of efforts made

to increase literacy and employability have
been disappointing. The authors provide some
general suggestions for research and for
programs. They conclude that the path to
solving the problems lies in relating
literacy to jobs and involving industry in
the process.

387. Tenopyr, Mary L. "Realities of Adult
      Literacy in Work Settings." Paper
      presented at the National Adult Literacy
      Conference, January 19-20, 1984,
      Washington, D. C. 20pp. (ED 240 290)

      Tenopyr raises a number of questions about
      the role business can and should play in
      meeting literacy requirements of jobs and of
      employees. Without more data, however, we
      cannot determine literacy requirements of
      jobs. They change in response to both
      changing technological needs and to problems
      raised by the literacy level of the
      employees. The author asserts that training
      efforts by business and industry have been
      spotty and the results have been
      inconclusive. She clearly identifies problem
      areas and concludes that at the present time
      the major efforts in literacy training must
      be provided by the educational system, not
      the workplace. Communication between
      business and education must be increased and
      more data collected in order to address the
      problem and determine the most effective role
      for business.

Instruction and Literacy Acquisition: Theory and Research

388. Auten, Anne. "The Challenge: Job Literacy in
      the 1980s." JOURNAL OF READING 23 (May
      1980): 750-754.

      Auten presents a summary of ERIC/RCS
      documents from 1970-1979 on the topic of job-
      related reading skills. She cites the need
      to identify reading skills in the military as
      well as in business and industry and reviews
      progress made in this area. Programs for

teaching these job-related reading skills are
described briefly. Research questions are
identified and explored.

389. Burkett, James R., and Lydia R. Hooke.
"Analysis of the Functional Literacy
Requirements of Air Force Jobs."
INNOVATIONS IN BASIC SKILLS EDUCATION FOR
MILITARY PERSONNEL. Proceedings of
Division of Military Psychology Symposium,
88th Annual Convention of the American
Psychological Assn., Washington, D.C.:
Office of the Assistant Secretary of
Defense, September 1980, pp. 28-40.

Although the Air Force has relatively
little need for remedial reading programs, it
recognizes the problem created by personnel
who "are by no means functionally illiterate
by usual standards, but are simply not
skilled enough to cope with the difficulty or
complexity of the reading materials and
literacy tasks that their jobs require" (p.
28). Traditionally, the Air Force has met
this problem by rewriting materials to a
lower readability level and/or placing the
personnel in academic remedial reading
programs similar to those offered in schools.
The difficulties with these solutions are
identified and a new approach suggested in
which the emphasis is on a functional, job-
related view of literacy. The authors
describe this approach and the results of a
pilot study are given in which the types of
reading tasks in various jobs are analyzed.

390. College Board, The. ACADEMIC PREPARATION FOR
THE WORLD OF WORK. New York, 1984.

The College Board reports on a series of
Business-Education Dialogues held in five
cities during 1982-83. "Business people from
coast to coast agreed that inadequate reading
levels among entering employees is the
largest single problem for employers" (p. 2).
Specific skills were identified. Although
the focus of the report is on preparing
high school students, much of the content is

also appropriate for those who work with
adults to use as a framework in developing
literacy skills for the work place.

391.   Diehl, William A., and Larry Mikulecky. "The
       Nature of Reading at Work." JOURNAL OF
       READING 24 (December 1980): 221-227.

       Diehl and Mikulecky report on a study of
the reading demands of 100 occupations. They
found that 99% of the subjects read on the
job and for an average of 113 minutes a day.
Reading was vital to job completion in only
26% of the cases and important but not vital
in 56% of the cases. It is often possible to
obtain needed information in other ways.
Reading at work is generally reading-to-do,
not reading-to-learn. This is a critical
difference from reading done in schools.

392.   Glauber, Anne, Victoriana Nichols, and
       Valerie Mann Watts. BASIC SKILLS IN THE
       U.S. WORK FORCE: THE CONTRASTING
       PERCEPTIONS OF BUSINESS, LABOR, AND PUBLIC
       EDUCATION. New York: Center for Public
       Resources, February, 1983.

       Glauber, Nichols, and Watts advocate the
involvement of American business in the
improvement of basic skills, since
businessmen are the ones who know the job
market and its demands most completely. The
authors conducted a survey of 184 businesses
and 123 school systems throughout the
country, examined the literature in the
field, and interviewed and corresponded with
the international offices of labor unions.
The product of this study is a list of
competencies needed by U.S. workers in the
areas of reading, writing, speaking and
listening, mathematics, science, and
reasoning that can provide a general
framework for designing programs. In
addition, the authors describe possible
alternative ways to deliver basic skills
instruction within a corporation or to
support programs outside the job setting.

The issue of contrasting perceptions is especially relevant in the area of reading skills. The authors identify the question of deficient reading levels among high school students as one of "nearly a crisis-proportion" (p. 18) according to national statistics. However, according to the survey companies believed that reading skills meet job requirements and schools believed that students were adequately prepared for reading demands of the market-place. Among reasons for the discrepency are the following: some jobs required such low level reading skills that there were few deficiencies; people with low levels of literacy were not hired--the survey dealt only with those hired; over a third of the companies responding to the survey did indicate a problem with reading level in a majority of job categories, but it may be that the other companies felt reading was a less important deficiency relative to other skills areas. The contrasting perceptions here highlight the nature of the problem of identifying job-related reading deficiencies and setting up appropriate programs.

393. Guthrie, John T. "Literacy for Science and Technology." JOURNAL OF READING 27 (February 1984): 478-480.

Guthrie examines general literacy requirements for different job categories in scientific and technological occupations. His concern is that we have expended so much effort in these fields in teaching people the content that we have neglected to insure that they have sufficient literacy skills for the tasks required. The implications for business and industry are obvious; jobs may not be done properly. The implications for the individual may not be so obvious but are serious. Even minor reading difficulties may prevent an applicant from obtaining a position emphasizing scientific knowledge. The author makes some general suggestions for instruction.

394.   _____, and Mary Seifert. "Profiles of
        Reading Activity in a Community." JOURNAL
        OF READING 26 (March 1983): 498-508.

        Guthrie and Seifert report on a study
        conducted to determine the reading activity
        of people in four occupational groups. They
        found that the amount of time spent and the
        media used varied according to occupation.
        Differences in the content and function of
        reading were also documented. The findings
        have applicability for adult reading
        programs. For example, the authors found
        that workers in unskilled occupations read
        for about 60 minutes a day and read a variety
        of materials. This is in contradiction to
        the "popular image that unskilled workers are
        nonreaders or are limited to the reading
        required by employment applications" (p.
        508).

395.   Levin, Beatrice J. "Reading Requirements for
        Satisfactory Careers." READING AND CAREER
        EDUCATION. Edited by Duane M. Nielsen and
        Howard F. Hjelm. Newark, Delaware:
        International Reading Assn., 1975, pp. 76-
        81.

        Levin asserts that reading is a requirement
        for any job. She identifies a list of basic
        reading and study skills that need to be
        learned and should be related to a program of
        career education. Her aim is to prepare
        readers who are able to work independently
        and can apply reasoning-thinking skills to
        the reading process.

396.   Mikulecky, Larry. JOB LITERACY: THE
        RELATIONSHIP BETWEEN SCHOOL PREPARATION AND
        WORKPLACE ACTUALITY. FINAL REPORT.
        Bloomington, Indiana: Indiana University,
        School of Education, February 1981. (Also
        available in summary in READING RESEARCH
        QUARTERLY XVII (No. 3, 1982): 404-419.)

        Mikulecky reports on a study designed to
        determine literacy demands and strategies
        required for a range of jobs and to

investigate school related experiences. The
question assumes importance because of the
large number of people labeled functionally
illiterate and the problems this can cause in
the workplace. In comparing high school
students and workers, the author found that
high school students in school did not read
as much or as well or attach as much
importance to the task as workers did on the
job. He concludes that literacy preparation
in schools has little relevance to the
workplace. The study also presents some
findings concerning the reading strategies
used by various categories of workers.

397. _____, and William A. Diehl. LITERACY
    REQUIREMENTS IN BUSINESS AND INDUSTRY.
    Bloomington, Indiana: Indiana University,
    July 1979.

    Mikulecky and Diehl present a summary of
    relevant literature (1969-1979) in order to
    determine literacy requirements of a variety
    of businesses and industries. The
    description of how the search was conducted
    may be helpful to those who want to update
    it. The authors examine the legal aspects of
    ability testing--particularly literacy
    testing--as well as the tests and procedures
    themselves. The reading and writing demands
    of specific civilian and military
    occupations are reviewed. An extensive
    bibliography is provided for both literacy
    requirements and literacy activities.

398. _____, and William A. Diehl. JOB
    LITERACY: A STUDY OF LITERACY DEMANDS,
    ATTITUDES, AND STRATEGIES IN A CROSS-
    SECTION OF OCCUPATIONS. Bloomington,
    Indiana: Indiana University, School of
    Education, January 1980.

    The authors review definitions of
    functional literacy and conclude that it "is
    really a _relationship_ between the reader, the
    context, and what is required to be read. It
    is a variable construct that can change from
    situation to situation and from person to

person" (p. 1). With this definition as a
framework a study was conducted to determine
the literacy "demands" of various
occupations. The conclusions are complex and
detailed. In general, it appeared that most
workers read on the job, but the reading
tended to be repetitive and was "important,
but not vital" (p. 60) to the task. Much of
the needed information could have been
obtained from the task itself or from the
form of the written information. It may be
that "literacy 'demands' of a job are really
not demands at all; rather, the literacy
materials are used, not so much out of
necessity, as because they make the job task
easier or more efficient" (ibid.). The
authors briefly explore the implications of
these findings for functional literacy and
for school related reading programs.

399.   _____, and Dorothy Winchester. "Job
        Literacy and Job Performance Among Nurses
        at Varying Employment Levels." ADULT
        EDUCATION QUARTERLY 34 (Fall 1983): 1-15.

        Mikulecky and Winchester analyzed job
demands, literacy abilities and the use of
these abilities on the job by nurses of
varying degrees of competence. They
concluded that there are significant
differences between literacy in the classroom
and literacy on the job. Therefore we ought
to train using specifically work-related
materials and tasks. The application of
literacy requires more than basic skills; it
requires thinking and problem solving. The
authors make a number of suggestions for
adult educators.

400.   Seifert, Mary. "Reading on the Job."
        JOURNAL OF READING 22 (January 1979): 360-
        362.

        Seifert summarizes the work of Sticht and
his colleagues on the nature of literacy
skills in the work place. A distinction is
made between reading-to-learn and reading-to-
do. For working adults, both tasks are

prevalent in job training programs; the
latter task is the prevalent on-the-job
reading task. The demands of both tasks are
discussed and compared.

401. Sticht, Thomas G., ed. READING FOR WORKING:
      A   FUNCTIONAL   LITERACY   ANTHOLOGY.
      Alexandria, Virginia: Human   Resources
      Research Organization, 1975.

      Functional literacy is defined as the
      "possession of those literacy skills needed
      to successfully perform some reading task
      imposed by an external agent between the
      reader and a goal the reader wishes to
      obtain" (p. 4). Within the framework of this
      definition, it is important to consider the
      demands of the workplace rather than the
      skill level of the reader. Methods for
      determining the literacy demands of a given
      job and for reducing these demands are
      examined in detail. Also discussed are ways
      of determining readability and strategies for
      writing job manuals. Such an approach, it is
      believed, can provide guidance in many job
      areas, although the focus of the book is on
      the military. The authors stress that time
      is needed for reading programs to be
      effective. Impressive, lasting results
      rarely occur in short periods of time.
      Needed research in a number of areas is
      identified, including specific reading
      requirements in specific occupations and
      delivery systems for recruiting and retaining
      students. Information is also included on
      career related reading and functional
      literacy in secondary schools.

402. _____, and John S. Caylor.   EVALUATION
      OF THE LITERACY ASSESSMENT BATTERY (LAB) AS
      A   PREDICTOR   OF   SUCCESS   IN   THE   ARMED
      SERVICES.   Alexandria, Virginia: Human
      Resources Research Organization, June 1982.

      Sticht and Caylor elaborate on the
      Developmental Model of Literacy by
      identifying and stressing the importance and
      role of cognitive processes in oral and

written language comprehension. In the current study of the effectiveness of the LAB, it was found that the Auding Paragraphs test was a useful addition to existing tests for predicting success in the military. In addition, the authors suggest further areas of evaluation, research, and concept development for improved practices in the armed services.

403. _____, Lydia R. Hooke, and John S. Caylor. LITERACY, ORACY, AND VOCATIONAL APTITUDE AS PREDICTORS OF ATTRITION AND PROMOTION IN THE ARMED SERVICES. Alexandria, Virginia: Human Resources Research Organization, March 1982. 82pp. (ED 217 169)

The authors propose a Developmental Model of Literacy in which learning to read requires closing of the gap between existing oral language comprehension and the desired reading comprehension. Based on this model a Literacy Assessment Battery was developed to measure the gap between auding and reading skills and to predict success in the military. While identifying the need for further research on the relationship of the variables, it was found that adding auding skills to reading skills was a positive step "for predicting success in the military" (p. 57).

404. _____, and Howard H. McFann. "Reading Requirements for Career Entry." READING AND CAREER EDUCATION. Edited by Duane M. Nielsen and Howard F. Hjelm. Newark, Delaware: International Reading Assn., 1975, pp. 62-76.

Sticht and McFann identify two basic approaches to determining the reading demands of jobs. One approach, a summary task statement, identifies the types of reading materials and reading tasks involved in the job. The other, a summary index number, shows the reading grade level needed to perform satisfactorily in the particular job.

Examples, advantages, and disadvantages of both approaches are discussed.

405. Stiggins, Richard J. "An Analysis of the Dimensions of Job-Related Reading." READING WORLD 21 (March 1982): 237-247.

Stiggins examines and compares the information processing requirements of reading-to-learn (school reading) and reading-to-do (job-related reading). The discussion is theoretical but has practical implications. Of particular interest is the discussion of differences in text structure between the two kinds of reading. The author also points out the problems of using an assessment instrument designed for reading-to-learn in order to measure reading-to-do skills and proficencies.

Instruction: Alternatives,   Materials,   and Instructors

406. Hattenhauer, Darryl. "On Teaching the Short Story in Prison." ILLINOIS ENGLISH BULLETIN 70 (Spring 1983): 26-34.

This article was written with a specific group in mind but many of the suggestions can be applied to any group of adults who are reading short stories in an instructional setting. Hattenhauer identifies and uses the characteristics of this particular population in planning instruction. He cites, for example, the self-centeredness of many students, their readiness to read ethnic fiction, their refusal to be "cowed" (p. 27) by what the teacher might want, and their success in "ferreting out evidence" (p. 28). He provides lists of short stories categorized according to themes and according to the elements of fiction. He also provides specific suggestions for inductive instruction, for writing assignments, and for class discussions.

407. Heinemann, Susan Turk. "Can Job-Related Performance Tasks Be Used to Diagnose

Secretaries' Reading and Writing Skills?"
JOURNAL OF READING 23 (December 1979): 239-
243.

Heinemann identified tasks engaged in by
secretaries that could be used to analyze
their reading and writing abilities. She
found patterns of errors that emerged across
all tasks, although there were "less
definitive patterns to the errors that a
single secretary made" (p. 242). Such a task
oriented analysis could be useful for
upgrading individuals as well as groups of
workers.

408. Mikulecky, Larry. "Preparing Students for
     Workplace Literacy Demands." JOURNAL OF
     READING 28 (December 1984): 253-257.

     In this article Mikulecky addresses
teachers who are preparing high school
students for the workplace. Many of the
suggestions are adaptable to adult literacy
students who have the same job-related
reading concerns. The author cites the
particular reading requirements associated
with the workplace and presents a number of
instructional alternatives. He proposes
using a variety of job-related materials,
emphasizing problem solving and abstract
thinking, and emphasizing writing as well as
reading.

409. Miller, Phyllis A. "Reading Demands in a
     High-Technology Industry." JOURNAL OF
     READING 26 (November 1982): 109-115.

     Miller reports on the results of a study
conducted in a high technology industry to
determine the job-related reading skills
required for a variety of positions within
the industry, ranging from supervisor to
system design engineers and senior
programmers. The analysis is presented in
some detail, with information on the content,
format, and readability features of various
types of material as well as the reading
outcomes and tasks required for each level of

position. Suggestions are made for
instruction to overcome identified reading
problems.   Miller recommends using job-
related materials as the basis for the
instruction, emphasizing appropriate text
structures, and stressing ways of reading
efficiently.   She also suggests teaching
workers how to make their own writing more
readable.   Reading is an important part of
these positions, yet the subjects in this
study identified "many problems connected
with the reading and report that much of
their reading time is not spent efficiently"
(p. 115).

410.   Noe, Katherine Schlick.   "Technical Reading
       Technique: A Briefcase Reading Strategy."
       JOURNAL OF READING 27 (December 1983): 234-
       237.

       Noe identifies job-related reading needs
       for those whose students are "time-pressed
       working adults" (p. 234).   One way of helping
       these students prepare for specific job tasks
       and learn to monitor their own reading
       processes is by using actual work materials
       in instruction.   The author provides specific
       suggestions for a program using the Technical
       Reading Technique that includes both a
       prereading checklist to promote predictions
       about content and a postreading analysis to
       evaluate predictions and determine purposes
       of the reading.

411.   Rigg, Pat, and Francis E. Kazemek.   "A Last
       Chance at Literacy: Real World Reading
       Comes to a Job Corps Camp."   JOURNAL OF
       READING 27 (January 1984): 328-333.

       Rigg and Kazemek describe and analyze the
       reading program for young adults at a job
       corps camp.   It was a continuation of the
       kind of program many of these students had
       had in school with a notable lack of success.
       Stress was placed on mastery of decoding
       skills, the use of programmed materials with
       almost no real-world materials of interest to
       the students.   In addition, the authors

identify the lack of a literate environment as a major impediment to progress. They recommend an instructional program based on the interests of the students, using materials the students would choose to read and/or could use in the future. The focus of instruction should be on "reading, sharing, debating and listening" (p. 332) in order to create a literate environment in which students would want to read and would use reading to grow.

412.   Sticht, Thomas G., and Larry Mikulecky. JOB-RELATED   BASIC   SKILLS: CASES   AND CONCLUSIONS.   Columbus,   Ohio: ERIC Clearinghouse   on   Adult,   Career,   and Vocational Education, 1984. 54pp. (ED 246 312)

Sticht and Mikulecky examine job-related basic skills in general, looking at three particular cases. One of these, the Functional Literacy (FLIT) project of the Department of Defense is primarily concerned with the development of job-related literacy. The authors draw conclusions relevant to all basic skills, but readily applicable to literacy development. Citing the FLIT project, they suggest a psycholinguistic model in which language, cognition, and perception are critical in the development of literacy abilities. Students need knowledge of the job content as well as language and cognitive (reasoning) skills in order to read on higher levels. Learning occurs as "the result of an active, constructive process on the part of the learner" (p. 36). Program development must be related to this concept of the process of literacy acquisition. It ought to reflect the basic mission of the business, have a functional context, require active learning, and usually employ competency-based mastery learning.

413.   _____, Lydia R. Hooke, and John S. Caylor.   MANUAL FOR THE ADMINISTRATION AND INTERPRETATION OF THE LITERACY ASSESSMENT BATTERY (LAB). Alexandria, Virginia: Human

Resources   Research   Organization,   April 1982.

This   manual   provides   the   rationale   for   the development   of   a   test   battery   designed   as   a supplement   to   an   existing   military   test   in order   to   make   selection   and   classification decisions.   The   test   battery   measures   auding and   reading   comprehension.   The   manual includes   the   test   items,   normative   data,   and data   on   validity   and   reliability,   and suggests   diagnostic   uses.   It   is   particularly useful   as   a   means   of   examining   and   comparing the   two   comprehension   areas.

414.   Valentine, Lonnie D.   "Reading   Measurement Research   in   the   Air   Force."   INNOVATIONS   IN BASIC   SKILLS   EDUCATION   FOR   MILITARY PERSONNEL.   Proceedings   of   Division   of Military   Psychology   Symposium,   88th   Annual Convention   of   the   American   Psychological Assn.,   Washington,   D.C.:   Office   of   the Assistant   Secretary   of   Defense,   September 1980, pp. 7-24.

In   a   study   completed   in   the   spring   of   1978, Valentine   identifies   the   reading   grade   levels of   qualified   and   non   qualified   personnel   in the   four   military   services.   He   compares commercially   available   reading   tests, describes   the   Air   Force   Reading   Ability   Test developed   for   the   fifth   grade   through   college graduate   level,   and   provides   evidence   of   its reliability, validity, and usefulness.

Curriculum and Program Alternatives

415.   Anderson,   Clinton   L.   "Army   Basic   Skills Educational   Development   Efforts."   LIFELONG LEARNING   RESEARCH   CONFERENCE   PROCEEDINGS, February   12-13,   1982,   College   Park, Maryland.   272pp. (ED 215 198)

Anderson   describes   the   Army's   developing approach   to   meeting   the   problems   of   recruits who   read   at   a   low   level   and   experience difficulty   performing   job-related   tasks.

Literacy training is provided based on
competencies developed for job requirements
and tasks and the recruits' skills in
performing them, not on reading levels or
scores on adult basic education tests. In
addition, job materials are written to be
easily understood and used.

416. Bernick, Michael. "Illiteracy and Inner-City
Unemployment." PHI DELTA KAPPAN 67
(January 1986): 364-367.

The personnel of a privately funded program
designed to reduce unemployment in the inner
city discovered that they had to address the
problem of illiteracy and low levels of
literacy in addition to providing vocational
training. The success of the program is
attributed to: a strong assessment component;
a focus on the basic skills of reading,
writing, and problem solving; a rapport
between students and teachers; computer-
assisted instruction; and a strong connection
between instruction and work.

417. Bochtler, Stanley E. "Reading Goes to Jail--
and Sends a Word to All." READING AND THE
ADULT LEARNER. Edited by Laura S. Johnson.
Newark, Delaware: International Reading
Assn., 1980, pp. 25-29.

"Many of our students have been skilled to
death" (p. 29). This statement sums up the
philosophy and approach of the reading
program for inmates that Bochtler describes.
Students volunteer for the program, select
their materials, and read at their own pace.
The focus is on reading and obtaining
meaning, not on mastering individual skills.
The author includes lists of materials and
films that have been particularly successful.

418. Bowman, Harry L., et al. "Fundamental Skills
Training for U.S. Navy Recruits." Paper
presented at the Annual Meeting of the
College Reading Assn., October 26-28, 1984,
Washington, D.C. 15pp. (ED 250 657)

The Academic Remedial Training (ART)
program of the U.S. Navy is designed for
recruits reading below the sixth grade
reading level (raised to the eighth grade
level in 1985). The reading skills portion
of the program is based on a procedure
involving screening and diagnostic testing,
prescriptive instruction using ten modules,
and criterion-reference tests to insure
completion of the assigned modules. The
program is skill oriented, utilizes "elements
from commercial reading materials" (p. 4),
and can be completed in its entirety in five
weeks. It has been very successful in
remediating deficiencies when measured by a
program completion rate of over 90%.

419. Brennan, Mark, and Roslin E. Brennan.
      LITERACY AND LEARNING--THE HUMAN FACTOR. A
      REPORT TO THE CRIMINOLOGY RESEARCH COUNCIL
      OF THE AUSTRALIAN INSTITUTE OF CRIMINOLOGY
      ON THE LITERACY NEEDS AND ABILITIES OF
      PRISON INMATES [and] APPENDICES.
      Australian Institute of Criminology,
      Criminology Research Council, April 1984.
      354pp. (ED 242 891)

      This report is based on the premise that
      "if those concerned with education can
      understand and respond to the needs of
      inmates - indeed if they can see them as
      students rather than as prisoners - the
      status of education in penal institutions may
      be able to take on a less defensive stance"
      (p. 4). Inmates in this study were surveyed
      to determine their reading and writing needs,
      preferences for instruction and materials,
      and their perceptions of the role of literacy
      in rehabilitation. Literacy is viewed by the
      authors as more than the acquisition of basic
      skills, as is seen in the chapter on the role
      of literature in the acquisition and
      expansion of literacy.

420. Cooney, Joe. LINKING MATH, READING, AND
      WRITING SKILLS TO JOBS. Redwood City,
      California: San Mateo Office of Education,
      1981. 213pp. (ED 21 647)

This monograph documents the approach taken in a CETA program to link literacy skills to jobs but it has a wider application. Specific tasks that workers do in specific jobs are analyzed and the skills needed are identified. Detailed instructions on how to use the material is included which could be transferred to any literacy program aiming at work related skills. In addition, information is provided on the operation of skills centers for adults, assessment and instructional procedures, and instructional objectives.

421.   Duffy, Thomas M. "Literacy Instruction in the Military." Paper presented at the National Adult Literacy Conference, January 19-20, 1984, Washington, D.C. 61pp. (ED 240 288)

Duffy documents a shift in orientation of literacy instruction in the Armed Forces. The emphasis is no longer on mastering general decoding but on acquiring the ability to read materials required in specific job-related military tasks. The author reviews current programs in the Navy, Army, and Air Force and suggests directions for the future, such as the use of computers and videodisc systems.

422.   Emmitt, Robert J. and Barry J. Argento. THE JOB CORPS: BACK TO BASICS. A PROVEN PROGRAM FOR ACADEMIC ASSESSMENT. Country Manpower Report, October 1975. 25pp. (ED 215 137)

The authors describe a systems approach used to improve basic skills levels in reading, math, and high school equivalency subjects in Job Corps participants. Students receive an initial short assessment of their reading level and are then placed in one of three programs. Materials used include programmed readers in the beginning level and a variety of materials in the higher levels.

423.   Fleming, Lily, et al. "The Private Sector

Involvement in Literacy Efforts. Literacy:
Meeting the Challenge." Paper presented at
the National Right to Read Conference, May
27-29, 1978, Washington, D.C. 38pp. (ED
212 938)

This paper deals with models of corporate
involvement in literacy programs. It
provides a detailed description of an onsite
fundamental skills program that offers
reading instruction on three levels to
develop job-related literacy skills.
Emphasis in the beginning reading program is
on the use of language experience and
vocabulary and materials used on the job.

424. Gold, Patricia Cohen. "Literacy Training in
      Penal Institutions." Paper presented at
      the National Adult Literacy Conference,
      January 19-20, 1984, Washington, D. C.
      36pp. (ED 240 292)

Gold addresses four topics related to
literacy education in penal institutions: the
need for such programs, major issues, current
programs, and problems in improving programs.
She examines topics in some depth, presenting
evidence from the literature as well as
statistics from a variety of sources. The
picture is "dim" (p. 4). Because of an
inconclusive and inconsistent federal policy
on literacy training within penal
institutions we do not know exactly how many
inmates need literacy training. However, the
percent of inmates needing such training is
probably substantial. Major issues include:
the lack of a federal policy, insufficient
funds, inadequate facilities and equipment,
the lack of trained professionals, and the
failure to provide comprehensive literacy
programs. The author describes the two major
programs offered: volunteer literacy programs
and ABE programs. She also provides details
on unique and exemplary state programs. The
Federal Prison system is described and
problems within the penal system and within
the inmates themselves are identified. The
author concludes that there is a need for

both adequate attention to the problem and
resources.

425.   Huff, Kent H. "Development of a Job-Oriented
       Basic Skills Program for Navy Personnel."
       INNOVATIONS IN BASIC SKILLS EDUCATION FOR
       MILITARY   PERSONNEL.   Proceedings   of
       Division of Military Psychology Symposium,
       88th Annual Convention of the American
       Psychological   Assn.,   Washington,   D.C.:
       Office of the Assistant Secretary of
       Defense, September 1980, pp. 41-47.

       Because of a concern regarding the
       shrinking pool of recruits available for
       military service, the Navy developed a pilot
       program to upgrade lower aptitude personnel.
       Huff describes the program which is based on
       a task analysis of job-related reading
       requirements and combines technical skill
       training with literacy training.   Initial
       data is encouraging about the positive
       effects of the program.

426.   Kapel, Marilyn B.   "Improving   Reading
       Competence of City Housing Authority
       Personnel: A   Diversified   Approach."
       LIFELONG LEARNING 8 (November 1984): 16-20.

       Kapel places the reading problems and
       resulting difficulties of City Housing
       Authority employees within the context of a
       national problem that is of "major concern
       for both private and public employers" (p.
       16).   A local liberal arts college developed
       a program for the employees and provided the
       training. The program was designed to take
       into account current developments in reading
       theory and adult development and learning.

       The author provides a running account of
       the development of the program, highlighting
       procedures, employee resistance, testing,
       materials, and techniques used. Commercial
       materials formed the basis for the program,
       but the sessions were planned to include and
       involve the students.   The detailed
       discussion of the materials and instructional

techniques used give a picture of increasing confidence and enthusiasm on the part of the students. The gain in vocabulary and comprehension seen in the results of the post-tests gives evidence of increased ability.

427. Kokes, Loralyn B. "Reading Program Helps Employees Step Ahead." READING AND THE ADULT LEARNER. Edited by Laura S. Johnson. Newark, Delaware: International Reading Assn., 1980, pp. 20-24.

Kokes describes a program developed by and taught in a hospital in which the employees are given break or released time to attend. The program is designed to enable employees to obtain a high school degree and within that context they receive diagnosis and remediation in reading. That process is outlined and materials, instruction, and motivational strategies are suggested. The general conclusions are particularly interesting. The author concludes that: a reading program can be successful in a work setting; individualized instruction is valuable, particularly for the men; and the program need not be limited to one ability level.

428. Mayer, Linda A., John C. Ory, and Richard C. Hinckley. "Evaluation Research in Basic Skills with Incarcerated Adults." Paper presented at the Annual Meeting of the American Educational Research Assn., April 11-14, 1983, Montreal, Canada. 28pp. (ED 227 280)

The authors review sources that indicate an extremely low educational level and very high rate of functional illiteracy in federal prisons. They cite and examine a variety of instructional approaches that have been taken to meet this problem. They also report on a study conducted in six correctional institutions that compared student achievement from a traditional, although self-paced, instructional program and from a

computer-based program. The results showed
significant gains in Basic Skill instruction
in both delivery systems, with the most gains
occurring in language, the next highest gains
in mathematics and the least in reading
comprehension. The impact of high attrition
rate, probably due to Department of
Correction policy, is uncertain but "makes it
very difficult to assess the effectiveness of
the educational program" (p. 12).

429.   Newman, Anabel P., and Dorothy Winchester.
       LITERACY   ACTIVITIES: BUSINESS/INDUSTRY,
       VOLUNTEER ORGANIZATIONS.   Bloomington,
       Indiana: Indiana University, School of
       Education, July 1979.

       The authors conducted a search of relevant
       literature (1969-1979) to determine the
       extent, quality, cost, and philosophy of
       volunteer groups, libraries, the military,
       and business and industry engaged in literacy
       programs. An overview of the findings is
       provided for each category and specific
       programs are outlined.

430.   Robinson, Sandra F. "Basic Skills and Human
       Resources Development in the Army."
       INNOVATIONS IN BASIC SKILLS EDUCATION FOR
       MILITARY PERSONNEL.   Proceedings of
       Division of Military Psychology Symposium,
       88th Annual Convention of the American
       Psychological Assn., Washington, D.C.:
       Office of the Assistant Secretary of
       Defense, September 1980, pp. 48-52.

       Robinson describes the current Army Basic
       Skills Education Program which is based on
       job-related basic skills development as
       contrasted to the earlier approach that
       emphasized general literacy training.

431.   Sellman, Wayne S. "Pre-Enlistment Basic
       Skills Development: Preparing Youth to
       Enter Military Service." INNOVATIONS IN
       BASIC SKILLS EDUCATION FOR MILITARY
       PERSONNEL. Proceedings of Division of
       Military Psychology Symposium, 88th Annual

Convention of the American Psychological Assn., Washington, D.C.: Office of the Assistant Secretary of Defense, September 1980, pp. 2-6.

Sellman describes an ultimately unsuccessful program designed for applicants who failed to qualify for military service. Only 7 percent of the total population of 4061 who did not qualify permitted the military recruiters to refer them to an adult learning center. Of 267 referrals, only 98 actually enrolled in programs and only 28 enlisted in the military. The program was not continued. The article is useful in identifying possible reasons for the lack of success, such as lack of motivation to enter a program, failure of programs to teach specific military-related skills, similarity of programs to school situations, lack of financial assistance, and lack of transportation to the centers.

432. Sticht, Thomas G. BASIC SKILLS IN DEFENSE. Alexandria, Virginia: Human Resources Research Organization, June 1982. 69pp. (ED 237 776)

Sticht reports on the basic skills programs of the Armed Services for the Joint Service Working Group on Literacy/Basic Skills. The history of the programs is reviewed, present programs are identified and described, and suggestions are made for further directions. The emphasis is on linking basic literacy training with job-specific literacy tasks.

433. U.S. General Accounting Office. POOR DESIGN AND MANAGEMENT HAMPER ARMY'S BASIC SKILLS EDUCATION PROGRAM. REPORT TO THE SECRETARY OF THE ARMY. Washington, D.C., June 20, 1983. 37pp. (ED 233 179)

This report documents the substantial basic skills problem faced by the U.S. Army. At the end of 1981, 45% of the enlisted personnel had reading and mathematics abilities between the fourth and the ninth

grade level. The purpose of the report was
to examine the efforts of the Army to meet
the problem and to identify aspects of the
effort that needed to be improved or changed.
A major area of concern was in the whole
approach taken. Basic skills were not
related to job requirements and performance
but rather were "blanket literacy levels for
all jobs" (p. 7). It was agreed that the
thrust of the Basic Skills Education Program
(BSEP) would change to include the
fundamental skills needed to meet specific
Army job requirements. The report further
examines administrative reasons why the BSEP
has not been effective in reducing the
illiteracy problem. The issue of the amount
of time needed to remediate is addressed with
evidence submitted indicating "that adult
remedial programs used in DOD and in private
industry are ineffective in instilling
significant lasting improvements and that
substantial time and resources would be
required to bridge the gaps identified" (p.
19.).

Literacy in Postsecondary Institutions

The Extent and Implications of the Problem

434. Eurick, Alvin C., and Gayla A. Kraetsch. "A 50-Year Comparison of University of Minnesota Freshmen's Reading Performance." JOURNAL OF EDUCATIONAL PSYCHOLOGY 74 (October 1982): 660-665.

The authors report on a study that compared reading test results for university freshmen over a 50 year span. Eurick and Kraetsch warn against over-interpretation of the results which showed significant decline in the scores of the most recent group in the areas of vocabulary, comprehension, and reading rate. They point out that other studies, while not covering such a long time span, have also produced results showing a decline in reading performance. Suggested reasons for the decline include changes in the college population, in high school graduation requirements, in family and societal structure, and in the emphasis on reading.

435. Lederman, Marie Jean, Michael Ribaudo, and Susan R. Ryzewic. "Basic Skills of Entering College Freshmen: A National Survey of Policies and Perceptions." JOURNAL OF DEVELOPMENTAL EDUCATION 9 (Issue 1, 1985): 10-13.

Lederman, Ribaudo, and Ryzewic report on the results of a nationwide study conducted to determine the perceptions of colleges and universities regarding the level of basic skills of freshmen and the institutional

343

responses to those perceptions. They found
that the seriousness of the problem varied
according to the academic standards of the
institution. However, 85% of those
responding indicated that lack of preparation
in basic skills was "very much of a problem
or somewhat of a problem" (p. 11). The
authors discuss in some detail the steps that
institutions are taking to address the often
poor academic preparation of students,
including assessment, basic skills courses,
and other instructional support services.

436.   Maring, Gerald H., and Mary Ann Shea.
       "Skills are not Enough in College
       Developmental Reading." JOURNAL OF READING
       25 (May 1982): 786-790.

       Maring and Shea assert that college reading
       programs should develop reading maturity--
       defining "reading maturity as attitude toward
       leisure book reading, time spent in leisure
       book reading, and breadth of reading
       interests" (p. 788). Students in college
       programs have needs in the areas of reading
       maturity that the programs fail to address,
       stressing instead the skills and strategies
       needed for immediate success in college
       courses. The authors make a number of
       suggestions for improving reading maturity as
       well as reading abilities.

437.   Muehl, Lois B. "Trend in Test Results: An
       Analysis of Freshman Reading Competence."
       JOURNAL OF READING 26 (November 1982): 116-
       121.

       Muehl examines a variety of sources of
       information in analyzing the abilities of
       college freshmen to meet the literacy demands
       of postsecondary education. These sources
       include local and national test results and
       the statements of experts. She is optimistic
       that the recent downward trend in reading
       scores is, perhaps, being reversed. Part of
       the problem in college level reading may be
       attributed to the changing, more diverse
       college population.

438. Richardson, Richard C., Jr., Kathryn J.
      Martens, and Elizabeth C. Fisk. FUNCTIONAL
      LITERACY IN THE COLLEGE SETTING. AAHE-
      ERIC/Higher Education Research Report No.
      3.   Washington, D.C.: American Assn. for
      Higher Education, ERIC Clearinghouse on
      Higher Education, 1981.   52pp. (ED 211
      032)

      Richardson, Martens, and Fisk examine
      literacy from a variety of perspectives.
      They analyze language and the cognitive
      aspects of processing it, as well as the
      context in which literacy occurs and its
      functions.   Literacy is viewed as having a
      number of functions ranging from "helping to
      accomplish specific tasks" (p. 12) to "using
      language to learn" (ibid.) and promoting
      "larger goals and values of a society"
      (ibid.).   Various program models are
      discussed, demonstrating how colleges develop
      and structure literacy programs to develop a
      specific skill, prepare students for regular
      course work, or improve self-concept.

439. Simpson, Michele L.   "The Preparation of a
      College Reading Specialist: Some
      Philosophical Perspectives." READING WORLD
      22 (March 1983): 213-223.

      Simpson outlines a broad philosophical
      foundation for the rapidly expanding numbers
      of college reading programs. She advocates
      basing programs on an interactive model of
      learning and an andragogical model of the
      learner.   It is this approach that
      differentiates the college reading program
      from the elementary school model and that
      defines the field of college reading. In the
      first model, the learner is aware of and in
      control of the task, text, and learner
      characteristics and well as learner processes
      and strategies.   In the second, the
      instructor is "concerned with providing
      procedures/resources for self-directed
      learning" (p. 218).   In both areas, the
      author offers suggestions for training the
      instructor and for the process of instructing

the student.

440. Stahl, Norman A., Cynthia R. Hynd, and
      William A. Henk. "Avenues for Chronicling
      and Researching the History of College
      Reading and Study Skills Instruction."
      JOURNAL OF READING 29 (January 1986): 334-
      341.

      Stahl, Hynd, and Henk cite the need to
      examine and build on the past in developing
      reading and study skill programs for today.
      From this perspective they review major works
      which document the history of college reading
      instruction. They also suggest a number of
      directions to be taken and specific questions
      to be examined in developing historical
      research.

441. Tuchowski, Barbara, comp., and Genevieve
      Lopardo, ed. A TEN YEAR REVIEW OF THE
      RESEARCH IN DEVELOPMENTAL READING AT THE
      COLLEGE LEVEL. Illinois Assn. for
      Personalized Learning, 1982. 116pp. (ED
      222 872)

      This book is an overview of research from
      1971 to 1981 in a wide variety of areas
      related to college reading programs. Because
      developmental college reading programs are
      needed by many students, suggestions are made
      based on the research regarding
      characteristics of successful programs.

Instruction and Literacy Acquisition: Theory and
    Research

442. Anderson, Ora Sterling. "Comprehension of
      College Age Students: The State of the
      Art." READING WORLD 21 (March 1982): 213-
      225.

      Anderson reviews current research on the
      relationships between schema theory and
      reading comprehension and between
      metacognition and reading comprehension.
      Some specific strategies are highlighted,
      such as advanced organizers, questions, and

imagery.   Limitations of the studies and of
research in general on college level reading
are identified.

443. Chaplin,   Miriam   T.   "Rosenblatt Revisited:
      The Transaction Between Reader and Text."
      JOURNAL OF READING 26 (November 1982): 150-
      154.

      Chaplin examines theoretical aspects of
      reading both expository text and literature
      on the college level. Reading requires that
      students "be competent, efficient readers and
      thinkers" (p. 151) and that "until students
      can relate their personal experiences to
      academic experiences, they cannot internalize
      the content of the disciplines" (p. 152).
      Instructional   suggestions   are   made that
      encourage the active involvement of   the
      reader   in   creating   both objective and
      subjective   reactions   and   interpretations.
      Courses in developmental reading must relate
      closely to those in content area reading with
      ties between the two both in materials used
      and the setting.

444. College Board, The. ACADEMIC PREPARATION FOR
      COLLEGE. New York, 1983.

      The   College   Board has summarized "the
      combined judgments of hundreds of educators
      in every part of the country" (p. 1) in this
      outline of the basic academic competencies
      and   the   relevant content area abilities
      needed for success in college. The emphasis
      is on the student as an active, critical
      learner

445. Collins, Carmen. "The Use of Writing to
      Improve Reading Comprehension."   Paper
      presented at the Annual Meeting of the
      National Council of Teachers of English,
      November   20-25,   1981,   Boston,
      Massachusetts. 15pp. (ED 214 102)

      Collins reports on a study of the influence
      of writing on the reading comprehension of a
      group of college freshmen.   The   author

concluded that writing encouraged students to
see relationships, organize their thoughts,
and understand abstract ideas. As a result
reading comprehension improved as did the
students' attitudes about themselves and
about instruction. Collins suggests that
writing may also increase cognitive growth.

446. Drabin-Partenio, Ingrid, and Wendy Hall
      Maloney. "A Study of the Background
      Knowledge of Three Groups of College
      Freshmen." JOURNAL OF READING 25 (February
      1982): 430-434.

      After reviewing the critical importance of
      background knowledge in reading
      comprehension, the authors discuss a study
      conducted with remedial reading students,
      intermediate and advanced level speakers of
      English as a Second Language, and students in
      a nonremedial English 1 course. A
      questionaire was administered to determine
      the information students already held in the
      areas of geography, American history and
      civics, and current events. The results
      indicated that the first two groups differed
      significantly from the last group and
      suggested the need for "direct instruction by
      integrating into the remedial program the
      types of information often taken for granted
      as part of the information framework of the
      college student" (p. 434).

447. Driskell, Jeanette Lynn, and Edward L. Kelly.
      "A Guided Notetaking and Study Skills
      System for Use with University Freshmen
      Predicted to Fail." JOURNAL OF READING 23
      (January 1980): 327-331.

      Driskell and Kelly report on a study skills
      program that included instruction in focusing
      attention as well as on organizing and
      manipulating information. They provide some
      detail on the strategies that were used with
      a variety of content area reading materials.
      The results were positive, indicating that
      "training in how to select and organize
      material during study apparently helps many

students succeed" (p. 331).

448. Hayes, David A., and William Diehl. "What
     Research on Prose Comprehension Suggests
     for College Skills Instruction." JOURNAL
     OF READING 26 (April 1982): 656-661.

     Hayes and Diehl review the general lack of
     success of college reading programs in light
     of the "growing number of students whose
     reading and writing capabilities would
     scarcely have qualified them in earlier years
     for college study" (p. 656). They identify
     possible reasons for this situation, ranging
     from attempting too much in too short a time
     period to inappropriate instruction using a
     diagnostic-prescriptive model with little
     transfer to college reading. Research
     suggests, according to the authors, that
     there is a need to teach strategies that will
     enable students to develop persistence and
     flexibility in their reading and to monitor
     their own comprehension. Specific
     suggestions are made for instruction using
     selections from the students' college
     courses.

449. Horowitz, Rosalind. "Text Patterns: Part I."
     JOURNAL OF READING 28 (February 1985): 448-
     454.

     Horowitz reviews current research on the
     impact of text patterns--the rhetorical
     structure of text--on the reader's
     comprehension, recall, and reproduction of
     text. She identifies and illustrates five
     common types: time order, list, comparison
     and contrast, cause and effect, and problem
     and solution. She relates uses of these
     patterns in school, on-the-job, and in daily
     life. In addition the author indicates areas
     needing further research. See also 450.

450. _____. "Text Patterns: Part II."
     JOURNAL OF READING 28 (March 1985): 534-
     541.

     Horowitz continues examining text structure,

looking specifically at research dealing with
the awareness of it on the part of readers
and attempts to train students in text
patterning and pattern processing. She
provides details on a training study in
recognizing and using cause and effect with
community college students. The study
concluded that this training did have a
significant effect on "the extent to which
students elaborate upon ideas in history
essay exam writing, and can significantly
improve student ability to produce cause-
effect patterns in essay examinations" (p.
540). The author raises questions that need
to be answered in instructing students in
text structure. See also 449.

451.   Kennedy, Mary Lynch. "Reading and Writing:
       Interrelated Skills of Literacy on the
       College Level." READING WORLD 20 (December
       1980): 131-141.

       Kennedy examines the difficulties college
       students have because of an "inexperience
       with written language" (p. 132). She
       identifies a wide variety of reading and
       writing skill deficiencies including "one of
       the greatest problems the inexperienced
       college reader-writer faces: the inability to
       organize his thought, especially his thought
       about his reading, in a cohesive, coherent
       manner" (p. 134). She advocates instructing
       in reading and writing together, providing
       reasons why they are mutually beneficial.

452.   Nist, Sherrie L., and C. Ruth Sabol.
       "Disparities Among Reading, Writing, and
       Oral Language: A Look at Underprepared
       College Students." READING WORLD 24
       (December 1984): 96-104.

       Nist and Sabol review research and theories
       concerned with the relationship between oral
       and written language processes. They
       conclude that, although the exact nature of
       the relationship is unclear and uncertain,
       college students can read and, in fact, can
       read at a more complex syntactic and semantic

level than they can speak. Because of this,
the authors advocate teaching reading and
writing at a college level even though the
student does not have appropriate oral
language skills. They provide insights into
the similarities and differences between
reading and writing, highlighting the
importance of background information and
thinking skills.

453. Osburn, Bess, and Cleborne D. Maddux.
      "Reading Ability and Knowledge of the
      Reading Process Among Remedial and Non-
      Remedial Readers at the Post-Secondary
      Level." RESEARCH ON READING IN SECONDARY
      SCHOOLS. Monograph Number 10-11. Edited
      by Patricia L. Anders. Tucson, Arizona:
      University of Arizona, College of
      Education, Reading Department, Fall-Spring,
      1983, pp. 95-106.

      Osburn and Maddux highlight the importance
      of the reader having knowledge and control of
      the reading process. Unfortunately, as they
      point out, instructional materials for
      college students do not address this aspect
      of the process. The results of a study using
      80 college students indicated that students
      in low ability remedial and non-remedial
      groups were word-centered as compared to
      middle and high ability students who were
      meaning-centered. After instruction, which
      included the metacognitive aspects of
      reading, remedial students indicated that
      they had become more meaning centered. The
      authors conclude that "a good reader's
      reading ability, no matter what the age, is
      related to his or her perception of 'good'
      reading behavior" (p. 104). This means that
      we must not only instruct in basic skills but
      also instruct in the reading process,
      enabling students to control the process as
      well as emphasize reading as meaning.

454. _____. "What is Reading?
      Student Viewpoints." JOURNAL OF
      DEVELOPMENTAL AND REMEDIAL EDUCATION 6
      (Winter 1983): 8-9.

Osburn and Maddux interviewed college
students from educational psychology classes
and from remedial classes in order to
determine the view of reading held by good
and poor readers (as identified by the
Nelson-Denny Reading Test). They found that
good readers viewed reading as comprehending,
using meaning units and context to obtain
word meaning. Poor readers, on the other
hand, emphasized decoding, pronouncing each
word, and using the dictionary if needed to
obtain word meaning. The authors suggest
that, rather than stress words and the
decoding of words in instruction, we might
better emphasize "the function and control of
reading behavior" (p. 9).

455.   Palmer, James C. "Do College Courses Improve
        Basic Reading and Writing Skills?"
        COMMUNITY COLLEGE REVIEW 12 (Fall 1984):
        20-28.

        Palmer examines both the current literature
        and the results of a study conducted in three
        urban community college districts to
        determine whether specific courses and/or
        general content courses will improve the
        basic reading and writing skills of college
        students. He concludes that there is
        evidence of improvement in specific areas
        such as "reading rate and the ability to put
        together cohesive essays on complex topics"
        (p. 27). However, the findings are "guarded"
        for improvement in reading comprehension and
        in the mechanics of writing. Colleges must
        find more effective ways of upgrading student
        skills if they are to retain students and/or
        avoid lowering academic standards.

456.   Roberts, Judy, and Nancy Kelly. "The Keyword
        Method: An Alternative Vocabulary Strategy
        for Developmental College Readers."
        READING WORLD 24 (March 1985): 34-39.

        Roberts and Kelly compared the
        effectiveness of a keyword method and a
        dictionary method for immediate and long term
        recall of vocabulary. Significant results

were obtained favoring the keyword method of student developed imagery and mnemonics. This result is attributed to the development of meaning, the involvement of the student, and the relevance of the image. Because students need alternative strategies for learning, the keyword method is proposed as one possibility.

457. Simpson, Michele L. "Recent Research on Independent Learning Strategies: Implications for Developmental Education." FORUM FOR READING 15 (Fall-Winter 1983): 22-28. (See also ERIC document ED 247 528.)

Simpson reviews current research relating to the independent learning strategies of college students. No one strategy is judged superior. Instead, it is the student's act of attending, interacting, reconstructing, and elaborating that will make a strategy effective. The student needs to analyze the variables involved in learning, including task, text, and learner characteristics as well as learner processes and strategies and to assume control of his own learning. The author provides suggestions for instruction.

458. Smith, Sharon L. "Learning Strategies of Mature College Learners." JOURNAL OF READING 26 (October 1982): 5-12.

Based on the premise that "instruction in reading and study strategies relates to larger issues of intellectual development in college" (p. 5), Smith presents a detailed analysis of the learning strategies used by college readers. They reflect a problem-solving approach to reading and learning and illustrate the significance of flexibility, active participation, and control and self-monitoring on the part of the reader. Suggestions for instruction include: using long text selections, synthesizing multiple texts, modeling strategies, using affective strategies, encouraging decision-making, and promoting active control by the reader.

459.   _____. "Comprehension and Comprehension
        Monitoring   by   Experienced   Readers."
        JOURNAL OF READING 28 (January 1985): 292-
        300.

        Smith reviews the results of two prior
        studies on the comprehension of experienced
        readers and presents the results of a third
        study.   Previously she found that mature
        readers "proceed on a trial-and-error basis
        but within a systematically organized
        repertoire of strategies" (p. 292) and use
        outside information from a variety of sources
        to build meaning through scaffolding, defined
        as "building a structure of meaning around
        the text" (ibid.). The current study, using
        a long, difficult, unfamiliar text, suggests
        that "the student's perception of ownership
        of a task can affect choice of learning
        strategies and depth of comprehension" (p.
        299). A student was more inclined to produce
        a product by using "bootstrapping" techniques
        consisting of "building a structure of
        meaning within the text" (p. 292) when that
        appeared to be the expectation of the
        instructor rather than using scaffolding
        techniques.

Instruction: Alternatives,   Materials,   and Instructors

460.   Baechtold, Shirley, Terrel O. Culross, and
        Gwendolyn Gray. "The News Magazine in the
        College Reading Classroom." JOURNAL OF
        READING 29 (January 1986): 304-310.

        Baechtold, Culross, and Gray identify a
        number of goals of college reading programs
        including the need to teach reading
        comprehension, to "stimulate students'
        awareness of national and world problems" (p.
        305) and to "try to reconcile what they read
        with what they already think ... to explore
        their assumptions and frameworks of thought"
        (p. 308). Specific details are provided for
        a variety of instructional strategies using a
        weekly news magazine to accomplish these
        aims.

461. Brittain, Mary M., and Clay V. Brittain.
      "Means of Assessing Remedial Reading Needs
      of College Students." Paper presented at
      the Annual Meeting of the College Reading
      Assn., October 28-30, 1982, Philadelphia,
      Pennsylvania. 14pp. (ED 222 871)

          Brittain and Brittain relate means of
      assessment to two categories of college
      reading programs. The first type of program
      offers self-contained courses and course
      sequences and uses standardized tests to
      identify students needing instruction. The
      authors raise questions concerning the use of
      survey and diagnostic tests and make some
      brief suggestions for other alternatives.
      The second type of program links reading
      instruction to content area instruction and
      generally does not rely on information from
      standardized tests. A few programs are
      briefly reviewed with the suggestion that
      they "reflect theoretical-philosophical
      orientations which require a more incisive
      and holistic view of the reader than
      standardized tests currently provide" (p.
      10).

462. Brozo, William G., and Norman A. Stahl.
      "Focusing on Standards: A Checklist for
      Rating Competencies of College Reading
      Specialists." JOURNAL OF READING 28
      (January 1985): 310-314.

          Brozo and Stahl present a checklist based
      on 19 identified sources in the literature
      and suggest it can be used as one element in
      assessing the competencies of college reading
      specialists. The categories included are
      undergraduate training, instruction, research
      and measurement, administrative and
      counseling, and personal characteristics.
      (See also entry 484.)

463. Cooper, Jan, Rick Evans, and Elizabeth
      Robertson. TEACHING COLLEGE STUDENTS TO
      READ ANALYTICALLY: AN INDIVIDUALIZED
      APPROACH. Urbana, Illinois: National
      Council of Teachers of English, 1985.

Cooper, Evans, and Robertson advocate the development of critical reading in every class by "reading journals" written by the student after reading a text, and responded to by the instructor using questions designed to probe and to sharpen thinking about the text. The emphasis is on a dialogue between student and instructor. Examples illustrate the procedures used and the student responses.

464.   Flynn, Peggy. "Speed is the Carrot." READING AND THE ADULT LEARNER. Edited by Laura S. Johnson. Newark, Delaware: International Reading Assn., 1980, pp. 63-68. (Also printed in JOURNAL OF READING 20 (May 1977): 683-687.)

Flynn relates the details of planning a reading improvement course covering reading and study skills for college freshmen who were labeled "special Freshmen" because of their low SAT scores. "The students, however, had only one thing on their minds-- speed reading. For them, these were the magic words" (p. 65). Flynn capitalized on what must be the motivation for many college students, the desire and need to read faster. She describes how she used this motivation to teach comprehension, comprehension strategies, flexibility, and speed.

465.   Frager, Alan M., and Loren C. Thompson. "Conflict: The Key to Critical Reading Instruction." Paper presented at the Annual Meeting of the Ohio Council of the International Reading Assn., October 18-20, 1984, Columbus, Ohio. 18pp. (ED 251 806)

Frager and Thompson identify the dissonance of conflicting ideas as an important motivator and variable in developing and activating critical reading and thinking skills. They present a specific plan and include examples to teach critical reading as a meaning-driven, hypothesis generating process, with the teacher modeling the process and guiding the student in the application of thinking skills.

466. _____. "Teaching College
Study Skills with a News Magazine."
JOURNAL OF READING 28 (February 1985): 404-
407.

Frager and Thompson identify as a top
priority in college study programs the need
to "help the students learn study skills that
can be applied in their other courses" (p.
404). Because of the practical difficulties
of using college texts with students enrolled
in a variety of courses, the authors advocate
using a weekly news magazine that will
include topics related to a variety of
college majors. They provide suggestions for
summarizing and synthesizing information as
well as critical reading and inference
making. The focus is on "the critical
thinking and research skills so vital for
success in college" (p. 407).

467. Gordon, Belita. ITEM SPECIFICATIONS FOR A
COLLEGE LEVEL BASIC SKILLS READING TEST.
1981. 35pp. (ED 205 893)

Gordon presents guidelines for choosing and
wording the items and text to be included in
statewide competency testing programs or
college basic skills tests. Skill levels
range from the literal to the interpretative
and critical. The discussion is detailed and
specific with numerous clear examples. The
monograph also provides a framework for
examining existing tests and questions.

468. _____, and Rona F. Flippo. "An Update
on College Reading Improvement Programs in
the Southeastern United States." JOURNAL
OF READING 27 (November 1983): 155-163.

Generally, Gordon and Flippo conclude that
the conditions of a decade ago still hold
true for college reading programs. They
found that teachers require specific
training, that reading tests are not used
appropriately, and that a diagnostic-

prescriptive model prevails. In examining
the training and background of instructors,
they found them to be highly trained and
experienced, with the majority having a
background in reading instruction. The
authors suggest "that because of daily
demands these teachers have made instruction
their raison d'etre, placing little emphasis
on research or on the theory that underpins
instructional methods and materials" (p.
158). This was found to be "unfortunate"
(ibid.). Teachers also did not participate
in college reading associations and
professional activities. The prevalent model
of instruction was a teacher-directed one,
based on a diagnostic-prescriptive approach,
with the diagnosis frequently based on
inappropriate use of tests. Course content
was concerned with vocabulary and
comprehension skills. "The skills taught
were those tested by published tests" (p.
162). The need for professional growth is
clearly stated; the need for improvement in
instruction and curriculum is strongly
implied.

469. Harrison, David, and Barbara Little.
      ASSESSING ENGLISH SKILLS: READING. A
      RESOURCE BOOK FOR ADULT BASIC EDUCATION.
      Victoria, British Columbia, Canada:
      Ministry of Education, Continuing Education
      Division, 1984.

      This resource book is designed to be used
      by those working with students from a grade
      10 Adult Basic Education program to a
      beginning college level. The assumptions are
      clearly stated. "All students--and
      especially all adult students--have the right
      to be tested in a fair, judicious and humane
      way" (p. 3). "Testing must be at the service
      of teaching" (p. 2). Within this framework
      the authors examine reading theory as the
      basis for testing and provide specific
      suggestions and examples for assessing
      attitudes and interests as well as content
      area reading, study skills, and
      comprehension.

470. Holbrook, Hilary Taylor. "Reading Needs at
      the 2-Year College Level." JOURNAL OF
      READING 29 (May 1986): 770-772.

      Holbrook reviews a number of recent
      materials listed in the ERIC system
      documenting the variety of reading needs of
      2-year college students and related
      instructional suggestions. The review
      examines relevance of materials, critical
      reading and self-monitoring skills, the use
      of right brain activities, and suggestions
      for utilizing computers.

471. Hunter, Jill S. "Reading: The Key to Quality
      in Higher Education." READING WORLD 23
      (March 1984): 255-264.

      Hunter affirms the need for reading
      instruction on the college level based on an
      interactive model of reading and suggests
      ways of insuring that it is successful.
      Effective programs include an emphasis on the
      affective domain as well as on the cognitive,
      the involvement of students in the process of
      self-evaluation, a linking of reading
      instruction to academic course content, and
      instruction in strategies such as
      questioning, comprehension monitoring,
      networking and mapping, imagery, key ideas,
      decision making, text structure, and critical
      thinking. Hunter reviews selected programs.

472. Johnson, Linda L. "PGR: Problem-Guided
      Reading for College Math-Related Courses."
      JOURNAL OF READING 27 (April 1984): 602-
      608.

      Johnson identifies the emphasis on problem-
      solving in mathematics and the physical
      sciences as a major difference between
      reading texts in those areas and texts in the
      fields of English and the social sciences.
      Detailed instructions are given for Problem-
      Guided Reading (PGR) in mathematics courses.
      Students read the text to solve a particular
      problem. After solving a number of different
      problems they will have read and used most of

the information in the text. The procedure
is based on an active, constructive view of
reading, with the student analyzing,
reasoning, and relating new information to
prior knowledge.

473. Mullen, Jo-Ann. "Reviews of Test Materials."
      JOURNAL OF DEVELOPMENTAL AND REMEDIAL
      EDUCATION 4 (Winter 1981): 29-32.

      Mullen describes four tests in use with
      college students, three of them related to
      the assessment of reading and verbal skills.
      They are the Davis Reading Test, the
      Descriptive Tests of Language Skills, and the
      Nelson-Denny Reading Test. The author
      provides an overview of the administration,
      student directions, uses, and difficulties
      of each.

474. Nist, Sherrie L. "A Holistic Approach to
      Teaching College Reading." READING WORLD
      24 (March 1985): 82-87.

      Nist squarely identifies her assumptions
      before making instructional recommendations.
      Reading is a complex activity that "must be
      taught, not as a series of so-called skills
      or subskills but as an integration of three
      types of processes--cognitive, attitudinal,
      and manipulative" (p. 83). We must be
      concerned not just with the product of
      comprehension (the number of questions
      answered correctly) but also with the process
      of comprehension (the reasons for errors and
      the self-monitoring of the process).
      Finally, we must be aware of the
      characteristics of college students who have
      reading difficulties. In teaching reading
      Nist advocates a holistic approach that deals
      with the student as a total person.

      The author makes a number of suggestions
      for reading instruction including: linking
      instruction to content area texts as well as
      various other types of reading; integrating
      oral language development and writing into
      reading instruction; using a variety of

techniques for processing large amounts of written material; stressing critical thinking and reasoning in reading; and teaching vocabulary "in conjunction with the reading material, never using isolated word lists" (p. 86). Nist recognizes that although a holistic approach requires much more commitment and work on the part of the instructor than the use of a "prescription" and readily available commercial materials, it is more effective.

475. Oritz, Rose Katz. "Generating Interest in Reading." JOURNAL OF READING 27 (November 1983): 113-119.

Oritz addresses the problem of "boring" text by asserting that the reader has a "responsibility to generate interest" (p. 113) and that the designation "boring" may be a "cover up for difficult or inaccessible" (p. 116). She provides a wealth of practical suggestions for involving students in the process of generating interest in text and in analyzing how they are doing this. She also provides ideas for a teacher workshop to address the pedagogical issue of whether we should entertain students to maintain their interest.

476. Pigott, Margaret B. "Who's Afraid of the Wicked Witch? Reading for College Students." JOURNAL OF READING 23 (March 1980): 534-538.

Pigott advocates instruction in the process of critical reading for college students as a component of a course in writing. She describes in some detail instruction in an honors writing class based on a careful reading of an editorial, including prereading, examining diction, syntax, sentence structure and paragraph development, and analyzing the writer's argument.

477. Prager, James. "Helping Students Understand Their Textbooks." JOURNAL OF COLLEGE READING AND LEARNING XVI (1983): 89-94.

Prager identifies the lack of emphasis on "the thinking processes necessary for reading" (p. 89) as an important failure of materials and programs in college reading. He advocates instruction in the use and application of text patterns as a means of enabling students to understand what they are reading and to monitor their comprehension processes. He provides specific suggestions for the instructor including the development of student questions and diagrams.

478.   Rodriguez, Joan Hughes. "When Reading Less Can Mean Understanding More." JOURNAL OF READING 28 (May 1985): 701-705.

Rodriguez makes two suggestions for improving reading abilities on the college level, both of which require less time reading. In the first, she advocates spending more time discussing what has been read, coaching students in how to read a selection, and encouraging them to discuss and analyze why and how meaning is obtained. In the second suggestion, after identifying the impact of prior knowledge on comprehension, she advocates developing missing prior knowledge through easier reading materials or through other media. The need for close ties between the reading teacher and the subject area faculty is critical if skills and strategies are to be reinforced and applied.

479.   Shenkman, Harriet. "Psycholinguistic Awareness: A Mini-Workshop for Students." JOURNAL OF DEVELOPMENTAL AND REMEDIAL EDUCATION 2 (Winter 1979): 20-22.

Shenkman describes a series of exercises to be used with students that are designed to demonstrate that reading is an active process, with the reader engaged in predicting text information and using prior knowledge.

480.   Simpson, Michele L. "A Diagnostic Model for Use with College Students." JOURNAL OF

READING 26 (November 1982): 137-143.

Simpson bases the discussion of diagnosis
of college students reading abilities on a
clear statement of theory. The elementary
school model of evaluation and diagnosis is
examined and rejected because of its emphasis
on quantitative analysis and lack of
appropriate information. The author proposes
a model using informal evaluation that
assumes "that learning from text involves a
complex interaction of four major variables:
task characteristics, the learner's
strategies and processes, text
characteristics, and the learner's
characteristics" (p. 140). She provides
specific suggestions for questions that need
to be investigated in each area and ways of
investigating them.

481. _____. "PORPE: A Writing Strategy for
      Studying and Learning in the Content
      Areas." JOURNAL OF READING 29 (February
      1986): 407-414.

Simpson describes and illustrates a study
strategy, PORPE (Predict, Organize, Rehearse,
Practice, Evaluate) designed to develop
"effective and mature readers" (p. 408) who
"have some awareness and control of their own
cognitive activities while they read and
study" (ibid.) in preparation for essay
exams.

482. Smith, Ellen R. "Community College Reading
      Tests: A Statewide Survey." JOURNAL OF
      READING 28 (October 1984): 52-55.

Smith reports on the results of a survey of
the reading tests used and their uses in
community colleges in the state of
Washington. The findings indicated that
testing was widespread but "conducted
haphazardly" (p. 54), with no one test
identified as "best". She cautions
instructors about the need to use tests and
resulting scores appropriately.

483.   Solon, Carol.   "The Pyramid Diagram: A
        College Student Skills Tool." JOURNAL OF
        READING 23 (APRIL 1980): 594-597.

        Solon provides a rationale and detailed
        instructions for teaching students to develop
        and   use   a pyramid diagram to organize,
        relate,   and   recall   text   and   lecture
        information visually.

484.   Stahl, Norman A., et al. THE PROFESSIONAL
        PREPARATION OF COLLEGE READING AND STUDY-
        SKILLS SPECIALISTS.   College Reading and
        Learning Assistance Technical Report 84-05.
        Atlanta, Georgia: Georgia State University,
        1984. 18pp. (ED 248 761)

        The   preparation of college reading and
        study-skills specialists must be broad and
        include a scholarly academic background   as
        well   as   knowledge of the characteristics of
        adults, the adult learning process, and the
        theory and research of adult reading. The
        specialist must also be familiar with the
        administration   of   a   reading   program,
        instructional methods and materials and with
        the   literature and methods of research. The
        personal characteristics of the specialist
        are critical. (See also entry 462.)

485.   State University of New York. READING IN
        POSTSECONDARY   OCCUPATIONAL   EDUCATION:
        FACULTY   DEVELOPMENT   RESOURCES   MANUAL.
        BASICS OF CAREER PROGRAM   ACHIEVEMENT:
        EMPHASIS ON READING. Albany, New York: Two
        Year College Student Development Center,
        September 1981. 104pp. (ED 232 009)

        This manual contains numerous samples and
        examples of inservice workshops for two-year
        college faculty, staff, and administration.
        Included, for example, is information on
        readability formulas, text selection, the
        cloze procedure, reading-study skills, and
        program evaluation. The emphasis is on the
        use of a team approach to developing and
        implementing college reading programs.

486. Watson, Dorothy J. "In College and in
      Trouble--with Reading." JOURNAL OF READING
      25 (April 1982): 640-645.

      Watson describes the approach used in
      individual tutoring with a college student
      who had poor reading skills. The approach
      emphasizes success, not failure, and uses
      interesting, relevant materials with real
      language. The author focuses on meaning and
      provides suggestions to encourage
      comprehension. Writing is an integral part
      of the program.

487. Webb, Melvin W. "A Scale for Evaluating
      Standardized Reading Tests, with Results
      for Nelson-Denny, Iowa, and Stanford."
      JOURNAL OF READING 26 (February 1983): 424-
      429.

      Webb establishes a list of 10 criteria for
      judging college level reading tests and rates
      three widely used tests, The Nelson-Denny
      Reading Test, the Iowa Silent Reading Tests,
      and the Stanford Diagnostic Reading Test,
      Blue Level, based on these criteria. He
      suggests using test results in conjunction
      with other information. The criteria,
      according to the author, may be applied to
      other tests.

Curriculum and Program Alternatives

488. Brantley, Jerry, Bart Fiumano, Stuart Morton,
      and James Smarr. A MODEL FOR TEACHING
      BASIC SKILLS IN A COMMUNITY COLLEGE
      SETTING. Warren, Michigan: Macomb County
      Community College, September 1981. 239pp.
      (ED 215 719)

      The authors provide an extensive overview
      of the field of postsecondary developmental
      education programs for vocational/technical
      students. They include a review of recent
      literature concerned with literacy and the
      student in these programs, a comparison of
      six CETA basic skills programs, and a
      detailed description of the Macomb County

Community College program.

489. Brittain, Mary M.   "Developmental   and
      Remedial Reading Instruction for College
      Students." Paper presented at the Annual
      Meeting of the World Congress on Reading,
      July 26-30, 1982, Dublin, Ireland.   16pp.
      (ED 227 439)

      Brittain reviews the results of a survey of
      the reading programs of 50 colleges and of
      current literature in the field.   She
      concludes that these programs are growing in
      number and in scope, with a changing emphasis
      from general reading and study skills to
      reading in the content areas and learning in
      general.   She also identifies issues of
      concern to administrators and instructors.

490. Chand, Sunil. "The Impact of Developmental
      Education at Triton College." JOURNAL   OF
      DEVELOPMENTAL EDUCATION 9 (Issue 1, 1985):
      2-5.

      Chand describes a total developmental
      program designed to integrate basic skills
      into the content areas as well as to foster
      "students'   self-confidence,   skills   and
      awareness necessary to negotiate the college
      environment" (p. 3). Within the context of a
      total program of courses and learning support
      services,   the   reading and study skills
      instruction had recently changed its emphasis
      from product to process.   Other changes
      included   the use of academic texts, as
      opposed to commercially prepared materials,
      in instruction and the use of a test that
      "addresses reading as a process rather than
      as a set of skills" (ibid.) for pre- and
      post-testing.

491. Chaplin, Miriam T. "Where Do We Go from
      Here?   Strategies for Survival of College
      Reading Programs." JOURNAL OF READING 21
      (April 1978): 586-589.

      Chaplin suggests directions that may enable
      college reading programs to survive in the

late 1970's and into the 1980's.   In doing
so, she provides us with some benchmarks
against which we can examine current
programs.   She looks toward less emphasis on
remediation and more on the growth and
development of all students.   Her view of
reading and reading instruction is broad,
focusing on the tasks of analyzing,
organizing, and synthesizing ideas and
concepts.   She advocates application of these
strategies through the use of the student's
own text books and through cooperation
between the reading specialist and the
academic faculty.

492.   Cheek, Dallas H. "The Evolving Definition of
        College Reading."   JOURNAL OF READING 26
        (March 1983): 556-558.

        The aim of college reading programs,
according to Cheek, is to remediate reading
and study skill difficulties in
underachieving undergraduates.   The author
maintains that college reading is developing
its own instructional methodology.   The focus
on student-perceived relevancy of reading
instruction is one current trend in this
direction that is discussed in some detail.
Instructional strategies to promote this
include student input into the curriculum,
integration of reading into the content
areas, and student tutoring.

493.   Coleman, Jerry, and Anna Berg.   "Integrating
        Cognitive Development and the Basic
        Skills."   Paper presented at the Annual
        Meeting of the Conference on College
        Composition and Communication, March 17-19,
        1983, Detroit, Michigan.   32pp.   (ED 229
        725)

        Coleman and Berg "believe that to continue
to provide our students with only the surface
competencies in reading and writing when so
much more will be required of them is both
ineffective and misguided" (p. 2).   As a
result, they have identified twelve cognitive
strands that provide "a process-oriented

structure for the basic skills" (p. 6).
These include: "inferential reasoning,
changing frames of reference, generating
possibilities, hypothetical reasoning,
problem solving, decision making,
understanding and making coherent arguments,
metaphoric reasoning, classifying, seriating,
understanding complex relationships, and
reflection upon internal processes" (ibid.).
The authors provide detailed examples of
activities designed to involve students in
cognitive learning and in basic skill
acquisition.

494. Erlich, Howard, and Mary Lynch Kennedy.
      "Skills and Content: Coordinating the
      Classroom." JOURNAL OF DEVELOPMENTAL AND
      REMEDIAL EDUCATION 6 (Spring 1983): 24-27.

      Faced with an increasing number of
      inadequately prepared students, particularly
      in the areas of language communication and
      reasoning, a four-year college developed a
      project that would address these needs in
      humanities and science courses. The academic
      faculty were instructed in skill areas and
      were expected to develop their own strategies
      for including them in the content courses.
      Erlich and Kennedy describe the project and
      provide some detail on strategies used and
      skills stressed in reading and studying,
      writing, speaking and listening, and language
      and reasoning. The last area is the "pivot
      upon which the other skills turn" (p. 26).
      Training of the academic faculty is ongoing,
      focusing on the blending of content and
      skills.

495. Friedlander, Jack.   "Should Remediation be
      Mandatory?" COMMUNITY COLLEGE REVIEW 9
      (Winter 1981-82): 56-64.

      Friedlander examines both sides of this
      issue, considering the large number of
      students who need help in basic skills and
      the relatively small number who actually ask
      for help when remediation is voluntary. He
      points out, however, that when remediation is

required in a developmental education program
it may or may not be effective. The author
describes a variety of programs in which
remediation has been effectively integrated
into a regular college course, thus reducing
the stigma attached to remedial classes and
insuring that the remediation takes place.

496. Granschow, Leonore. "Integrating Basic
      Reading, Writing, and Study Skills in
      Content Areas." JOURNAL OF DEVELOPMENTAL
      AND REMEDIAL EDUCATION 3 (Spring 1980): 24-
      26.

      Granschow describes a program which offers
      reading and study skills in conjunction with
      one or more content areas. The emphasis of
      the program is on involving students in the
      process of learning and of becoming
      independent learners through interaction with
      the instructor and with other students.
      Students are encouraged to examine the
      reasoning process involved in reacting to
      text as well as to acquire vocabulary,
      comprehend text, and apply study skills. The
      author forsees that some students may require
      a more traditional basic skills course in
      reading before succeeding in this course.
      Faculty members from all disciplines need to
      become involved with learning about the
      literacy needs of students.

497. Gruenberg, Diane E. "College Basic Skills
      Programs: A National Survey." JOURNAL OF
      DEVELOPMENTAL AND REMEDIAL EDUCATION 6
      (Spring 1983): 2-4, 30-32.

      Gruenberg reports on the results of a
      survey of colleges with basic skills programs
      that was designed to elicit "information on
      organization, skills emphasis, placement and
      exit criteria, staff training and
      professional development, program evaluation,
      effective teacher qualities and relationships
      between the skills program and other college
      programs" (p. 2). The author relates the
      results with some descriptive detail,
      emphasizing in particular the importance of

the teacher in effective programs.

498.   Harding, Ida Beal.   "Adjunct   Courses:
        Integrating   Study   Skills into Content
        Courses." Paper presented at the Annual
        Meeting of the Western College Reading
        Assn., April 9-12, 1981, Dallas, Texas.
        10pp. (ED 208 339)

        Harding describes in some detail a program
        designed to teach reading and study skills as
        they relate to particular content courses.
        The program aims at insuring that transfer
        from the reading classroom to the content
        classroom will take place and that students
        will have the skills needed to succeed.   The
        content instructor and the reading teacher
        alternate at providing instruction.   The
        program also offers a variety of support
        services.

499.   Henrichs, Margaret. "Strategies for Language
        Expansion: A College Reading Program."
        Paper presented at the Annual Meeting of
        the International Reading Assn., April 27-
        May 1, 1981, New Orleans, Louisiana. 11pp.
        (ED 207 034)

        Henrichs   describes   a   college   reading
        program based on a psycholinguistic model of
        reading,   emphasizing   a   whole   language
        approach and incorporating writing, speaking,
        and   listening   as   well   as   reading.
        Instruction requires that students develop
        problem-solving, reasoning skills and self-
        monitoring techniques.   College texts are
        used as the basis of the instruction in order
        to insure transfer of strategies to the
        content classroom. A sample lesson designed
        to foster prediction strategies is included.

500.   Katz, Ina C.   "Adjunct Classes: Teaching
        College Students Strategies for Learning
        from Texts." JOURNAL OF COLLEGE READING
        AND LEARNING 16 (1983): 75-80.

        Katz describes reading classes offered as
        an adjunct to and in conjunction with

particular content classes that are designed to develop metacognitive strategies, strategies for learning from text and knowledge of a subject. Learning from both lectures and text is emphasized.

501. Monteith, Mary K. "Beyond Basic Skills Courses in Colleges to Courses in Basic Concepts and Content Area Reading." JOURNAL OF READING 22 (October 1978): 74-77.

Monteith reviews literature from 1975 to 1978 on the need to meet the problems presented by the underprepared and/or high risk college student. She also looks ahead and predicts trends for the future. At the time of writing the article, the author identifies basic skills courses as the most prevalent approach but predicts that we will see more courses offered in basic subject matter concepts in conjunction with a literacy program that includes reading and writing as well as study skills.

502. Mullen, Jo-Ann. "College Reading Programs: Some Perennial Questions." Paper presented at the Annual Meeting of the International Reading Assn., April 27-May 1, 1981, New Orleans, Louisiana. 14pp. (ED 205 904)

Mullen presents a series of questions that need to be addressed in planning and improving college reading programs. Among her concerns are: the selection and retention of students, evaluation of students and programs, and the content and structure of curricula. She suggests that programs should not be limited to poor students reading at low levels. Pros and cons are discussed, with conclusions often left to the reader.

503. Nist, Sherrie L. "Developmental Versus Remedial: Does a Confusion of Terms Exist in Higher Education Reading Programs?" JOURNAL OF DEVELOPMENT EDUCATION 8 (Issue 3, 1985): 8-10.

Nist addresses an area that has been
fraught with confusion in the literature on
college reading. She examines the related
questions of whether there is a distinction
to be drawn between remedial and
developmental college reading programs and
whether there should be such a distinction.
She suggests that there has, in fact, been a
shift in terminology from remedial to
developmental although the "description of
programs using both terms was similar in
theoretical approach, content, and pedagogy"
(p. 9).

Nist makes a distinction between those
students who have received prior reading
instruction but have have not mastered basic
skills and those students who have not
received instruction in the advanced skills
needed for college level reading. The former
are remedial students; the latter are
developmental students. Based on a set of
distinctions between the two groups, the
author proposes guidelines for developing
programs for each group regarding materials,
instructional techniques, and the time
required.

504.   _____, and Cynthia R. Hynd. "The
College Reading Lab: An Old Story with a
New Twist." JOURNAL OF READING 28 (January
1985): 305-309.

Nist and Hynd review the traditional
program developed by college reading labs
based on a diagnostic-prescriptive,
individualized instructional approach. They
cite a number of procedures not conducive to
promoting student progress: the use of faulty
tests; instruction in skills as opposed to
strategies; and minimal feedback for the
student. The authors advocate that "reading
should be taught using a holistic, content
based approach" (p. 306) and suggest a number
of techniques used in their program that
foster student involvement with the process
and thinking about the text. They stress
that the teacher and the approach are more

important than materials and machines in obtaining student growth in reading.

505. Richardson, Richard C., et al. A REPORT ON LITERACY DEVELOPMENT IN COMMUNITY COLLEGES: TECHNICAL REPORT. Tempe, Arizona: Arizona State University, Department of Higher and Adult Education, May 1982. 558pp. (ED 217 925)

Literacy is defined by the authors as "the use of reading and writing as operations in the service of a goal to accomplish transactions within a specific context" (p. 13). This definition provides the basis for the detailed study of literacy in community colleges in general and in two specific programs in particular. The scope is broad, covering, for example, administration, planning, faculty support, staff development, the varieties of reading and writing found in colleges, and the motivations of students. Further research needs are indicated.

506. Richardson, Richard C. Jr., Elizabeth Fish and Morris A. Okun. LITERACY IN THE OPEN ACCESS COLLEGES. San Francisco, California: Jossey-Bass Inc., 1983.

The authors report on a three year study of the program in one open-access community college that emphasized the development of critical reading and writing skills. In general, college programs were found not to have an emphasis on critical literacy involving the highest levels of thinking and not to stress student achievement of independence and self-direction in critical literacy.

Richardson, Fish, and Okun provide a graphic picture of a college placing reading and writing in the context of the total college and relating literacy to students' motives and motivation. They examine the relation of reading and writing to the demands of the instructional situation as well as to the requirements and goals of the

student. It is not sufficient to determine a
student's   speed,   vocabulary,   and
comprehension level and then to require or
suggest that he take a general remedial
reading and/or writing course. We must also
look   at   the   teacher's   requirements,   the
demands of the textbook, and the student's
purpose in taking the course and reading the
material. One way of accomplishing this is
by   offering   remedial   courses   within   the
academic departments. The authors' go beyond
course content and reach into the very fabric
of   academia,   touching   upon   admissions,
financial aid, educational programs, course
designations, academic progress, and faculty
conditions.   A   useful   and   extensive
bibliography completes the book.

507. Roueche, John E. "Between a Rock and a Hard
      Place."   COMMUNITY   AND   JUNIOR   COLLEGE
      JOURNAL 54 (April 1984): 21-24.

      Roueche   cites   the   fact   that   although
      instruction   in   literacy   skills   has existed
      for a number of years in community colleges,
      there   has   been   little program evaluation by
      the colleges themselves. The author   reports
      on   a   series   of   studies   designed   to
      investigate practices in successful   literacy
      programs.   He discusses 11 elements related
      to   instruction,   curriculum,   and   program
      structure   that   appear   to contribute to the
      retention and achievement of   students.   In
      addition, he discusses the difficulties of
      raising literacy levels in colleges where
      there   is   not   a total commitment throughout
      the curriculum to requiring high   levels   of
      basic skills.

508. _____, George A. Baker, III, and Suanne
      D. Roueche. "College Responses to Low-
      Achieving Students: A National Study."
      AMERICAN EDUCATION 20 (June 1984): 31-34.

      The authors report on a national study of
      two   and   four   year   colleges   conducted   to
      assess   programs   for   the   underprepared
      student.   They "report with accuracy and

confidence that very few American colleges
and universities have escaped the problem of
underprepared students on their campuses"
(pp. 31-32). Roueche, Baker, and Roueche
describe the policies and procedures that
govern many of these programs and the
organizational structures and strategies used
to manage them.

509. Roueche, Suanne D., and Veronica Nora
Comstock. A REPORT ON THEORY AND METHOD
FOR THE STUDY OF LITERACY DEVELOPMENT IN
COMMUNITY COLLEGES. Austin, Texas: Texas
University, Department of Educational
Administration, November 1981. 505pp. (ED
211 161)

Roueche and Comstock examine literacy
demands of the reading classroom and the
content classroom, the structure of literacy
programs, and the relation of these programs
and literacy development to a variety of
aspects of college life and curriculum. The
authors conclude that "for systematic
literacy development to occur in the
community college, there must be organized
and concerted administrative and
instructional effort to effect it" (p. xiii).
The discussion is detailed, with many
examples of present problems and suggestions
for the future.

510. Sadler, Wilbert L., Jr. "Is The College
Reading Program Worth Saving?" READING
IMPROVEMENT 21 (Winter 1984): 262-266.

Sadler describes current college reading
programs necessitated by the "upsurge of
students entering college deficient in
reading skills" (p. 262). Current practices
include the use of a survey test for
diagnostic purposes, diagnostic-prescriptive
based instruction, and completion based on
achievement level. He details both the
positive and negative attitudes of students
and teachers toward these programs. The
author cites as characteristics of successful
programs the support of the college, an

atmosphere based on humanism and self-worth,
content dealing with reading skills related
to specific disciplines, and the use of a
variety of methods and materials. There is a
need for these supportive reading programs if
high risk students with potential are to
succeed in college, make sufficient income to
raise their living standards, and improve the
quality of their lives.

511.   Schmelzer, Ronald, and William G. Brozo.   "A
        Skills Therapy Approach for Developmental
        Learning in College." JOURNAL OF READING
        25 (April 1982): 646-655.

        Schmelzer and Brozo place basic skills
        instruction in the context of skills therapy,
        defined as "the process of effecting change
        in personality variables through skills
        training" (p. 646). This approach requires
        teachers who are competent and comfortable
        working in the area of counseling as well as
        in instructing reading, writing, studying,
        and basic math. The authors describe the
        procedure, provide a detailed example, and
        review relevant research.

512.   Sherman, Debora, and Clark Taylor.   "Basic
        Skills for the Diversely Prepared."
        DIVERSE STUDENT PREPARATION: BENEFITS AND
        ISSUES.   NEW DIRECTIONS FOR EXPERIENTIAL
        LEARNING.   Edited by Pamela J. Tate.   San
        Francisco, California: Jossey-Bass Inc.,
        September 1982, pp. 61-69.

        Sherman and Clark focus on a generic,
        problem-solving model and define basic skills
        as those that "are basic to the task at hand"
        (p. 62).   Thus, problems with basic
        communication and learning skills must be
        addressed at every point in the undergraduate
        and graduate program. Suggestions are made
        for instruction and assessment that reflect
        the importance both of involving students in
        the process of basic skills acquisition and
        control and of using relevant course content
        for instruction.   Skills specialists must
        work with content area faculty in order to

integrate basic skills into a total curriculum. A number of models for achieving this are proposed.

513. Smith, Jeffery K., Carl J. Schavio, and Donald B. Edge. THE EVALUATION OF COLLEGE REMEDIAL PROGRAMS. Princeton, New Jersey: Educational Testing Service, ERIC Clearinghouse on Tests, Measurement, and Evaluation, November 1981. 107pp. (ED 211 607)

The authors caution that "this paper is not the be all and end all of evaluating college basic skills remedial programs" (p. 2). It does however provide a readable overview of a complex topic and includes numerous specific examples of evaluative activities. Pros and cons are included for most suggestions and techniques as well as ideas on how to employ them.

514. Soll, Lila, and Cecelia McCall. BASIC SKILLS PROGRAMS AT THE CITY UNIVERSITY OF NEW YORK: READING. New York: City University of New York, Office of Academic Affairs, 1981. 156pp. (ED 207 029)

Soll and McCall present an overview of the reading programs at the seventeen colleges that comprise the City University of New York. They categorize the programs into two main groups. The first is based on a skills model of reading and consists of programs based on a bottom-up theory in which decoding, vocabulary, and comprehension skills are diagnosed and remediated. The second is based on a psycholinguistic model of reading and considers the reader's background information and his cognitive and linguistic processing strategies. Writing skills are frequently integrated into these programs reflecting the interaction of the processes of writing and reading. The variety of programs makes this a useful resource for the practitioner. Detailed descriptions are given of populations served, administrative structure, entrance and exit criteria, support services, faculty, and instruction provided.

515. Stasz, Bird. "Problem Solving/Reading Modules for Trade Students." JOURNAL OF COLLEGE READING AND LEARNING 16 (1983): 96-99.

Stasz describes modules developed for community college students with low levels of literacy who are enrolled in trade programs. Students need help in developing reading skills, in learning to read technical job manuals, and in solving problems in the workplace. The author provides examples from job manuals to illustrate the techniques used.

516. Sutherland, Betty J., and David Sutherland. "Read Writers: A Sensible Approach to Instruction." JOURNAL OF DEVELOPMENTAL AND REMEDIAL EDUCATION 6 (Fall 1982): 2-5, 32.

After reviewing research concerned with the relationships between reading and writing, Sutherland and Sutherland describe a course developed to integrate instruction in these two areas. A team teaching approach is used; materials included are teacher- or student-generated texts and novels. The authors conclude that this approach is educationally effective as well as cost effective.

517. Weinstein, Claire E., and Brenda T. Rogers. "Comprehension Monitoring: The Neglected Learning Strategy." JOURNAL OF DEVELOPMENTAL EDUCATION 9 (Issue 1, 1985): 6-9, 28-30.

Weinstein and Rogers describe in some detail a program for college students that focuses on teaching students to use and apply learning strategies. Included in this course is instruction on comprehension monitoring. The authors clearly relate reviews of the literature in general and research in particular to the development of the course content.

518. Whimbey,   Arthur.   "Reading,   Writing,
      Reasoning Linked in Testing and Training."
      JOURNAL OF READING 29 (November 1985): 118-
      123.

      Whimbey   examines   the   mental   processes
      involved in reasoning, expository writing,
      and   reading   and   concludes   that   the
      correlations between them suggest the need
      for   instruction   focusing   on analytical
      reasoning. He describes such a program that
      uses Thinking Aloud Paired Problem Solving as
      an   important   instructional   strategy.
      Students form pairs and alternate between
      reading   and   solving problems aloud and
      listening   for   errors   and asking   for
      clarification.

519. Whimbey, Arthur, J.W. Carmichael, Jr., Lester
      W. Jones, Jacqueline T. Hunter, and Harold
      A. Vincent. "Teaching Critical Reading and
      Analytical   Reasoning in Project   SOAR."
      JOURNAL OF READING 24 (October 1980): 5-10.

      The authors describe a five week precollege
      summer   program for freshmen that emphasizes
      the connections between critical reading and
      analytical reasoning. The students engage in
      verbal and mathematical problem-solving with
      each student thinking aloud as he solves the
      problem.

Literacy Around the World

The Extent and Implictions of the Problem

520. Fisher, E. A. "Illiteracy in Context."
      PROSPECTS XII (No. 2, 1982): 155-162.

      Fisher compares countries with high rates
      of illiteracy to countries with low rates in
      the areas of demographics, education,
      communications, nutrition and health,
      agriculture, and consumption and economics.
      The author concludes that countries with high
      rates of illiteracy are worse off according
      to every indicator than countries with low
      rates.

521. Fordham, Paul, ed. CO-OPERATING FOR
      LITERACY. Report of an International
      Seminar, October 1983, Berlin. 41pp. (ED
      237 755)

      This report advocates the use of
      cooperative efforts in order to solve the
      problems associated with eradicating
      illiteracy throughout the world. Literacy is
      essential if an individual is to participate
      in the work place and in the larger society.
      It is also essential for the development of
      the society itself. Examples from various
      countries are provided to demonstrate the
      need for "sustained national programmes, if
      possible on a mass scale" (p. 19). A major
      weakness in many literacy programs is the
      failure to go beyond basic skills and provide
      for post-literacy training. Literacy
      programs must work with other agencies to
      provide extension and application of skills
      in relevant and significant settings. Areas
      of concern are identified and specific

suggestions are made for cooperation on a national, regional, and international basis.

522. Gayfer, Margaret, Budd L. Hall, J. Ruby Kidd, and Virginia Shrivastava. THE WORLD OF LITERACY POLICY, RESEARCH AND ACTION. Ottawa, Canada: International Council for Adult Education, 1980.

This book is a compilation of issues and actions in the field of literacy around the world. A wide range of topics is addressed, from administration, costs, and staffing of programs to curriculum, contents, and methods for teaching. Examples are provided from a variety of countries documenting various alternatives.

523. International Reading Assn. "First IRA Literacy Award 1979." JOURNAL OF READING 23 (February 1980): 397-400.

The article includes a brief description of the award winners and reprints the speech of Amadou-Mahtar M'Bow, Director-General of UNESCO, delivered at the the awards ceremony. He provides an overview of the discouraging statistics on adult illiteracy worldwide and presents highlights of areas where progress is being made. Implications of illiteracy in terms of poverty, democracy, and the future of the world's children are outlined. M'Bow concludes that "the struggle against illiteracy must be waged on a world-wide scale" (p. 399).

524. Lange, Bob. "World Literacy's Vital Signs." JOURNAL OF READING 25 (December 1981): 278-282.

Lange examines the bad news and the good news of worldwide literacy efforts. The bad news is that illiteracy has by no means been eradicated and, in absolute numbers, has in fact been increasing because of population increases. The good news is that we can recognize factors indicative of effective attempts to develop literacy and we can point

to some successful programs. Lange quotes
Bhola's finding that successful programs
require a national commitment, dynamic
interaction between social and economic
structures, and motivation and participation
of the illiterates. Examples from a number
of recent ERIC documents are provided.

525. Malmquist, Eve. "Developing Reading Ability-
      -A Worldwide Challenge: The Present
      Situation and an Outlook for the Future."
      Paper presented at the Biannual Meeting of
      the International Reading Association World
      Congress on Reading, August 5-7, 1980,
      Manila, Philippines. 24pp. (ED 208 341)

      Malmquist examines definitions of literacy
      and illiteracy and concludes that literacy
      must be viewed within a particular context as
      a "relative concept" (p. 13). Literacy
      problems exist in developed, industrialized
      countries as well as in underdeveloped
      countries. The author reviews trends in
      worldwide literacy programs and suggests that
      there is a need for cross-national
      comparative studies on reading methods.

526. Michigan State University. "Select
      Bibliography on Literacy." THE NFE EXCHANGE
      17 (1980): 11-19.

      This bibliography includes a wide range of
      topics and sources related to problems and
      programs in literacy. Each item is annotated
      and addresses to write to for further
      information are generally provided.

527. _____.   SUPPLEMENTAL LISTING #3.
      LITERACY AND BASIC EDUCATION: 1981-1984.
      East Lansing, Michigan: Non-Formal
      Education Information Center, 1985.

      This bibliography contains 69 items
      covering a wide range of topics related to
      the development of basic literacy in various
      countries. Addresses are provided for use in
      obtaining each item. A list of the names and
      addresses of international organizations

concerned with the development of literacy is
also included.

528. Power, Sara Goddard. "The Politics of
     Literacy." LITERACY FOR LIFE: THE DEMAND
     FOR READING AND WRITING. Edited by Richard
     W. Bailey and Robin Melanie Fosheim. New
     York: The Modern Language Association of
     America, 1983, pp. 21-29.

     Power traces the evolution of a definition
     of literacy that enables the reader to
     function within a context and that links
     literacy to the quality of life and the
     possession of power. The reader can enlarge
     his experience, assume control over his rates
     of reading and comprehension, and engage in
     complex cognitive tasks. The role of the
     press in the creation and distribution of
     written information is explored in some
     depth. Numerous examples from developing and
     Third World countries are provided.

Instruction and Literacy Acquisition: Theory and
Research

529. Deckert, Glenn D. "Sociocultural Barriers to
     the Reading Habit: the Case of Iran."
     JOURNAL OF READING 25 (May 1982): 742-749.

     Deckert examines the reasons why adult
     Iranians do not read even though they are
     literate. He identifies seven cultural
     barriers to reading that range from the time-
     consuming activities of Iranian life and the
     confined role of women to the emphasis on
     rote memorization while reading.
     Implications for the development of
     curriculum, materials, and programs for other
     cultures and societies are suggested.

530. Junge, Barbara Jackson, and Debebe Tegegne.
     "The Effects of Liberation from Illiteracy
     on the Lives of 31 Women: A Case Study."
     JOURNAL OF READING 28 (April 1985): 606-
     611.

     Junge and Tegegne describe the effects of

the Ethiopian literacy campaign on the lives
of women in a rural village and in a town.
The results are not reported statistically,
although the authors do give some indication
of numbers. The article instead focuses on
the responses of the women to questions in an
interview. These responses give the reader a
vivid sense of the effects of moving into
literacy in terms of the women's feelings
about themselves and the attitudes of others
towards them. The difficulties they
experience overcoming their illiteracy come
through in their remarks and provide
suggestions for the development of future
literacy programs.

531. Lazarus, Ruth. "Reflections on Creating a
     'Literate Environment.'" CONVERGENCE XV
     (1982): 67-72.

     Lazarus addresses the problem of retaining,
     expanding, and applying newly acquired
     literacy skills within the context of a broad
     definition of literacy. Literacy is viewed
     as a means of personal development as well as
     a way "of enabling the new literates to
     participate more effectively in the
     qualitative transformation of their
     environment" (p. 68). Based on this premise
     the author suggests ways of creating an
     environment conducive to literacy. This
     might be done by producing written materials
     of interest to the reader and by creating
     motivating and useful reading situations.
     The adult must be involved in all steps of
     the process, including the development of
     continuing education facilities. A number of
     examples from various countries are provided.

532. Macedo, Donaldo P. "The Politics of an
     Emancipatory Literacy in Cape Verde."
     JOURNAL OF EDUCATION 165 (Winter 1983): 99-
     111.

     Macedo holds that literacy is much more
     than "simply the development of skills aimed
     at acquiring the dominant standard language"
     (p. 99). Rather, it is "an integral part of

the way in which people produce, transform, and reproduce meaning" (ibid.). Literacy is "an eminently political phenomenon" (ibid.). Within this context, the author examines the history of literacy education in Cape Verde where both the content and the language of instruction have created "functional literates in the Portuguese language" (p. 101) but not in the Capeverdean language. The author also examines major approaches to reading instruction and finds that, while the cognitive and the interactionist approaches encourage the active role of the reader in the construction of meaning, all approaches fail to account for the role of language in literacy programs. Because of the social, political, and idealogical features of the Capeverdean language, it, rather than Portuguese, must be the language of instruction. Macedo accepts Freire's concept of emancipatory literacy. In order to achieve this literacy, instruction must be in the language of the people.

533. Noor, Abdun. "Managing Adult Literacy Training." PROSPECTS XII (No. 2, 1982): 163-184.

Within the context of a world view of literacy Noor examines definitions, addresses a variety of related issues, and proposes a research agenda. Literacy instruction requires the active participation of a motivated adult using relevant materials. Instruction should not be limited to school settings, but can be provided anywhere using literacy instructors, primary school teachers, and non-professional teachers. Motivation to continue in the program can come from the group of learners as well as from the materials and incentives used. Examples from many countries are included to support and clarify the discussion.

534. Obah, Thelma Y. "Prior Knowledge and the Quest for New Knowledge: The Third World Dilemma." JOURNAL OF READING 27 (November 1983): 129-133.

Obah addresses an issue of concern to much
of the Third World. She examines the
discrepency between the prior knowledge held
by native college students and the knowledge
required by many of the texts they read. The
author cites current research and theory
related to the importance of prior knowledge
in reading comprehension and identifies a
"culture-concept gap" (p. 131) as being
responsible for many reading difficulties.
Shee provides suggestions for overcoming this
problem.

Instruction: Alternatives and Materials

535. Bogaert, Michael V. d. A CONCEPTUAL FRAMEWORK
     FOR DESIGNING LITERACY MATERIALS FOR
     INDIGENOUS AUDIENCES. Occasional Paper #9.
     East Lansing, Michigan: University of
     Michigan, Non-Formal Education Information
     Center, no date.

     Bogaert accepts the notion that "the Medium
     is the Message" (p. 3). He presents a
     detailed analysis of the theory, particularly
     in relation to indigenous groups in India,
     and concludes that literacy materials must be
     developed as a result of mutual cooperation
     between students and teachers and should use
     the local language and folk methods of
     education such as stories, songs, and
     informal chats. The author provides ten
     questions that can be used to assess both the
     medium and the message of literacy materials.

536. Daswani, C.J. MOTIVATIONAL MATERIALS
     DEVELOPMENT. Monograph No. 2. Literacy
     Curriculum and Materials Development.
     Portfolio of Literacy Materials. Bangkok,
     Thailand: UNESCO, 1981. 57pp. (ED 228
     387)

     Citing the low motivation on the part of
     many illiterate adults to join an adult
     education program and the negative attitude
     toward such programs on the part of those who
     are already literate, Daswani suggests that
     there is a need to provide a variety of

motivational materials at different points in
the educational process. In addition to
developing materials that will encourage
literacy and that will link literacy to
curriculum, he proposes that materials must
be developed that will encourage adults to
join a program in the first place. Examples
of motivating materials from a variety of
countries are included.

537.   Michigan   State   University.   "Beyond
       Literacy." THE NFE EXCHANGE. Issue No. 17.
       East   Lansing,   Michigan: Non-Formal
       Education Information Center, 1980, pp. 5-
       6.

       This article explores ways in which the
       newly literate can create community-based
       reading materials to insure that the recently
       acquired reading skills are reinforced. More
       importantly, the newly literate begin to
       assume control over what is newsworthy and
       important. General suggestions are made;
       questions are raised; sources for further
       information are provided.

538. Richmond, Edmun B.   "Two Strategies for
       Selecting Vocabulary in Third World
       Illiteracy Programs." READING IMPROVEMENT
       22 (Spring 1985): 41-49.

       Richmond states his premises clearly. "The
       development of materials in the native
       language is ... mandatory. In addition,
       materials must be produced within the
       parameters of the culture to which the
       materials are directed" (p. 41). This means
       that the choice of vocabulary and the
       sequencing of vocabulary instruction must be
       appropriate to the target population. Words
       must not be taught in isolation. The author
       advocates using contrasting pairs of words
       within the reader's experience--for example,
       hot-cold. "There is a spectrum between hot-
       cold which refines the gradient between the
       two polarities" (p. 41). Teaching the
       contrasting pair and the spectrum enables the
       adult to learn words as related and as parts

of concepts. The author discusses in detail
the application of this approach to the
development of materials in The Gambia. In
general, materials in Third World literacy
programs must be developed by native speakers
familiar with the culture in question.

539. Thirumalai, M. S. INSTRUCTIONAL MATERIALS
     DEVELOPMENT. Monograph No. 3. Literacy
     Curriculum and Materials Development.
     Portfolio of Literacy Materials. Bangkok,
     Thailand: UNESCO, 1981. 97pp. (ED 228
     388)

     Thirumalai discusses in detail materials
     needed in a literacy program, issues related
     to their development, the process of
     development, and the evaluation of the
     materials. Samples from various countries
     are included.

540. _____. FOLLOWUP MATERIALS DEVELOPMENT.
     Monograph No. 4. Literacy Curriculum and
     Materials Development. Portfolio of
     Literacy Materials. Bangkok, Thailand:
     UNESCO, 1981. 64pp. (ED 228 389)

     Thirumalai examines the rationale and need
     for materials for remedial instruction and
     enrichment following a basic literacy
     program. The creation of follow-up materials
     is discussed and advantages and disadvantages
     of different kinds of materials are pointed
     out. Evaluation of materials is also
     discussed. Examples of a variety of print
     and non-print materials from various
     countries are included.

541. Valdehuesa, Manuel E. "Publishing for New
     Literates in Asia." JOURNAL OF READING 28
     (April 1985): 632-634.

     Valdehuesa identifies a serious problem in
     the area of adult literacy: the lack of
     suitable materials available to newly
     literate adults in Asia. He examines the
     roles and responsibilities of the various
     groups involved in developing, publishing,

and circulating materials and concludes that they need to coordinate their efforts and operate under a much needed "coherent and determined national policy" (p. 634).

542. Wendell, Margaret M. BOOTSTRAP LITERATURE: PRELITERATE SOCIETIES DO IT THEMSELVES. Newark, Delaware: International Reading Assn., 1982.

Wendell discusses in detail the process of writing appropriate text for preliterate and newly literate people. She identifies four stages of literature related to the experience of the reader and the author ranging from known and personal to unknown and vicarious in which the form of presentation ranges from free to translated text. Examples are drawn from a variety of cultures. The author also addresses issues related to training writers to create their own text.

Curriculum and Program Alternatives

543. Adams, Roy J. "The Functional Illiterate Worker and Public Policy." TESL TALK 13 (Fall 1982): 9-16.

Adams addresses the dual problem of functional illiteracy and lack of command of English faced by individuals, employers, and the Canadian government. The problem is a "major" (p. 11) one that needs a national solution. The author makes suggestions for work-based, employer-sponsored plans and reviews current suggestions made by a number of commissions charged with investigating issues related to functional literacy.

544. Anzalone, Stephen J, and Stephen D. McLaughlin. MAKING LITERACY WORK: THE SPECIFIC LITERACY APPROACH. Amherst, Massachusetts: University of Massachusetts, Center for International Education, 1983. 79pp. (ED 236 413)

The authors advocate an approach to

curriculum development and material selection that relates to specific literacy needs in a specific context as contrasted to a general functional literacy approach. Examples from Third world countries illustrate the need for this approach and the process to be used in developing it.

545. Arnove, Robert F. "The Nicaraguan National Literacy Crusade of 1980." PHI DELTA KAPPAN 62 (June 1981): 702-706.

Arnove describes the Nicaraguan National Literacy Crusade as "perhaps the single most impressive basic literacy campaign" (p. 702), citing the reduction of illiteracy in the population over 10 years of age from 50% to 23% in five months and to 15% in nine months. The project represented a total effort, with literates teaching illiterates in small, local units. Reading materials were developed in consultation with political leaders and were designed to "prepare people to play a more active role in creating a more prosperous and just society" (p. 705). The author also discusses the implications and consequences of the program.

546. Asian-South Pacific Bureau of Adult Education. CAMPAIGNING FOR LITERACY. Courier No. 25. Papers presented at the Seminar on Campaigning for Literacy, January 4-11, 1982, Udaipur, Rajasthan, India. 80pp. (ED 222 775)

The papers in this issue examine a variety of literacy programs throughout Asia, reviewing definitions of literacy, aims and objectives of programs, and procedures for establishing and maintaining programs. The emphasis is on establishing mass campaigns to meet "the problems of mass illiteracy" (p. 6).

547. _____. SPECIAL ISSUE IN PREPARATION FOR THE FOURTH INTERNATIONAL CONFERENCE ON ADULT EDUCATION CONVENED BY UNESCO, PARIS, 1985. Courier No. 31. July 1984. 125pp.

(ED 248 388)

The papers in this special issue address three major topics: definitions and implications of literacy, an overview of adult education in Asia, and specifics of adult education programs in various Asian countries with a particular emphasis on literacy efforts.

548. Atucha, Luis Maria Aller, and Catherine D. Crone. "A Participatory Methodology for Integrating Literacy and Health Education in Honduras." CONVERGENCE XV (No. 2, 1982): 70-81.

The authors describe a Honduran program based on concepts developed by J.L. Lebret and Paulo Freire. The program combined literacy training, health education, and family planning. Its aim was not only to develop literacy skills but also to promote acceptance of family planning and to institute community action in the area of preventative medicine and sanitation. Skills taught had to be relevant and needed and the methodology used had to be appropriate to adult learners. For example, instruction in this program took place in small literacy circles, each composed of groups of adults with leaders chosen by their peers. The discussion is detailed and relates the program to the principles advocated by Freire.

549. Behrstock, Julian. "Reaching the Rural Reader." JOURNAL OF READING 24 (May 1981): 712-718.

Behrstock identifies the need to disseminate printed materials into rural areas around the world and describes efforts that are being made to accomplish this goal. Problems of printing, developing the format and content, and distributing the materials are addressed. Suggestions are made on ways to promote readership of books in rural areas including, for example, mini-libraries, local "learning groups" (p. 718), and the rotation of books among schools.

550. Bendor-Samuel, David H., and Margaret M. Bendor-Samuel. COMMUNITY LITERACY PROGRAMMES IN NORTHERN GHANA. Dallas, Texas: Summer Institute of Linguistics, 1983. 90pp. (ED 241 676)

The authors describe the program of the Summer Institute of Linguistics, 1972-1979, designed to advance the literacy levels of six language groups in Northern Ghana. Details are provided on the particular program for each group. Each program was developed within a particular local context and all were developed within a national context.

551. Bhola, H.S. "Adult Literacy Policy and Performance in Malawi: An Analysis." Paper presented at the Workshop in Political Theory and Policy Analysis, January 14, 1985, Bloomington, Indiana. 35pp. (ED 253 728)

Bhola discusses the recent history of adult literacy education in Malawi as a background for understanding its current status. Agencies have been established to deal with the problem but, as he points out, there must be a national commitment to the development of adult literacy as well as cooperation between agencies to insure future success. The author also points out that the lack of training materials has hindered success in the past and will continue to do so.

552. Bordia, A., and G. Carron. TRAINING OF LOCAL-LEVEL ADMINISTRATIVE PERSONNEL IN NATIONAL LITERACY PROGRAMMES. METHODOLOGICAL REPORT OF A TRAINING WORKSHOP, November 20-0, 1981, Nazareth, Ethiopia. 70pp. (ED 238 091)

This practical, detailed document was developed from a workshop held for local African administrators of literacy programs.

Training for local administrators must include field experience, opportunity for thorough discussions, and a recognition of the importance of their role in literacy development. Bordia and Carron include a general discussion of organizational and educational issues, a description of field visits, and related case studies. Materials from the workshop are included.

553. Butterfield, P.H. BLACK LITERACY IN SOUTH AFRICA--A COMPARISON OF THE CONTRIBUTION OF THE PUBLIC AND THE PRIVATE SECTOR. 1981. 30pp. (ED 240 494)

Butterfield notes the substantial size of the black illiterate population of South Africa and examines some of the private organizations and public agencies that have been formed to overcome the problem. He has isolated a number of reasons why the problem is so difficult to solve, among them: lack of cooperation among agencies, failure to agree on the definition and criteria for illiteracy and methods for eradicating it, incomplete government commitment to solving the problem, and few opportunities for literate blacks. However, the picture is not altogether bleak. The author cites some indications for optimism, including: an increased commitment of money, more university opportunities for blacks, and stepped-up state efforts.

554. Canfux, Jaime. "A Brief Description of the 'Battle for the Sixth Grade.'" JOURNAL OF READING 25 (December 1981): 226-233.

The "Battle for the Sixth Grade" addressed the problem of promoting the literacy skills developed in the brief, intensive Literacy Campaign in Cuba in 1960. The program, which was in operation at the time of the article, provides instruction in work settings, on television, in night school, and through independent study. Canfux describes the efforts of the program to meet the needs of the students, develop relevant materials, and train teachers.

555. Cardenal, Fernando, and Valerie Miller. "Nicaragua: Literacy and Revolution." PROSPECTS XII (No. 2, 1982): 201-212.

Cardenal and Miller cite reasons why the eradication of illiteracy was not possible under the Somoza government. However, under the Sandinista government, literacy has assumed priority status as a basic human right and as a prerequisite for political and economic change. The National Literacy Crusade is described in some detail from the planning stages to the management and organization of programs, the development of curriculum content, methodology and volunteer training, and, finally, program evaluation and monitoring.

556. Chandrasekhar, Rajkumari. ASPECTS OF ADULT EDUCATION. Raja Annamalaipuram, Madras, India: New Era Publications, 1982. 158pp. (ED 237 634)

Chandrasekhar describes the problem of adult illiteracy in India, reviews a variety of issues, and provides suggestions for initiating and implementing particular programs. The scope of topics is broad, ranging from statistics on the extent of illiteracy to suggestions for training teachers, developing teaching aids, and planning for evaluation.

557. Chauhan, Malikhan S. "Farmers' Functional Literacy Program in India." Paper presented at the National Adult Education Conference, November 12-16, 1982, San Antonio, Texas. 30pp. (ED 234 147)

Chauhan describes a functional literacy program for farmers in India in which three governmental agencies cooperated to link education and agriculture. The Ministry of Education provided the literacy training. The Ministry of Agriculture provided training and field demonstrations. The Ministry of Information and Broadcasting provided special programs for the participants. The author

discusses   methodology,   teachers,   and
accomplishments of the program.

558.   Comings, John, and David Kahler.   PEACE CORPS
       LITERACY   HANDBOOK.   APPROPRIATE
       TECHNOLOGIES FOR DEVELOPMENT.   MANUAL M-21.
       Washington, D.C.: Peace Corps,   Information
       Collection and Exchange Division, October
       1984.   176pp.   (ED 251 696)

       This manual provides an   overview of the
       development, organization, and implementation
       of literacy programs operated by the Peace
       Corps. It includes descriptions of various
       approaches as well as theories and procedures
       for setting up and evaluating programs. Case
       studies and sample materials are included.

559.   Dalglish,   Carol.   "Illiteracy and the
       Offender."   ADULT   EDUCATION (London)   56
       (June 1983): 23-26.

       Dalglish   sets   the   stage   for   examining
       literacy problems of British offenders by
       examining the implications of illiteracy for
       the individual and the principles of Paulo
       Freire for literacy training.   The illiterate
       offender is trapped into a cycle of poverty
       and delinquency. The author believes that
       the prison system in Britain has failed to
       take Freire's ideas into account and has not
       been effective in solving the illiteracy
       problem.   Dalglish   makes   some   general
       suggestions for change.

560.   Deiner, John T.   "The Nicaraguan Literacy
       Crusade." JOURNAL OF READING 25 (November
       1981): 118-125.

       Deiner acknowledges the "highly political
       nature of the Literacy Crusade and the
       partisan   nature   of   that   political
       involvement" (p.   118),   recognizing   the
       reasons for this as well as the impact it has
       had on the crusade.   The author provides
       background on the development of the program,
       describes the format of the crusade, the
       training given to volunteers, the financial

challenges of the campaign, the
implementation of the campaign, and the
textbook used. The methodology grew out of
that developed by Freire. A future challenge
will be to develop continuing adult education
and to involve the newly literate in the
decision-making process as "liberated,
critical, free-thinking political actors" (p.
125).

561. Freire, Paulo. PEDAGOGY IN PROCESS: THE
     LETTERS TO GUINEA-BISSAU. New York:
     Seabury Press, 1978.

     This book explains and documents Freire's
     views on literacy, literacy education, and
     the application of these views in a
     developing country with a high rate of
     illiteracy (90% of the population in 1974).
     The process of learning must involve the
     learner in an active creative manner.
     Reading is more than the mechanics of
     decoding; reading is a means of enabling
     critical thinking, problem-solving, and
     political action. The introduction to the
     book and the letters tell the story of the
     process used, the problems encountered, and
     the thoughts and reflections of the
     principals in the application of theory to
     practice.

562. Hargreaves, David. ADULT LITERACY AND
     BROADCASTING, THE BBC'S EXPERIENCE. New
     York: Nichols Publishing Company, 1980.

     Hargreaves gives an account of the BBC's
     involvement in the national literacy campaign
     in England between 1974 and 1978 as well as
     the beginnings of the campaign in 1972 to
     1974. Its focus was on reducing the adult's
     anxiety and stigma, not primarily on
     providing instruction. Toward this end,
     short programs were offered on prime time
     television. In addition the programs
     provided a telephone referral service, tutor
     training, and books for isolated readers and
     for tutors. The broadcasts were found to be
     particularly important and recruiting

suggests directions for future involvement of
broadcasting in literacy campaigns. Examples
of broadcasts are included as well as a
review of research projects conducted by the
National Institute of Adult Education, the
BBC, and the Adult Literacy Resource Agency.

563.   Hirshon, Sheryl L., with Judy Butler. AND
       ALSO TEACH THEM TO READ. Westport,
       Connecticut: Lawrence Hill and Company,
       1983.

       This book describes an American teacher's
       participation in the Sandinista's literacy
       crusade in Nicaragua. The crusade was based
       on the idea of Paolo Freire that control of
       the "word" also gives the reader the notion
       that he can effect change in the social
       order. "The literacy crusade was one
       expression of the Nicaraguan revolution's
       determination to give power to the people, to
       make them actors in their own social destiny.
       And it also taught them to read" (p. xii).
       The author fits the crusade into its larger
       setting by describing the people, the
       countryside, the participants in the crusade,
       and the difficulties encountered.

       The ten-step teaching methodology is
       described in some detail. The procedure
       begins with the use of a photograph to
       stimulate dialogue based on the students'
       life experiences. Knowledge of phonics and
       syllables is developed. Words used are
       related to other words. Finally, reading and
       dictating words and sentences are important
       parts of the program. This is not a dry,
       academic account, but rather an account from
       the inside out, showing the participants'
       frustrations, successes, and areas of growth
       as well as the dawning of "lights of
       understanding" (p. 201). According to the
       author, the illiteracy level dropped from 50%
       of the population to 12%. For the reader who
       wants more information, a current
       bibliography on the Nicaraguan literacy
       crusade is included.

564.   International Reading Association.   "Moroccan
        Group Wins IRA Literacy Award."   READING
        TODAY 3 (October/November 1985): 1.

        The Literacy and Adult Education Division
        of Morocco received the IRA Literacy Award
        for 1985 because of its "critical evaluation
        of past experience and rigorous testing of
        materials and methods" (p. 1) as well as for
        the emphasis it placed on working with women.
        In addition the recipient was cited for
        developing a program that includes a follow-
        up stage designed to insure retention of
        literacy skills.

565.   Kozol, Jonathan. CHILDREN OF THE REVOLUTION:
        A YANKEE TEACHER IN THE CUBAN SCHOOLS. New
        York: Delacorte, 1978.

        Kozol recounts the story of the Cuban
        Literacy Campaign of 1961 as well as the
        subsequent campaign designed to insure
        literacy for all adults. He also describes
        current Cuban schools. Interviews with some
        of the original instructors as well as with
        school personnel working at the time this
        book was published give the account a sense
        of reality and immediacy.

566.   Larrabee, Marva J.   "A Challenge for Third-
        World   Education: Changing   Male/Female
        Literacy in Pakistan." Paper presented at
        the Annual Meeting of the American
        Educational Research Association, April 23-
        27, 1984, New Orleans, Louisiana. 23pp.
        (ED 249 469)

        Larrabee reviews the history of primary
        level education and adult literacy education
        in Pakistan, showing how they are related and
        how the problems of the first has an impact
        on the second. The author examines efforts
        that have been made in raising the level of
        adult literacy and the reasons for their
        limited success. In addition, the National
        Literacy Programme, in effect from 1983-1993,
        is discussed.   One particular emphasis of
        this program is on the reduction of levels of

female illiteracy. Larrabee identifies the
need to develop measurement techniques,
instructional materials, and teacher
qualification standards.

567. Longley, Chris, ed.   BBC ADULT LITERACY
      HANDBOOK.   London: British Broadcasting
      Corporation, 1975.

      This handbook details how to organize and
      develop a program for teaching adults to read
      and how to go about teaching them.   It was
      designed to accompany the programs developed
      by the BBC for the Adult Literacy Campaign in
      the 1970s.   There is an emphasis on the
      development of decoding skills and on the
      importance of the use of relevant materials.
      Four case studies that relate tutoring to
      student needs included illustrating different
      literacy problems.

568. Mammo, Gudeta.   "The National Literacy
      Campaign in Ethiopia." PROSPECTS XII (No.
      2, 1982): 193-199.

      Mammo provides background on the origin and
      development of literacy programs in Ethiopia.
      Literacy programs have been greatly
      influenced by the definition of literacy
      developed at the World Conference of
      Ministers for Education on the Eradication of
      Illiteracy held in Tehran in 1965. Literacy
      is more than the acquisition of basic skills;
      it is a means of participating in the
      cultural, political, social, and economic
      life of the country.   The current National
      Literacy Campaign of Socialists Ethiopia is
      described in detail. Efforts have centered
      on providing basic literacy instruction,
      working with drop-outs, and insuring
      application of acquired skills.

569. Michigan State University.   "Literacy and
      Development." THE NFE EXCHANGE.   No. 17.
      East Lansing, Michigan: Non-Formal
      Education Information Center, 1980,
      pp. 1-4.

This article was developed from resources at the Non-Formal Education Information Center Library. It provides a brief overview of the many possible ways of instructing and of providing instruction. There are specific descriptions of a number of programs reflecting varying definitions of literacy. The implications of these differences are explored in terms of content, instruction, and instructors. Seven questions concerning goals, assumptions, instructors, language, delivery systems, evaluation, and follow-up are suggested for consideration when developing programs.

570.   _____. "Project Highlights." THE NFE EXCHANGE. No. 17. East Lansing, Michigan: Non-Formal Education Information Center, 1980, pp. 7-10.

A variety of international literacy projects are described, giving the reader an overview of the different instructional approaches that are used as well as the different contexts and settings in which instruction takes place. Addresses are provided for the various projects.

571.   Miller, Robert. "Mexican Literacy Education Today." JOURNAL OF READING 29 (November 1985): 132-135.

Miller describes the current efforts of the Mexican government to provide literacy training for adults in both their native languages and in Spanish. The program is based on the concepts of Paulo Freire, with instruction taking place in small groups using relevant words and concepts. Television programs used in conjunction with a workbook provide instruction and practice. In addition, the program includes the help of a literacy worker and the use of a toll-free number to answer questions and solve problems. A particular program is also described in which Indian women receive training in literacy in their native language and in Spanish as well as training in health and primary education.

572.   Mujica, Rene J.   "Some Recollections of my
        Experiences   in   the   Cuban   Literacy
        Campaign." JOURNAL OF READING 25 (December
        1981): 222-225.

        Mujica   details   his experiences as a young
        tutor   in   the   Cuban   Literacy   Campaign,
        discussing   the   people   he   tutored   and his
        contributions to   the   development   of   their
        literacy   skills.   Of particular interest is
        the impact the campaign had   on   the   author.
        He   states   that   "it   was   a   tremendous
        experience in the sense that   it   helped   me
        become   better   aware   of the problems of our
        country .... It gave   me   a   chance   to   grow
        tremendously   as an individual and as a human
        being" (p. 224).

573.   Napitupulu, W.P.   "Each   One   Teach   Ten:
        Literacy in Indonesia." PROSPECTS XII (No.
        2, 1982): 213-220.

        Napitupulu   describes the   literacy campaign
        in Indonesia initiated under General   Suharto
        in   1978.   The   program   utilized   Latin
        characters,   Arabic   numbers,   and   the
        Indonesian   language   and also provided basic
        education   in   functional   information,   work
        skills,   and   the   development   of   a   mental
        attitude toward innovation   and   development.
        The   delivery   system   was   a   non-formal
        education program, generally in rural   areas.
        Instruction   was   provided to learning groups
        by   educated   people   serving   as   volunteer
        tutors.   The   author   describes   the
        organization of the program, its content, and
        evaluation procedures.

574.   O'Neill, Julie.   "Literacy   Groups   in   a
        Probation   Department."   ADULT   EDUCATION
        (London) 55 (June 1982): 49-54.

        As part of the adult   literacy   campaign   in
        Britain,   O'Neill   ran   two   groups   in   the
        Probation service that were designed to serve
        as a "bridge" for those who were reluctant or

unable   to   participate   in   the   usual
instructional facilities. In order to enroll
such students in the first place, the efforts
of an organizer are essential. To retain
students the program must be   flexible,   with
the   student   participating,   belonging,   and
controlling. The failure of the   program   to
serve   as   a   bridge to normal facilities is
seen not as a   failure   of   the   student   but
rather   as   a   failure of the adult education
system.

575.   Ouane, Adama. "Rural Newspapers and Radio
       for Post-Literacy in Mali." PROSPECTS XII
       (No. 2, 1982): 243-253.

       Ouane describes the history of literacy
       education in Mali beginning with the first
       mass campaign in 1961-1967 that used the
       French language as its basis. The author
       points out the problems with that project in
       terms of the difficulty of the language and
       the inappropriateness of content and   methods
       used. More recently the emphasis has been on
       using   the   national   language,   linking
       instruction to the social and economic
       aspects of the workplace, and developing a
       rural information newspaper.   Currently,
       because of the growth in literacy as a result
       of this program, stress is now being placed
       on post-literacy development. The production
       of reading materials, particularly the rural
       newspaper, is critical to this effort and is
       discussed in some detail. Educational radio
       has developed programs to link tutors and
       learners with issues and ideas. The aim of
       all these efforts has been to create a
       "literate environment" (p. 253).

576.   Prieto, Abel.   "Cuba's National Literacy
       Campaign." JOURNAL OF READING 25 (December
       1981): 215-221.

       Prieto describes the beginnings of the
       National Literacy Campaign in 1960 and its
       development.   The examples he gives clarify
       the philosophy behind the program: the adult
       literate has an obligation to teach the

illiterate; the teaching must done be in an
accessible place; the materials used must be
meaningful and must relate to the economic,
political, and social concerns of the people
in Cuba.

577. Rivera, William M.   EVALUATION   IN   ADULT
      EDUCATION: AN INTERNATIONAL PERSPECTIVE.
      THEORY,   INNOVATION,   AND   PRACTICE   IN
      ANDRAGOGY.   No. 4.   Tallahassee, Florida:
      Florida State University,   International
      Institute of Andragogy, December 1982.
      38pp. (ED 228 464)

      Rivera   identifies   the   critical   role   of
      evaluation   and   evaluation   research   in the
      field of adult education at the international
      level.   Until   recently,   "literacy   was
      primarily   a   sphere   of   action   rather than
      analysis"   (p.   24).   In   looking   at   the
      analysis of literacy, the author provides an
      overview of the topic of evaluation, what   it
      is   and   how to approach it. He examines its
      role in program planning and   the   impact   of
      the   particular   socioeconomic   structure   in
      establishing evaluation criteria.   Finally,
      he   looks at questions related to large-scale
      evaluation   research   and   at   the   need   to
      consider   both   "short-term   economic
      considerations"   (ibid.)   and   "long-term
      educational payoff" (ibid.).

578. Saraf, S.N.   FUNCTIONAL LITERACY PROJECT OF
      INDIA, 1968-1978--A DECADE OF EVALUATION--
      PROCEDURES, PROBLEMS, AND PROSPECTS. The
      Fundamentals   of   Educational   Planning:
      Lecture-Discussion   Series   No. 67.   Paris,
      France: UNESCO, April 1980. 34pp. (ED 213
      094)

      Saraf   describes   the   Functional   Literacy
      Project   of   India   that   in   1978   was
      incorporated   into   a   larger   program,   the
      National   Adult   Education   Programme.   He
      reviews the format of the project as well   as
      its problems. Much of the discussion centers
      on   evaluation   procedures.   He details the
      need   for   both   formative   and   summative,

qualitative   and   quantitative   evaluation
procedures.

579. _____.   LITERACY   IN   A   NON-LITERACY
      MILIEU: THE   INDIAN   SCENARIO.   Paris,
      France: UNESCO, International Institute for
      Educational Planning, 1980.   184pp.   (ED
      238 087)

      Saraf   presents   an overview of the current
      status of literacy   in   India   and   describes
      specific   programs,   particularly   the   local
      "Village Literacy Movement" and the   national
      "Functional   Literacy   Project."   Because of
      differences in areas within the country,   the
      author   suggests   a   decentralized,   area-
      specific   approach   that   would   adapt   the
      program   to   the locality, while also linking
      it to local and   national   development.   He
      includes detailed, specific lists of steps to
      be   taken   in the planning and implementation
      of a literacy campaign   and   in   the   process
      makes   an   analogy   to   a   well   organized,
      structured military campaign.

580. Scottish   Adult   Literacy   Agency.   ADULT
      LITERACY IN SCOTLAND.   Edinburgh, Scotland:
      Her Majesty's Stationery Store, 1980.

      This   publication   provides   a   detailed
      overview of a literacy program in a developed
      country.   The program   was   adapted   to   meet
      local   needs   from   one   that   originated   in
      England using the resources of the   BBC.   A
      variety   of   programs   are described, such as
      one in a women's center and one in   a   short-
      term   prison.   The   problems of a developed
      country are identified and incorporated   into
      the   various   programs.   There is a need, for
      example, to use   the   newly   acquired   skills
      that   must   be addressed by the programs.   In
      addition, there is a demand for more advanced
      skills.   Programs   cannot   deal   solely   with
      beginning   literacy   levels but must identify
      the needs of adults in a particular   context.
      A   list   of   publications   available from the
      Agency is included.

581.   Smith, Arthur E. "An Adult Literacy Campaign
        in Great Britain." READING WORLD 20
        (December 1980): 119-122.

        Smith summarizes the major elements of the
        adult literacy program in Great Britain.
        Instruction was provided on the local level
        with the Adult Literacy Resource Agency
        giving information and seed money and with
        the BBC providing publicity to increase
        public awareness. Instruction using the
        language experience approach was conducted
        both by volunteers and by paid tutors. Smith
        cites the achievements of the program while
        emphasizing the substantial number of adults
        who still need literacy training.

582.   Spaulding, Seth. "Evaluation of Adult
        Nonformal Education Programs: An
        International Perspective." Paper
        presented at the Annual Meeting of the
        Comparative and International Education
        Society, March 18-21, 1982, New York.
        18pp. (ED 222 658)

        Spaulding presents an historical overview
        of evaluation programs and procedures for
        specific international nonformal adult
        education programs. Many of the programs
        reviewed deal with literacy development. The
        reasons for program evaluation and the
        problems associated with it are discussed.
        The author advocates active participatory
        evaluation, both for its usefulness in
        program improvement and for its value as an
        educational tool for the participants.

583.   Stock, Arthur. "Post-Literacy Educational
        Strategies: The United Kingdom Experience."
        CONVERGENCE XIV (No. 4, 1981): 44-52.

        According to Stock, British literacy
        programs are firmly grounded in the notion
        that literacy skills must take place in a
        "life" context. This has been very
        influential in the development of post-
        literacy techniques that are designed to
        maintain and apply literacy skills already

acquired. Stock discusses possible
strategies such as suitable books, links with
work, contributions of the media, the role of
continuing education, the place of literacy
in non-literacy programs, and the involvement
of students in programming.

584. _____. "The United Kingdom: Becoming
      and Staying Literate." PROSPECTS XII (No.
      2, 1982): 221-232.

      Stock reviews the recent history of adult
      literacy efforts in the United Kingdom,
      describing the role of national agencies as
      well as of district and local groups. A
      particular focus for the author is the need
      for post-literacy techniques to maintain,
      apply, and enhance literacy skills. These
      techniques include, for example, locally
      created periodicals and pamphlets, textbooks
      for adults, rewritten classics, novels and
      plays, and the involvement of local libraries
      and various labor oriented groups. The role
      of the media in post-literacy programs and in
      the production of print materials is
      discussed.

585. Thomas, Audrey M. ADULT ILLITERACY IN
      CANADA--A CHALLENGE. Occasional Paper No.
      42. Ottawa, Canada: Canadian Commission
      for UNESCO. 1983. 150pp. (ED 237 779)

      This paper places the Canadian literacy
      education experience within both a historical
      context and a framework of world literacy.
      Examples from other developed, industrialized
      countries are provided. This historical and
      worldwide background enables the reader to
      understand the influences on Canadian
      literacy and to view it from a comparative
      perspective. An overview of the responses
      of various Canadian agencies is provided and
      issues relating to organization, delivery
      systems, and methods are identified. Thomas
      stresses that a "variety of strategies has to
      be devised to service the under-educated
      adult" (p. 106). She advocates using the
      Language Experience Approach because it

"encourages the development of indigenous
materials by the students themselves"
(ibid.), although the final determination of
methodology must remain with the local
organization. The author identifies a need
for tutor training as well as for university
support for literacy programs.

586.   UNESCO. CURRICULUM DEVELOPMENT IN LITERACY.
        Monograph No. 1. Part A: Proceedings and
        Methods of the First Regional Literacy
        Workshop, November 29-December 20, 1979,
        Udaipur, India. Part B: Curriculum and
        Materials Development. Portfolio of
        Literacy Materials. Bangkok, Thailand,
        1981. 77pp. (ED 228 386)

        This monograph presents an overview of the
        hands-on process of curriculum development as
        it was experienced and summarized by the
        participants of the First Regional Literacy
        Workshop. The emphasis in developing a
        curriculum must be on the "felt needs" and
        "real needs" (p. 11) of the learners within
        the larger framework of particular national
        goals and objectives. Criteria and methods
        for developing curriculum are stated.
        Literacy problems and goals in various Asian
        countries are identified. Sample materials
        developed by the participants are included
        together with a discussion of
        teaching/learning strategies and evaluation
        requirements.

587.   _____. PLANNING OF LITERACY PROGRAMMES.
        PLANNING, ADMINISTRATION AND MONITORING IN
        LITERACY. Portfolio of Literacy Materials.
        Series 2, Monograph 1. Bangkok, Thailand,
        1982. 25pp. (ED 226 313)

        The participants at a Regional Literacy
        Workshop (Viet Nam, 1980) developed the ideas
        and information in this monograph. They
        identified the need to define literacy as a
        prerequisite to the planning of any literacy
        program. No country in attendance limited
        the definition of literacy to the 3 Rs. All
        countries included skills needed to improve

the quality of life. Since the exact
definition depends on local and national
concerns, it is essential that each country
determine a workable, acceptable definition
and set of related goals. The monograph
reviews the planning process, delivery
systems, and evaluation procedures.

588. _____. ADMINISTRATION OF LITERACY
PROGRAMMES. PLANNING, ADMINISTRATION AND
MONITORING IN LITERACY. Portfolio of
Literacy Materials. Series 2, Monograph 2.
Bangkok, Thailand, 1982. 23pp. (ED 226
314)

This monograph covers many areas of concern
to administrators, from developing support
for literacy education to organizing,
administering and staffing the program. The
emphasis is on decision making. The
monograph was developed from a Regional
Literacy Workshop held in Viet Nam in 1980.
The need for active participation and
cooperation at all levels, from learners to
leaders, is stressed.

589. Vijayendra, T. "Adult Education Integrates
Literacy, Health and Conscientization: The
Mandar Story." CONVERGENCE XV (No. 2,
1982): 35-42.

Vijayendra describes a literacy program in
a small isolated tribal village in India that
grew out of a need to develop preventative
medicine techniques and to promote outreach
from the local hospital to the surrounding
population. The literacy program was
developed on the village level with an
emphasis on local leaders, instructors, and
materials. The materials used all relate to
health or agricultural concerns.

590. Yong-Fan, Hong. "Continuing Literacy Work in
China." PROSPECTS XII (No. 2, 1982): 185-
192.

The level of literacy in China since 1949
has greatly improved among the working class.

The author cites the benefits of this in
terms of political, cultural, scientific, and
economic activities. Yong-Fan discusses the
recruitment and training of teachers, issues
related to instruction in Chinese characters
and teaching practice, ways of combining
literacy instruction with other activities,
financial resources, and evaluation systems.
Literacy training must be relevant to local
conditions and local priorities.

591.   Zaman, Rafe-uz. "Functional Literacy Through
        Television in Pakistan." PROSPECTS XII
        (No. 2, 1982): 233-241.

The author describes the establishment,
objectives, methods, problems, and costs of a
program designed to make adults functionally
literate. Students follow specially designed
television programs often in community
viewing centers. In spite of the problems
cited, this program appears to the author to
have merit.

AUTHOR INDEX

P. = Page Number(s), E. = Entry Number(s)

411

434 ADULT LITERACY